MAXIMUM RIDE

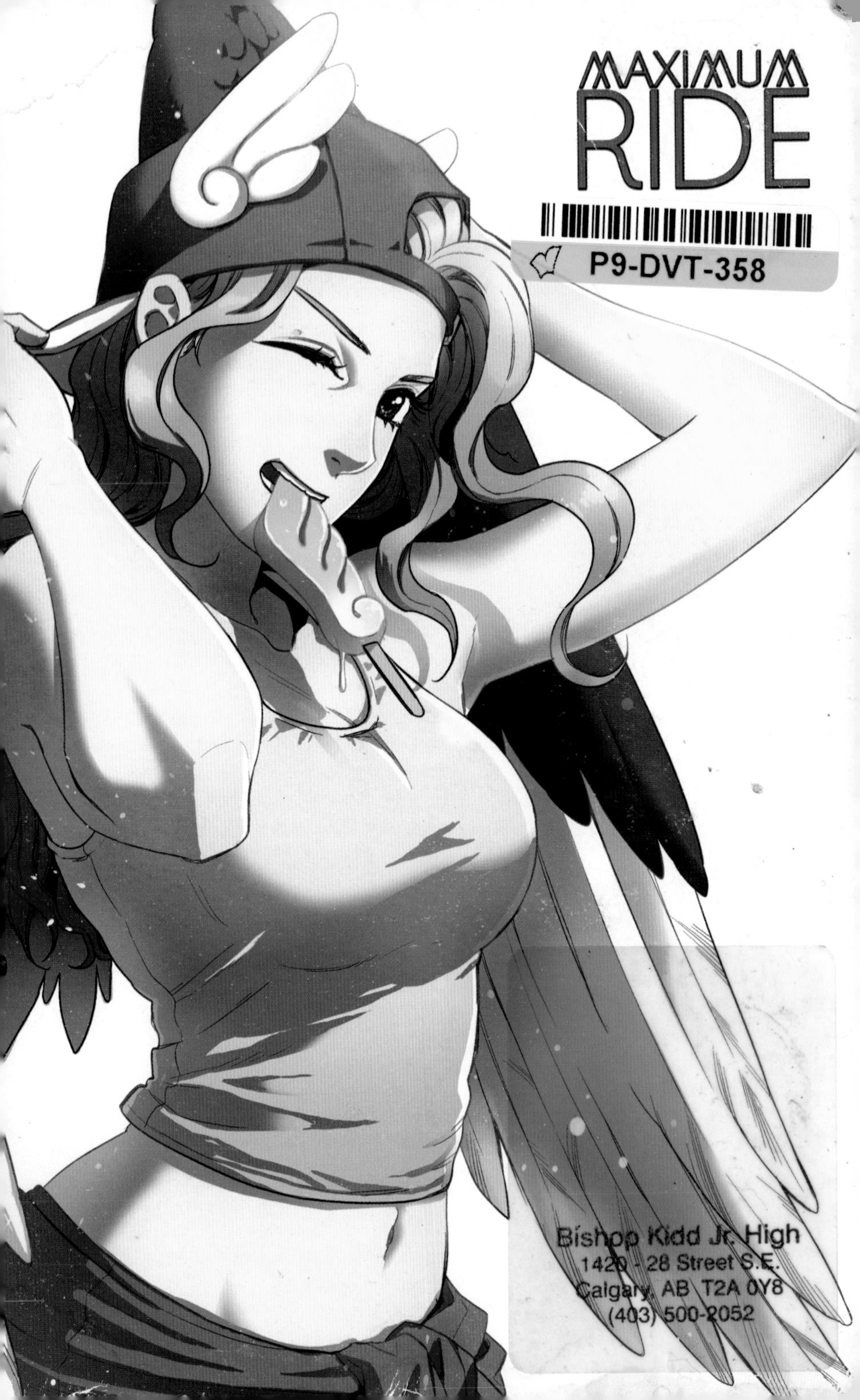

WHAT CAME BEFORE

Max and her flock are genetic experiments. Created by a mysterious lab known only as the "School," their genetic codes have been spliced with avian DNA, giving them wings and the power to soar. What they lack are homes, families, and memories of a real life.

The flock's long battle against ITEX — the corporation behind their creation — and its "By-Half" initiative that sought to wipe out half the world's population came to a head in Germany. Though Max and the girls emerged on top with the help of kids across the world, their victory came at a price: Ari sacrificed himself to protect Max, his half-sister. Enraged, Max made short work of ITEX's latest mutation and her "fake" mother and the facility's director, Marian Janssen.

With nowhere else to turn, Max and the flock are welcomed with open arms at the home of Valencia Martinez — Max's natural mother —in Arizona. But they were granted only a few short weeks of reprieve before Jeb turned up with an offer of aid and protection from the government higher-ups. Skeptical, Max agreed to a meeting, but when the talk turned toward building a special "school" where the flock could be studied, Max was quick to walk out the door, leery of their intentions.

On their own again, the flock discovered some surprising new developments in their already unique powers. Nudge uncovered a magnetic ability to draw metal toward her, Iggy was able to understand and process colors without seeing them, Fang became invisible if he stayed still long enough and Angel could change her appearance at will!

Following her instincts, Max led the flock to a remote desert area where they reunited with none other than Dr. Martinez. On her recommendation the flock agreed to take on a rescue mission in the South Pole. Fed, made warm, and fed again aboard the *Wendy K,* the flock decided to assist the scientists in their research of the effects of global warming. But the flock's newfound peace in the Antarctic comes to an end when a new enemy sets its sights on their powers...

MAXIMUM RIDE

Max is the eldest member of the flock, and the responsibility of caring for her comrades has fallen to her. Tough and uncompromising, she's willing to put everything on the line to protect her "family."

FANG

Only slightly younger than Max, Fang is one of the elder members of the flock. Cool and reliable, Fang is Max's rock. He may be the strongest of them all, but most of the time it is hard to figure out what is on his mind.

IGGY

Being blind doesn't mean that Iggy is helpless. He has not only an incredible sense of hearing, but also a particular knack (and fondness) for explosives.

NUDGE

Motormouth Nudge would probably spend most days at the mall if not for her pesky mutant-bird-girl-being-hunted-by-wolf-men problem.

GASMAN

The name pretty much says it all. The Gasman (or Gazzy) has the art of flatulence down to a science. He's also Angel's biological big brother.

ANGEL

The youngest member of the flock and Gazzy's little sister, Angel seems to have some peculiar abilities —— mind reading, for example.

ARI

Just seven years old, Ari is Jeb's son but was transformed into an Eraser. He used to have an axe to grind with Max but ends up losing his life protecting her.

JEB BATCHELDER

The flock's former benefactor, Jeb was a scientist at the School before helping the flock to make their original escape.

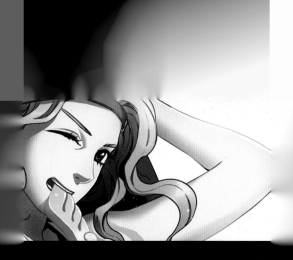

MAXIMUM RIDE

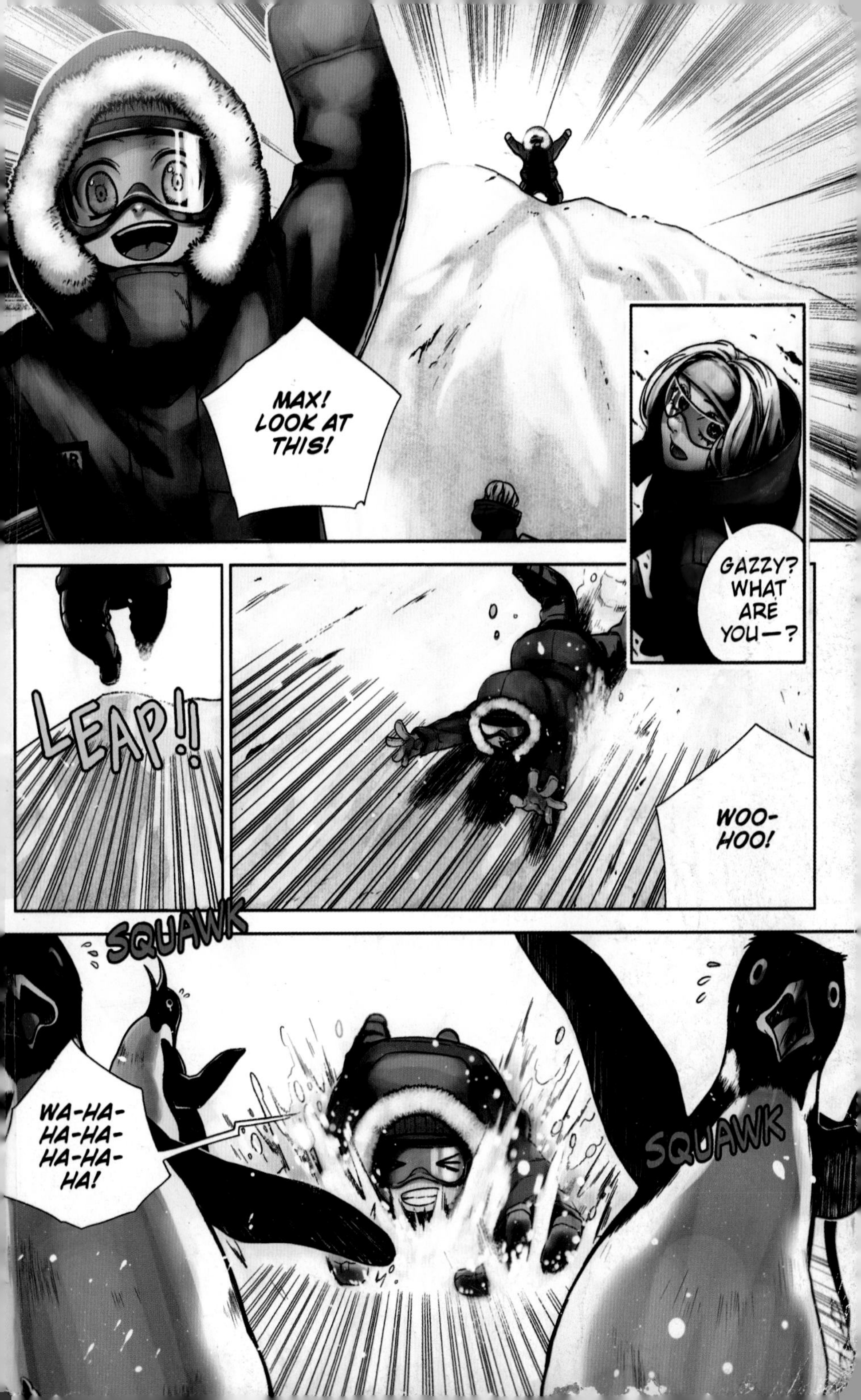
MAX! LOOK AT THIS!
GAZZY? WHAT ARE YOU—?
LEAP!!
WOO-HOO!
SQUAWK
WA-HA-HA-HA-HA-HA-HA!
SQUAWK

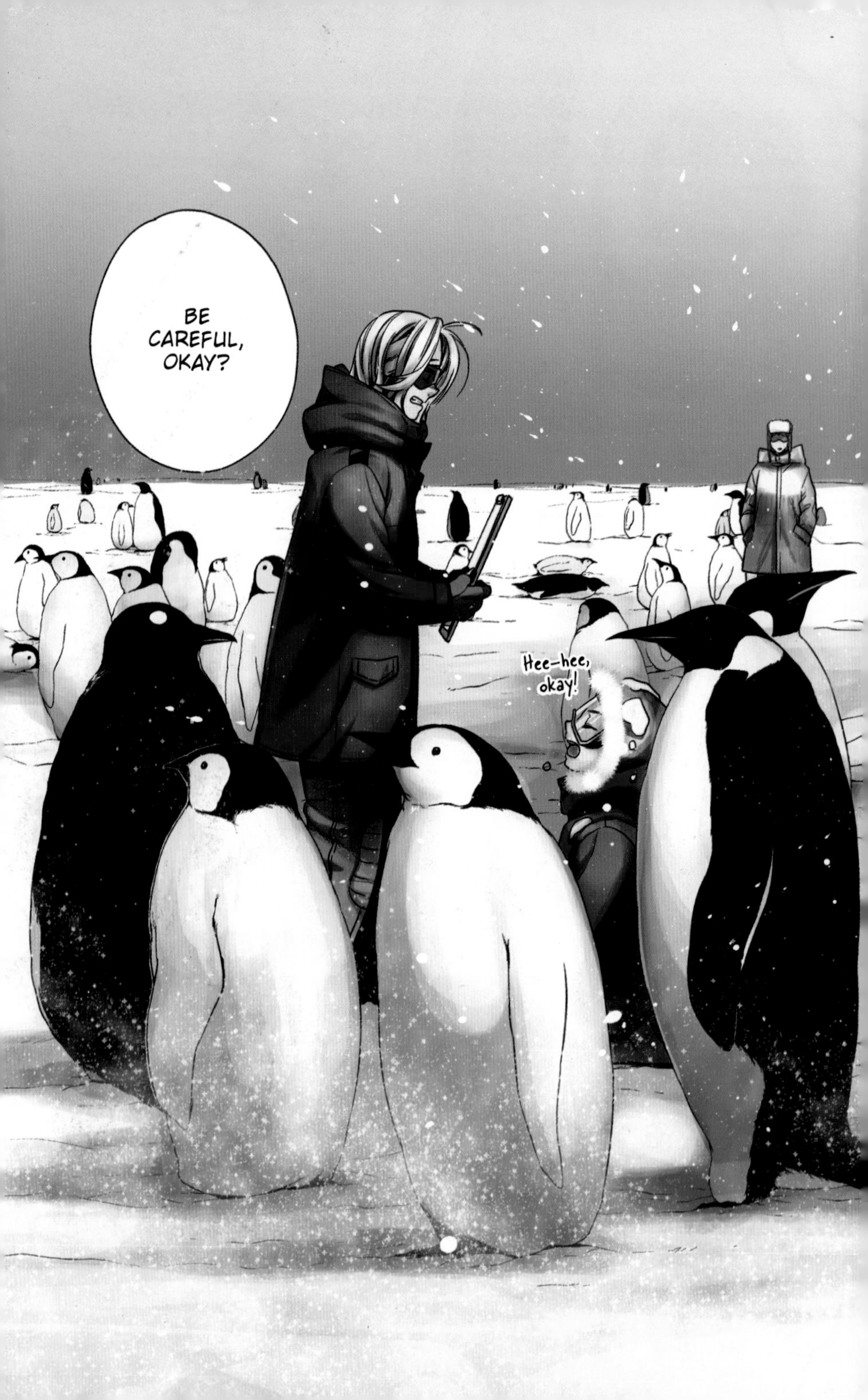
BE CAREFUL, OKAY?
Hee-hee, okay!

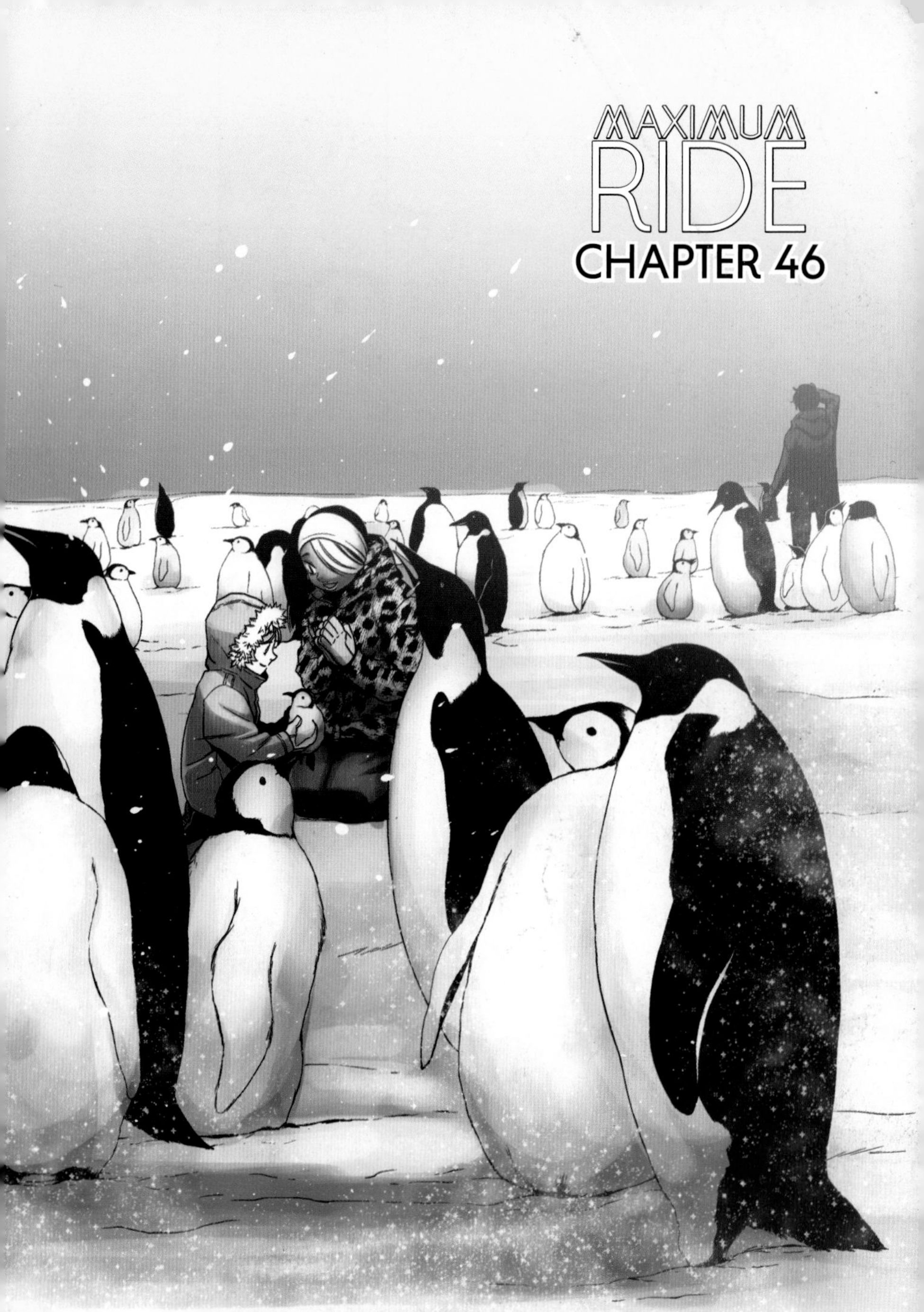
MAXIMUM RIDE
CHAPTER 46

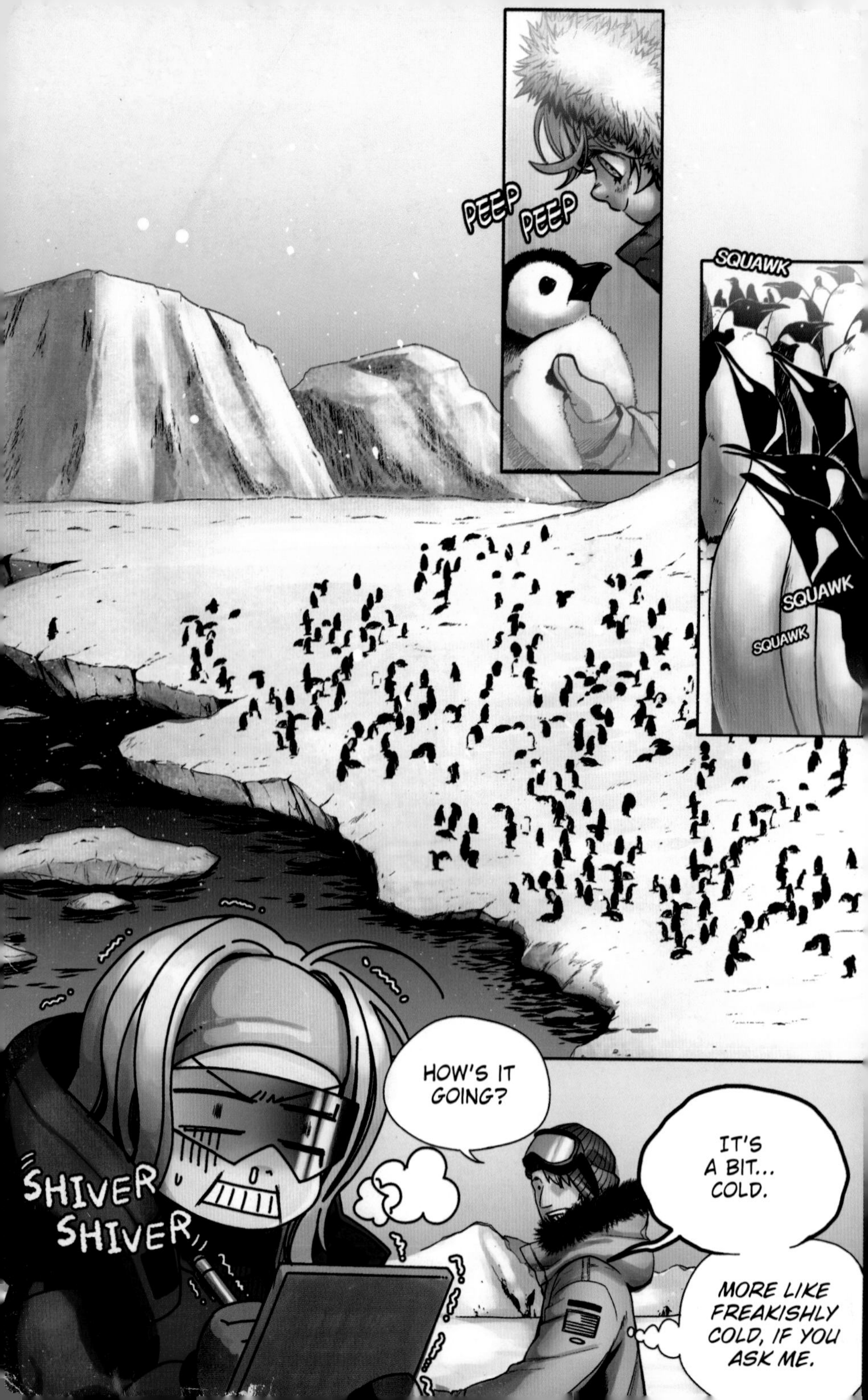
PEEP PEEP
SQUAWK
SQUAWK
SQUAWK
SHIVER SHIVER
HOW'S IT GOING?
IT'S A BIT... COLD.
MORE LIKE FREAKISHLY COLD, IF YOU ASK ME.

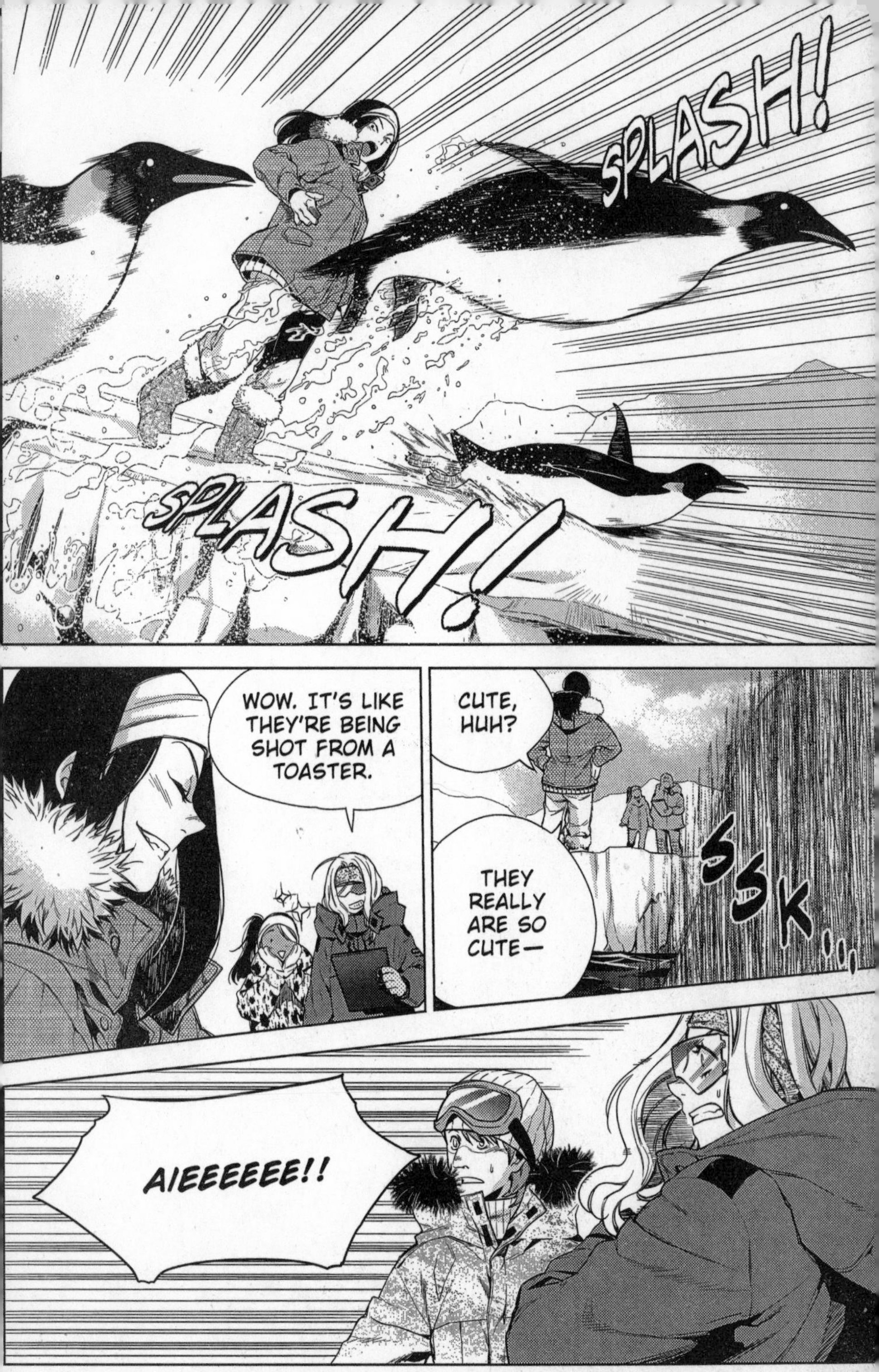
SPLASH!
SPLASH!
WOW. IT'S LIKE THEY'RE BEING SHOT FROM A TOASTER.
CUTE, HUH?
THEY REALLY ARE SO CUTE—
SSK...
AIEEEEEE!!

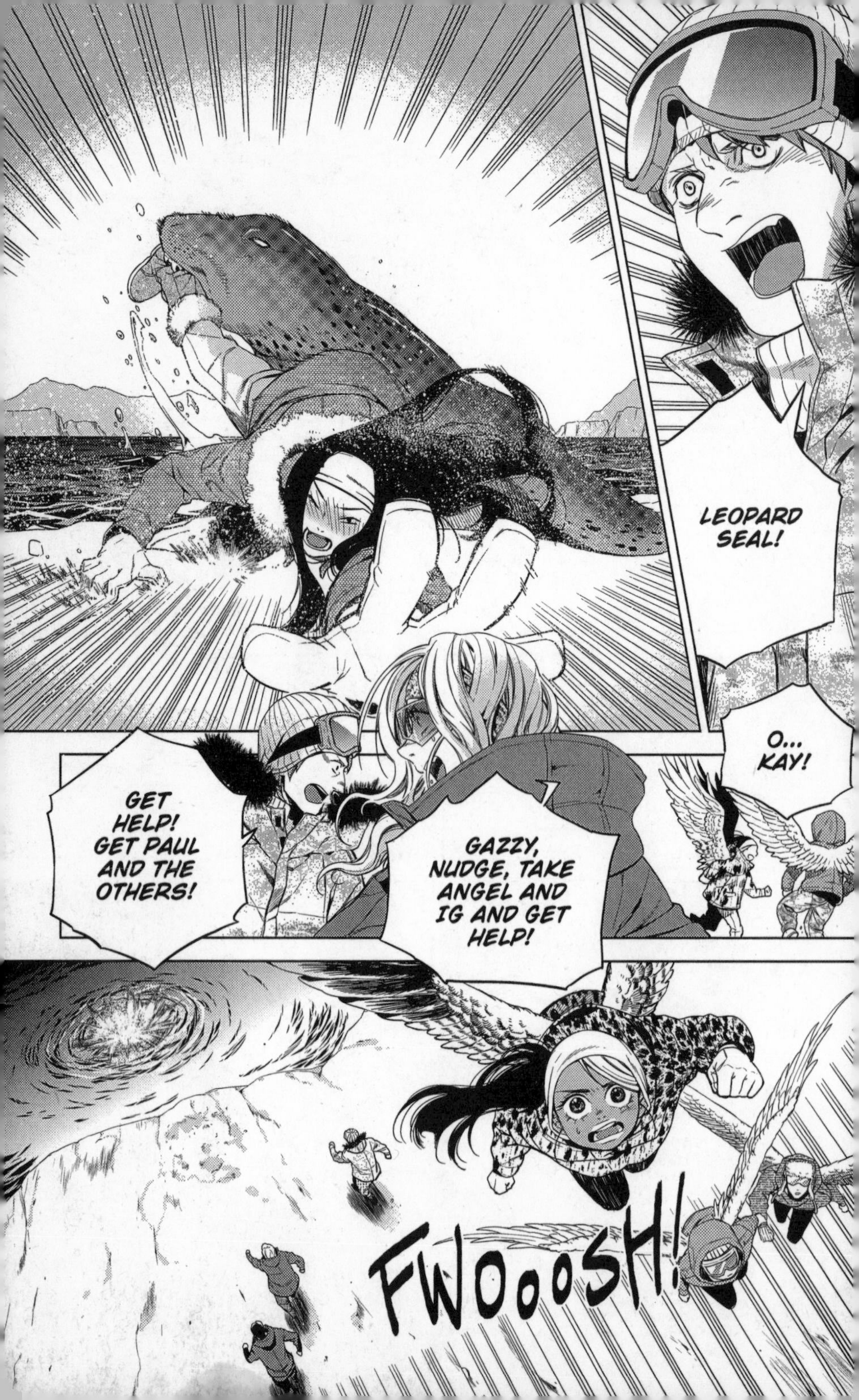
LEOPARD SEAL!
GET HELP! GET PAUL AND THE OTHERS!
GAZZY, NUDGE, TAKE ANGEL AND IG AND GET HELP!
O... KAY!
FWOOoSH!

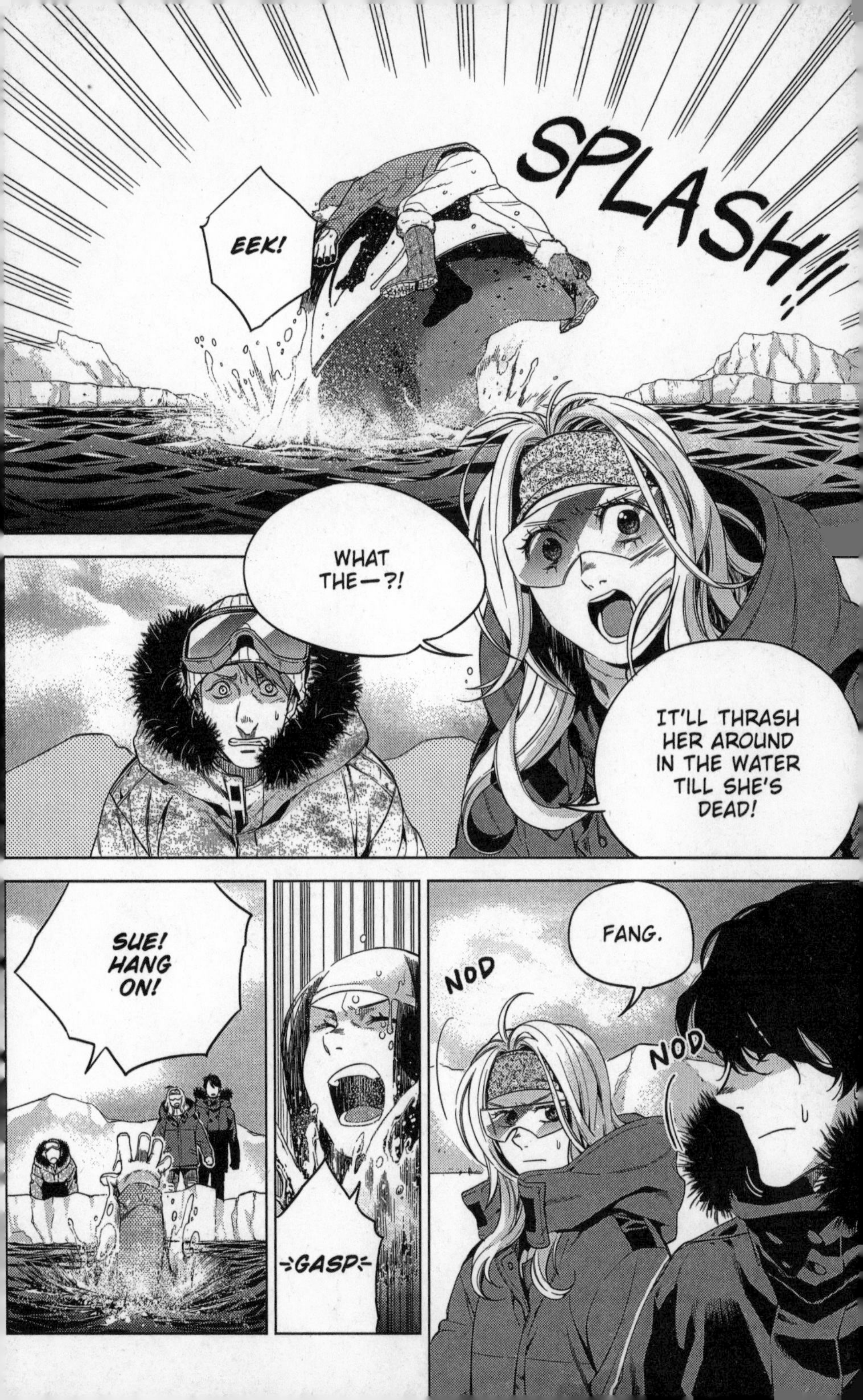
EEK!
SPLASH!!
WHAT THE—?!
IT'LL THRASH HER AROUND IN THE WATER TILL SHE'S DEAD!
SUE! HANG ON!
GASP
FANG.
NOD
NOD

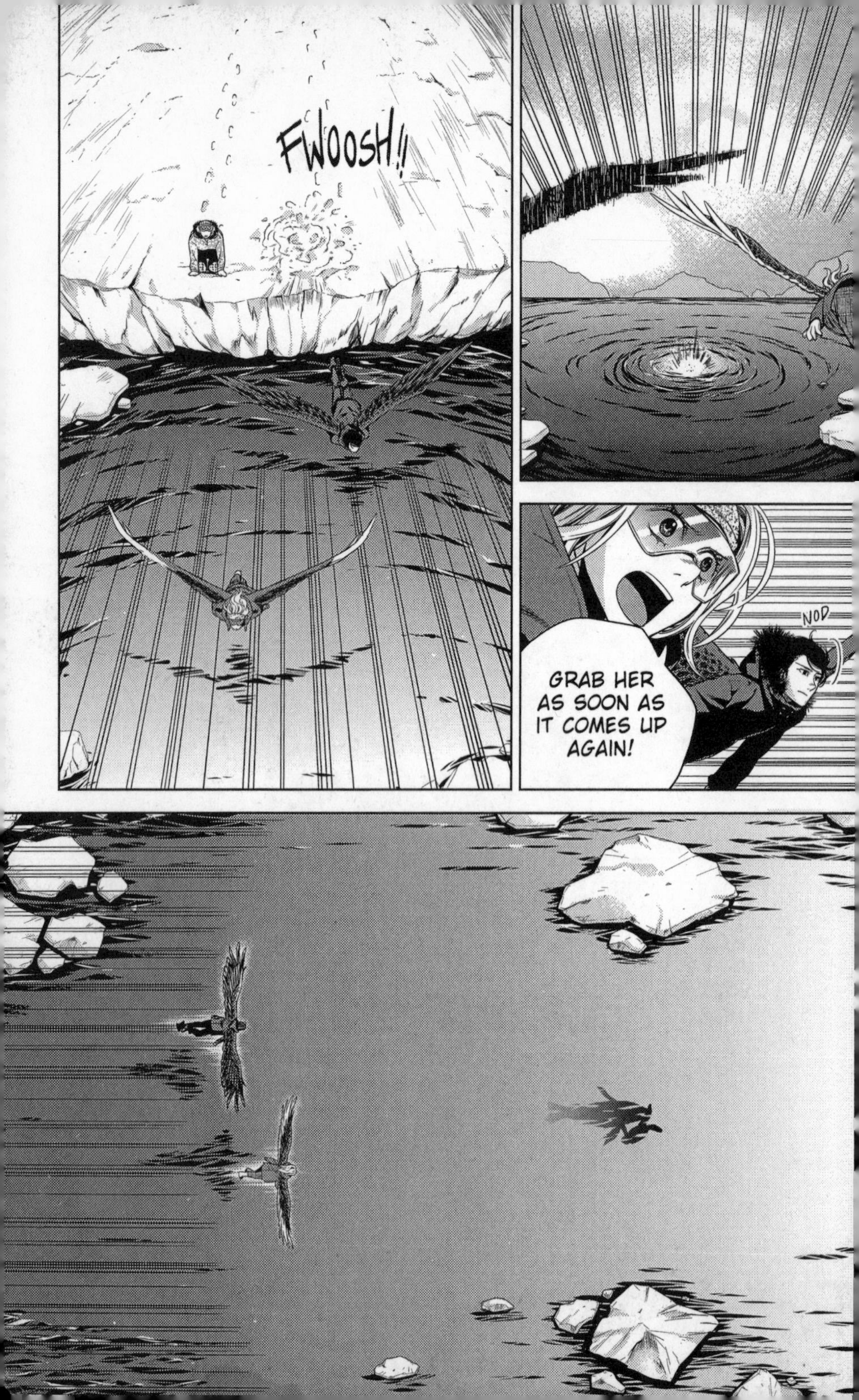
FWOOSH!!
GRAB HER AS SOON AS IT COMES UP AGAIN!
NOD

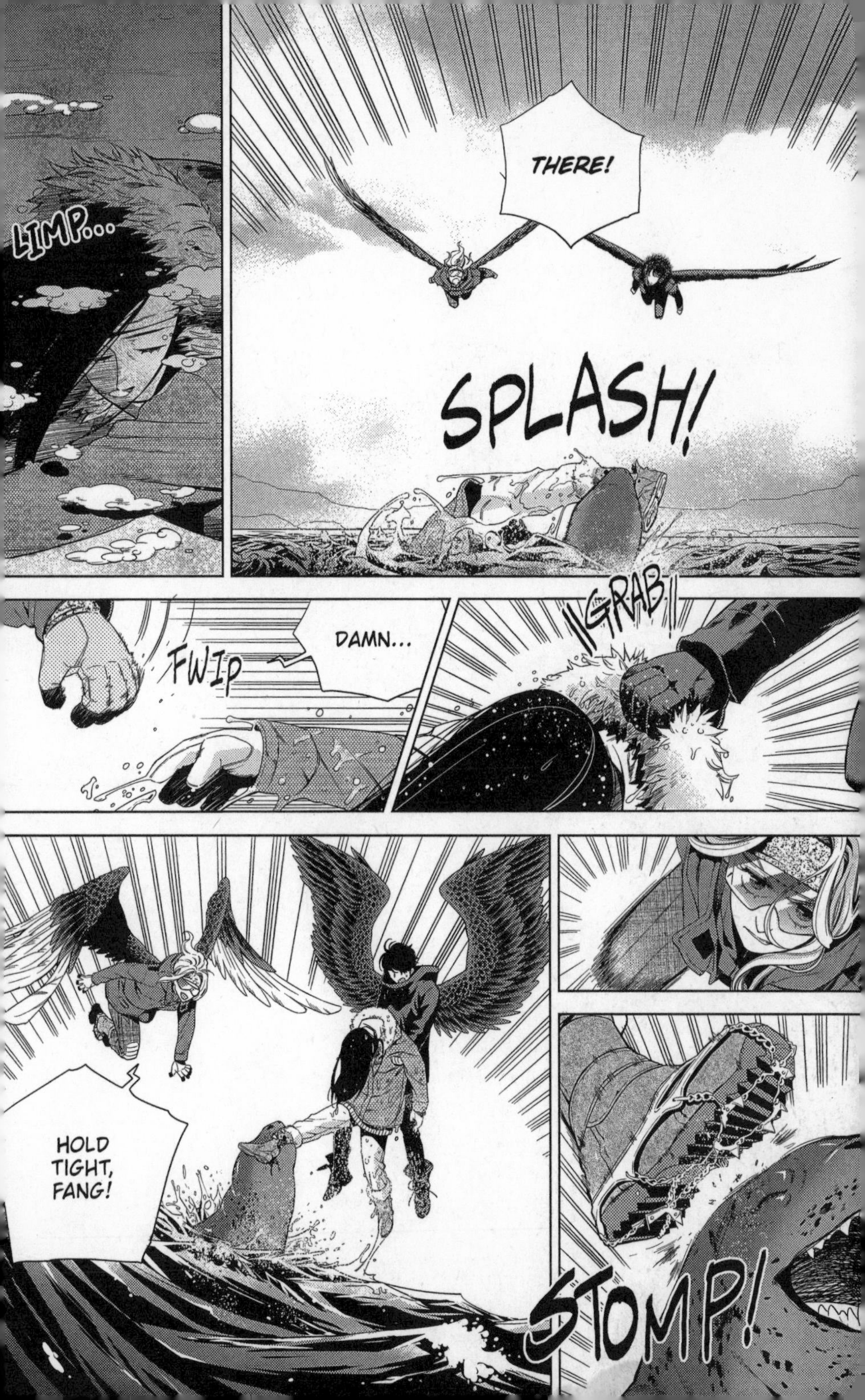
LIMP...
THERE!
SPLASH!
FWIP
DAMN...
GRAB
HOLD TIGHT, FANG!
STOMP!

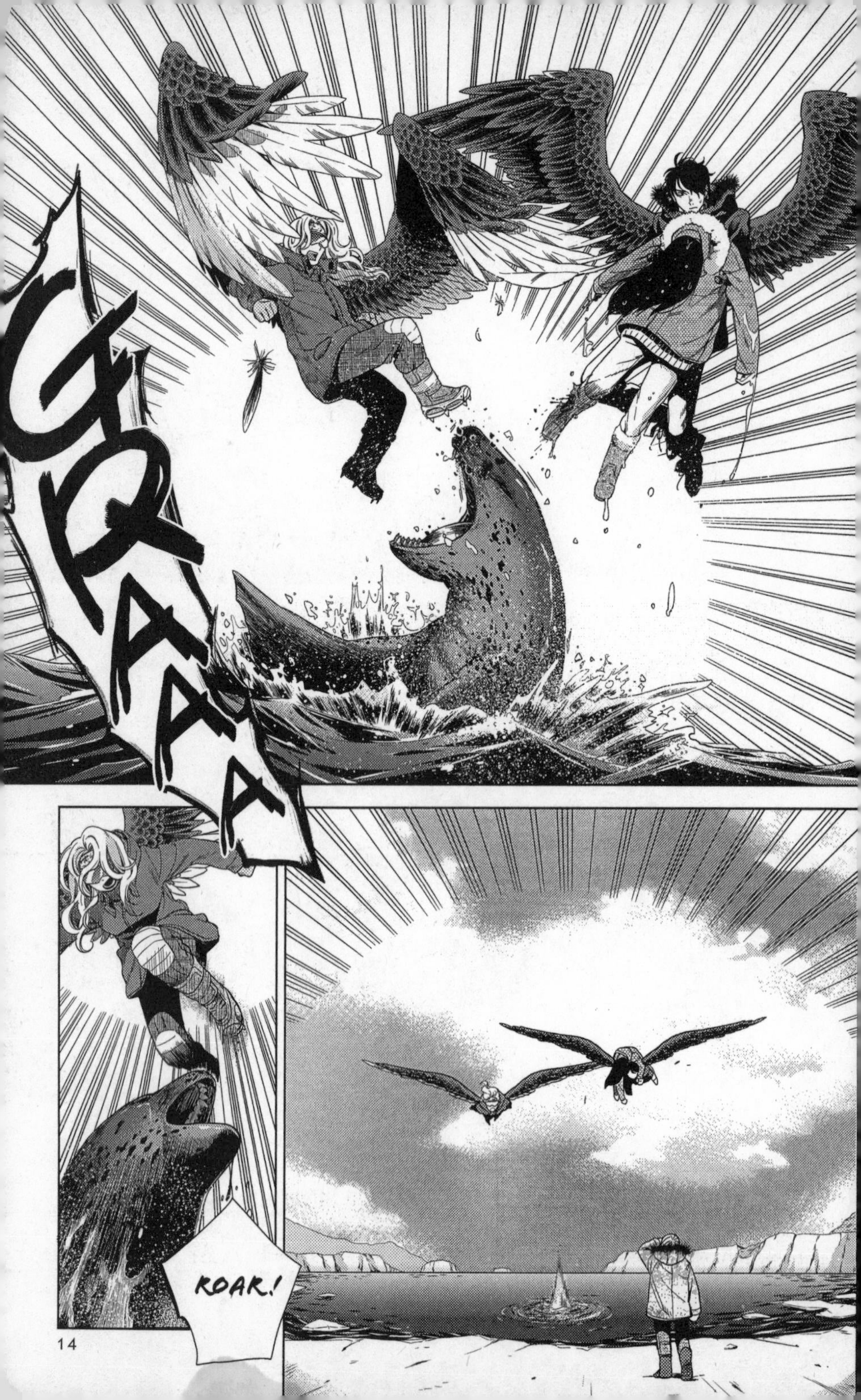
ROAR!

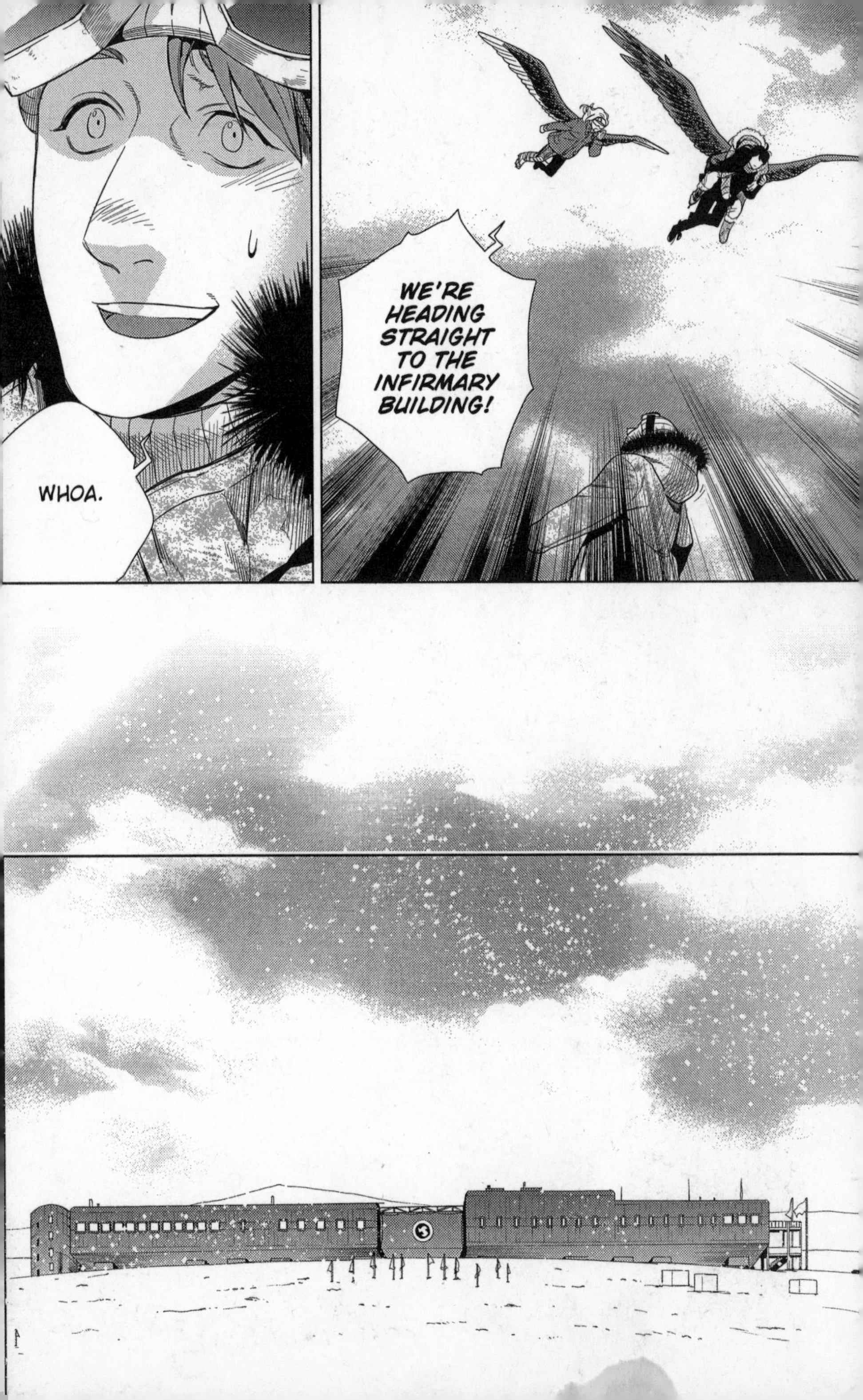
WHOA.
WE'RE HEADING STRAIGHT TO THE INFIRMARY BUILDING!

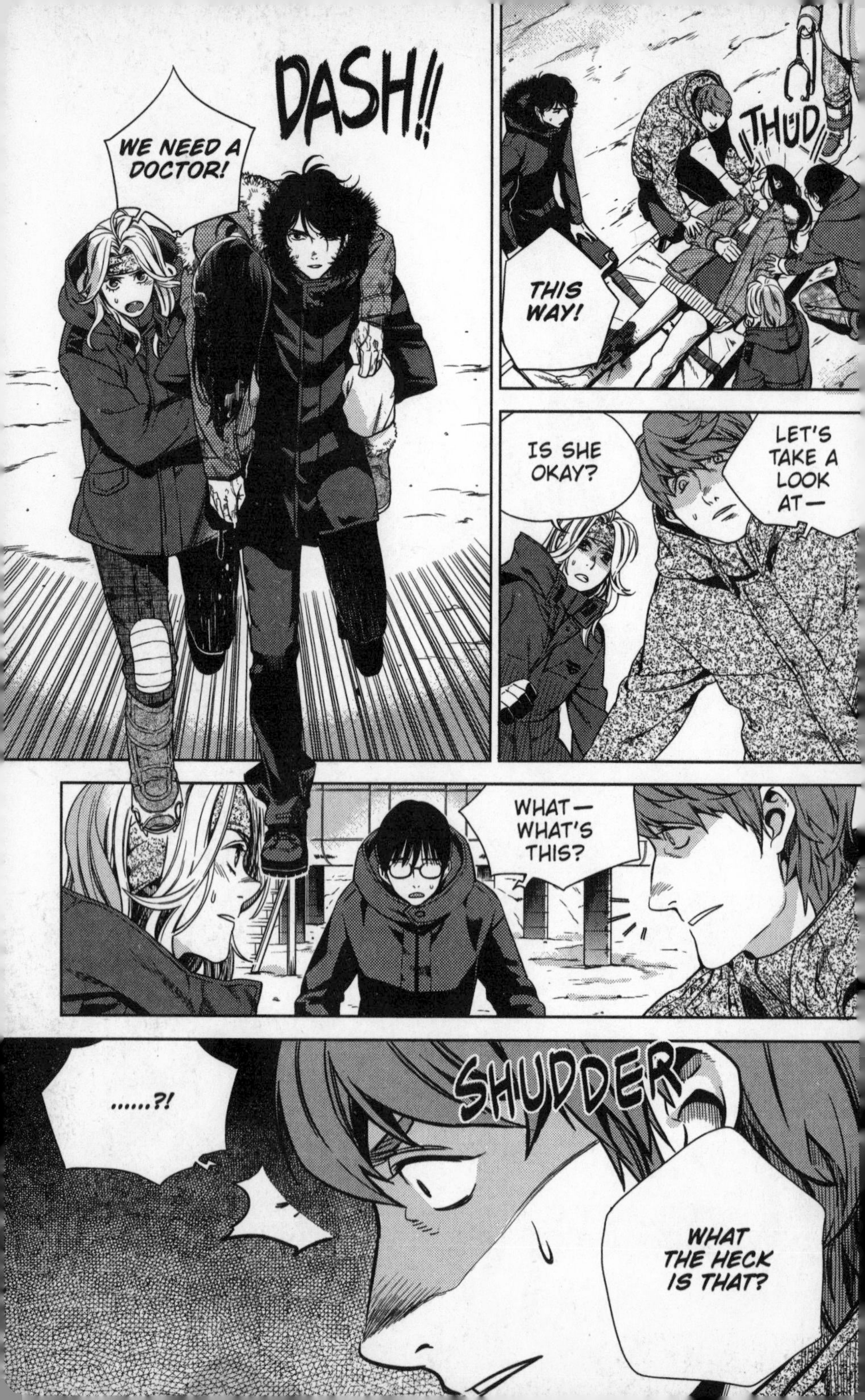

WE NEED A DOCTOR!
DASH!!
THUD
THIS WAY!
IS SHE OKAY?
LET'S TAKE A LOOK AT—
WHAT— WHAT'S THIS?
......?!
SHUDDER
WHAT THE HECK IS THAT?

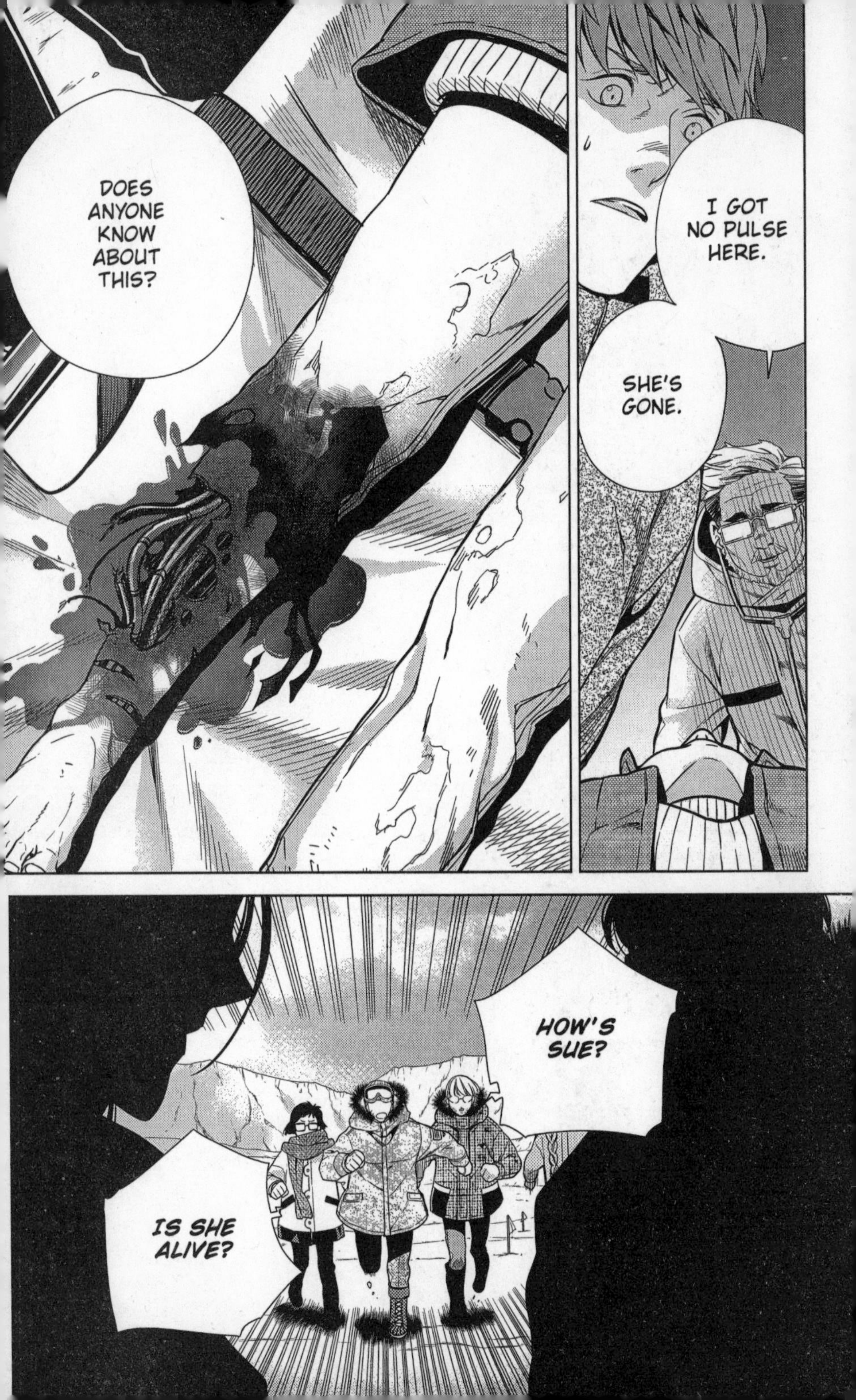
DOES ANYONE KNOW ABOUT THIS?
I GOT NO PULSE HERE.
SHE'S GONE.
HOW'S SUE?
IS SHE ALIVE?

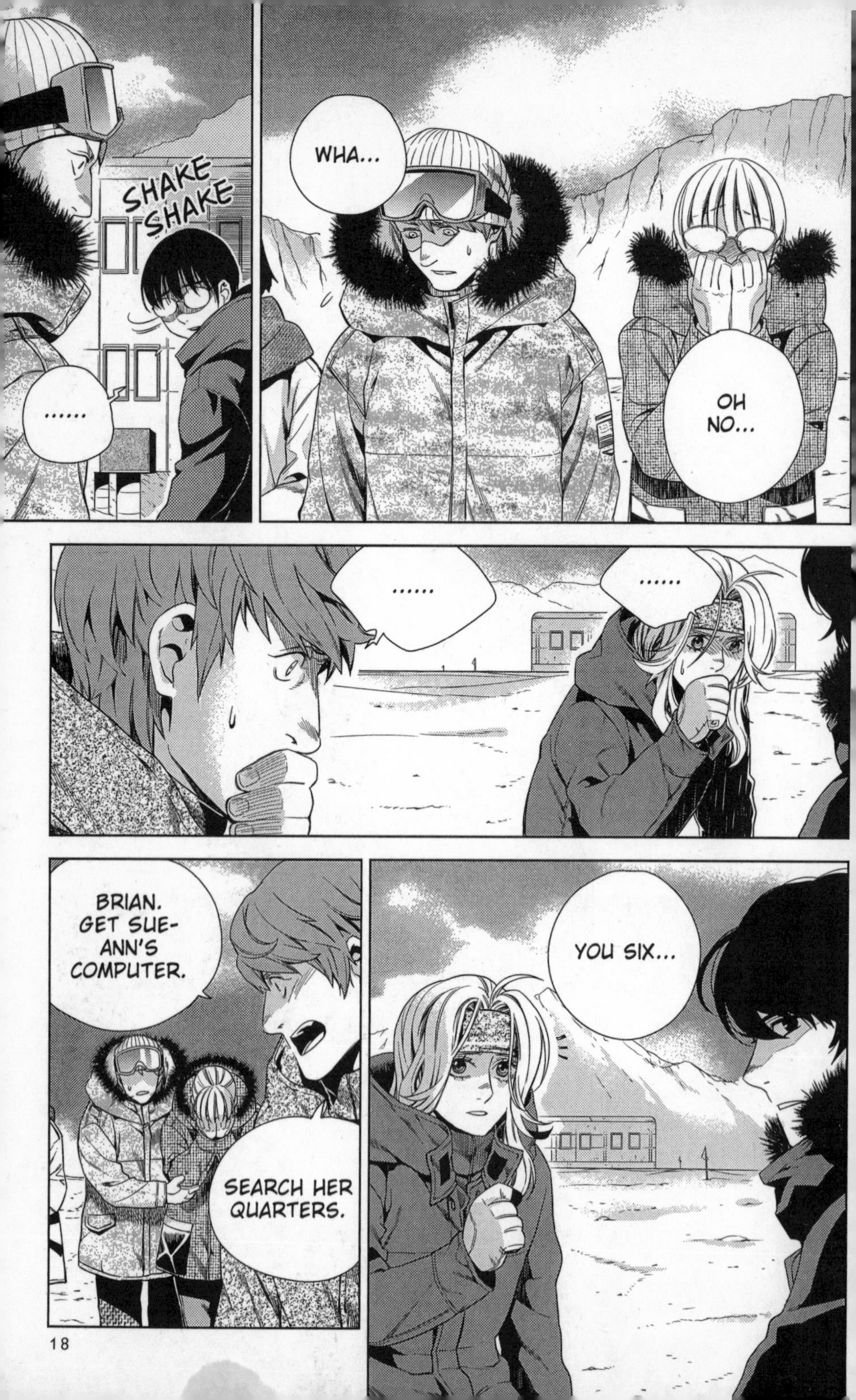
SHAKE SHAKE
......
WHA...
OH NO...
......
......
BRIAN. GET SUE-ANN'S COMPUTER.
SEARCH HER QUARTERS.
YOU SIX...

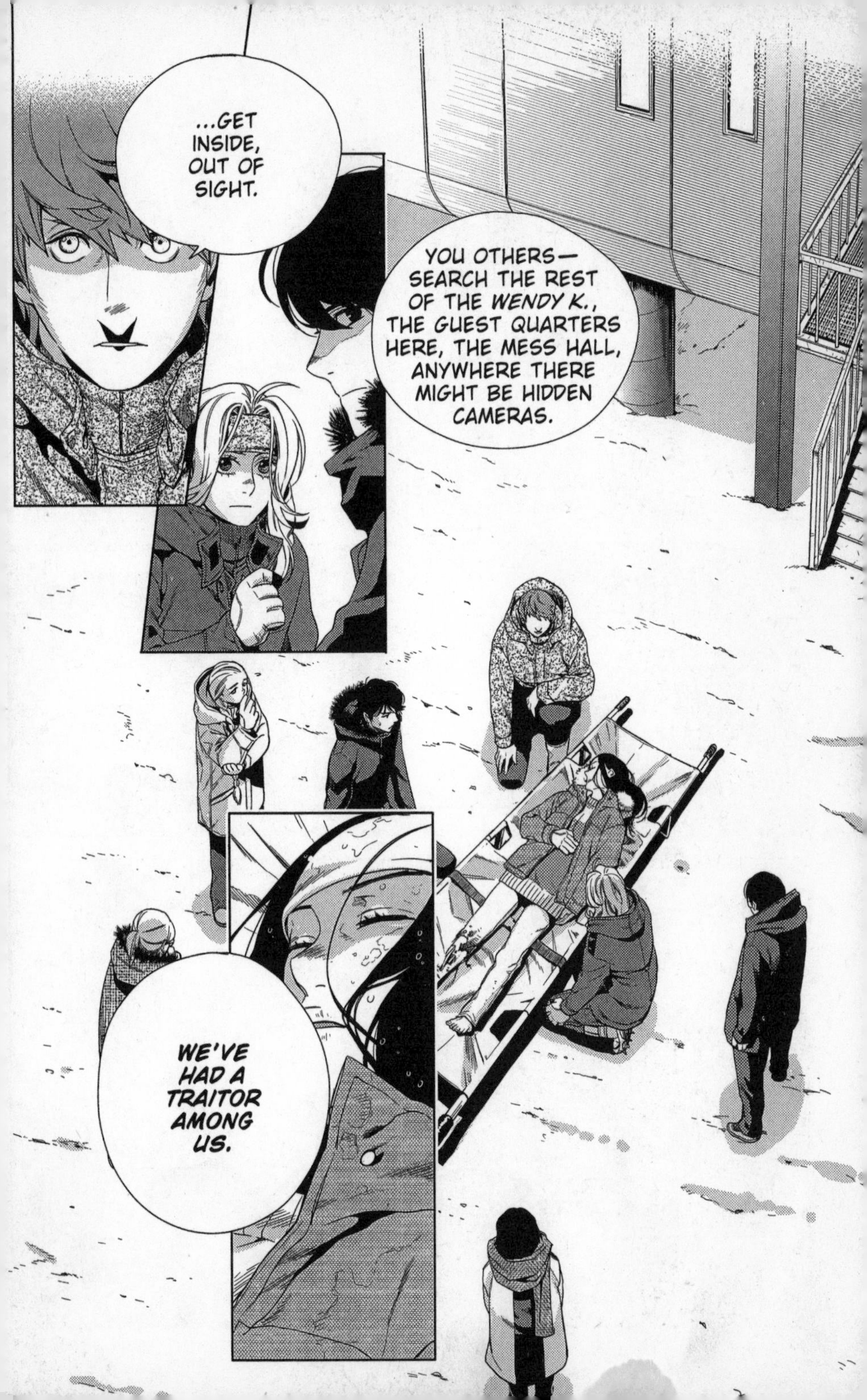
...GET INSIDE, OUT OF SIGHT.
YOU OTHERS— SEARCH THE REST OF THE *WENDY K.*, THE GUEST QUARTERS HERE, THE MESS HALL, ANYWHERE THERE MIGHT BE HIDDEN CAMERAS.
WE'VE HAD A TRAITOR AMONG US.

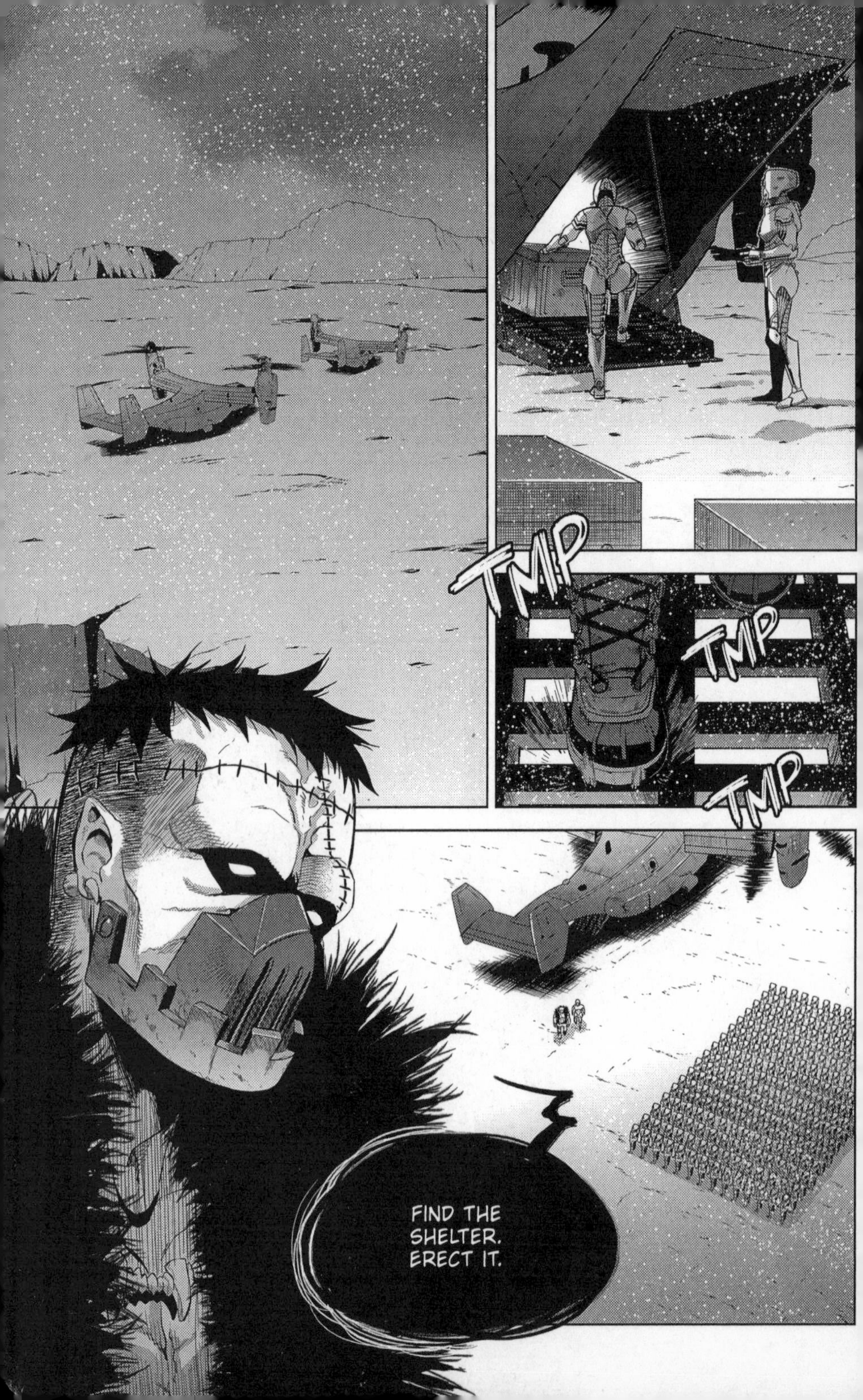
TMP
TMP
TMP
FIND THE SHELTER. ERECT IT.

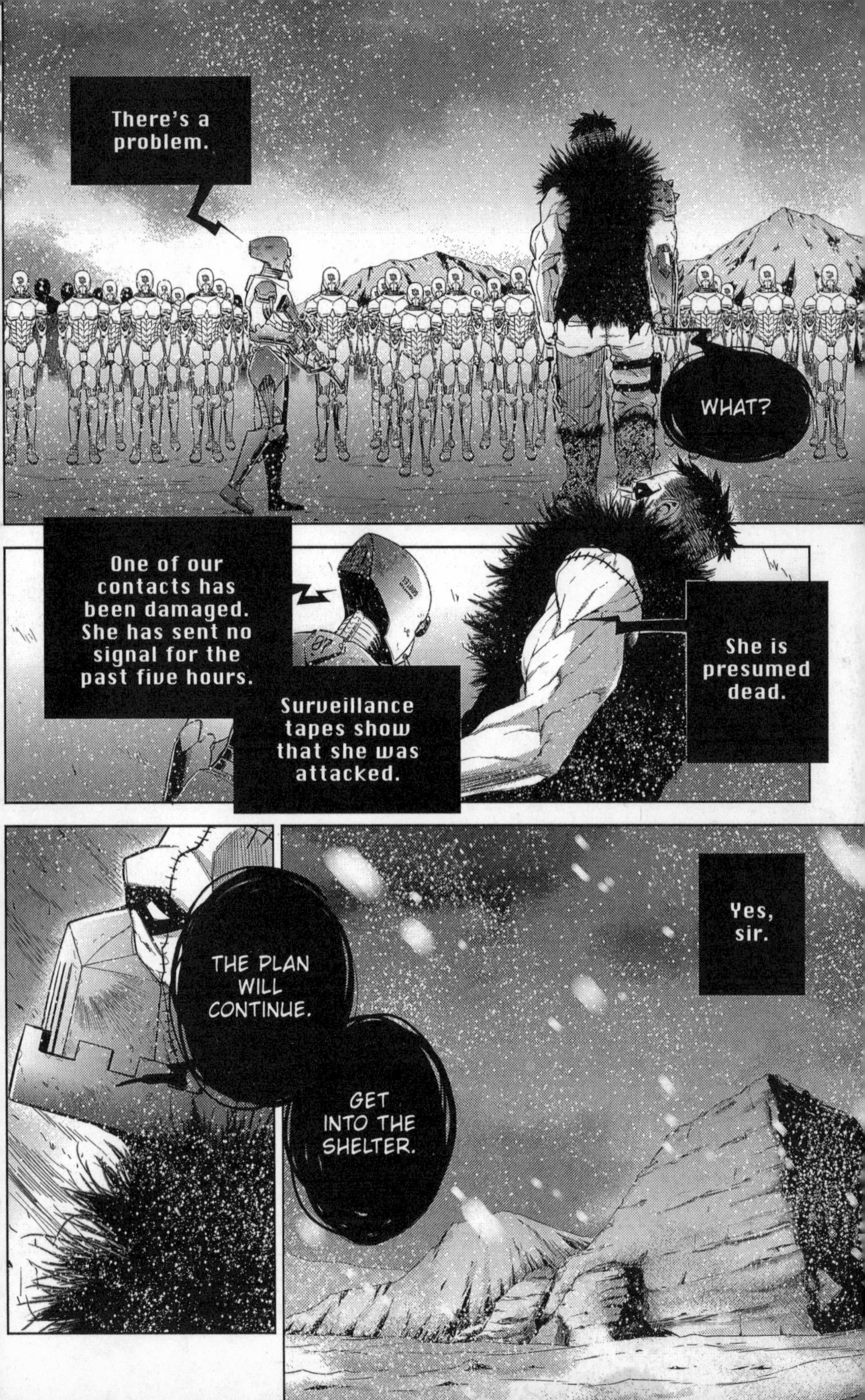
There's a problem.
WHAT?
One of our contacts has been damaged. She has sent no signal for the past five hours.
Surveillance tapes show that she was attacked.
She is presumed dead.
THE PLAN WILL CONTINUE.
GET INTO THE SHELTER.
Yes, sir.

Sign Up Sign In

Fang's Blog

HOME Blog Posts Discussions Groups Photos Chat BBS

TODAY'S THEME: WEIRDNESS AT THE BOTTOM OF THE WORLD.

Our lives are pretty freaking weird already — what with the wings, the fleeing for our lives, etc. And yet we can still be amazed when things get even weirder. Cool.

Some stuff has kept life interesting for us lately: (1) Iggy can see, off and on. He needs to be practically snow-blinded for it to kick in, but he's actually seen stuff. Made Max wish she'd brushed her hair sometime in the last month. (2) We've flown with snow petrels. They're beautiful white birds, about pigeon size, that are all over the place here. They're like flying pureness, to sound stupid and goofy. If Angel were an actual 100 percent bird, she'd be a snow petrel. The Gasman would be an emu. (3) There have been some penguin incidents, caused by uncautious belly-sliding down packed-snow slopes. Did you know that a penguin, if startled, might suddenly barf on you? We didn't either. Did you know how revolting regurgitated, half-digested krill and squid are? I do now. (4) We performed a daring rescue at sea, made possible by Max and yours featherly. Unfortunately, the person we rescued turned out to be a mole who's probably been spying on us for the past week. So now we're most likely in mortal danger, as per usual. Fortunately, the person we rescued didn't make it. So I'm guessing her reports have slowed way down. In the meantime, whoever's out there planning God knows what, we're on to you. We see you coming. We're not going to take it well.

I'll go ahead and tell you: We're in Antarctica. We're here checking out the signs of global warming. Global warming may sound comfy — no more winter coats — but everything on Earth right now kind of desperately relies on the climate staying as is. But if we give up our childish fears of catastrophic flooding, earthquakes, tsunamis, untold plant and animal extinctions, droughts, famines, and whatnot, we could just relax right now and let 'er rip!

However. For those of us who prefer the planet relatively undisastered, it seems clear that things have to change. I mean, we humans have to change our habits, our recklessness, our dependence on fossil fuels and beef.

Any questions?

Comment Wall (2,111 comments) ▼

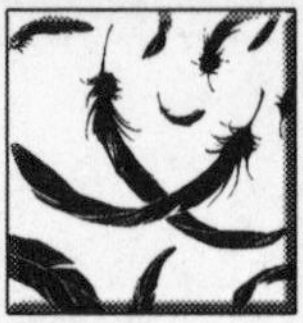

Fang

Welcome!

Visitor number

545,422

HOME Blog Posts Discussions Groups Photos Chat BBS

Comment ▼

Ali, Ju-Ju, Ariel, and Robin Bernstein from Palm Beach write:
Wassup up with no beef? No hamburgers?

Well, Ali, Ju-Ju, Ariel, and Robin Bernstein,
Good thing you asked. For myself, I'm totally about the burgers. And steak. Shish kebabs. Stew. You name it, if it's cow, it's for me.
But this incredibly cool scientist I know, Dr. Brigid Dwyer, told me that livestock is causing more damage to the Earth's climate than cars. All the cars. For one thing, cattle "release" more methane and other greenhouse gases than even the Gasman, which is saying something. Plus, cattle eat about fourteen pounds of grain to produce one pound of meat. Which is energy efficiency in reverse. Not to mention the deforestation for their grazing land, the water they consume. It all adds up hugely. Makes ya think, huh?
— Fang

BitterGummy from Honshu writes:
Get off ur soapbox, man! When I want a lecture, I'll go 2 school!

Sounds like you need it, BitterGummy. Try to stay awake this time.
— Fang

MinkyPuddin from Sydney writes:
Fang I miss u guyz so much. U haven't bin in the newz lately. I am all worried.
Your #1 fan.

No worries, MinkyPuddin. We're fine. More fine than we've been in a long time, actually.
— Fang

Shy Babe from Seattle writes:
Dear Fang, I wrote u last month. Do u have a girlfriend?

I recommend you stick to your own species, Shy Babe. Thanks anyway.
— Fang

Okay, guys, gotta go. Global disaster to document, scientists to talk to. And it's dinnertime. I'm guessing it's not beef.
— Fang

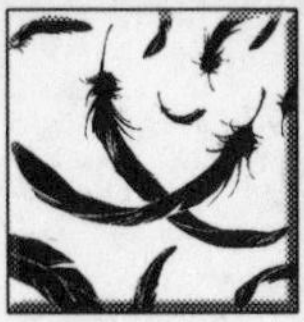

Fang
Welcome!

Visitor number
545,422

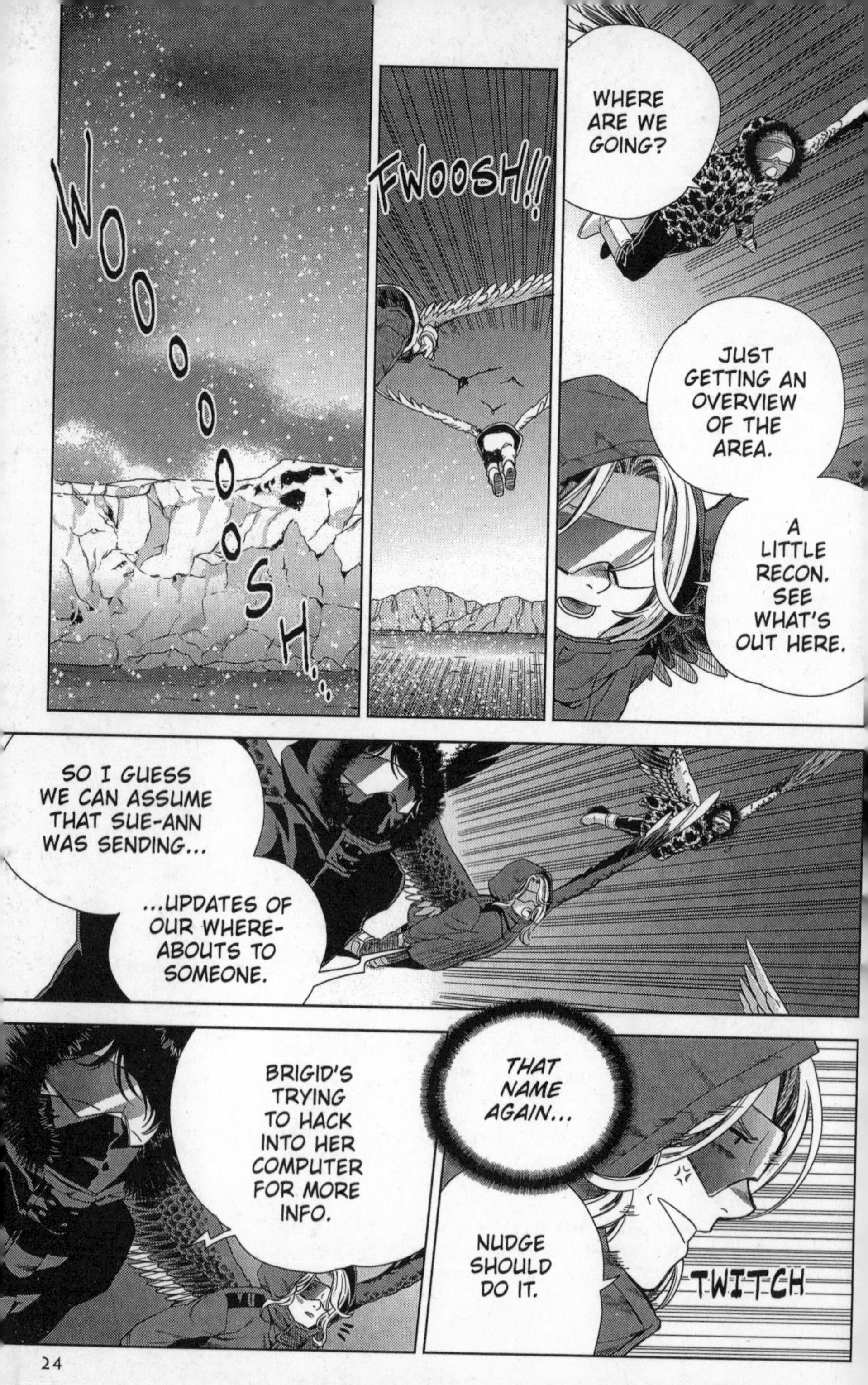
WOOOOOOSH...
FWOOSH!!
WHERE ARE WE GOING?
JUST GETTING AN OVERVIEW OF THE AREA.
A LITTLE RECON. SEE WHAT'S OUT HERE.
SO I GUESS WE CAN ASSUME THAT SUE-ANN WAS SENDING...
...UPDATES OF OUR WHERE-ABOUTS TO SOMEONE.
BRIGID'S TRYING TO HACK INTO HER COMPUTER FOR MORE INFO.
THAT NAME AGAIN...
NUDGE SHOULD DO IT.
TWITCH

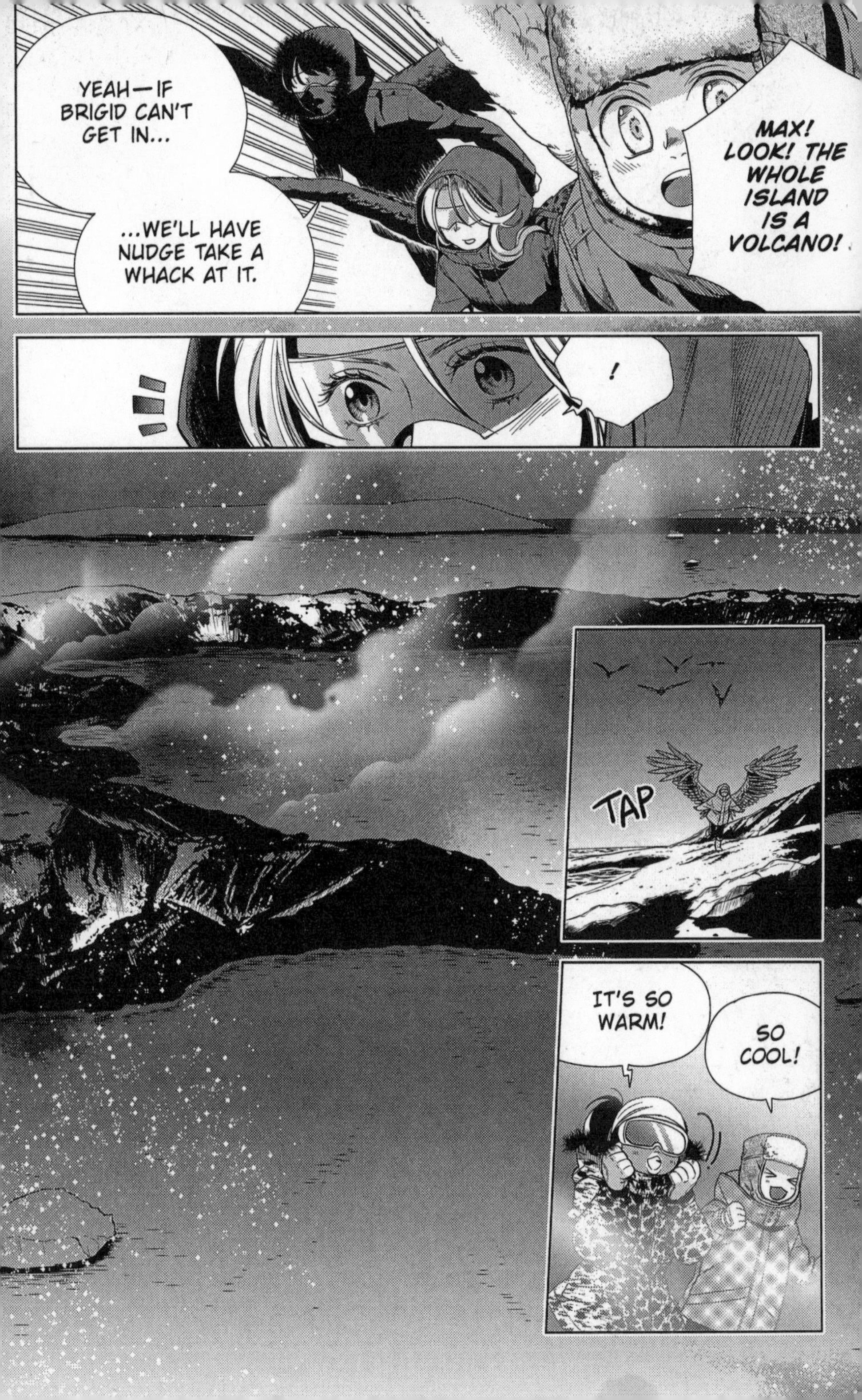
YEAH—IF BRIGID CAN'T GET IN...
...WE'LL HAVE NUDGE TAKE A WHACK AT IT.
MAX! LOOK! THE WHOLE ISLAND IS A VOLCANO!
!
TAP
IT'S SO WARM!
SO COOL!

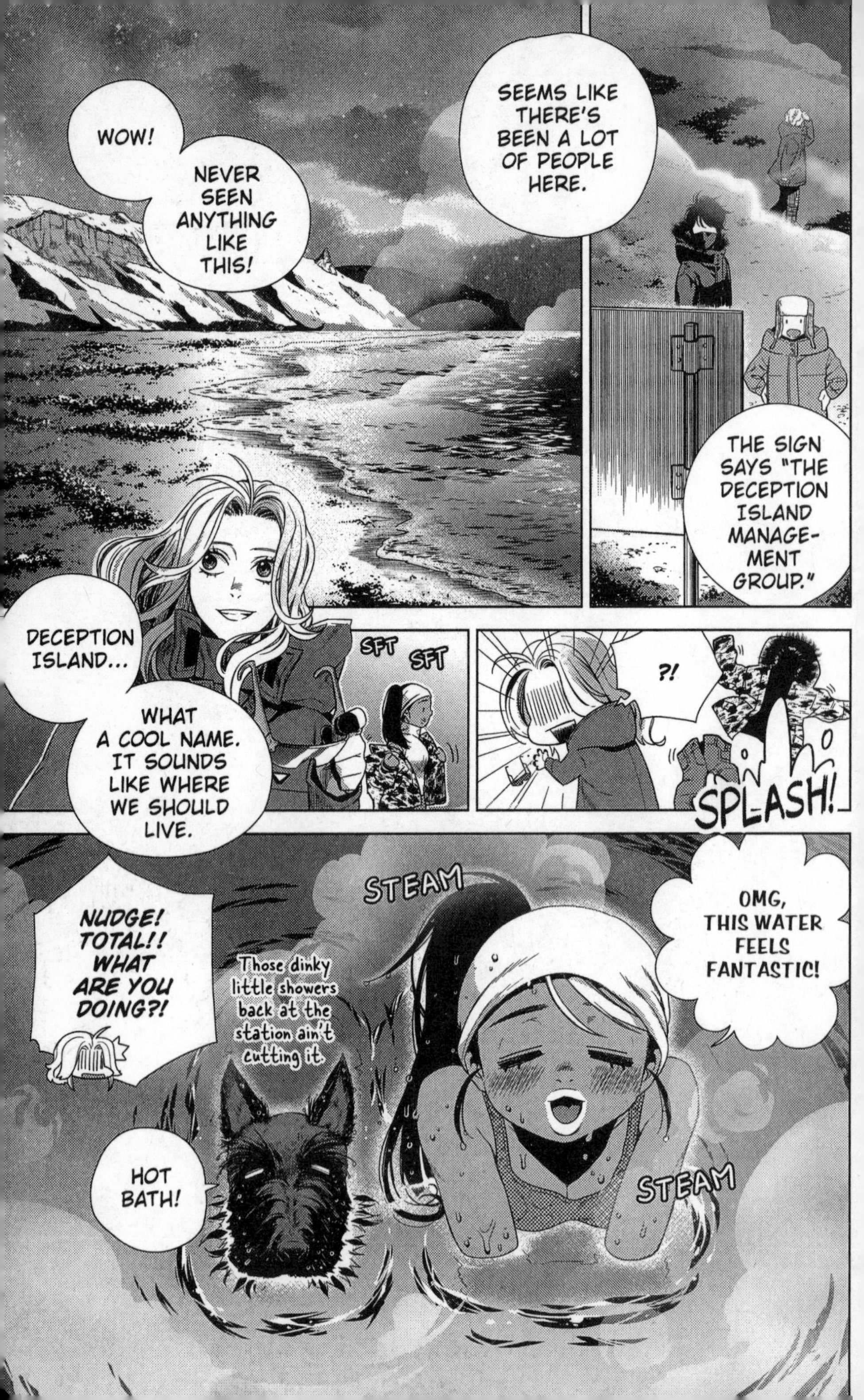
WOW!
NEVER SEEN ANYTHING LIKE THIS!
SEEMS LIKE THERE'S BEEN A LOT OF PEOPLE HERE.
THE SIGN SAYS "THE DECEPTION ISLAND MANAGE-MENT GROUP."
DECEPTION ISLAND...
WHAT A COOL NAME. IT SOUNDS LIKE WHERE WE SHOULD LIVE.
SFT SFT
?!
SPLASH!
NUDGE! TOTAL!! WHAT ARE YOU DOING?!
Those dinky little showers back at the station ain't cutting it.
STEAM
OMG, THIS WATER FEELS FANTASTIC!
HOT BATH!
STEAM

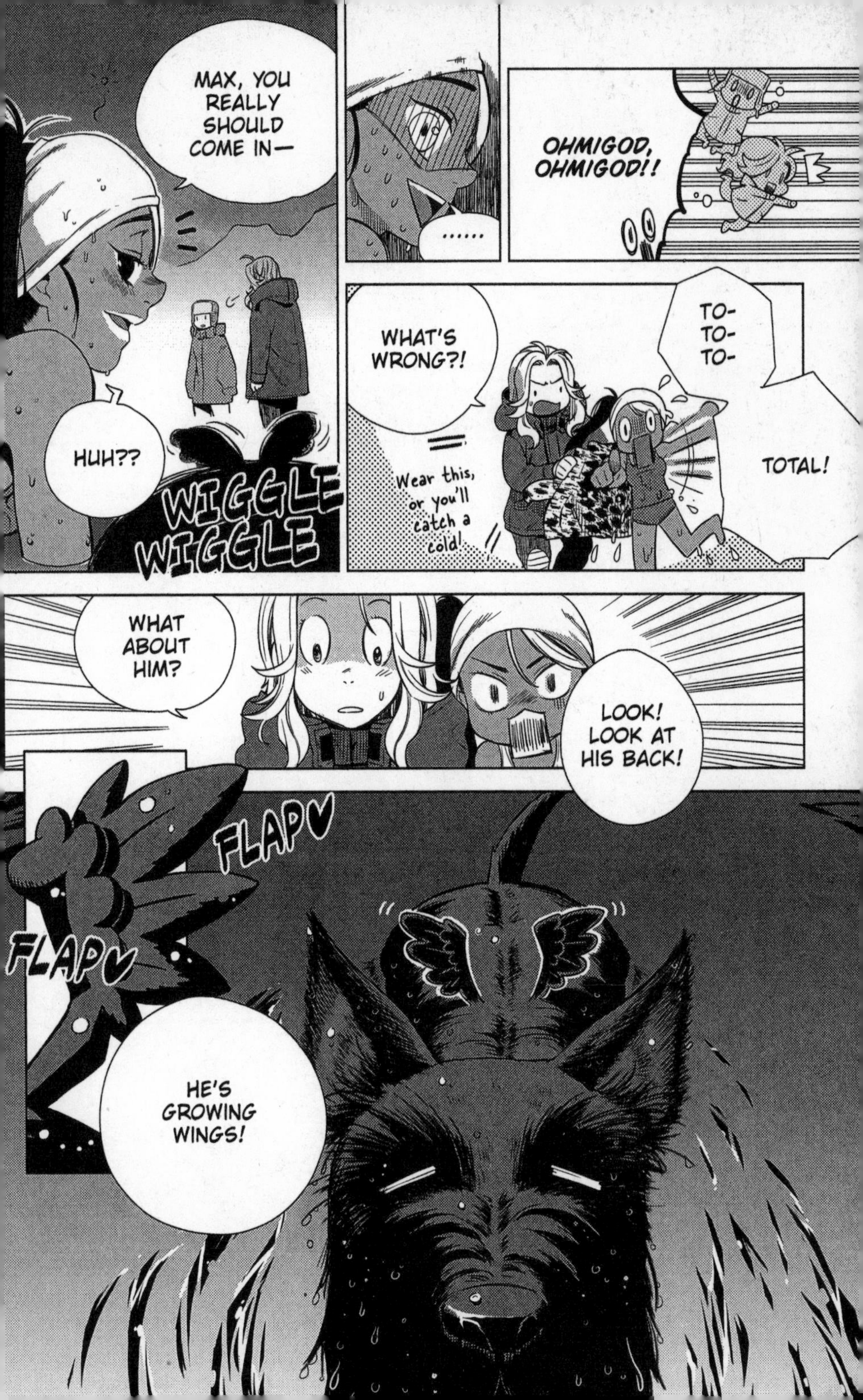
MAX, YOU REALLY SHOULD COME IN—
HUH??
WIGGLE WIGGLE
......
OHMIGOD, OHMIGOD!!
WHAT'S WRONG?!
Wear this, or you'll catch a cold!
TO-TO-TO-
TOTAL!
WHAT ABOUT HIM?
LOOK! LOOK AT HIS BACK!
FLAP♥
FLAP♥
HE'S GROWING WINGS!

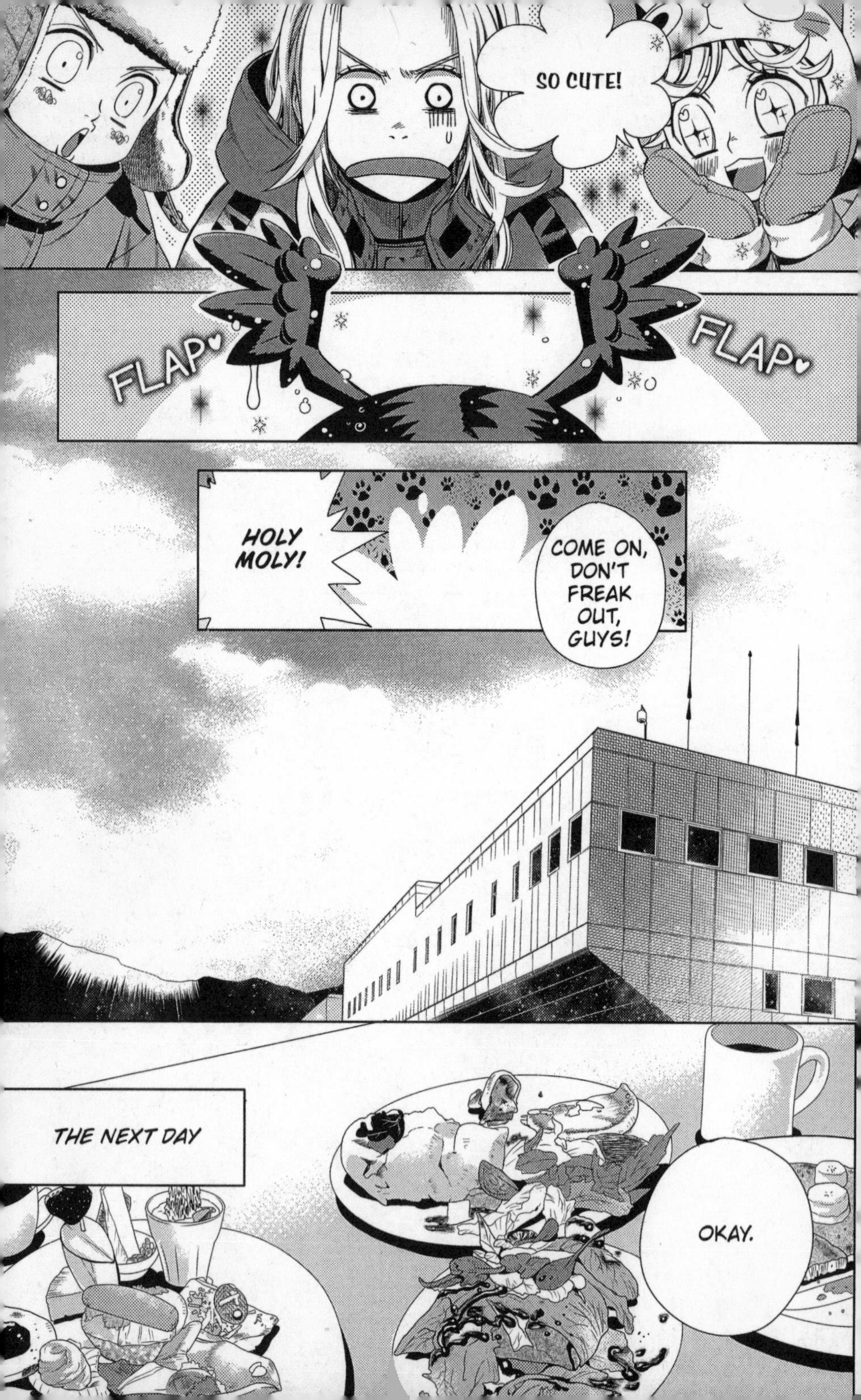
SO CUTE!
FLAP♥
FLAP♥
HOLY MOLY!
COME ON, DON'T FREAK OUT, GUYS!
THE NEXT DAY
OKAY.

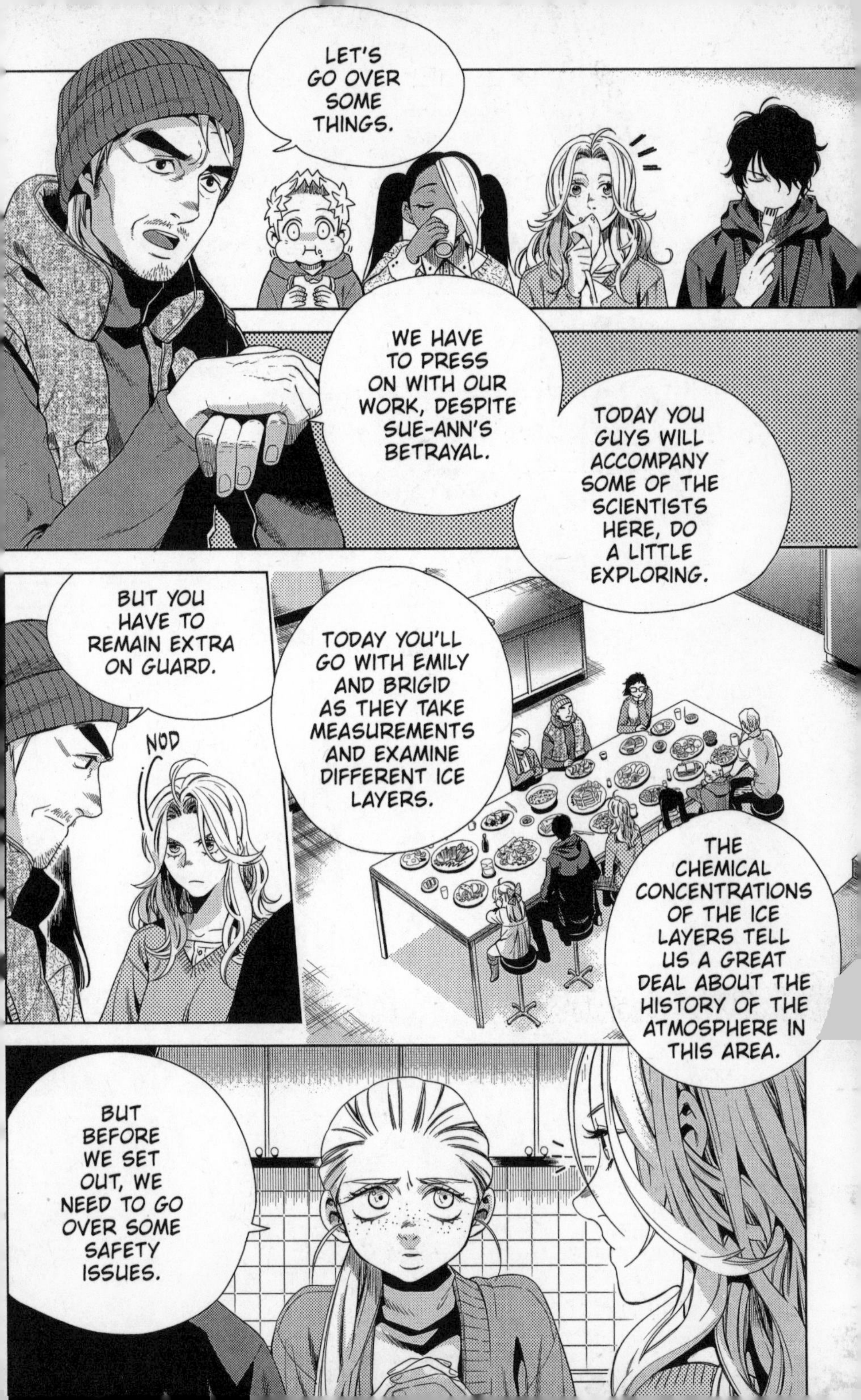
LET'S GO OVER SOME THINGS.
WE HAVE TO PRESS ON WITH OUR WORK, DESPITE SUE-ANN'S BETRAYAL.
TODAY YOU GUYS WILL ACCOMPANY SOME OF THE SCIENTISTS HERE, DO A LITTLE EXPLORING.
BUT YOU HAVE TO REMAIN EXTRA ON GUARD.
NOD
TODAY YOU'LL GO WITH EMILY AND BRIGID AS THEY TAKE MEASUREMENTS AND EXAMINE DIFFERENT ICE LAYERS.
THE CHEMICAL CONCENTRATIONS OF THE ICE LAYERS TELL US A GREAT DEAL ABOUT THE HISTORY OF THE ATMOSPHERE IN THIS AREA.
BUT BEFORE WE SET OUT, WE NEED TO GO OVER SOME SAFETY ISSUES.

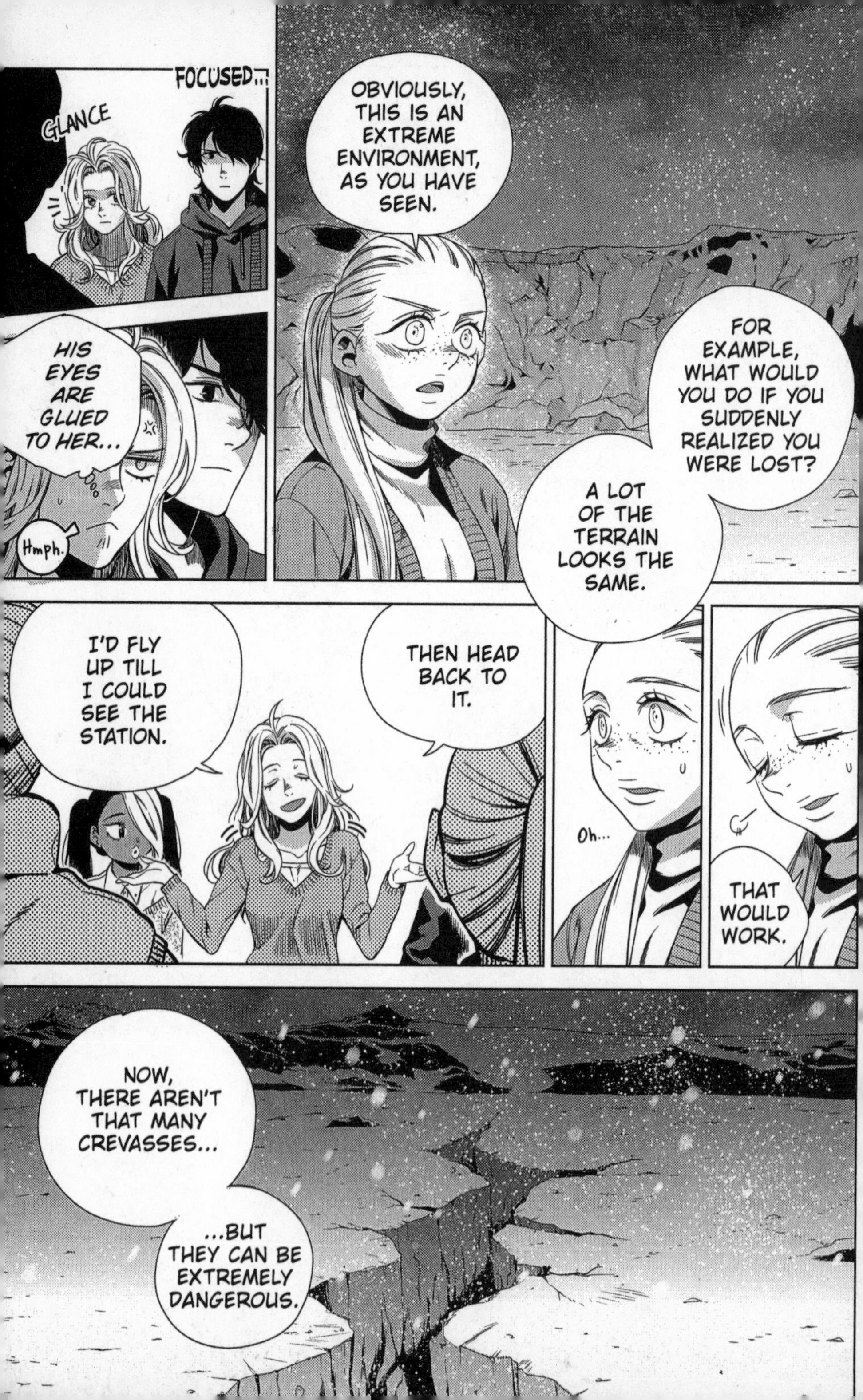
FOCUSED...
GLANCE
HIS EYES ARE GLUED TO HER...
Hmph.
OBVIOUSLY, THIS IS AN EXTREME ENVIRONMENT, AS YOU HAVE SEEN.
FOR EXAMPLE, WHAT WOULD YOU DO IF YOU SUDDENLY REALIZED YOU WERE LOST?
A LOT OF THE TERRAIN LOOKS THE SAME.
I'D FLY UP TILL I COULD SEE THE STATION.
THEN HEAD BACK TO IT.
Oh...
THAT WOULD WORK.
NOW, THERE AREN'T THAT MANY CREVASSES...
...BUT THEY CAN BE EXTREMELY DANGEROUS.

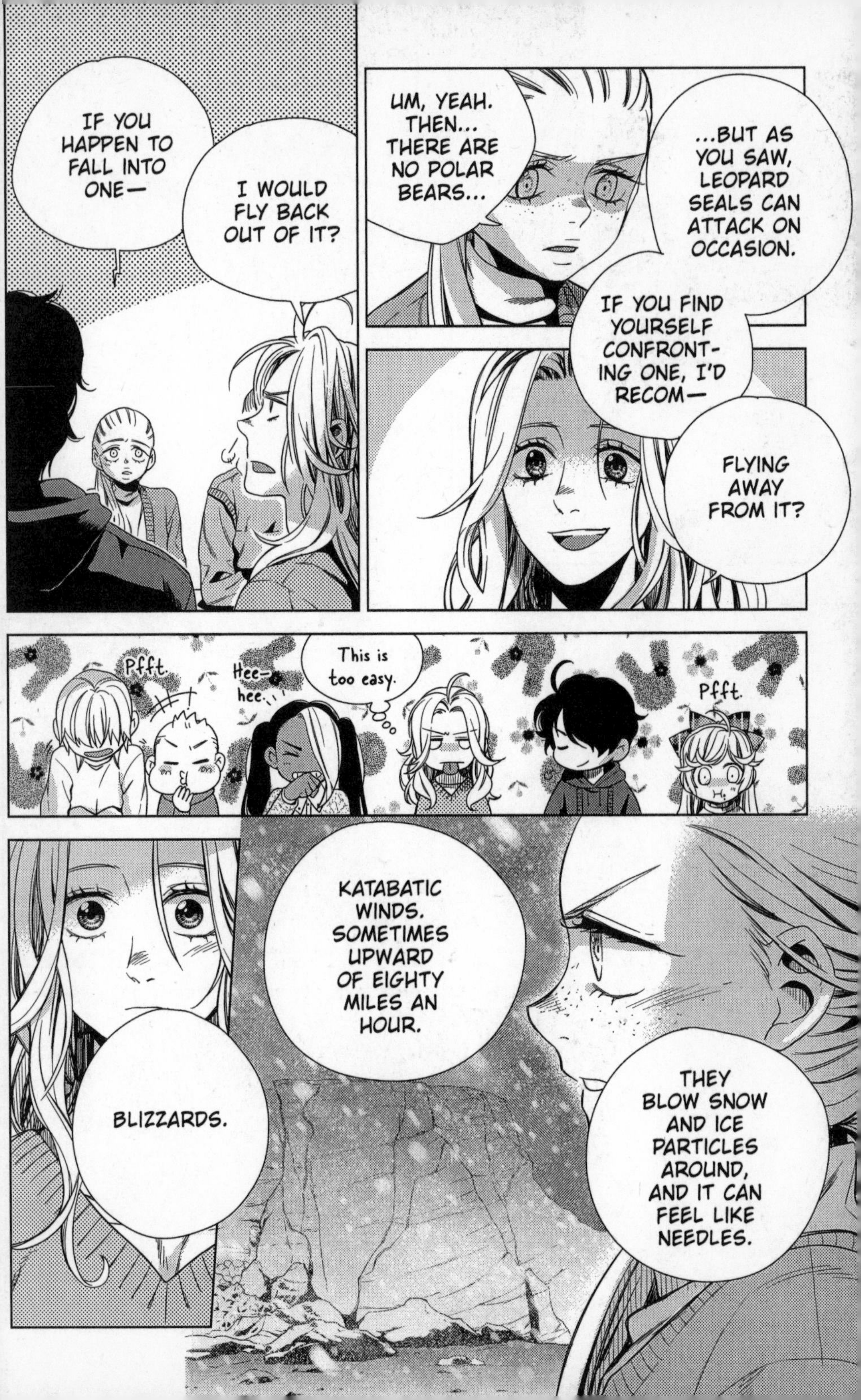
IF YOU HAPPEN TO FALL INTO ONE—
I WOULD FLY BACK OUT OF IT?
UM, YEAH. THEN... THERE ARE NO POLAR BEARS...
...BUT AS YOU SAW, LEOPARD SEALS CAN ATTACK ON OCCASION.
IF YOU FIND YOURSELF CONFRONT-ING ONE, I'D RECOM—
FLYING AWAY FROM IT?
Pfft.
Hee-hee.
This is too easy.
Pfft.
BLIZZARDS.
KATABATIC WINDS. SOMETIMES UPWARD OF EIGHTY MILES AN HOUR.
THEY BLOW SNOW AND ICE PARTICLES AROUND, AND IT CAN FEEL LIKE NEEDLES.

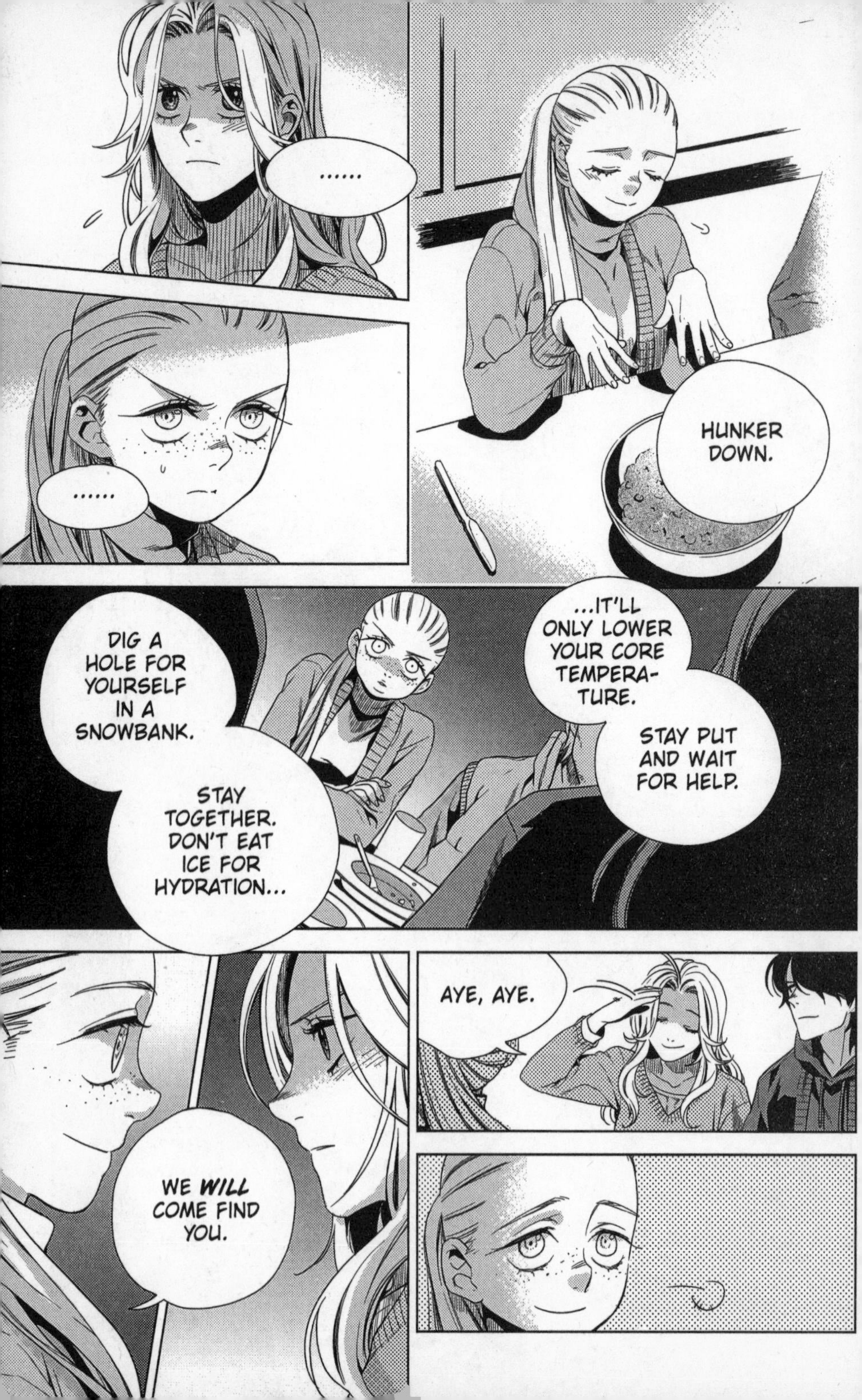
......
......
HUNKER DOWN.
DIG A HOLE FOR YOURSELF IN A SNOWBANK.
STAY TOGETHER. DON'T EAT ICE FOR HYDRATION...
...IT'LL ONLY LOWER YOUR CORE TEMPERA-TURE.
STAY PUT AND WAIT FOR HELP.
WE *WILL* COME FIND YOU.
AYE, AYE.

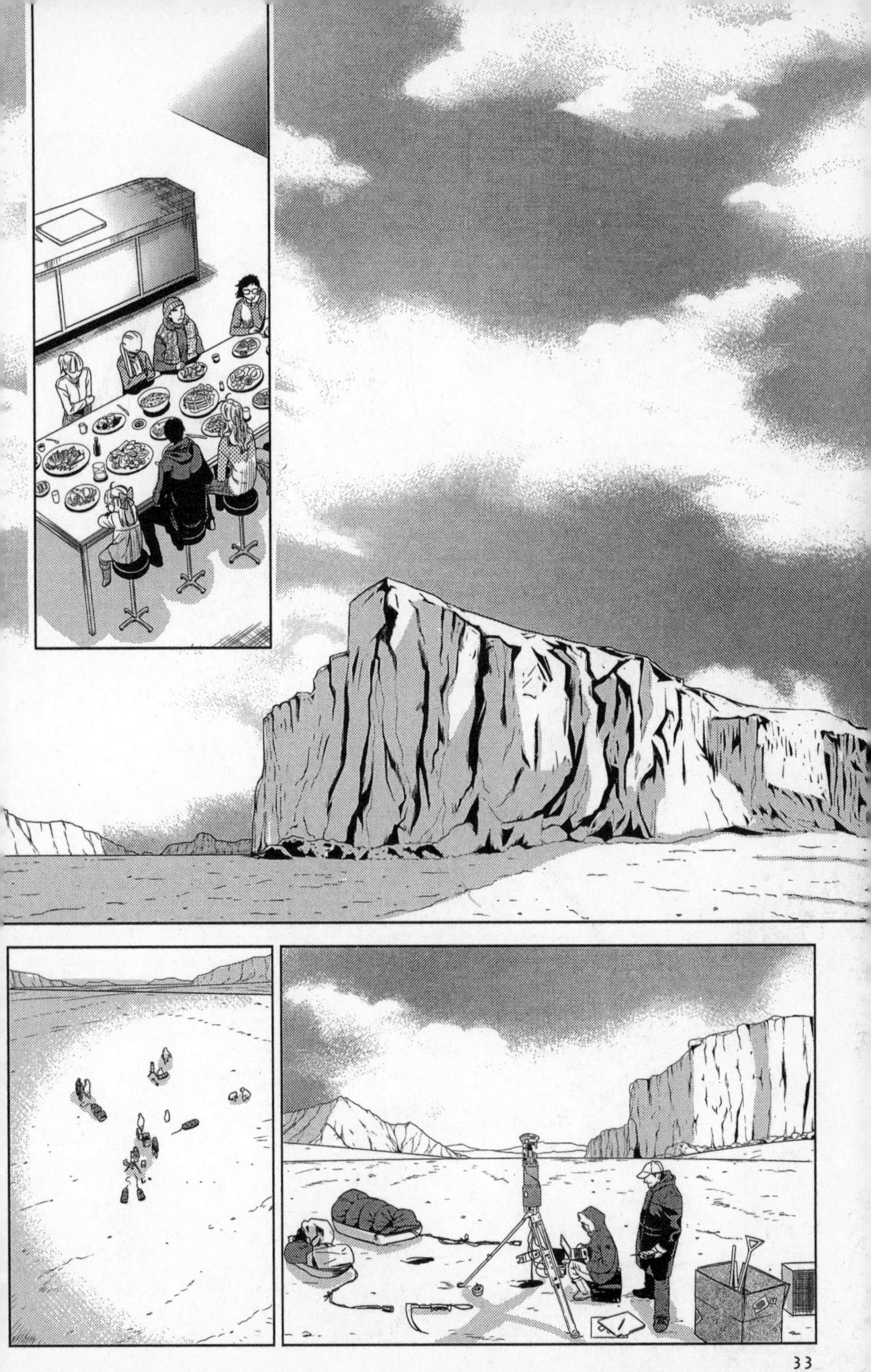

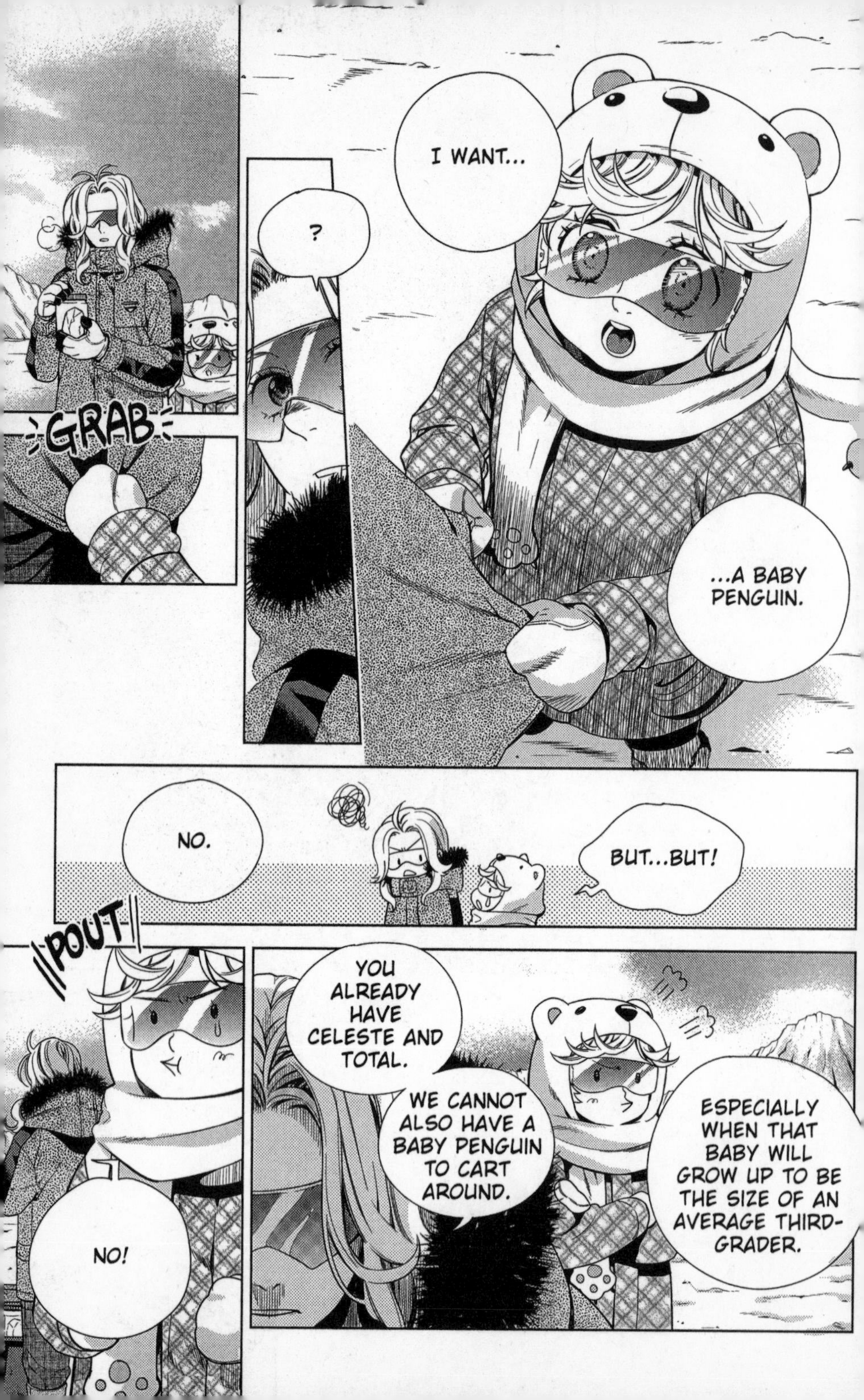
GRAB
?
I WANT...
...A BABY PENGUIN.
NO.
BUT...BUT!
POUT
NO!
YOU ALREADY HAVE CELESTE AND TOTAL.
WE CANNOT ALSO HAVE A BABY PENGUIN TO CART AROUND.
ESPECIALLY WHEN THAT BABY WILL GROW UP TO BE THE SIZE OF AN AVERAGE THIRD-GRADER.

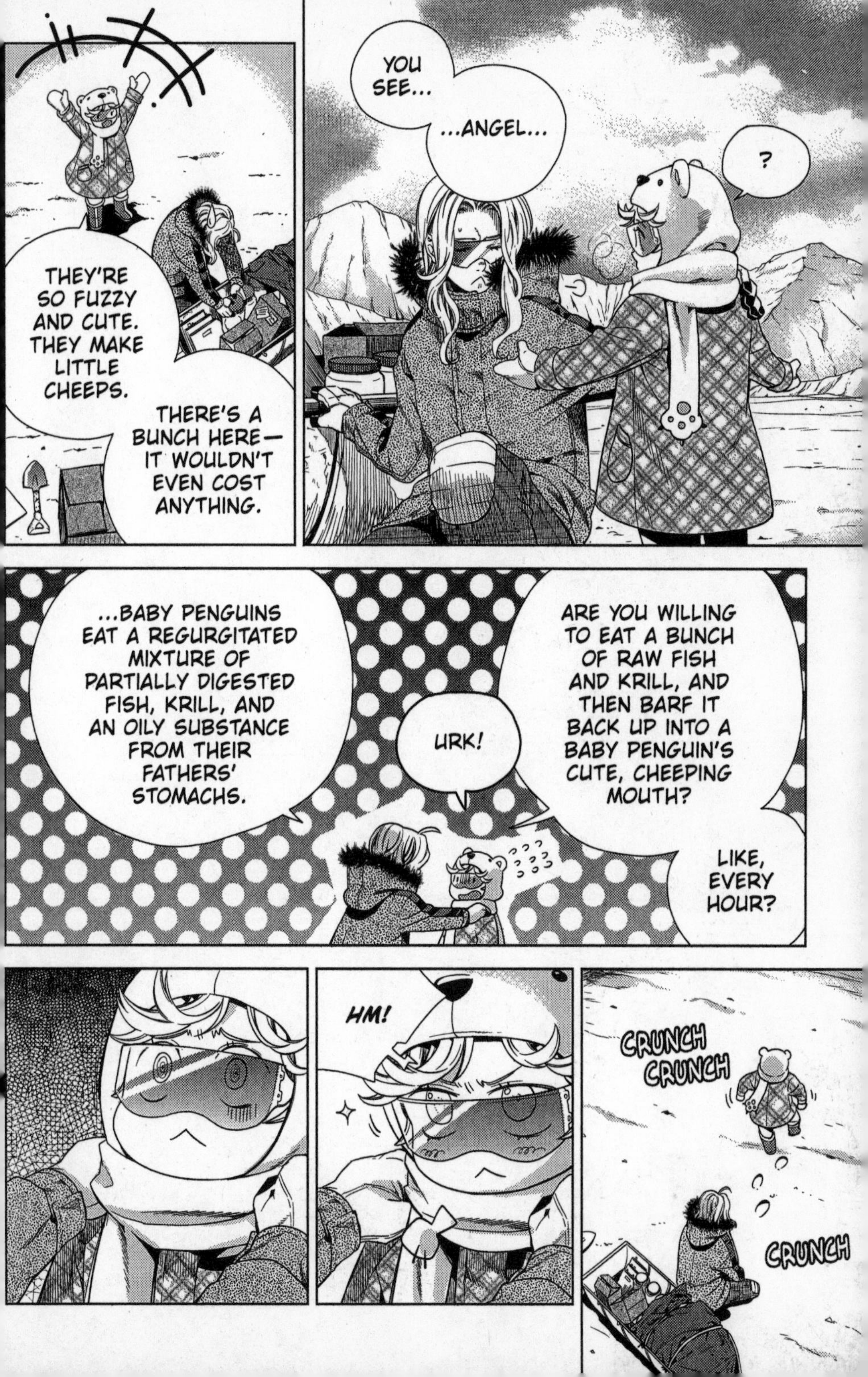
THEY'RE SO FUZZY AND CUTE. THEY MAKE LITTLE CHEEPS.
THERE'S A BUNCH HERE—IT WOULDN'T EVEN COST ANYTHING.
YOU SEE...
...ANGEL...
?
...BABY PENGUINS EAT A REGURGITATED MIXTURE OF PARTIALLY DIGESTED FISH, KRILL, AND AN OILY SUBSTANCE FROM THEIR FATHERS' STOMACHS.
URK!
ARE YOU WILLING TO EAT A BUNCH OF RAW FISH AND KRILL, AND THEN BARF IT BACK UP INTO A BABY PENGUIN'S CUTE, CHEEPING MOUTH?
LIKE, EVERY HOUR?
HM!
CRUNCH CRUNCH
CRUNCH

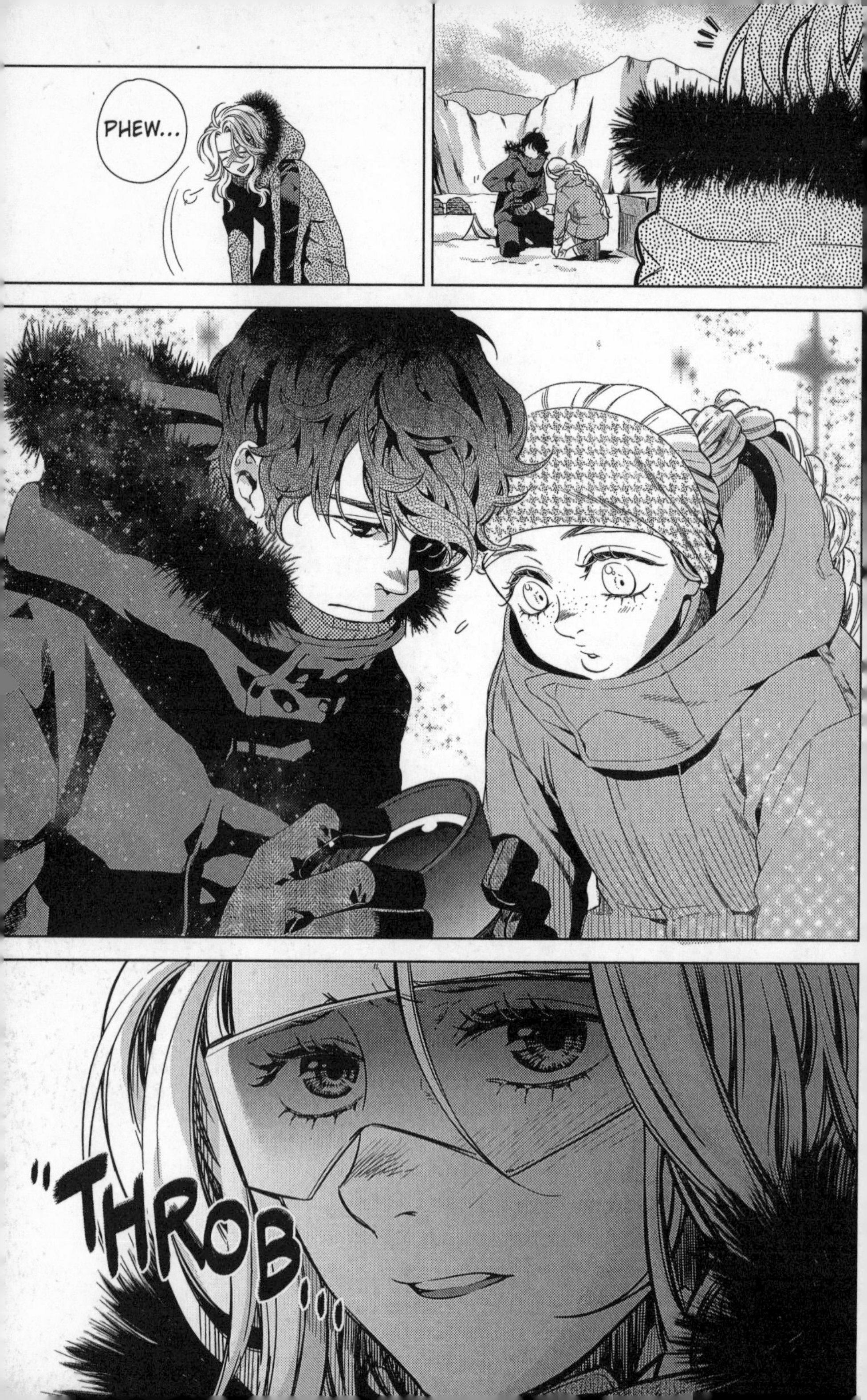
PHEW...
THROB...

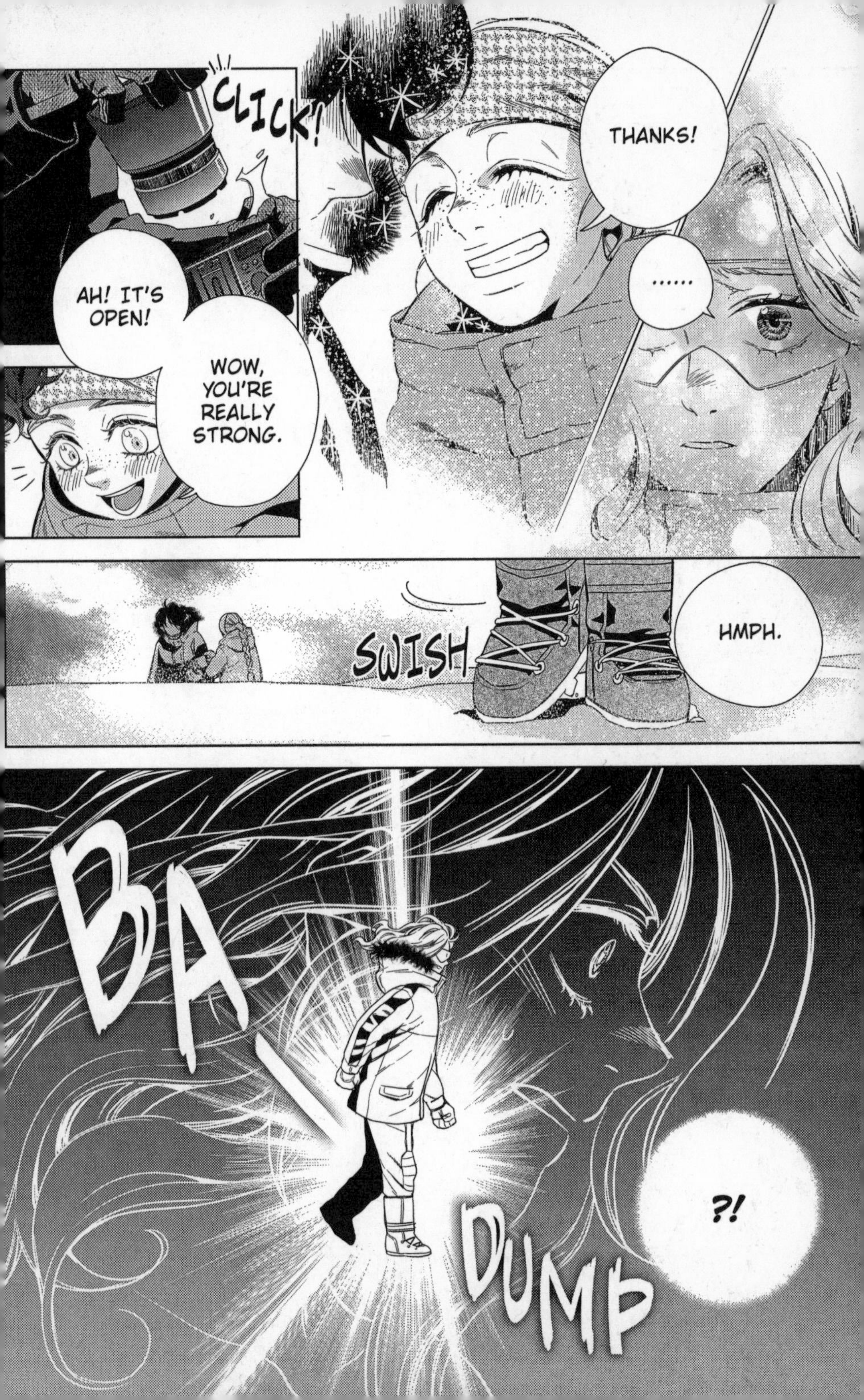
CLICK!
AH! IT'S OPEN!
WOW, YOU'RE REALLY STRONG.
THANKS!
......
SWISH
HMPH.
BA
DUMP
?!

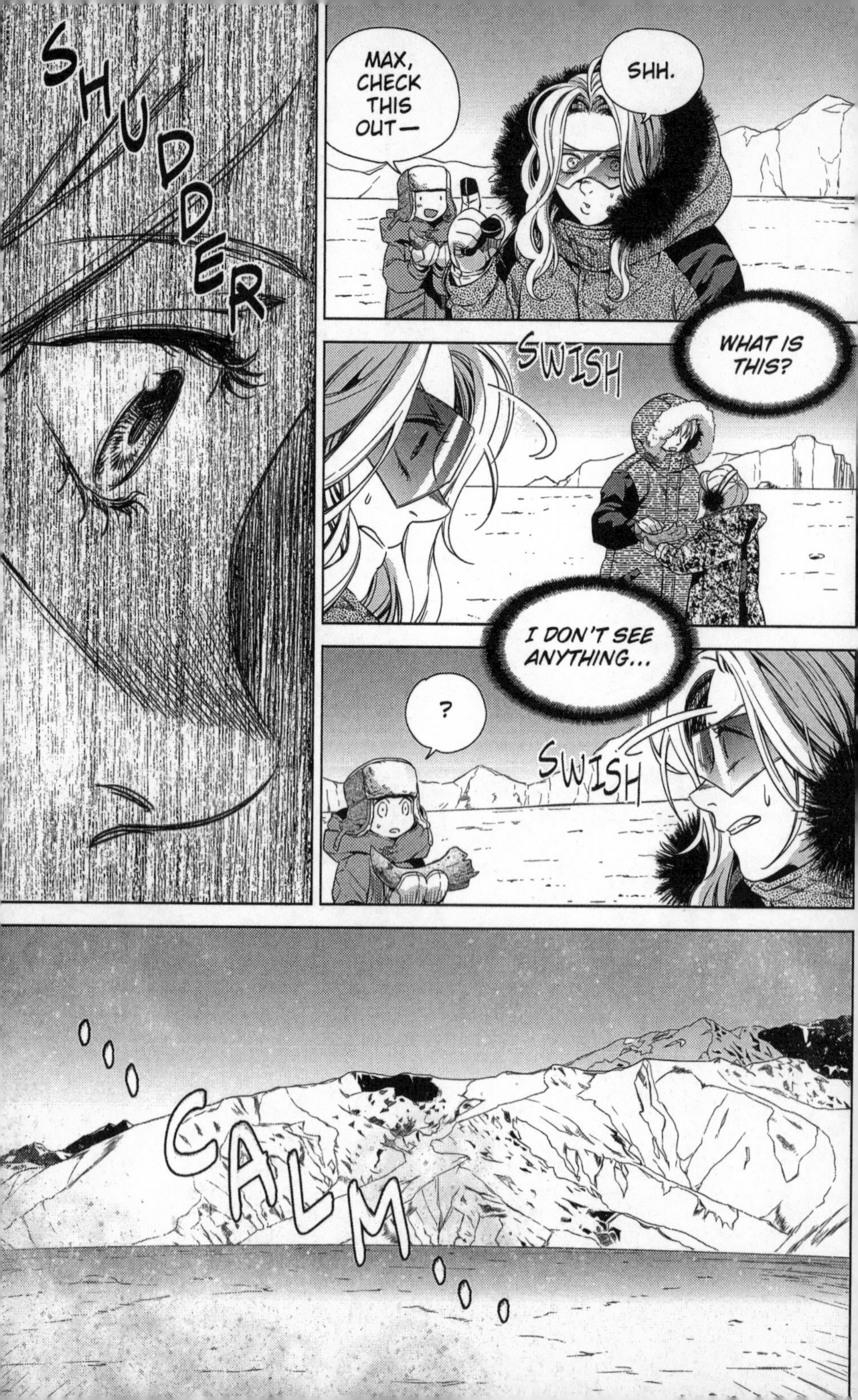
SHUDDER
MAX, CHECK THIS OUT—
SHH.
SWISH
WHAT IS THIS?
I DON'T SEE ANYTHING...
?
SWISH
CALM

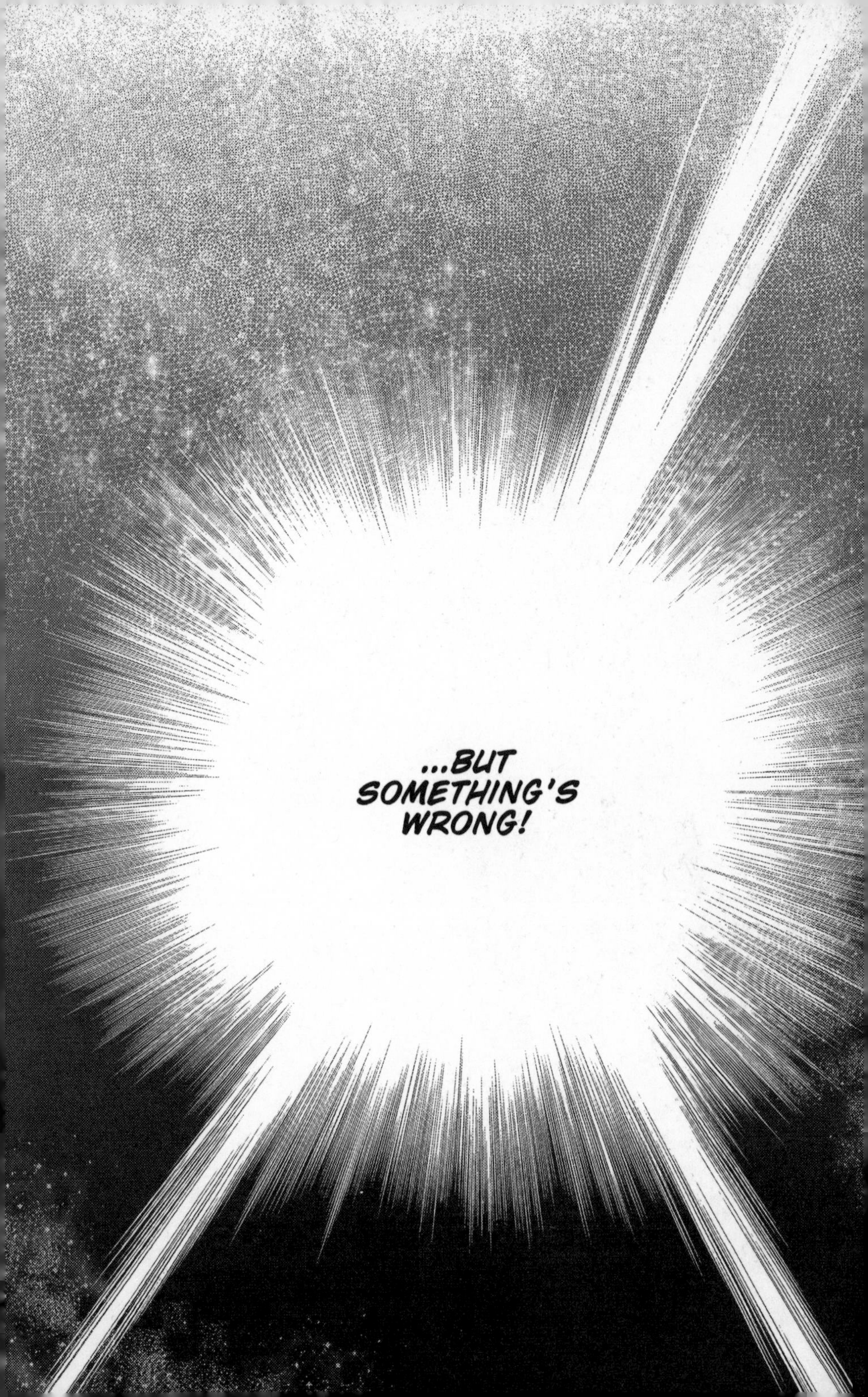
...BUT SOMETHING'S WRONG!

HOME Blog Posts Discussions Groups Photos Chat BBS

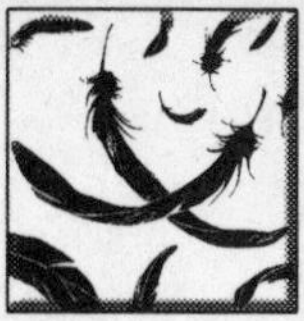

Fang

Welcome!

Visitor number

723,989

Yo, faithful readers. You know, when I was a kid, my big ambition was to someday not live in a dog crate. Some kids aim high, I don't know. But here's a thought, for those of you who haven't decided on a big ambition: How about being a scientist?

I know, we all think Bill Nye the Science Guy. Or maybe Dr. Bunsen Burner from that kids' show with the Muppets. But being a scientist (not the evil kind, obviously) can be awesome. I know, because I've met some non-evil scientists recently.

Right now we're working with a bunch of scientists that rock the house. One of them is only a little older than me, and not at all geekified. I have to say, a chick who's supersmart and super-brave, dedicated to her work, wanting to help people, save the world — well, there's nothing hotter than that.

So if you're not a total wastoid, consider checking out science. We're gonna need all the help we can get to save what's left of the planet. It'll be up to us. We'll need to have some real skills, real tools. Remember my "Useful Jobs" list from before? There were a lot of jobs on it that could help us in the future. Put down your air guitars, quit pretending to walk down a fashion runway. Go review it.

Comment ▼

Slimfan3 from Jacksonville writes:
What about all those guys who were after you?

Well, Slimfan3, either they haven't found us yet, or they all got wiped out. Either way, the past week has been a primo vacation. If you like cold weather.
— Fang

MissLolo from Tulsa writes:
Are you and Max gonna get married anytime soon? <Blushes.>

Uh, MissLolo? We're fourteen years old. We think. Who knows how much longer we'll be around? Who knows where we'll end up? We don't plan more than a day or two ahead.
— Fang

Googleblob from Holy Oak, CA, writes:
Fangalator —
Dude, you are the coolest. I wanna get a tat of your wings on my back. Like, life-size.

Googleblob, unless your back is fourteen feet across, you are out of luck, my friend.
— Fang. Just Fang.

S. Haarter from Johannesburg writes:
I really like hearing @ the stuff u r doin to save the planet. U r my hero. I m gonna txt u a pic of me. [pic deleted] I m reading ur blog 2 my science class as my ecology project. Keep it up!
Your #1 fan.

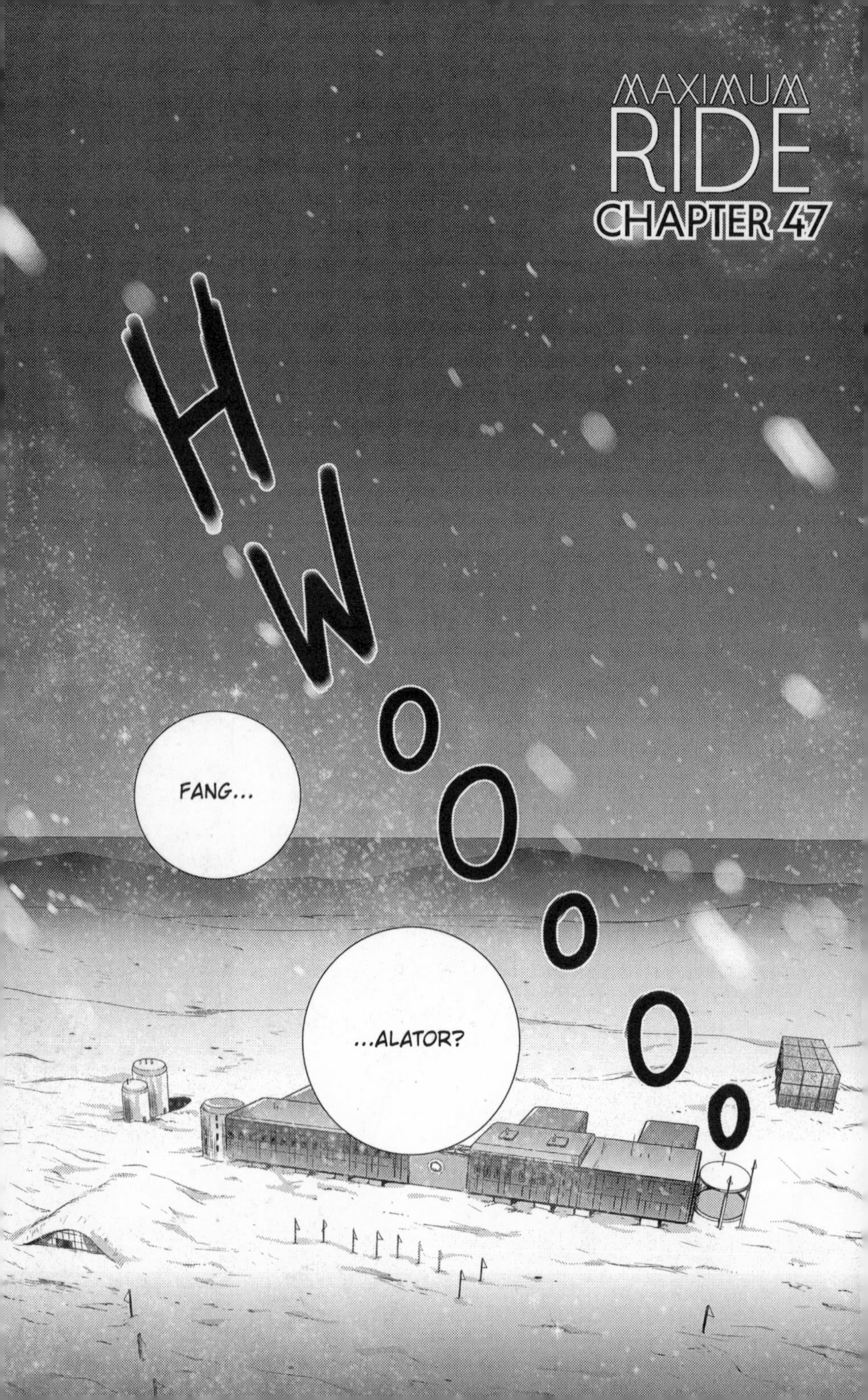
MAXIMUM RIDE
CHAPTER 47
HWOOoOo
FANG...
...ALATOR?

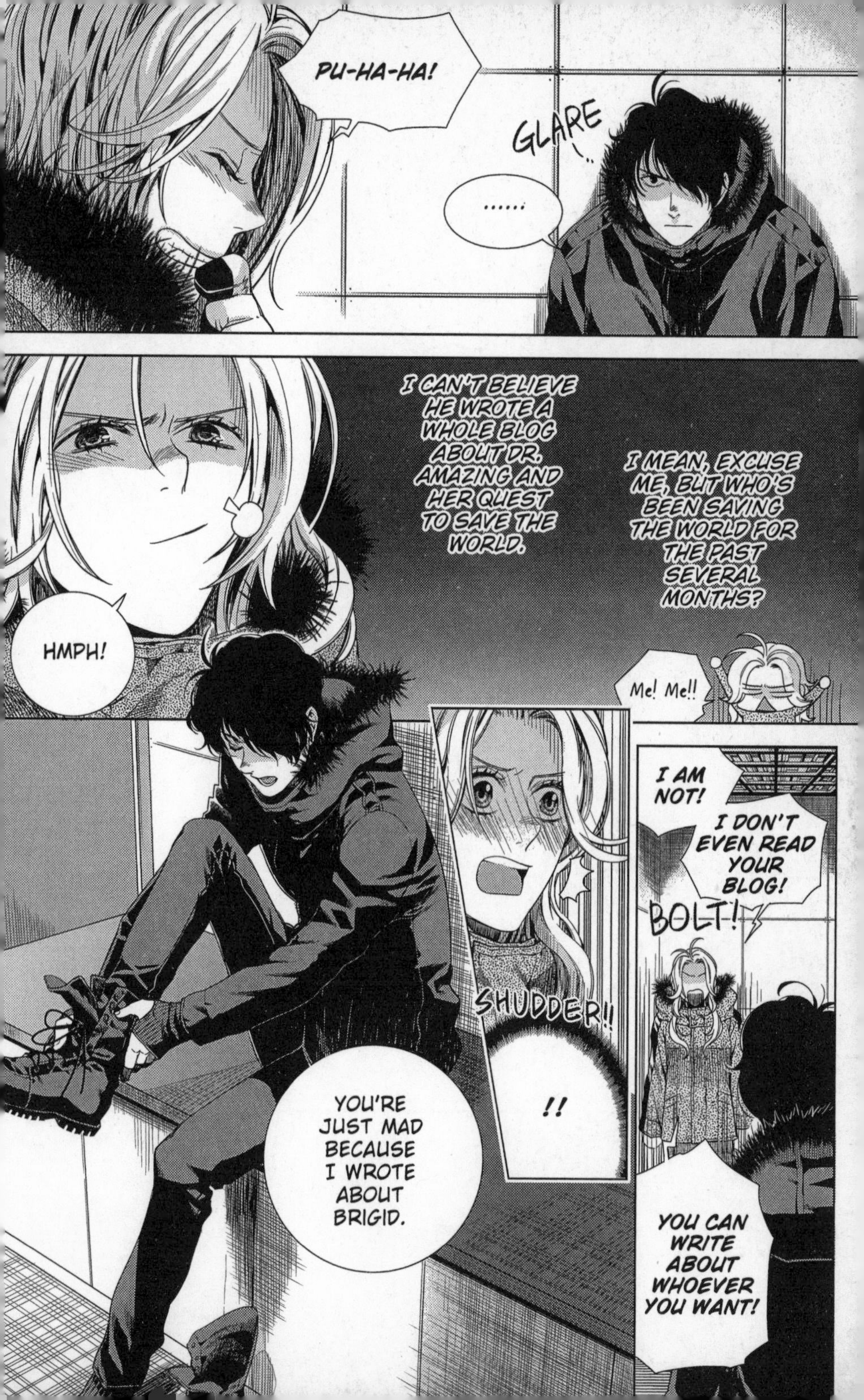
PU-HA-HA!
GLARE
......
I CAN'T BELIEVE HE WROTE A WHOLE BLOG ABOUT DR. AMAZING AND HER QUEST TO SAVE THE WORLD.
I MEAN, EXCUSE ME, BUT WHO'S BEEN SAVING THE WORLD FOR THE PAST SEVERAL MONTHS?
HMPH!
Me! Me!!
YOU'RE JUST MAD BECAUSE I WROTE ABOUT BRIGID.
SHUDDER!!
!!
I AM NOT!
I DON'T EVEN READ YOUR BLOG!
BOLT!
YOU CAN WRITE ABOUT WHOEVER YOU WANT!

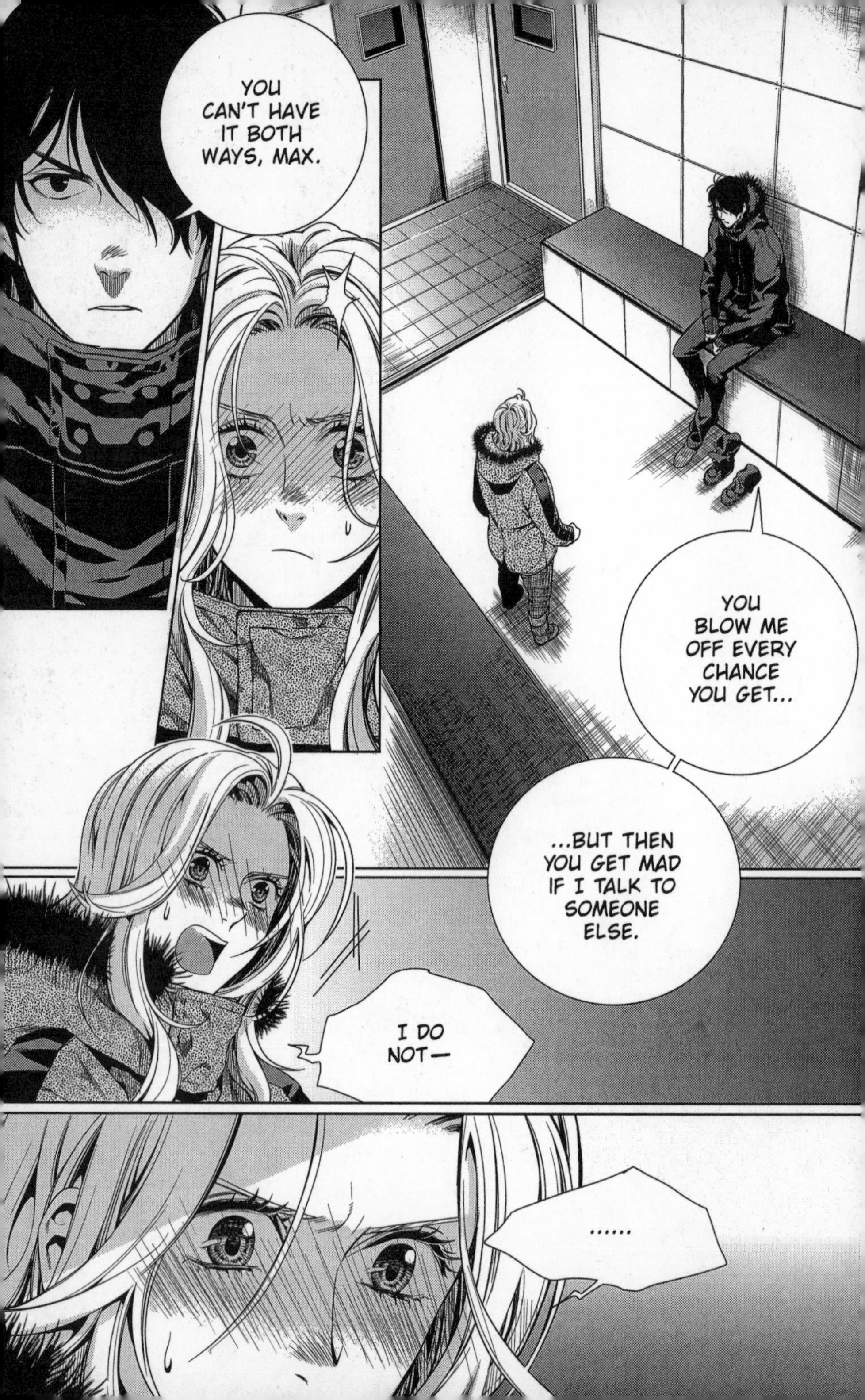
YOU CAN'T HAVE IT BOTH WAYS, MAX.
YOU BLOW ME OFF EVERY CHANCE YOU GET...
...BUT THEN YOU GET MAD IF I TALK TO SOMEONE ELSE.
I DO NOT—
......

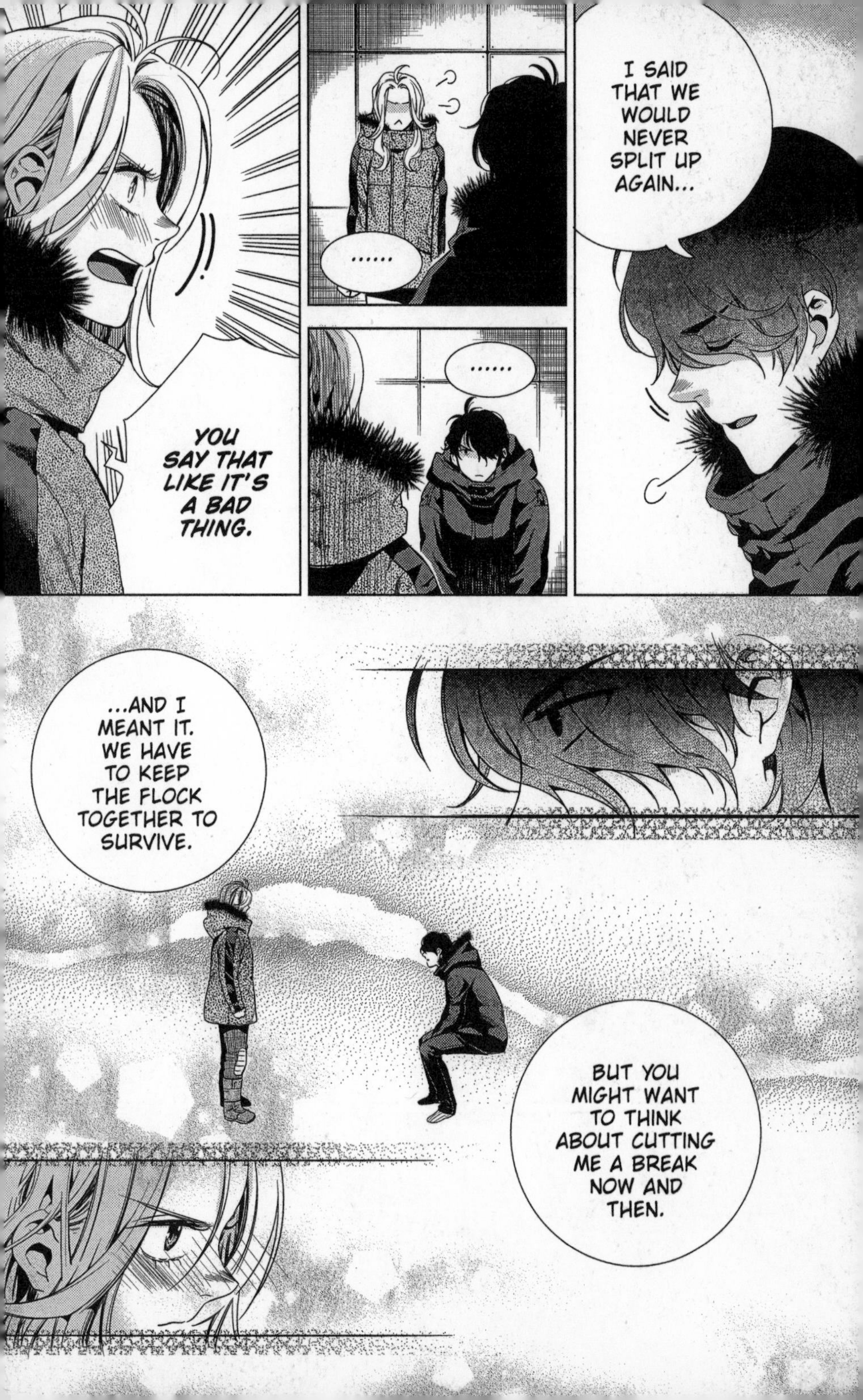
YOU SAY THAT LIKE IT'S A BAD THING.
......
......
I SAID THAT WE WOULD NEVER SPLIT UP AGAIN...
...AND I MEANT IT. WE HAVE TO KEEP THE FLOCK TOGETHER TO SURVIVE.
BUT YOU MIGHT WANT TO THINK ABOUT CUTTING ME A BREAK NOW AND THEN.

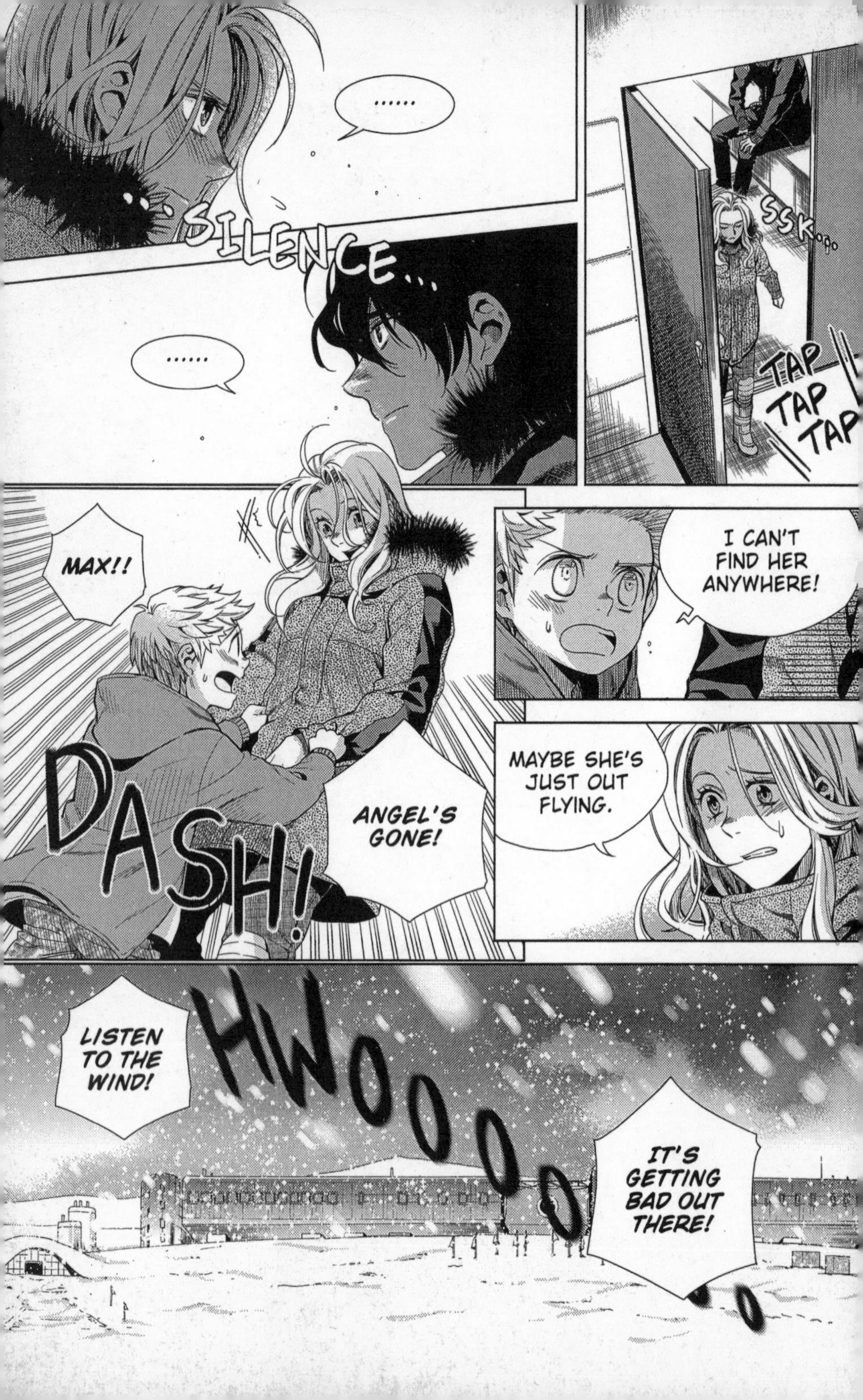
......
SILENCE...
......
SSK...
TAP
TAP
TAP
MAX!!
DASH!
ANGEL'S GONE!
I CAN'T FIND HER ANYWHERE!
MAYBE SHE'S JUST OUT FLYING.
LISTEN TO THE WIND!
HWOOOOO
IT'S GETTING BAD OUT THERE!

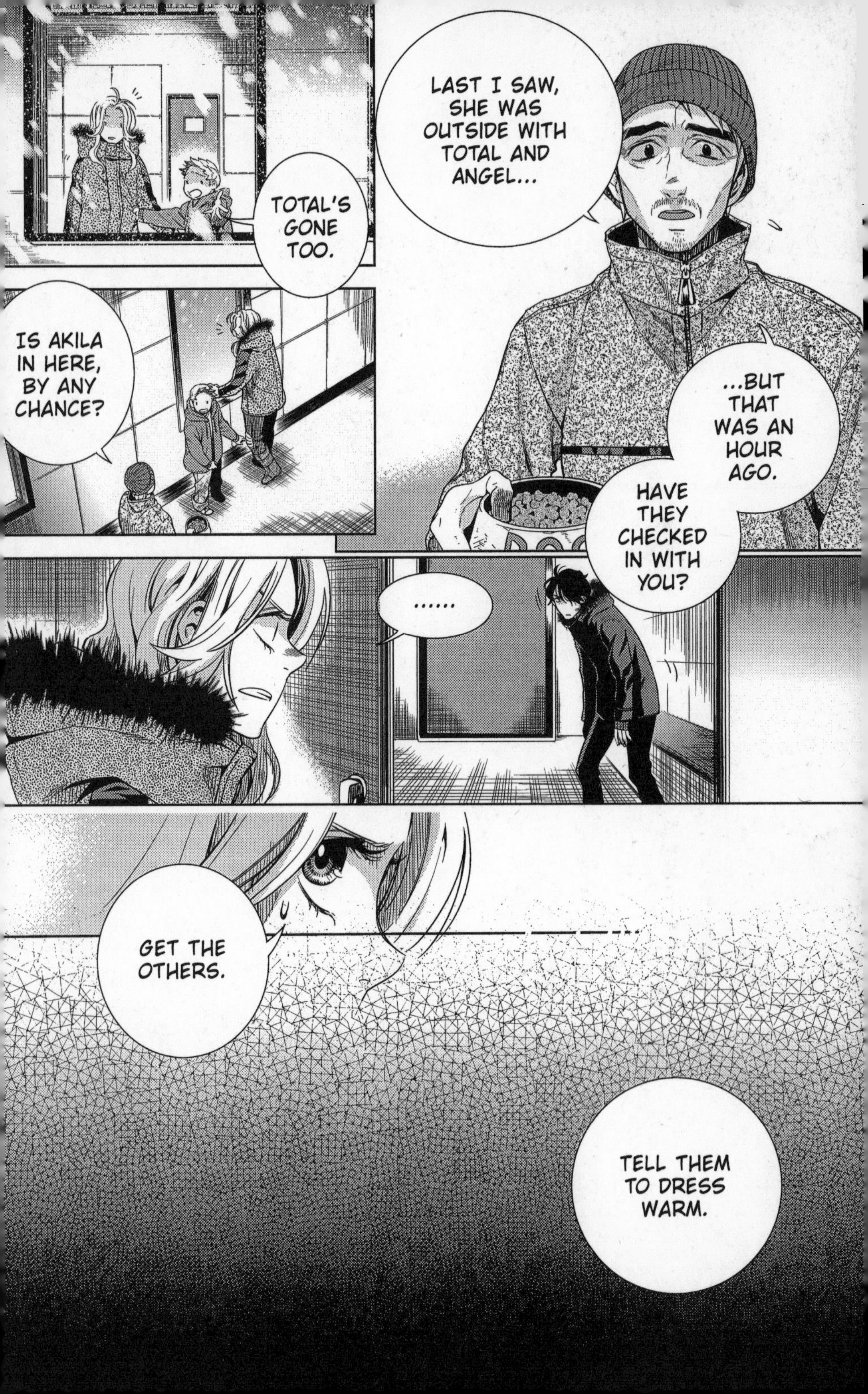
TOTAL'S GONE TOO.
IS AKILA IN HERE, BY ANY CHANCE?
LAST I SAW, SHE WAS OUTSIDE WITH TOTAL AND ANGEL...
...BUT THAT WAS AN HOUR AGO.
HAVE THEY CHECKED IN WITH YOU?
......
GET THE OTHERS.
TELL THEM TO DRESS WARM.

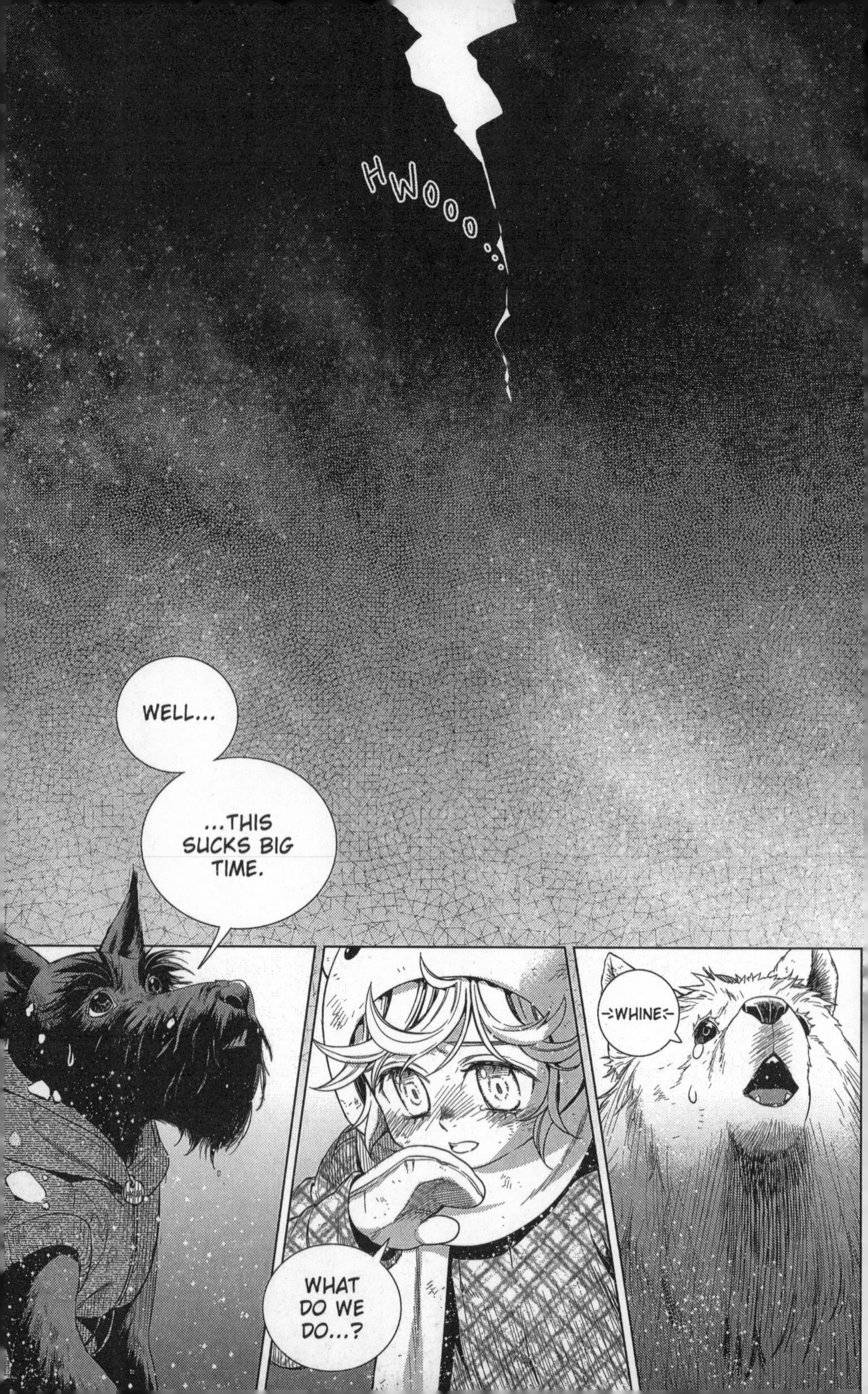
HWOOO...
WELL...
...THIS SUCKS BIG TIME.
WHAT DO WE DO...?
WHINE

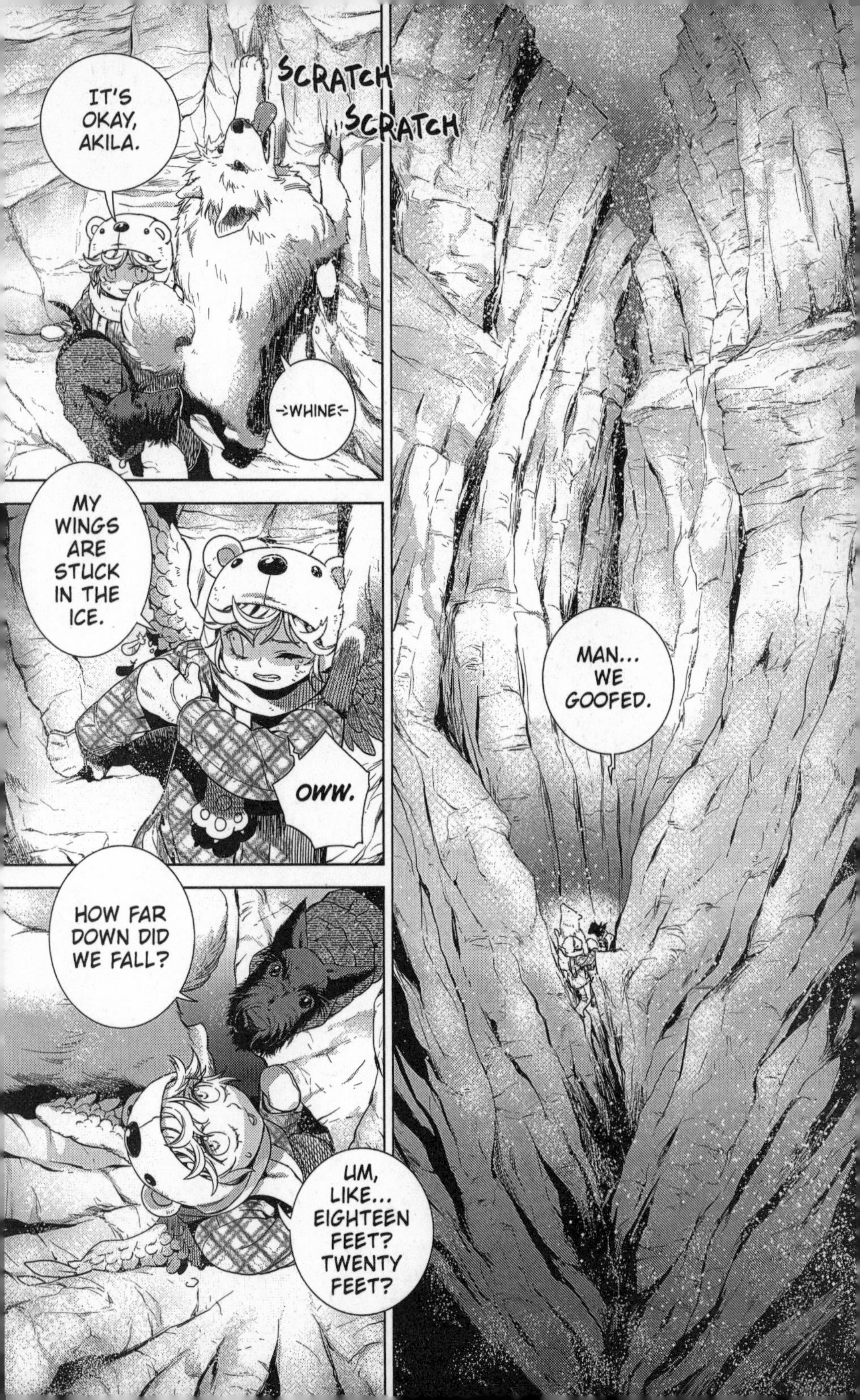
IT'S OKAY, AKILA.
SCRATCH
SCRATCH
-WHINE-
MY WINGS ARE STUCK IN THE ICE.
OWW.
HOW FAR DOWN DID WE FALL?
UM, LIKE... EIGHTEEN FEET? TWENTY FEET?
MAN... WE GOOFED.

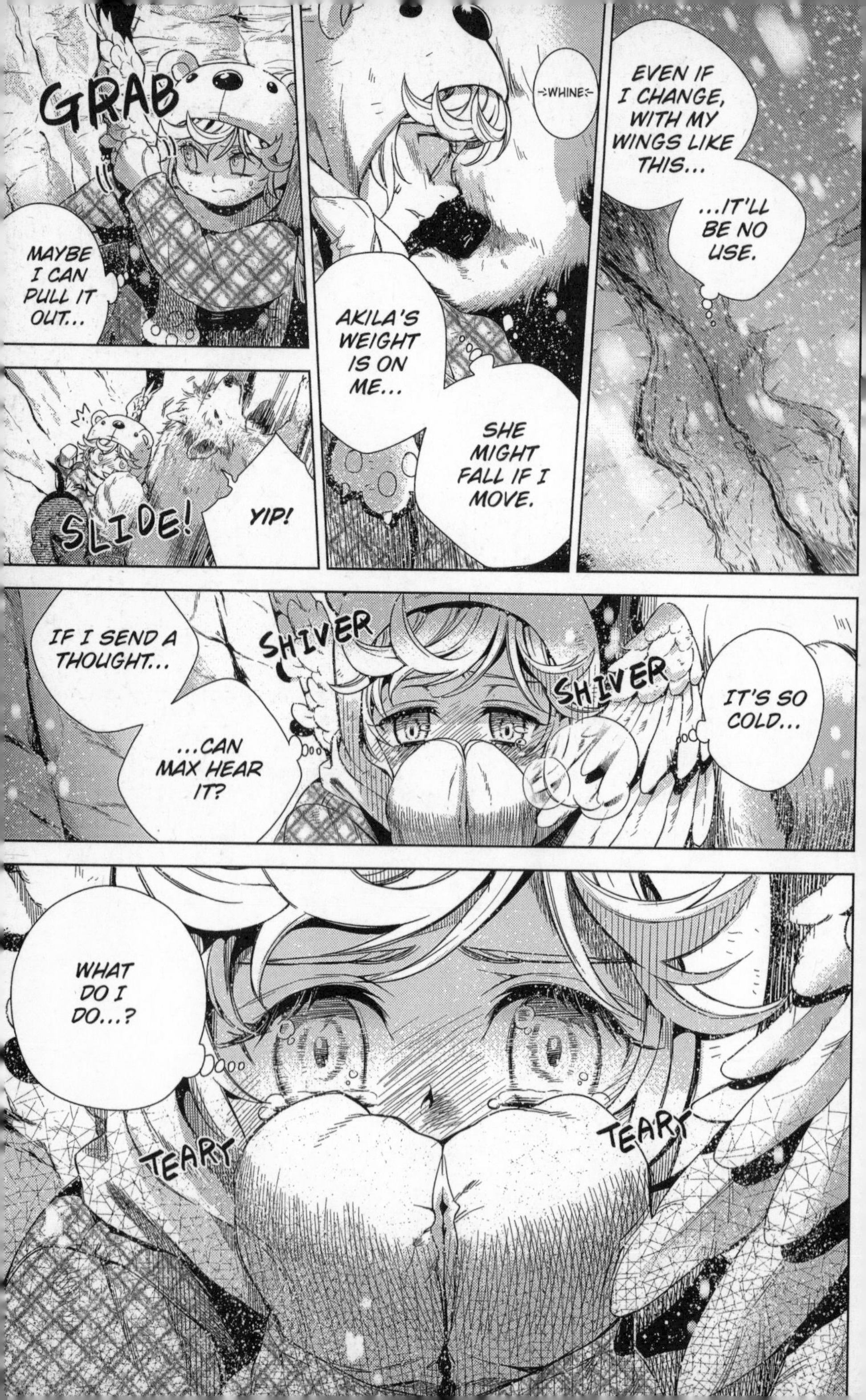
GRAB
MAYBE I CAN PULL IT OUT...
WHINE
AKILA'S WEIGHT IS ON ME...
SHE MIGHT FALL IF I MOVE.
EVEN IF I CHANGE, WITH MY WINGS LIKE THIS...
...IT'LL BE NO USE.
SLIDE!
YIP!
IF I SEND A THOUGHT...
...CAN MAX HEAR IT?
SHIVER
SHIVER
IT'S SO COLD...
WHAT DO I DO...?
TEARY
TEARY

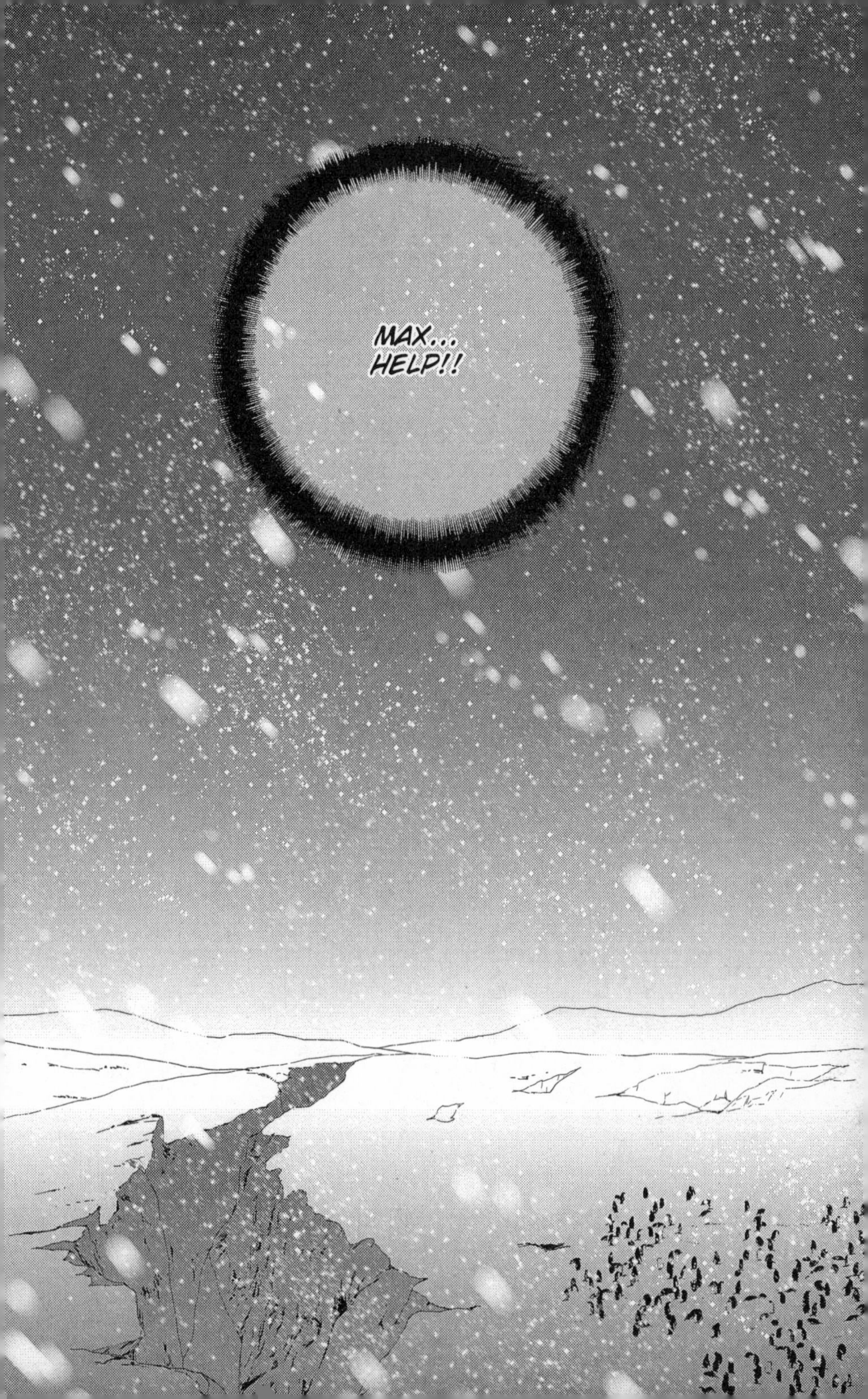
MAX... HELP!!

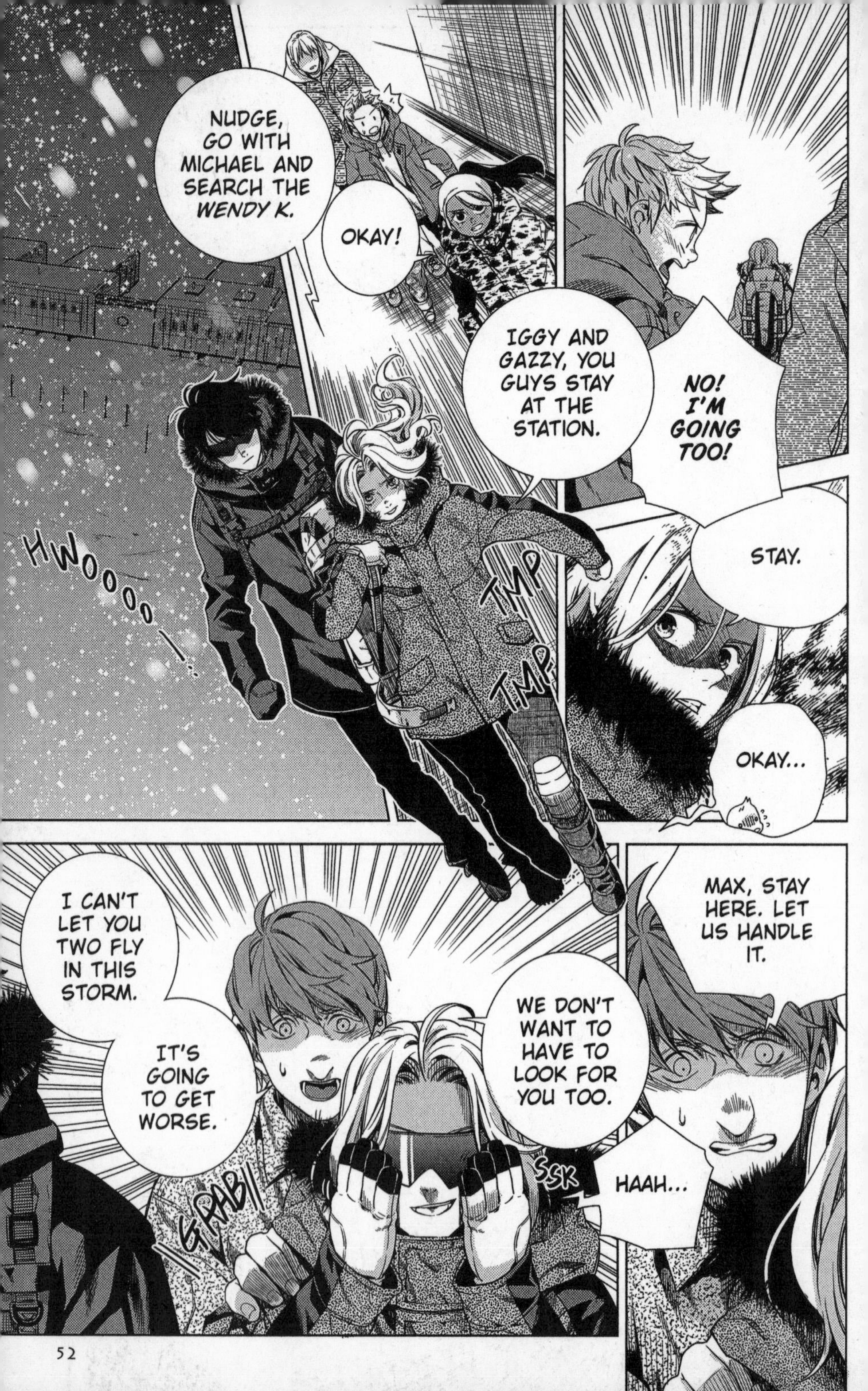
NUDGE, GO WITH MICHAEL AND SEARCH THE *WENDY K.*
OKAY!
HWOOOO...!
IGGY AND GAZZY, YOU GUYS STAY AT THE STATION.
TMP
TMP
NO! I'M GOING TOO!
STAY.
OKAY...
I CAN'T LET YOU TWO FLY IN THIS STORM.
IT'S GOING TO GET WORSE.
GRAB
WE DON'T WANT TO HAVE TO LOOK FOR YOU TOO.
SSK
MAX, STAY HERE. LET US HANDLE IT.
HAAH...

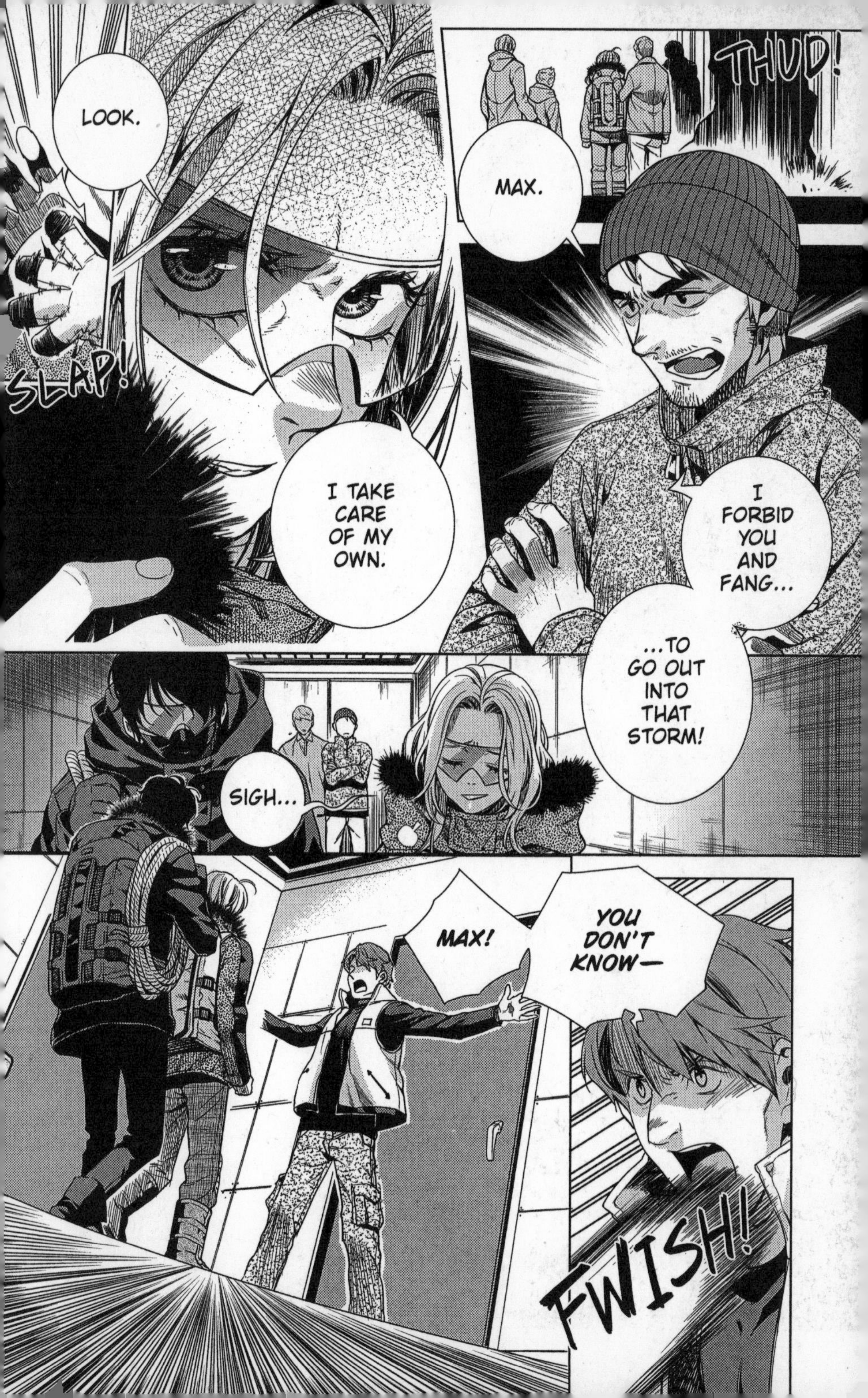
LOOK.
SLAP!
I TAKE CARE OF MY OWN.
THUD!
...
MAX.
I FORBID YOU AND FANG...
...TO GO OUT INTO THAT STORM!
SIGH...
MAX!
YOU DON'T KNOW—
FWISH!

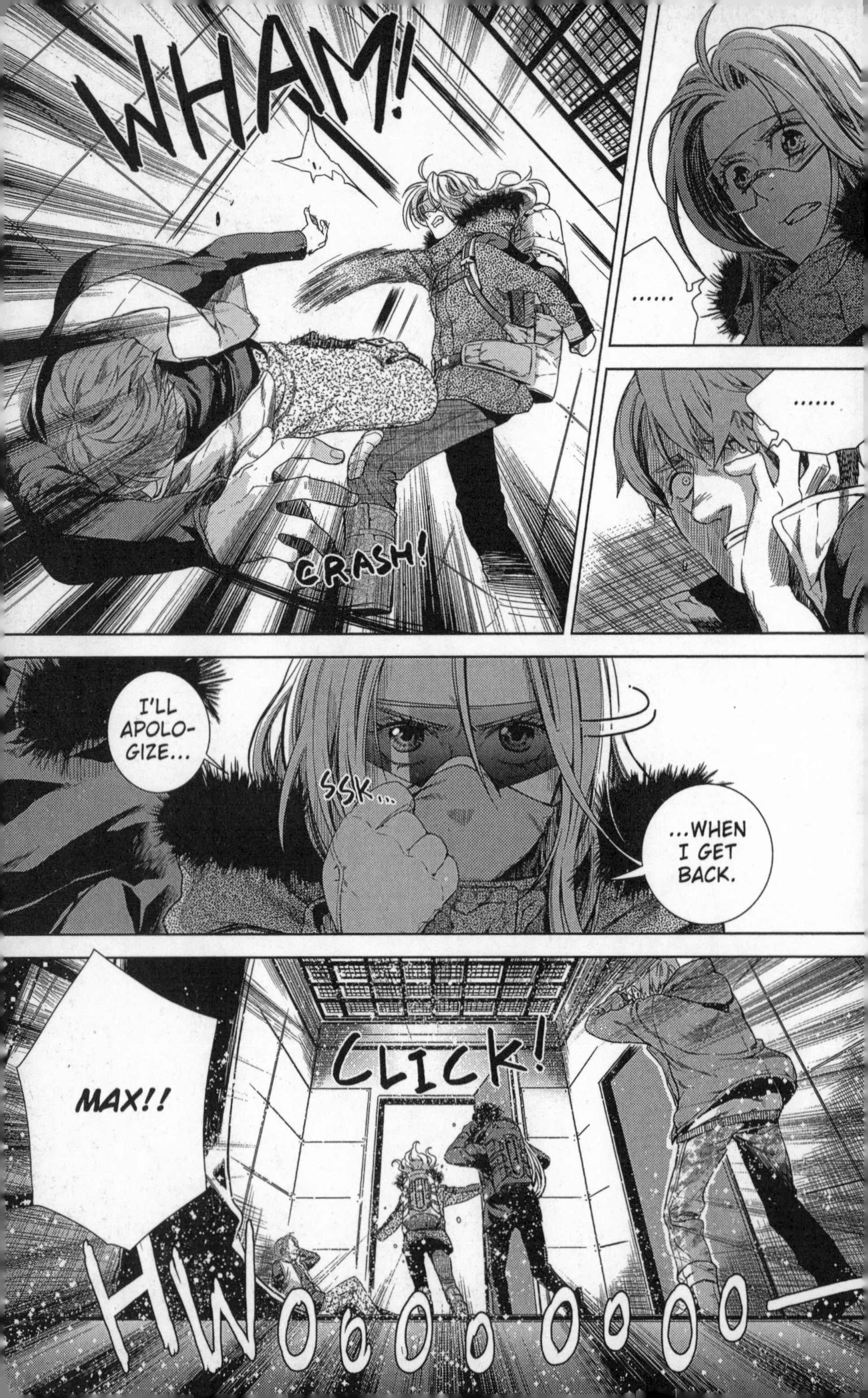
WHAM!
CRASH!
......
......
I'LL APOLOGIZE...
SSK...
...WHEN I GET BACK.
MAX!!
CLICK!
HWOOOOOOOOO

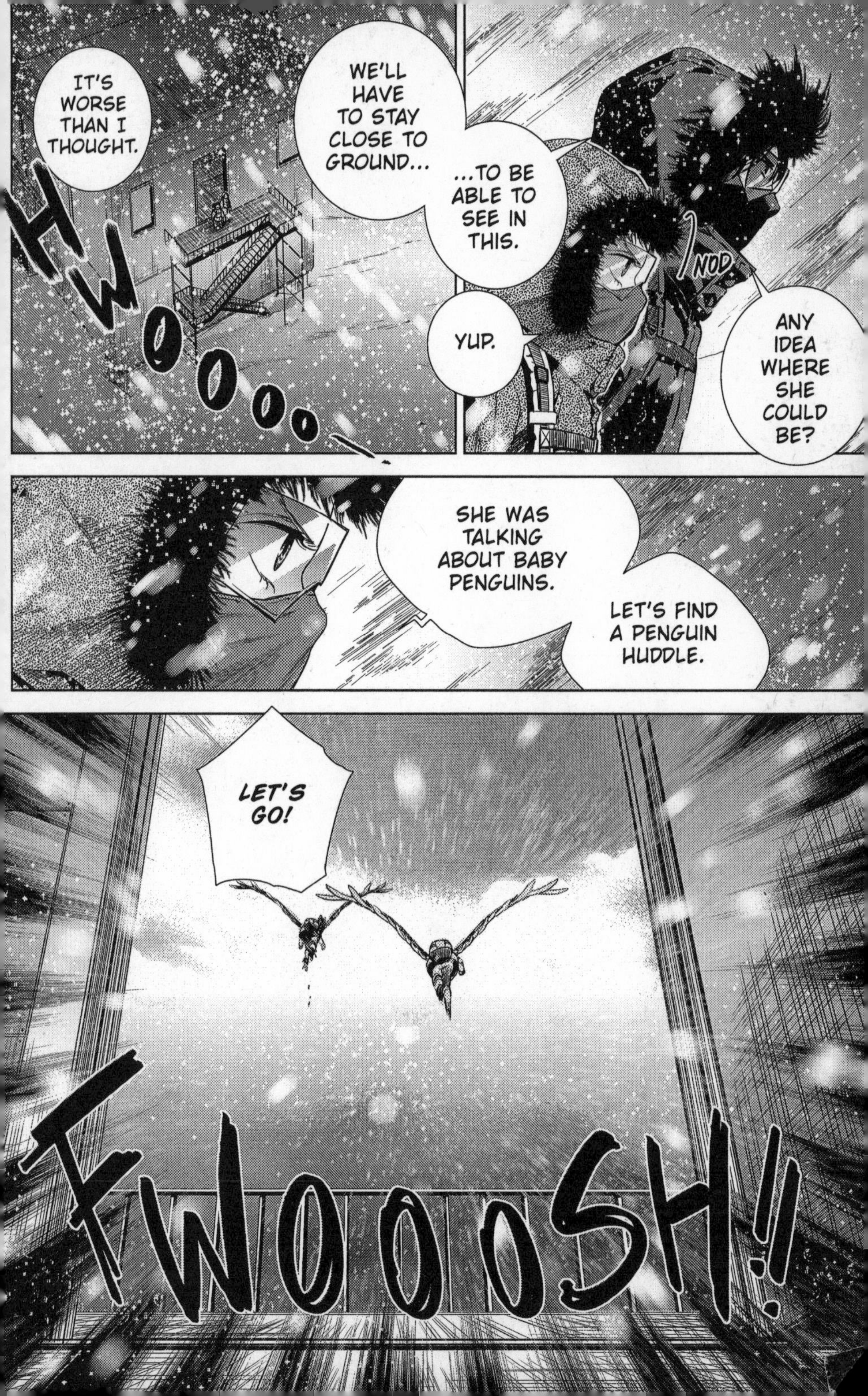
HWOOOOO...
IT'S WORSE THAN I THOUGHT.
WE'LL HAVE TO STAY CLOSE TO GROUND...
...TO BE ABLE TO SEE IN THIS.
NOD
YUP.
ANY IDEA WHERE SHE COULD BE?
SHE WAS TALKING ABOUT BABY PENGUINS.
LET'S FIND A PENGUIN HUDDLE.
LET'S GO!
FWOOOSH!!

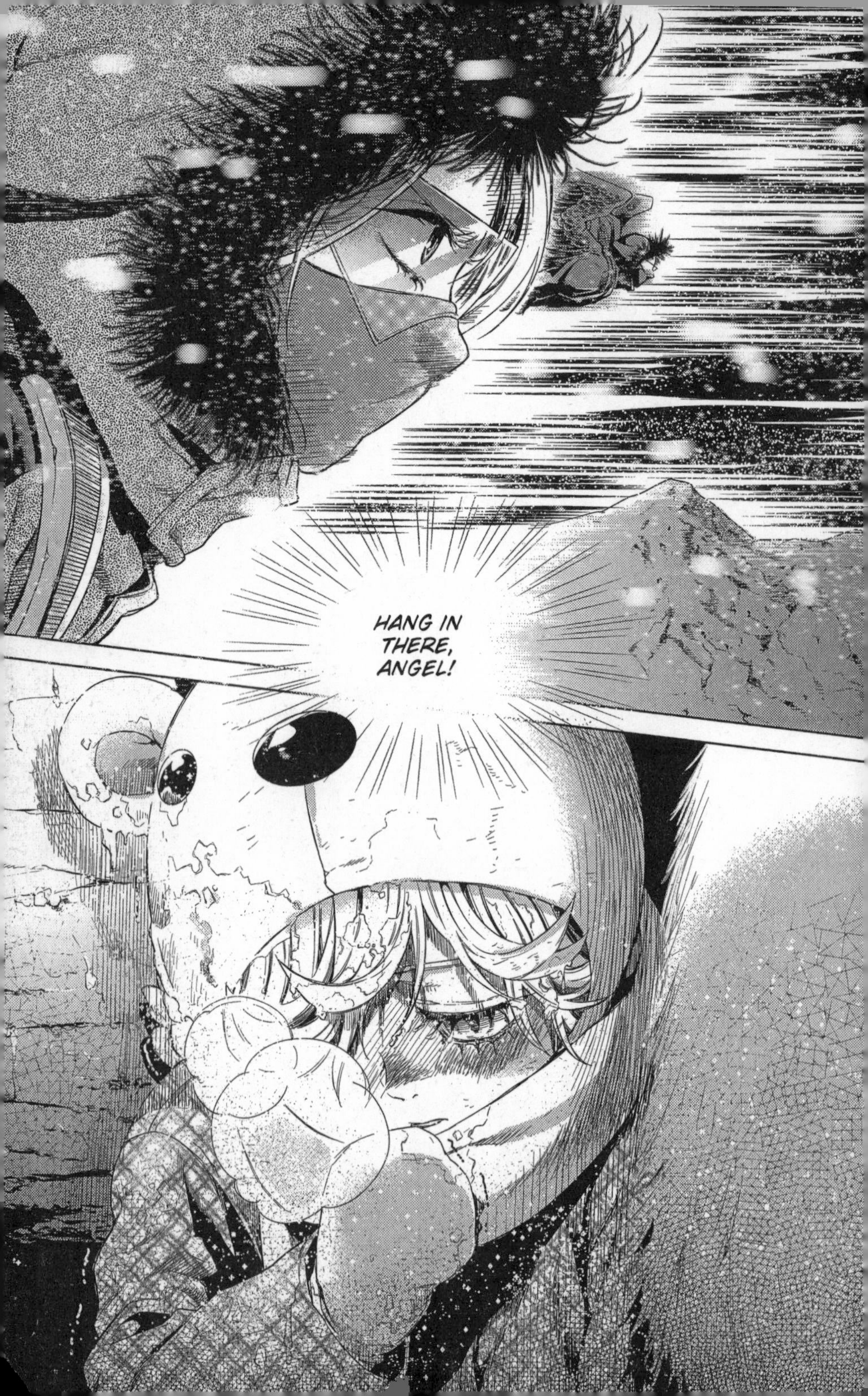
HANG IN THERE, ANGEL!

MAXIMUM
RIDE

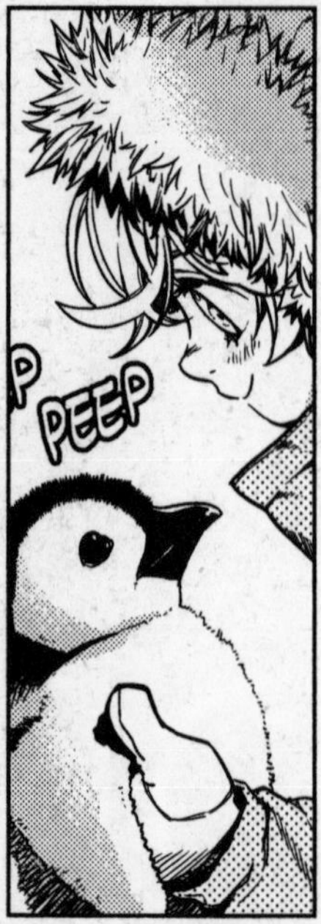
P
PEEP

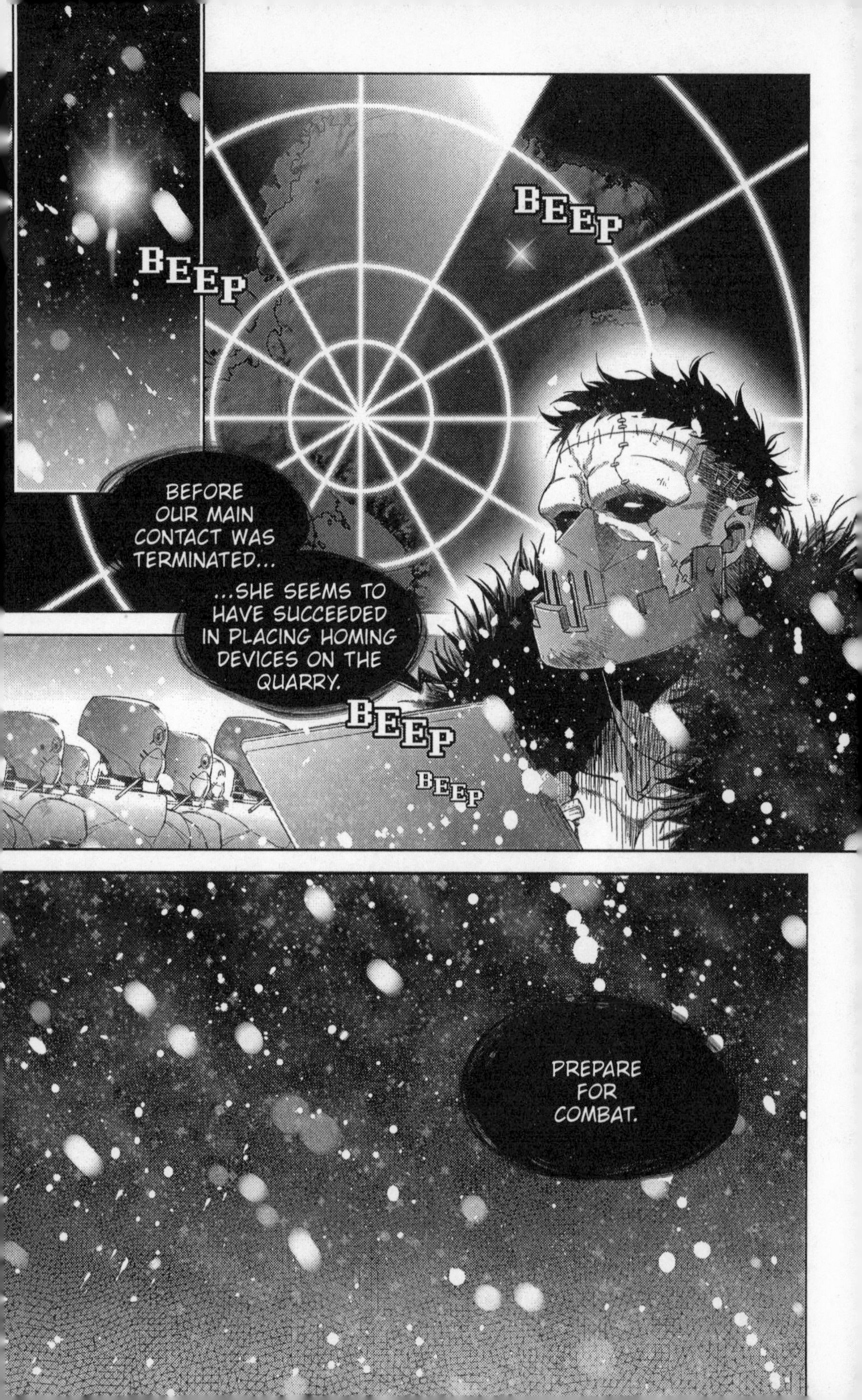
BEEP
BEEP
BEFORE OUR MAIN CONTACT WAS TERMINATED...
...SHE SEEMS TO HAVE SUCCEEDED IN PLACING HOMING DEVICES ON THE QUARRY.
BEEP
BEEP
PREPARE FOR COMBAT.

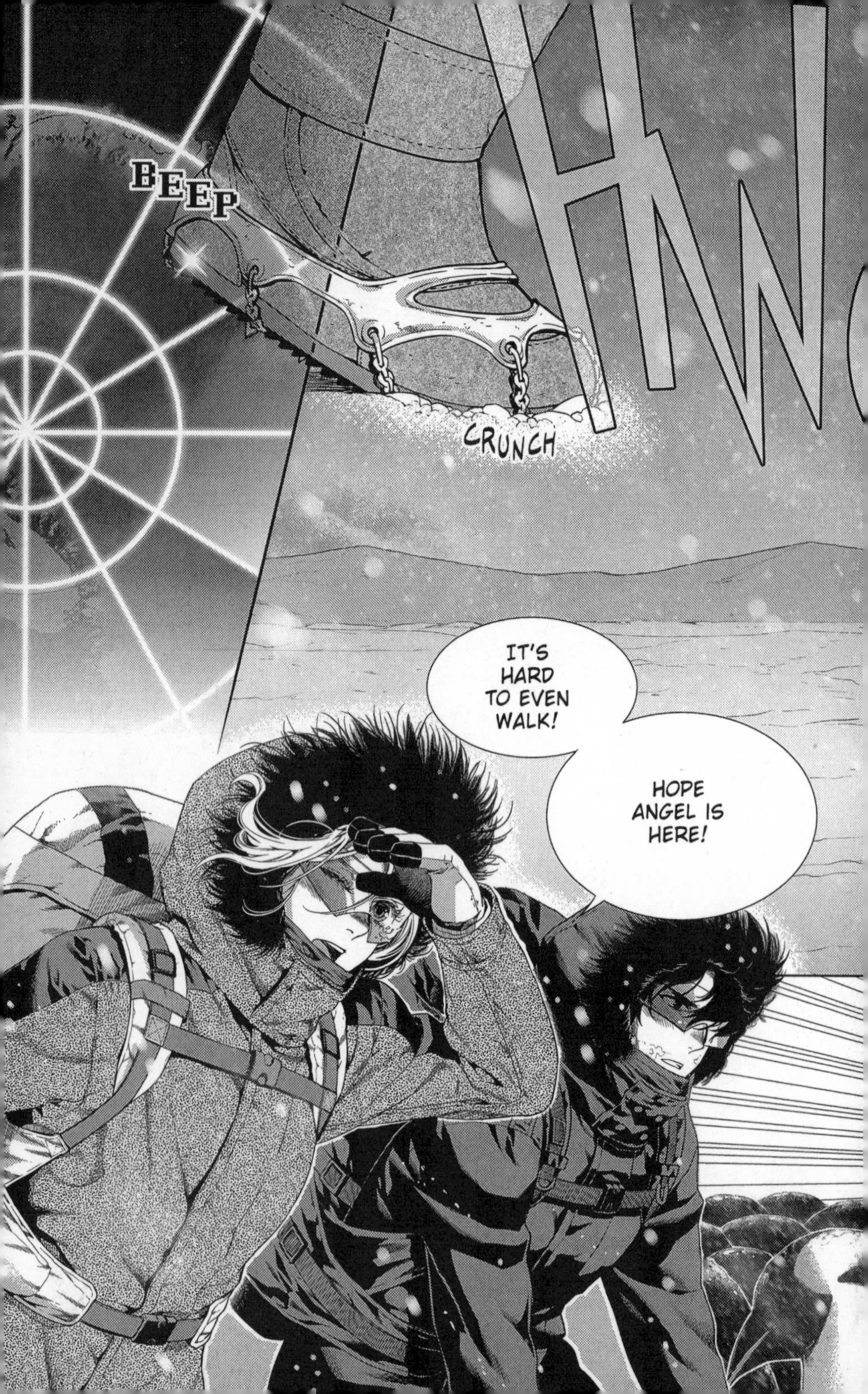
BEEP
CRUNCH
HWO
IT'S HARD TO EVEN WALK!
HOPE ANGEL IS HERE!

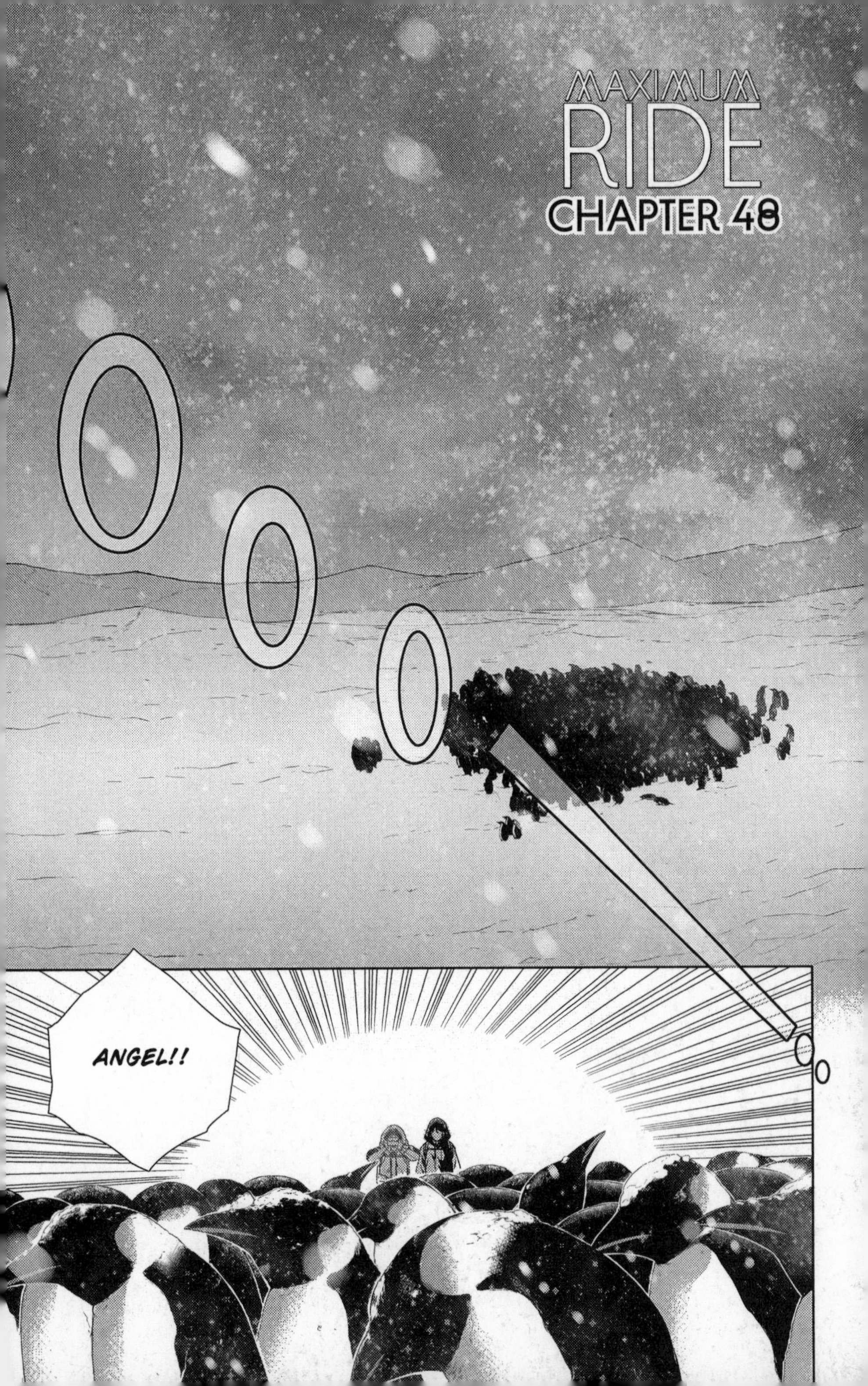
MAXIMUM RIDE
CHAPTER 48
ANGEL!!

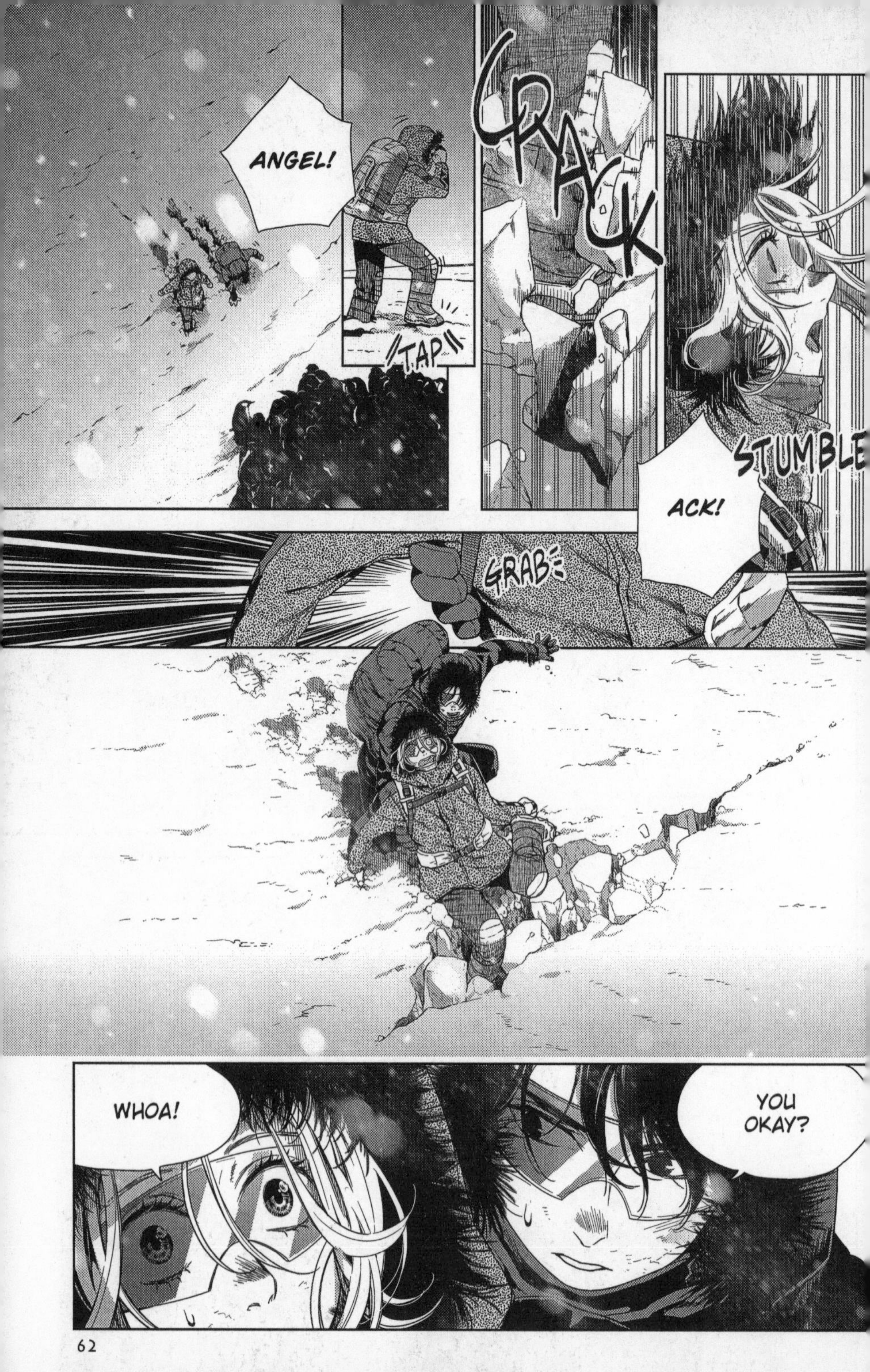
ANGEL!
TAP
CRACK
STUMBLE
ACK!
GRAB
WHOA!
YOU OKAY?

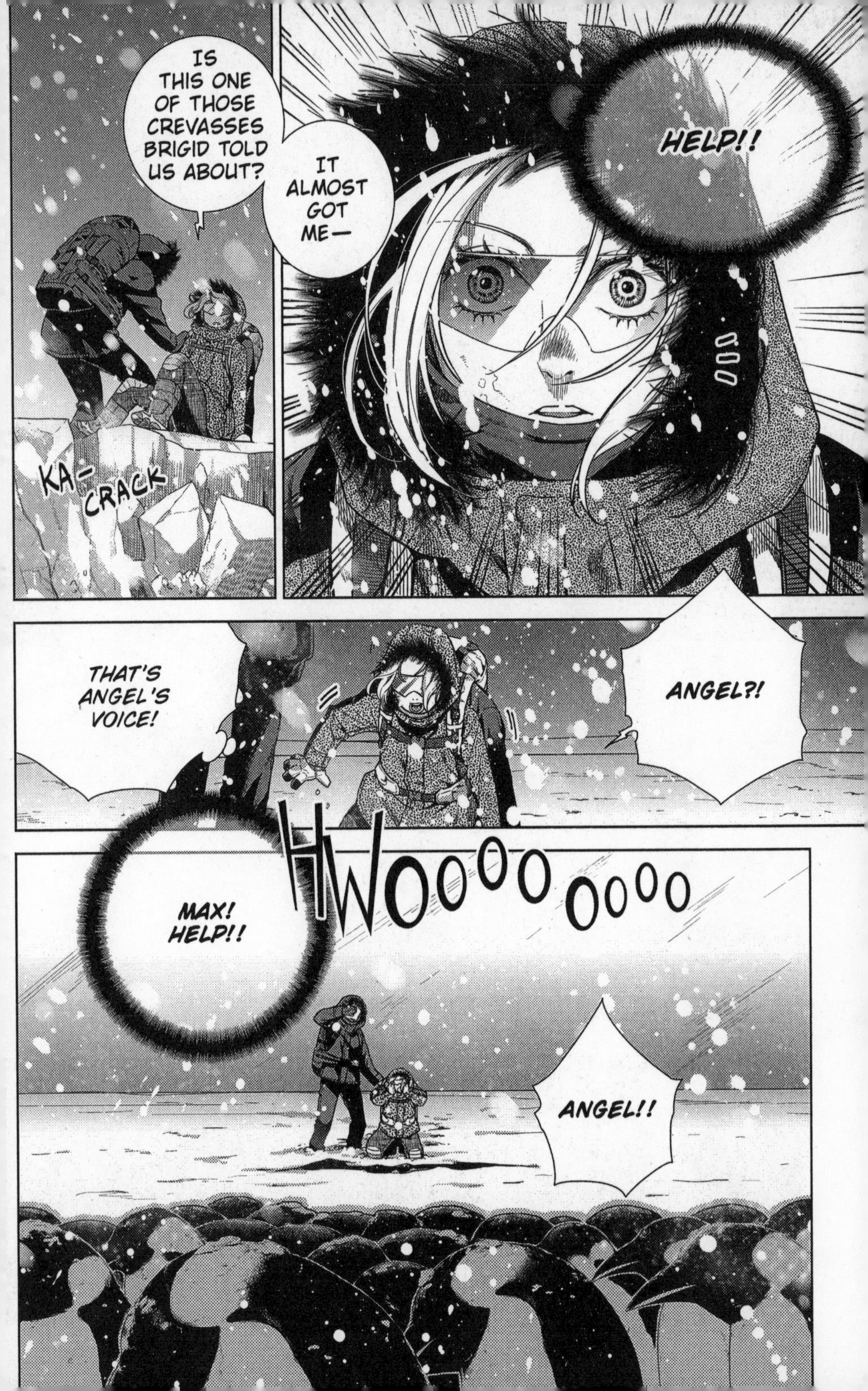
IS THIS ONE OF THOSE CREVASSES BRIGID TOLD US ABOUT?
IT ALMOST GOT ME—
KA-CRACK
HELP!!
THAT'S ANGEL'S VOICE!
ANGEL?!
MAX! HELP!!
HWOOOO OOOO
ANGEL!!

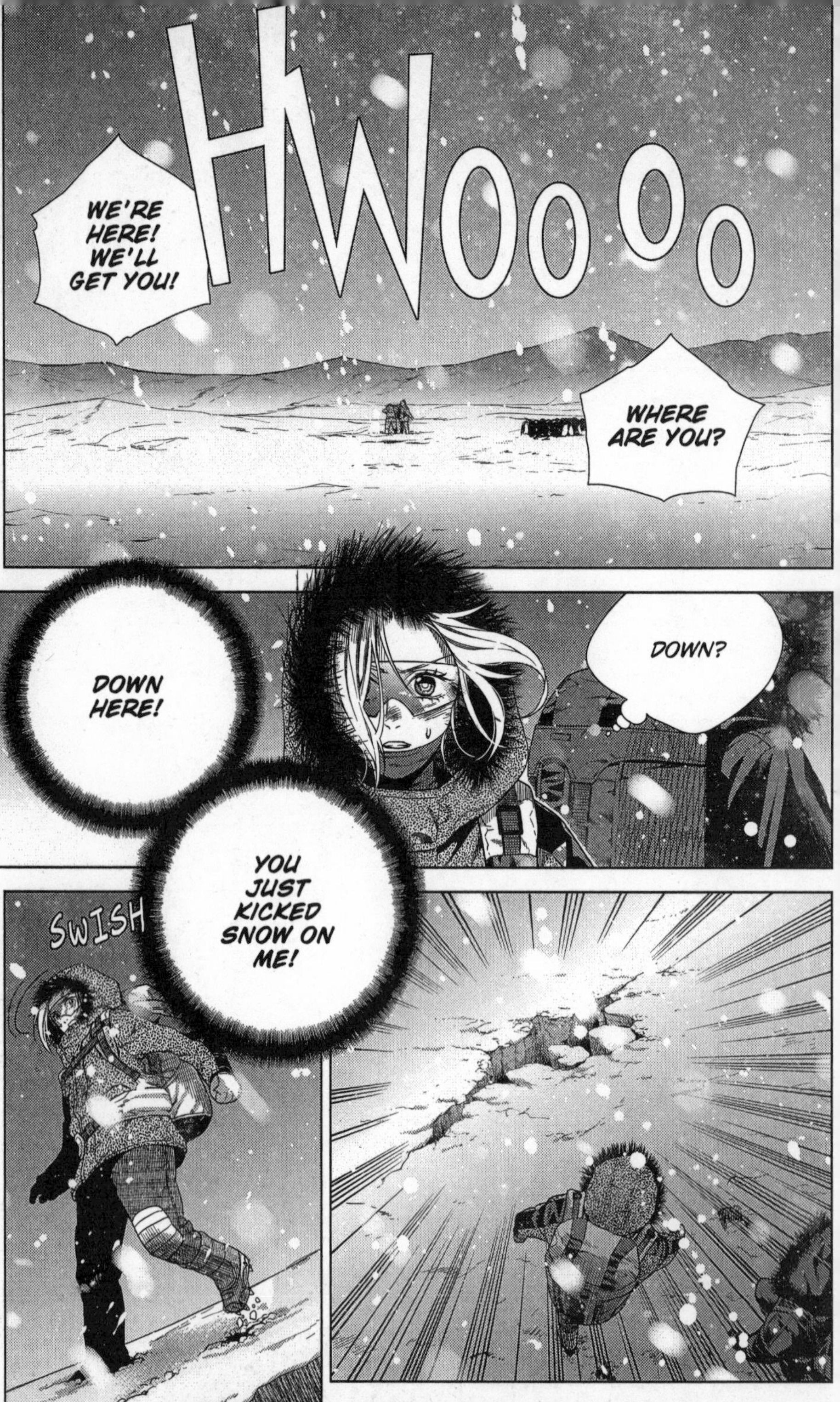
WE'RE HERE! WE'LL GET YOU!
HWOOOO
WHERE ARE YOU?
DOWN HERE!
DOWN?
YOU JUST KICKED SNOW ON ME!
SWISH

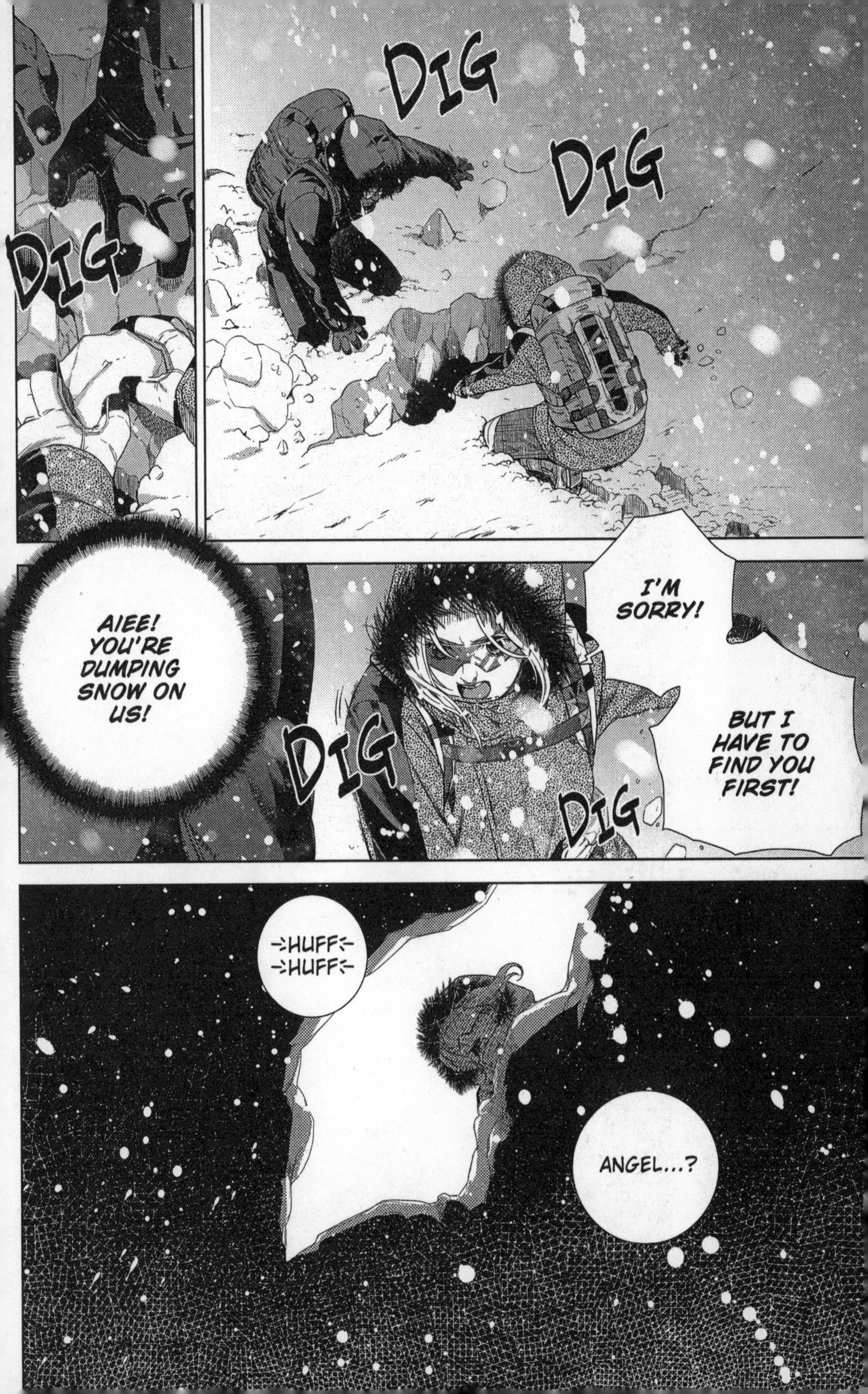
DIG
DIG
DIG
AIEE! YOU'RE DUMPING SNOW ON US!
I'M SORRY!
DIG
DIG
BUT I HAVE TO FIND YOU FIRST!
HUFF HUFF
ANGEL...?

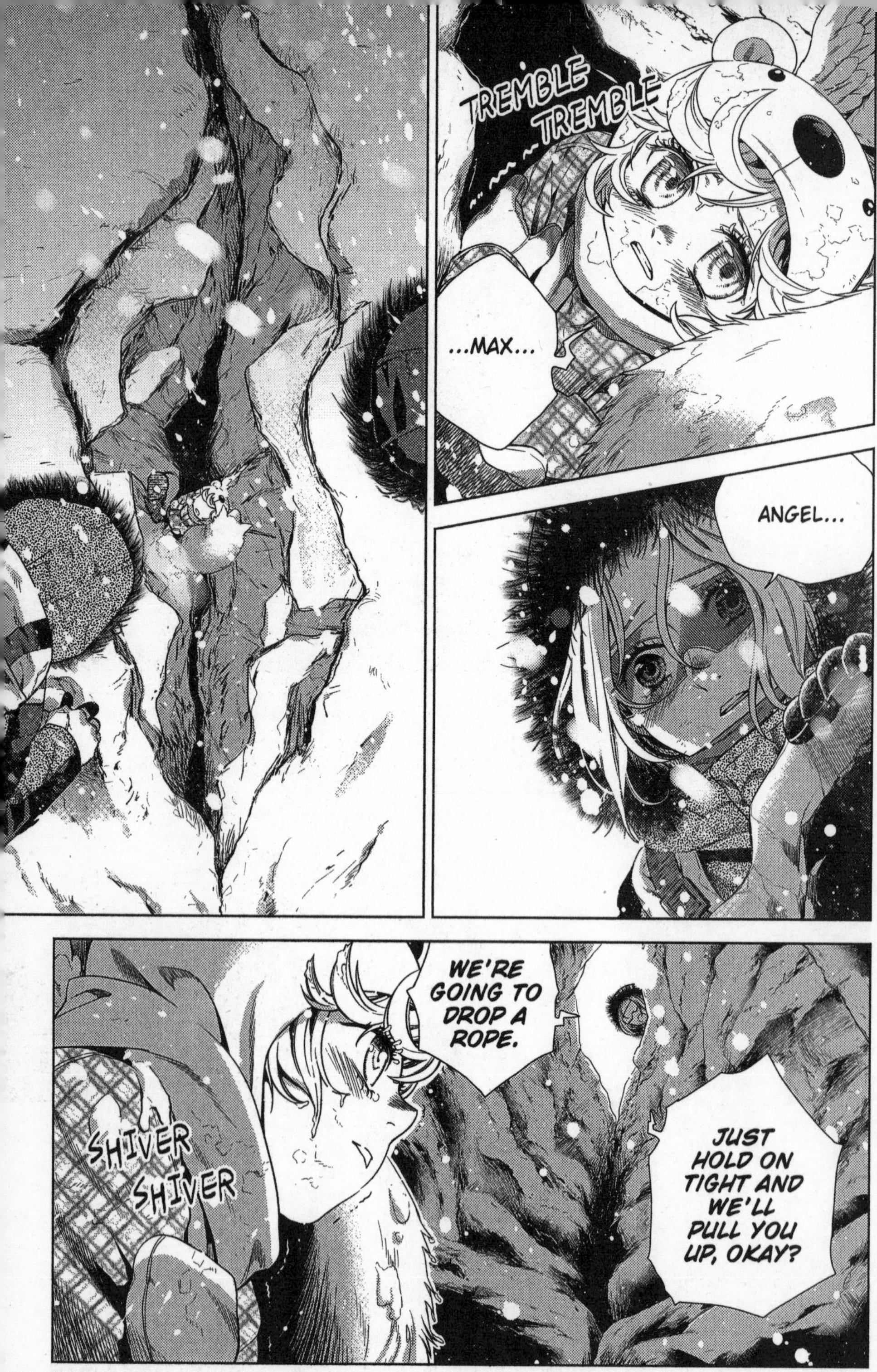
TREMBLE TREMBLE
...MAX...
ANGEL...
WE'RE GOING TO DROP A ROPE.
SHIVER SHIVER
JUST HOLD ON TIGHT AND WE'LL PULL YOU UP, OKAY?

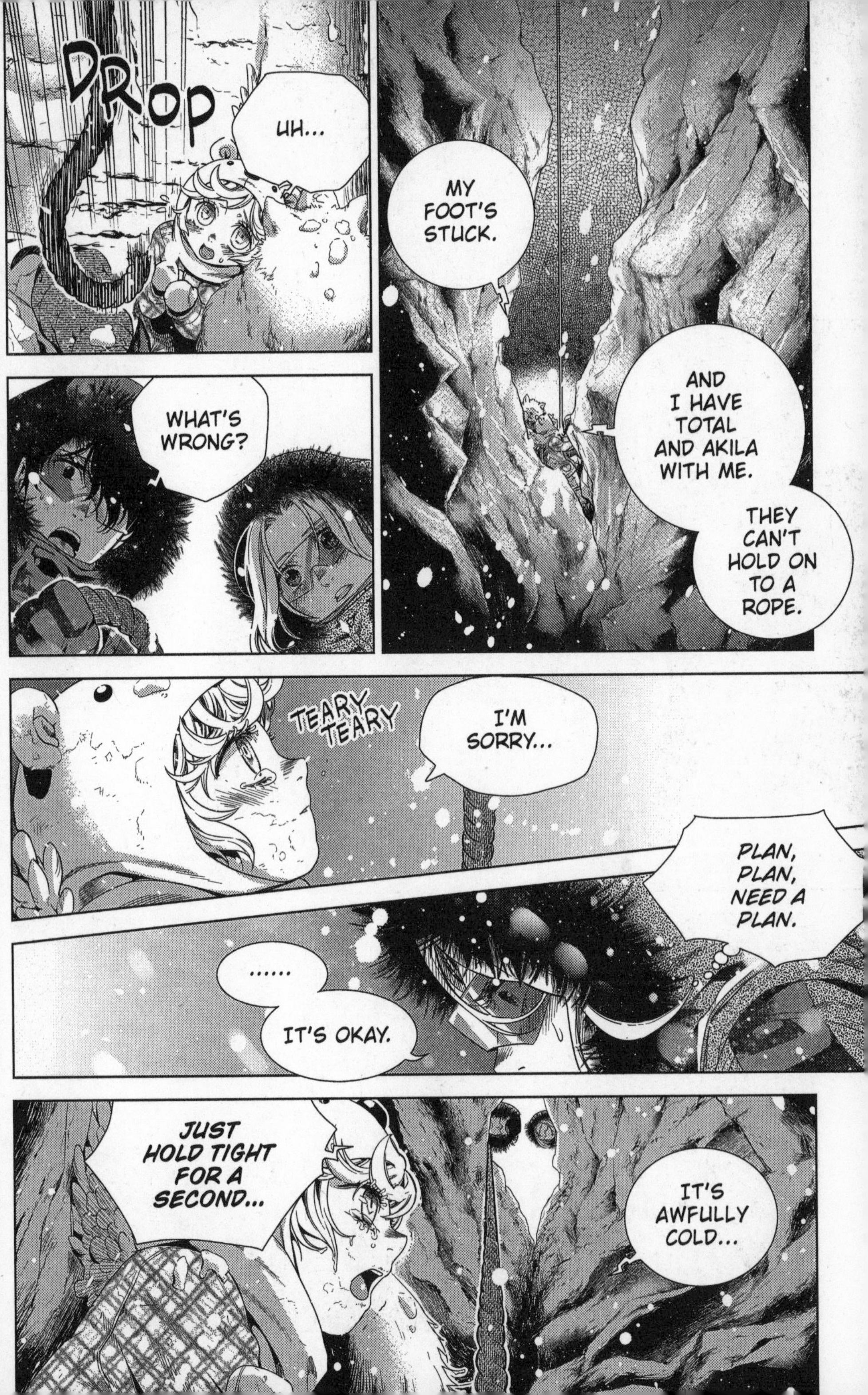
DROP
UH...
WHAT'S WRONG?
MY FOOT'S STUCK.
AND I HAVE TOTAL AND AKILA WITH ME.
THEY CAN'T HOLD ON TO A ROPE.
TEARY TEARY
I'M SORRY...
PLAN, PLAN, NEED A PLAN.
......
IT'S OKAY.
JUST HOLD TIGHT FOR A SECOND...
IT'S AWFULLY COLD...

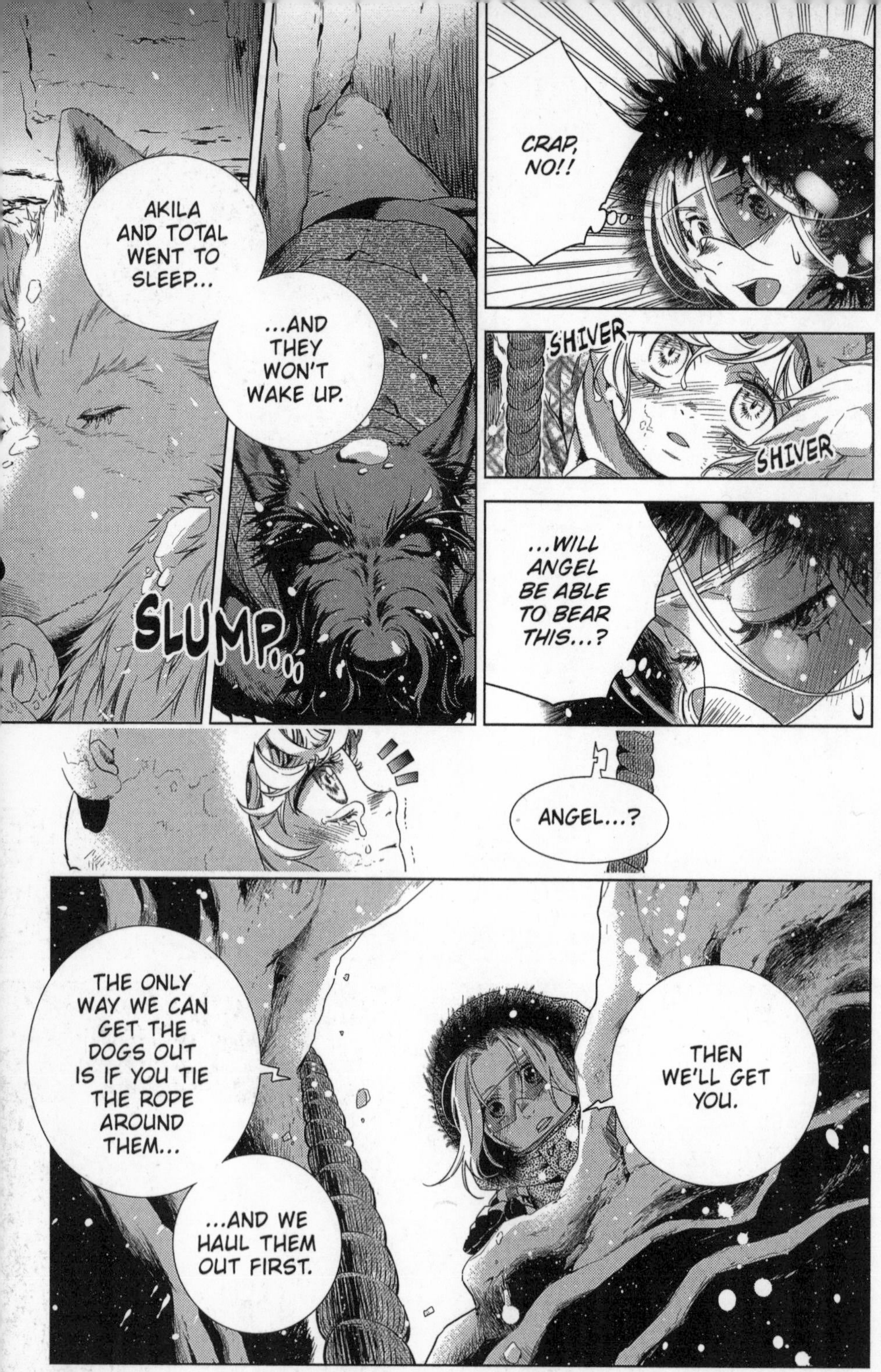
AKILA AND TOTAL WENT TO SLEEP...
...AND THEY WON'T WAKE UP.
SLUMP...
CRAP, NO!!
SHIVER
SHIVER
...WILL ANGEL BE ABLE TO BEAR THIS...?
ANGEL...?
THE ONLY WAY WE CAN GET THE DOGS OUT IS IF YOU TIE THE ROPE AROUND THEM...
...AND WE HAUL THEM OUT FIRST.
THEN WE'LL GET YOU.

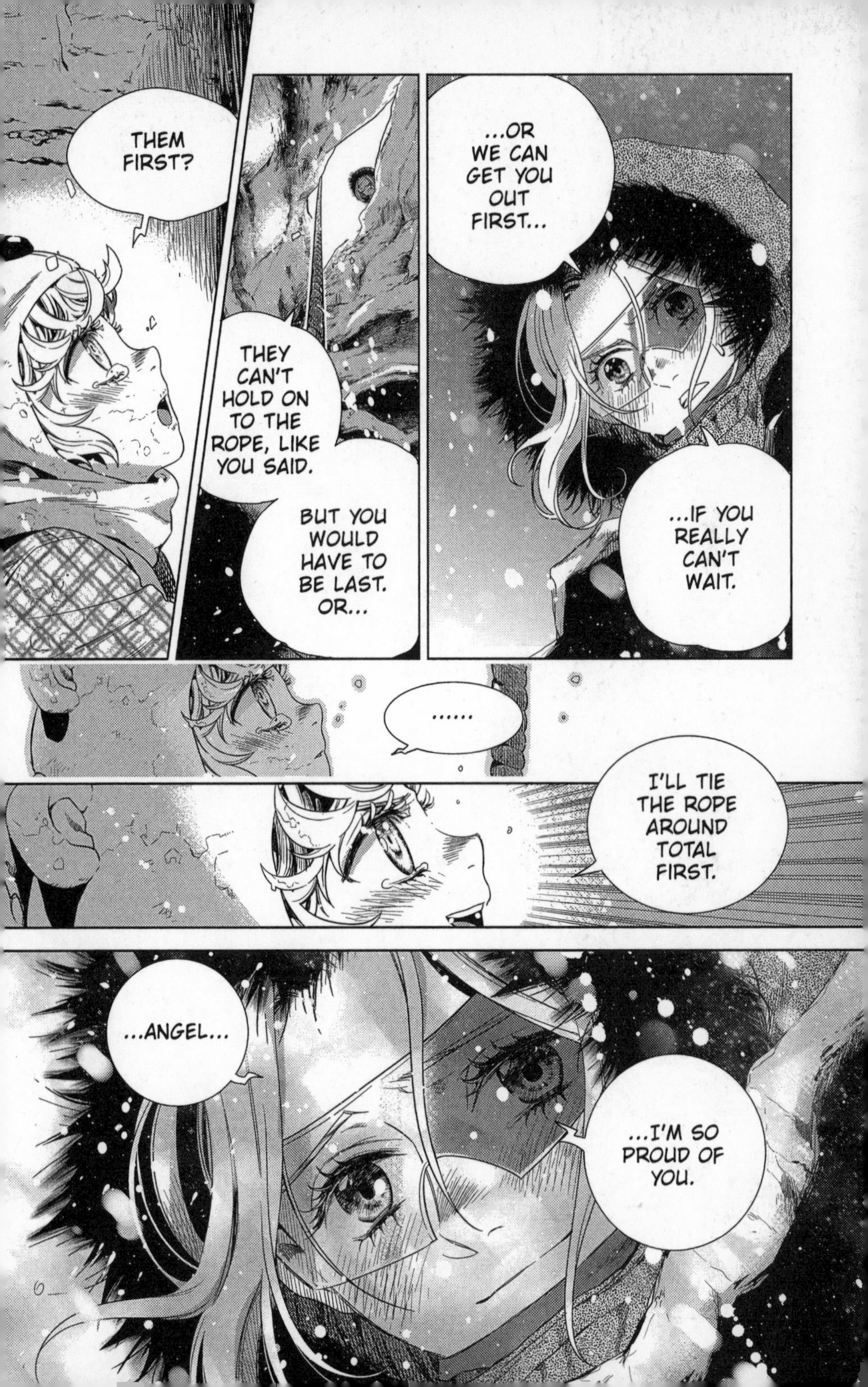
THEM FIRST?
THEY CAN'T HOLD ON TO THE ROPE, LIKE YOU SAID.
BUT YOU WOULD HAVE TO BE LAST. OR...
...OR WE CAN GET YOU OUT FIRST...
...IF YOU REALLY CAN'T WAIT.
......
I'LL TIE THE ROPE AROUND TOTAL FIRST.
...ANGEL...
...I'M SO PROUD OF YOU.

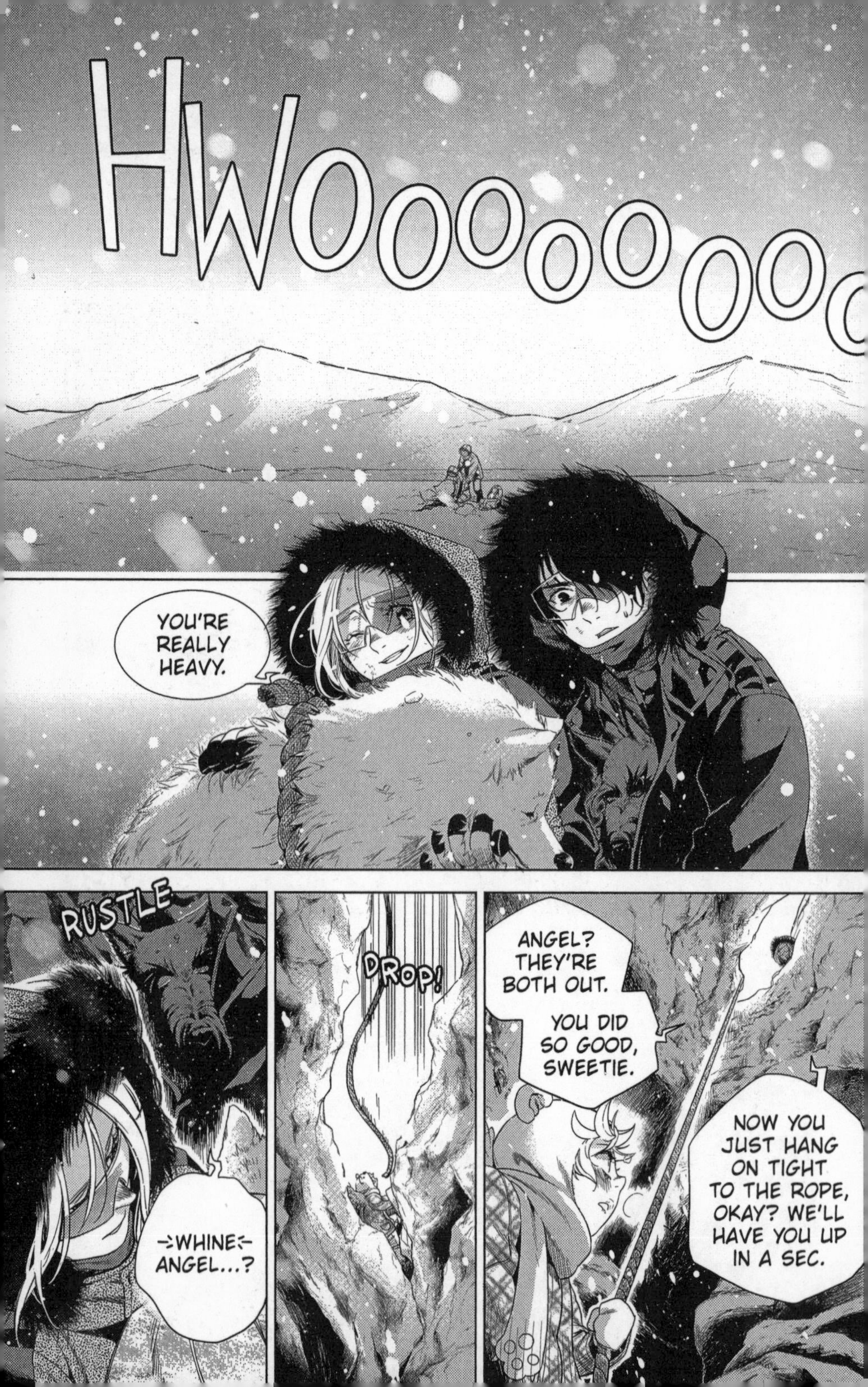
HWOOOOOOOO
YOU'RE REALLY HEAVY.
RUSTLE
≈WHINE≈ ANGEL...?
DROP!
ANGEL? THEY'RE BOTH OUT.
YOU DID SO GOOD, SWEETIE.
NOW YOU JUST HANG ON TIGHT TO THE ROPE, OKAY? WE'LL HAVE YOU UP IN A SEC.

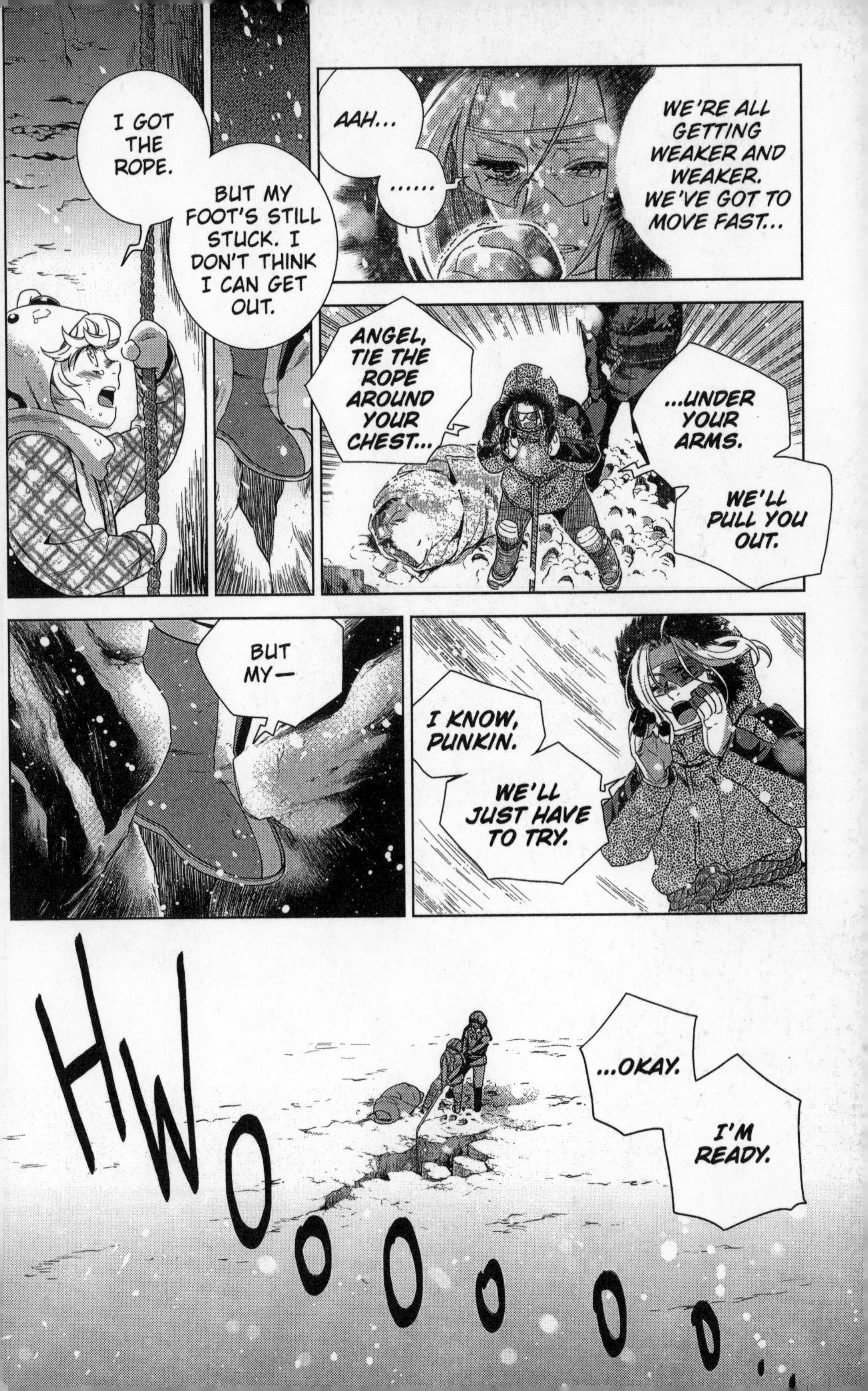
I GOT THE ROPE.
BUT MY FOOT'S STILL STUCK. I DON'T THINK I CAN GET OUT.
AAH...
......
WE'RE ALL GETTING WEAKER AND WEAKER. WE'VE GOT TO MOVE FAST...
ANGEL, TIE THE ROPE AROUND YOUR CHEST...
...UNDER YOUR ARMS.
WE'LL PULL YOU OUT.
BUT MY—
I KNOW, PUNKIN.
WE'LL JUST HAVE TO TRY.
HWOOOOOOO...
...OKAY.
I'M READY.

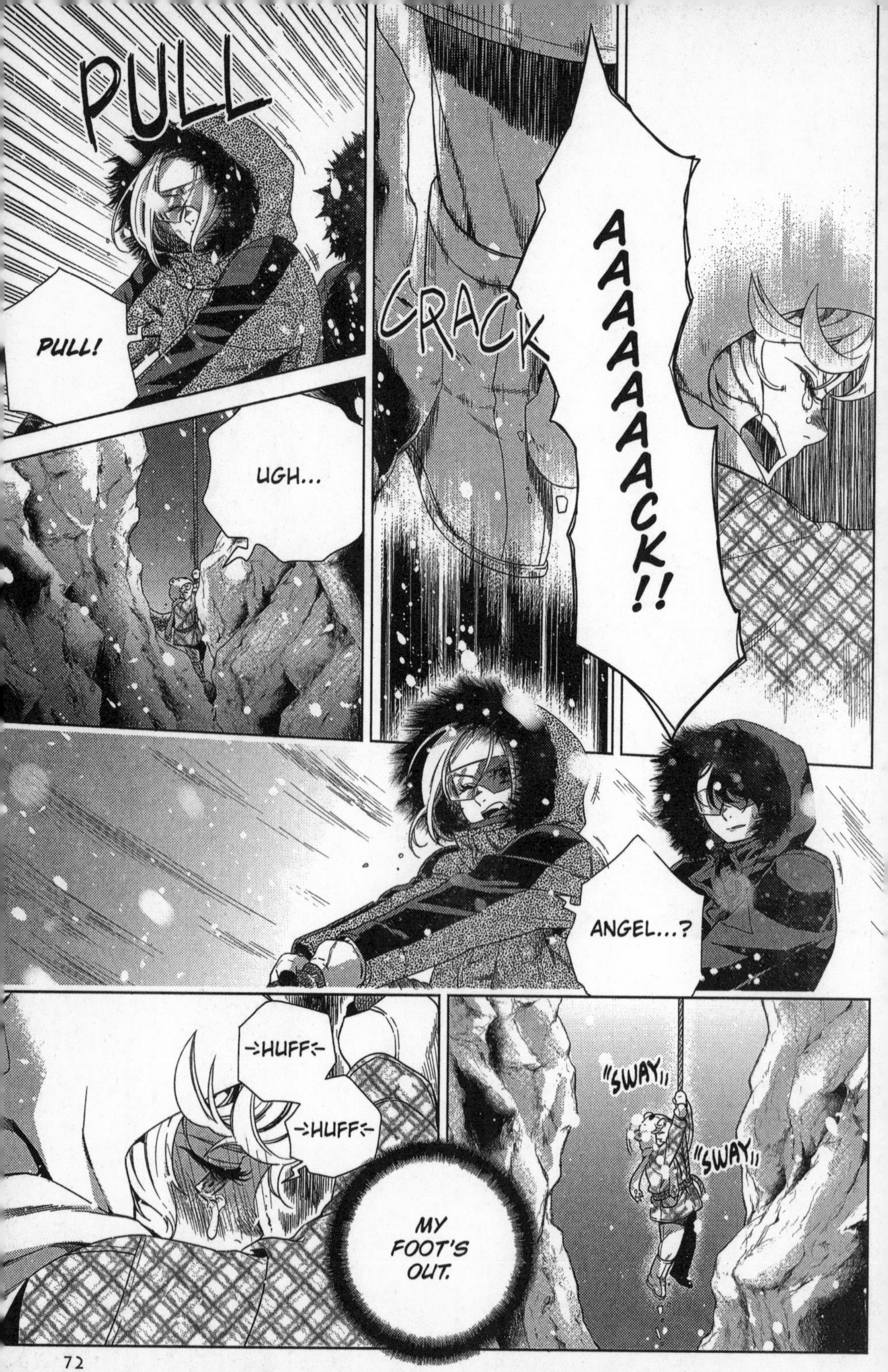
PULL
PULL!
UGH...
CRACK
AAAAAAAACK!!
ANGEL...?
HUFF
HUFF
MY FOOT'S OUT.
SWAY
SWAY

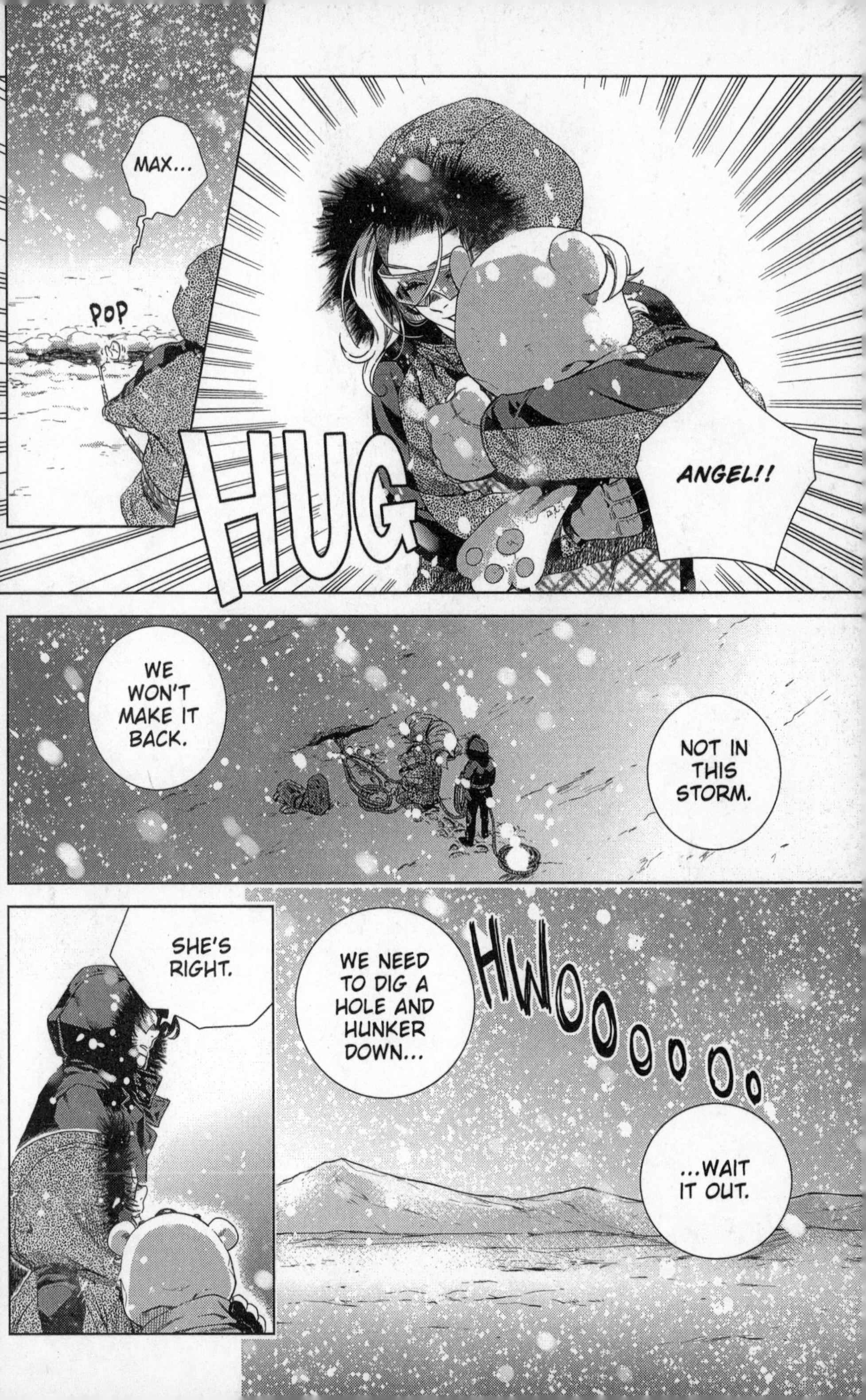
MAX...
POP
HUG
ANGEL!!
WE WON'T MAKE IT BACK.
NOT IN THIS STORM.
SHE'S RIGHT.
WE NEED TO DIG A HOLE AND HUNKER DOWN...
HWOOOOO..
...WAIT IT OUT.

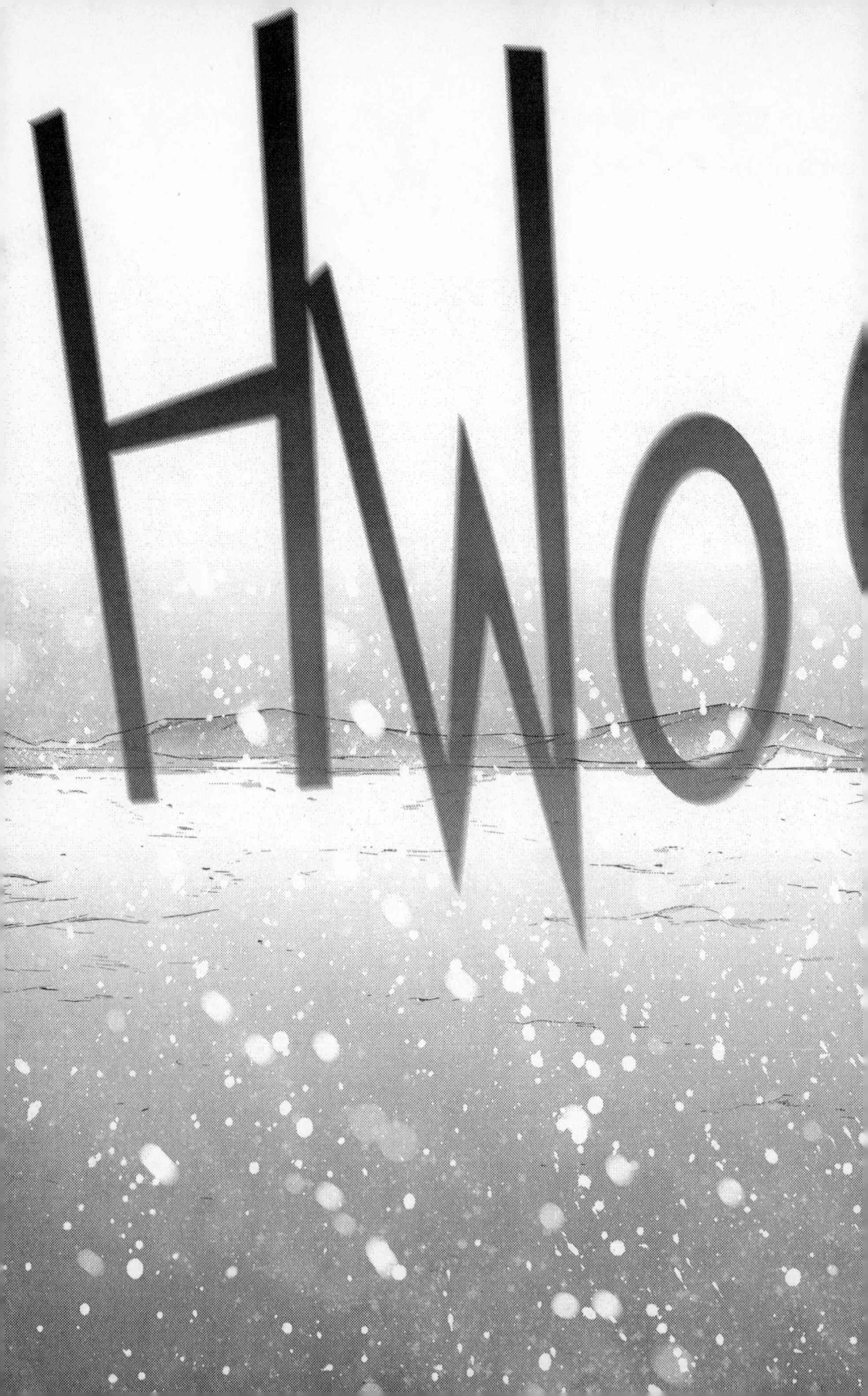
HWO

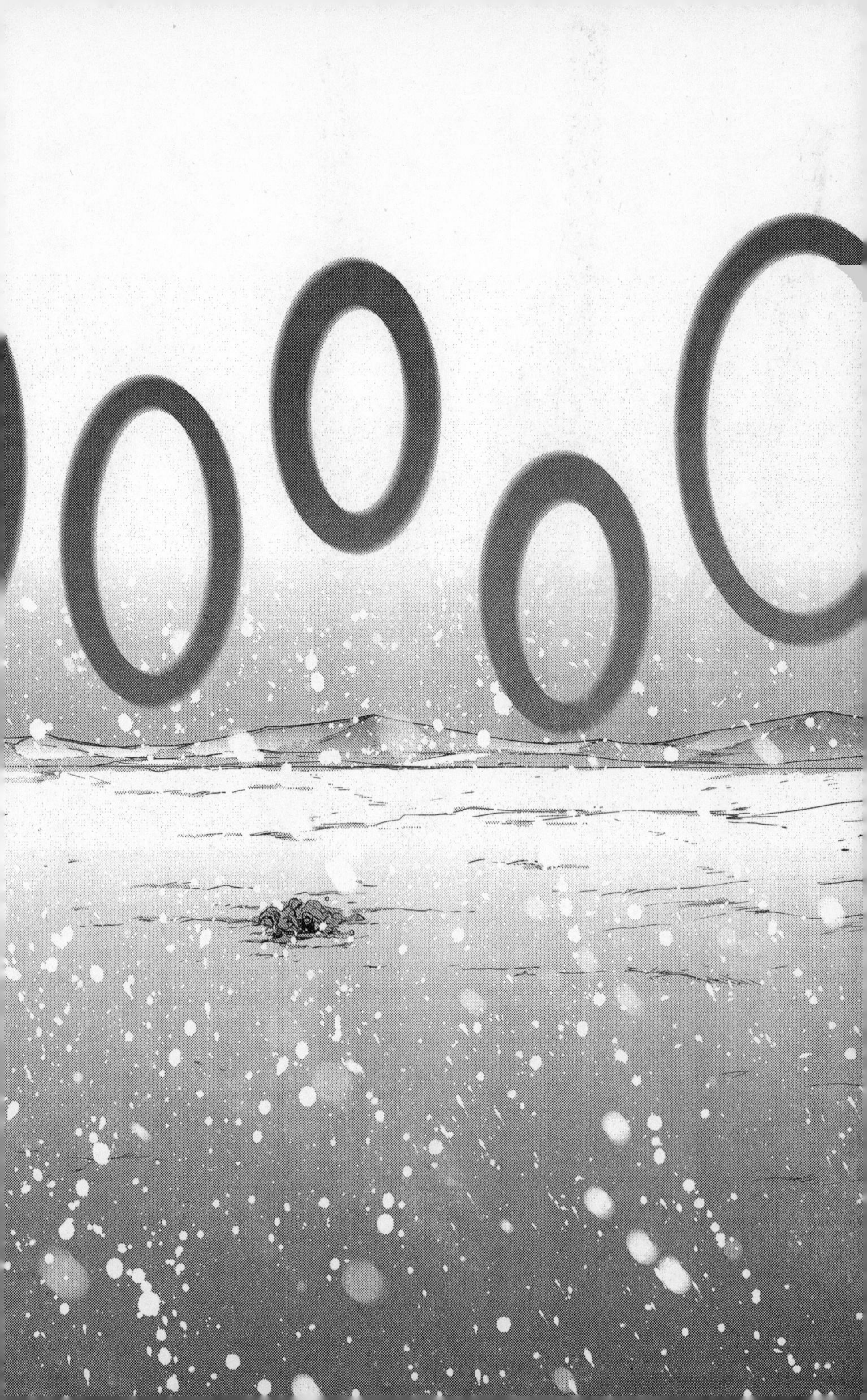
OOOOO

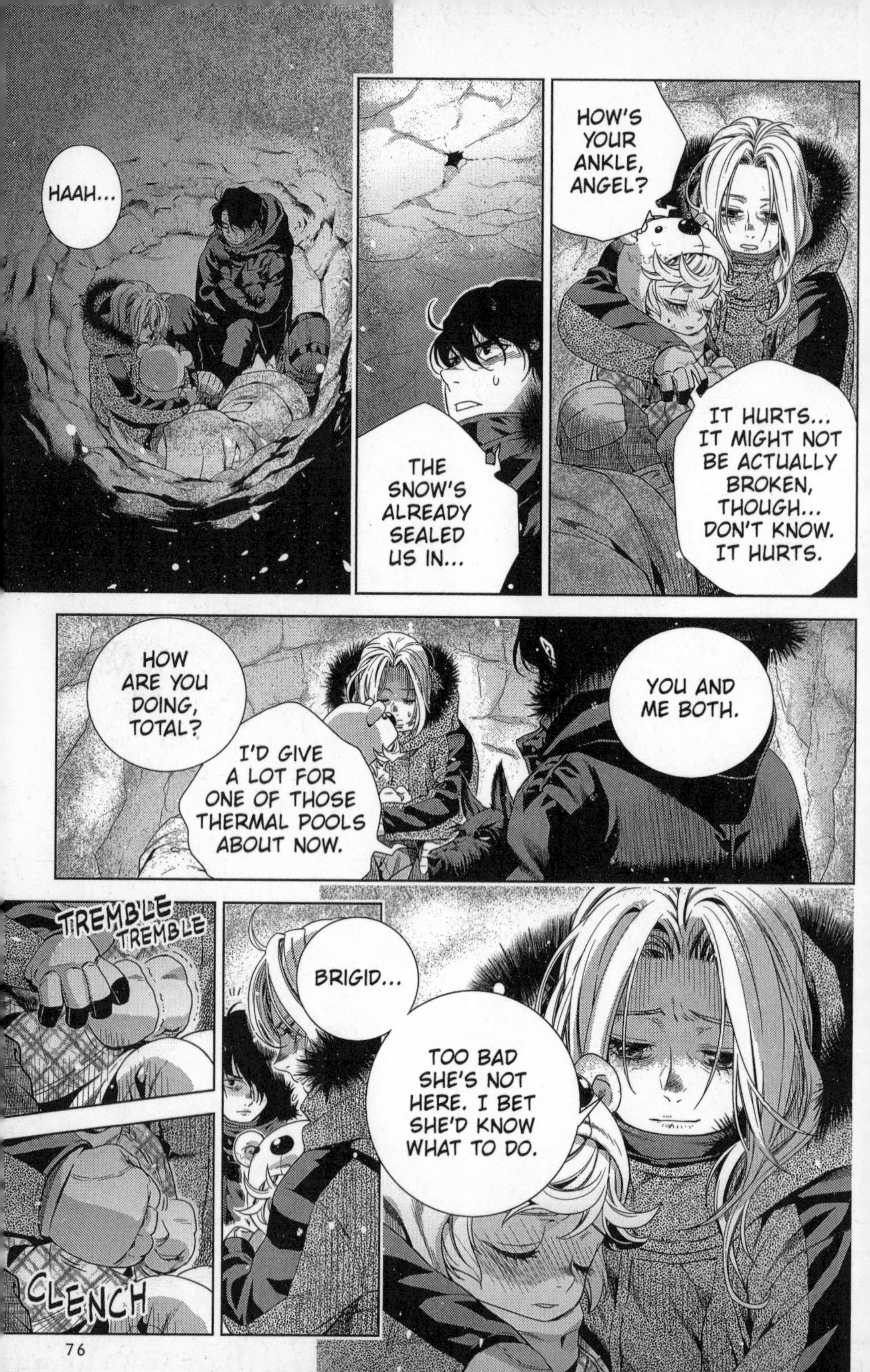
HAAH...
THE SNOW'S ALREADY SEALED US IN...
HOW'S YOUR ANKLE, ANGEL?
IT HURTS... IT MIGHT NOT BE ACTUALLY BROKEN, THOUGH... DON'T KNOW. IT HURTS.
HOW ARE YOU DOING, TOTAL?
I'D GIVE A LOT FOR ONE OF THOSE THERMAL POOLS ABOUT NOW.
YOU AND ME BOTH.
TREMBLE TREMBLE
CLENCH
BRIGID...
TOO BAD SHE'S NOT HERE. I BET SHE'D KNOW WHAT TO DO.

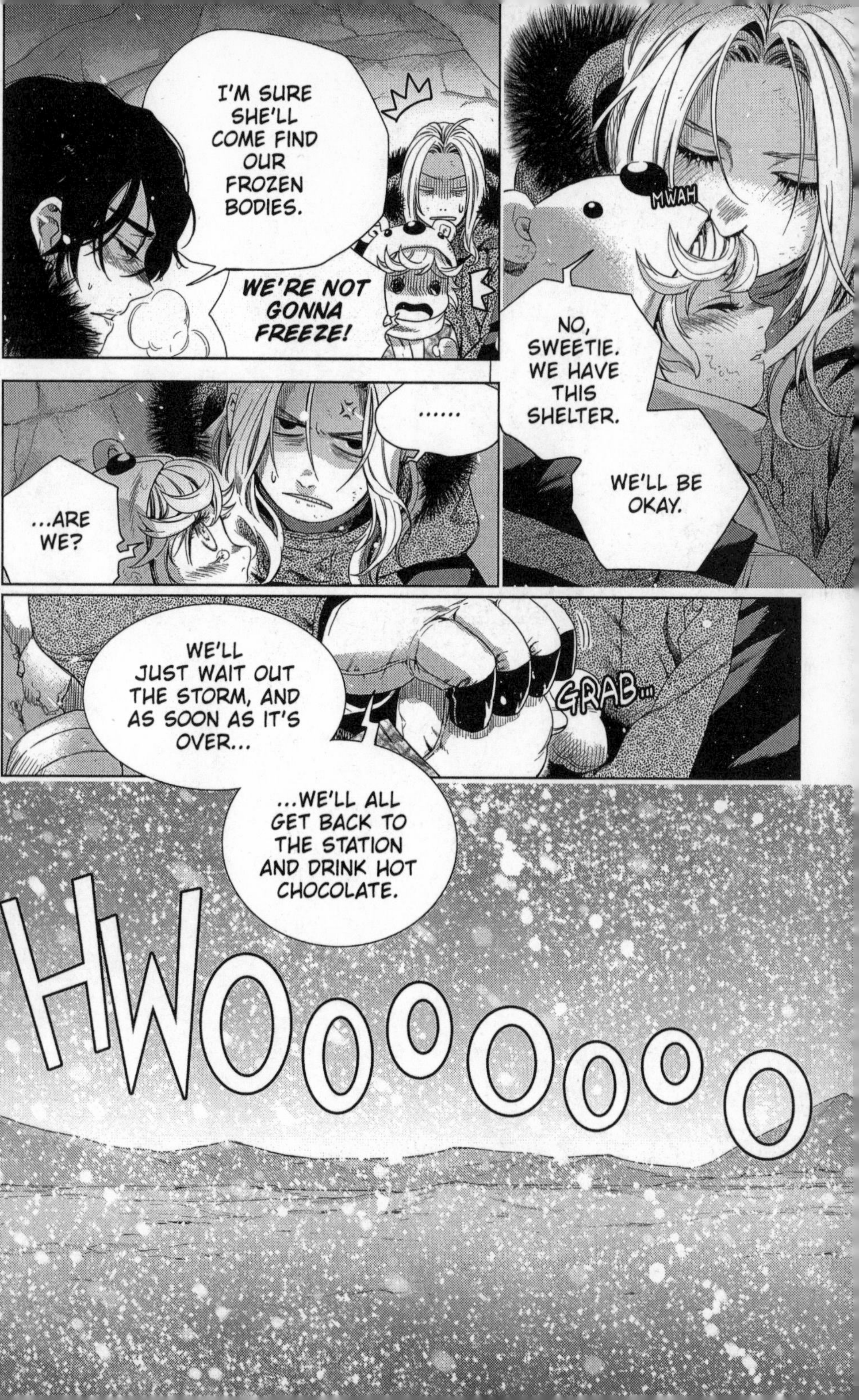
I'M SURE SHE'LL COME FIND OUR FROZEN BODIES.
WE'RE NOT GONNA FREEZE!
MWAH
NO, SWEETIE. WE HAVE THIS SHELTER.
WE'LL BE OKAY.
...ARE WE?
......
WE'LL JUST WAIT OUT THE STORM, AND AS SOON AS IT'S OVER...
GRAB...
...WE'LL ALL GET BACK TO THE STATION AND DRINK HOT CHOCOLATE.
HWOOOOOOO

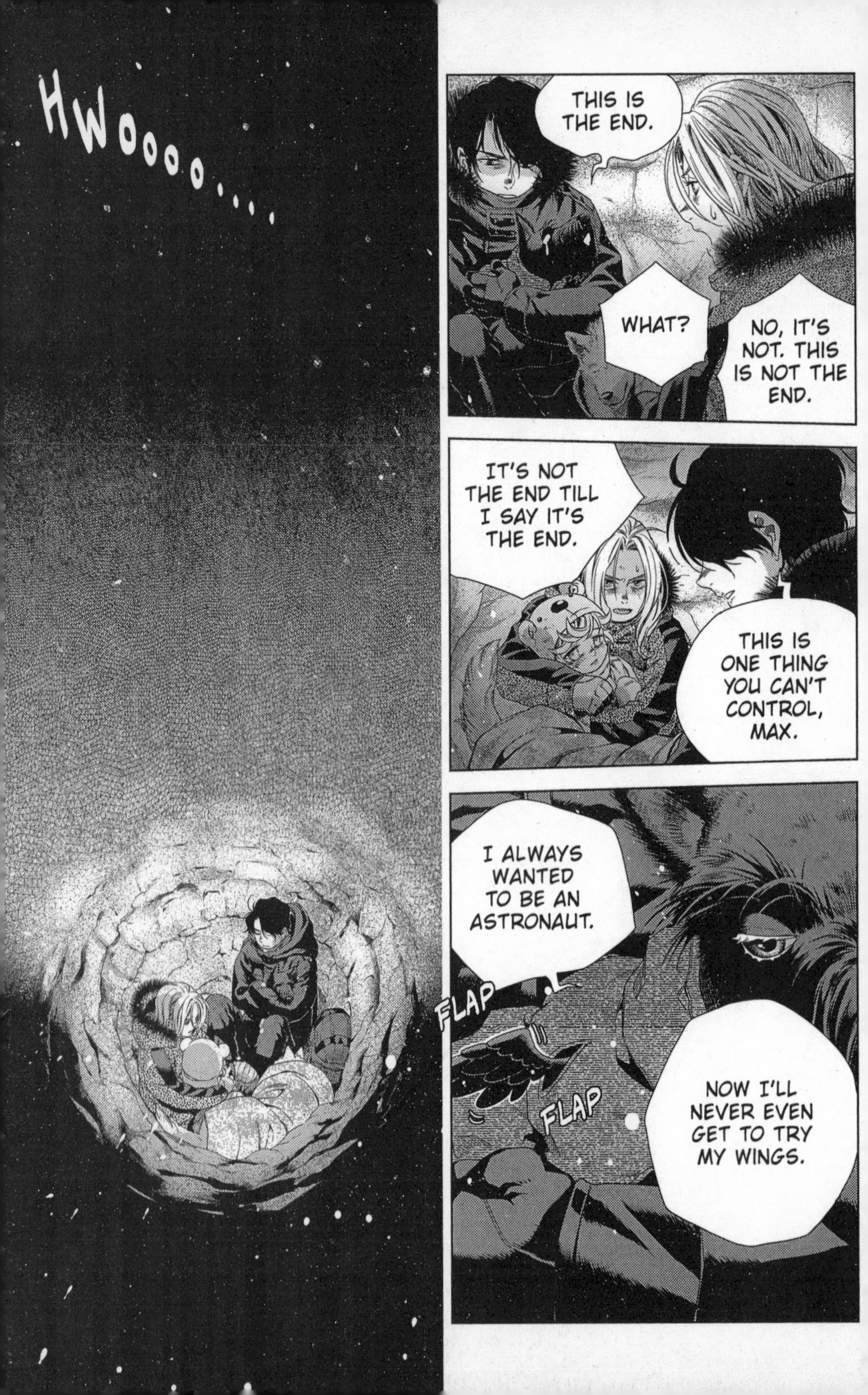
HWOOOO....
THIS IS THE END.
WHAT?
NO, IT'S NOT. THIS IS NOT THE END.
IT'S NOT THE END TILL I SAY IT'S THE END.
THIS IS ONE THING YOU CAN'T CONTROL, MAX.
I ALWAYS WANTED TO BE AN ASTRONAUT.
FLAP
FLAP
NOW I'LL NEVER EVEN GET TO TRY MY WINGS.

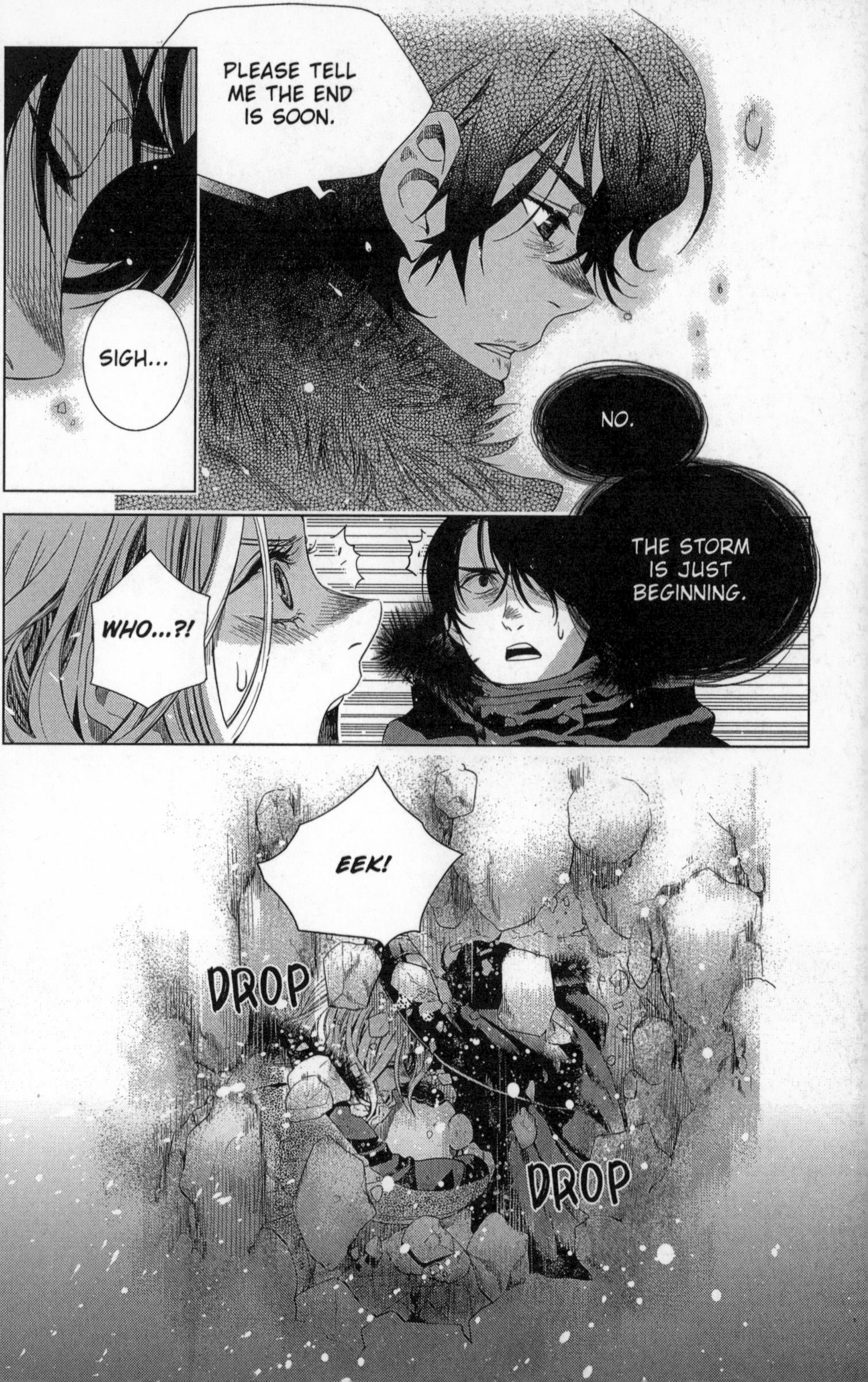
SIGH...
PLEASE TELL ME THE END IS SOON.
NO.
THE STORM IS JUST BEGINNING.
WHO...?!
EEK!
DROP
DROP

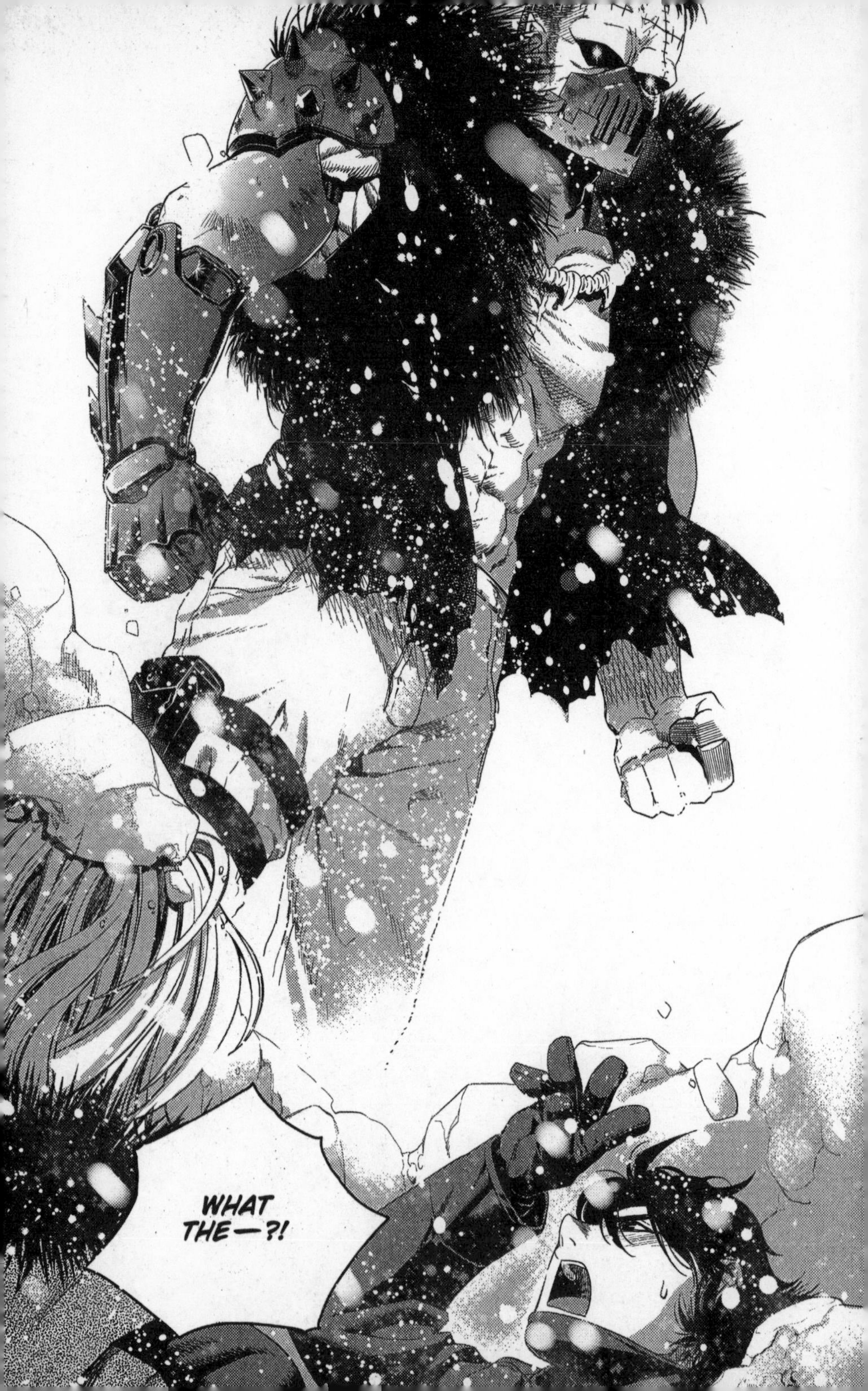
WHAT THE—?!

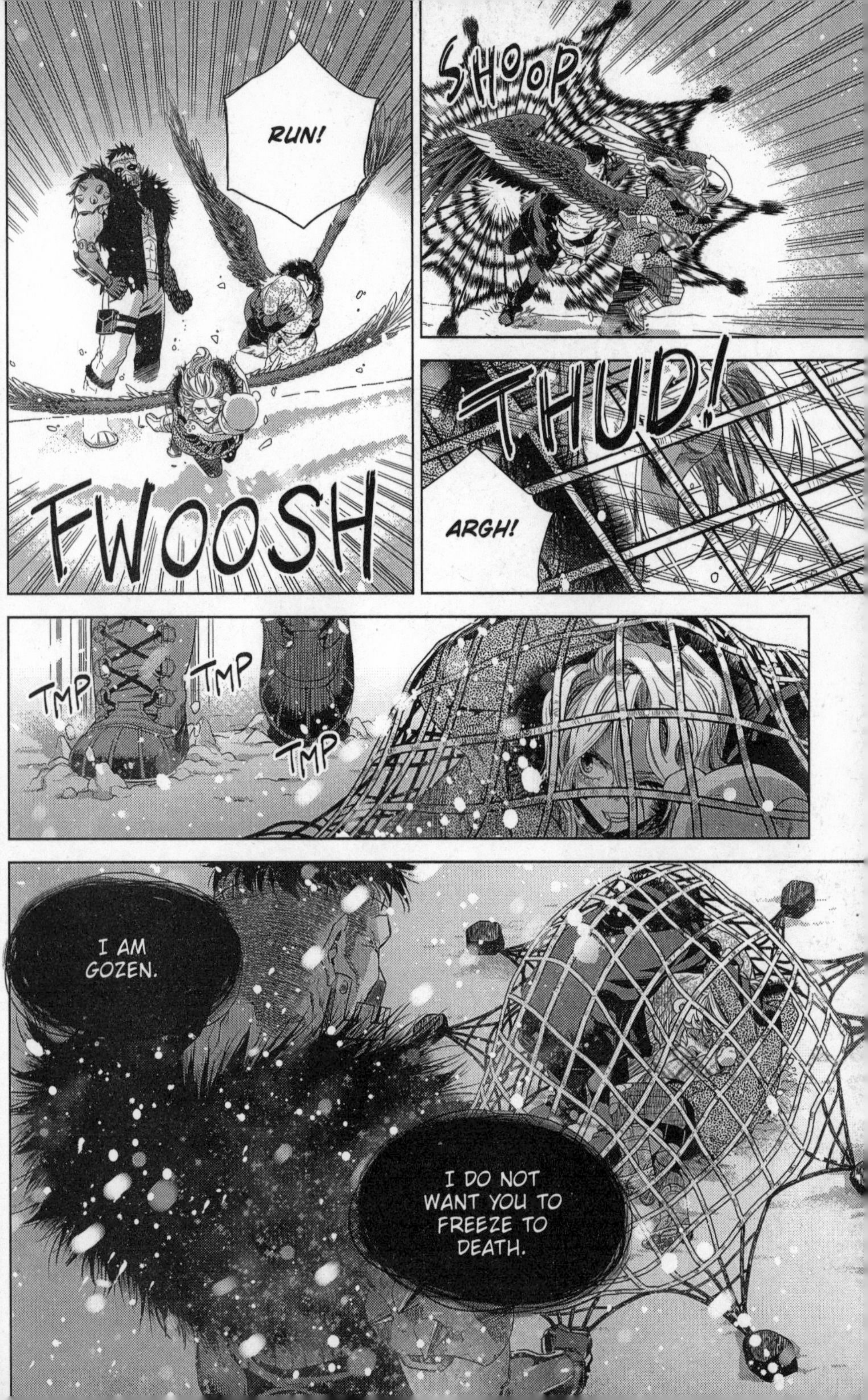
RUN!
FWOOSH
SHOOP
THUD!
ARGH!
TMP
TMP
TMP
I AM GOZEN.
I DO NOT WANT YOU TO FREEZE TO DEATH.

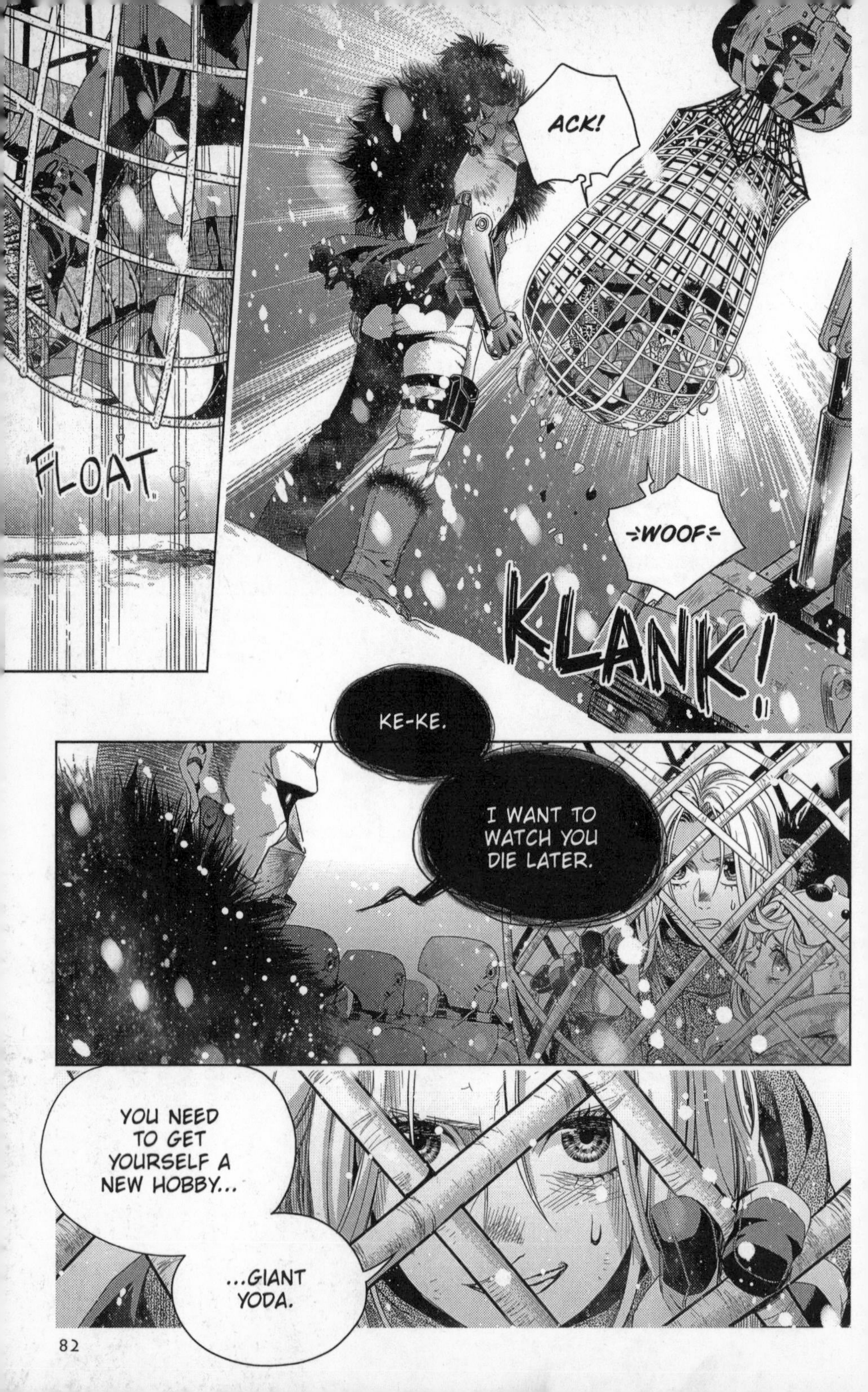
FLOAT
ACK!
WOOF
KLANK!
KE-KE.
I WANT TO WATCH YOU DIE LATER.
YOU NEED TO GET YOURSELF A NEW HOBBY...
...GIANT YODA.

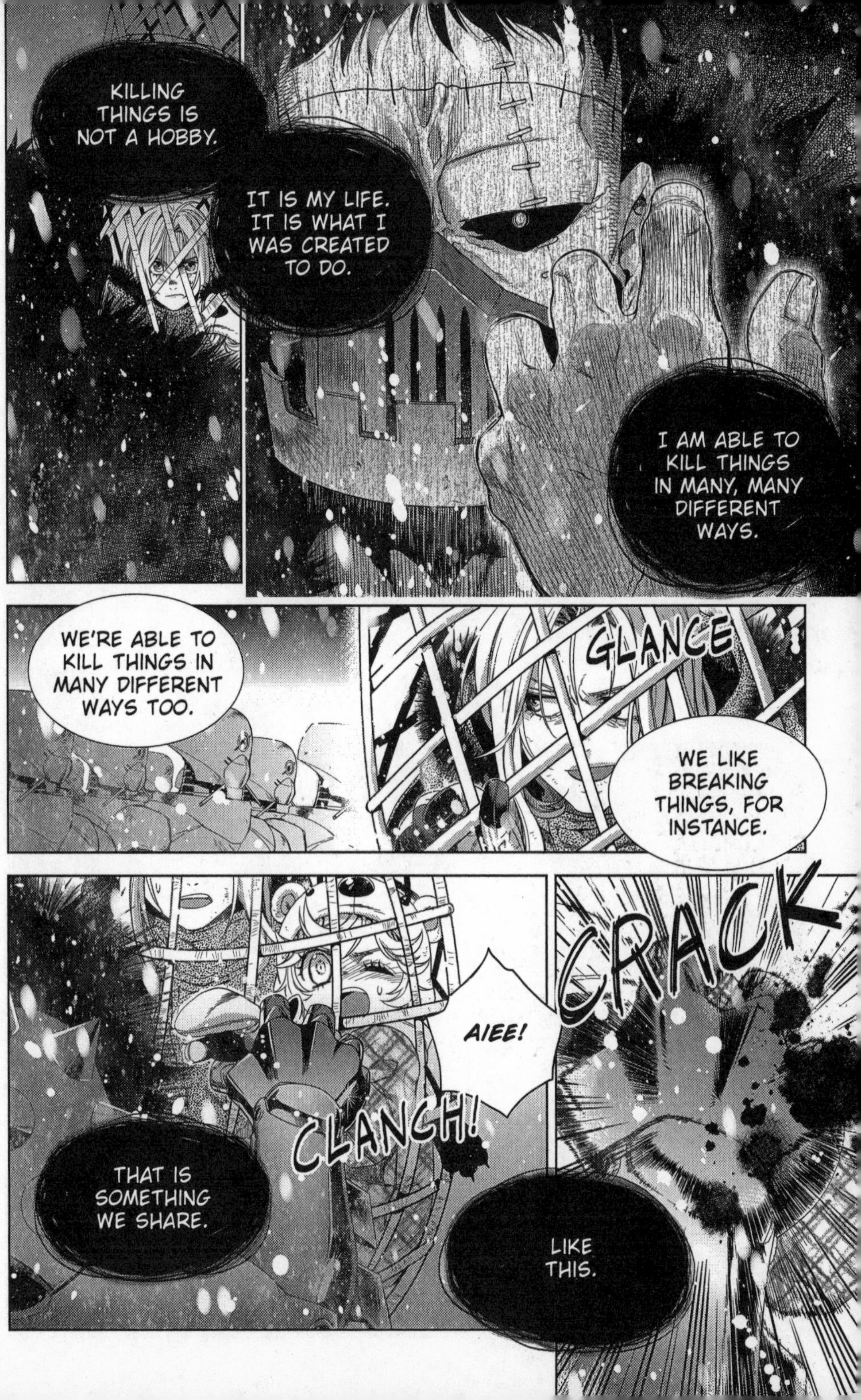
KILLING THINGS IS NOT A HOBBY.
IT IS MY LIFE. IT IS WHAT I WAS CREATED TO DO.
I AM ABLE TO KILL THINGS IN MANY, MANY DIFFERENT WAYS.
WE'RE ABLE TO KILL THINGS IN MANY DIFFERENT WAYS TOO.
GLANCE
WE LIKE BREAKING THINGS, FOR INSTANCE.
AIEE!
CLANCH!
THAT IS SOMETHING WE SHARE.
CRACK
LIKE THIS.

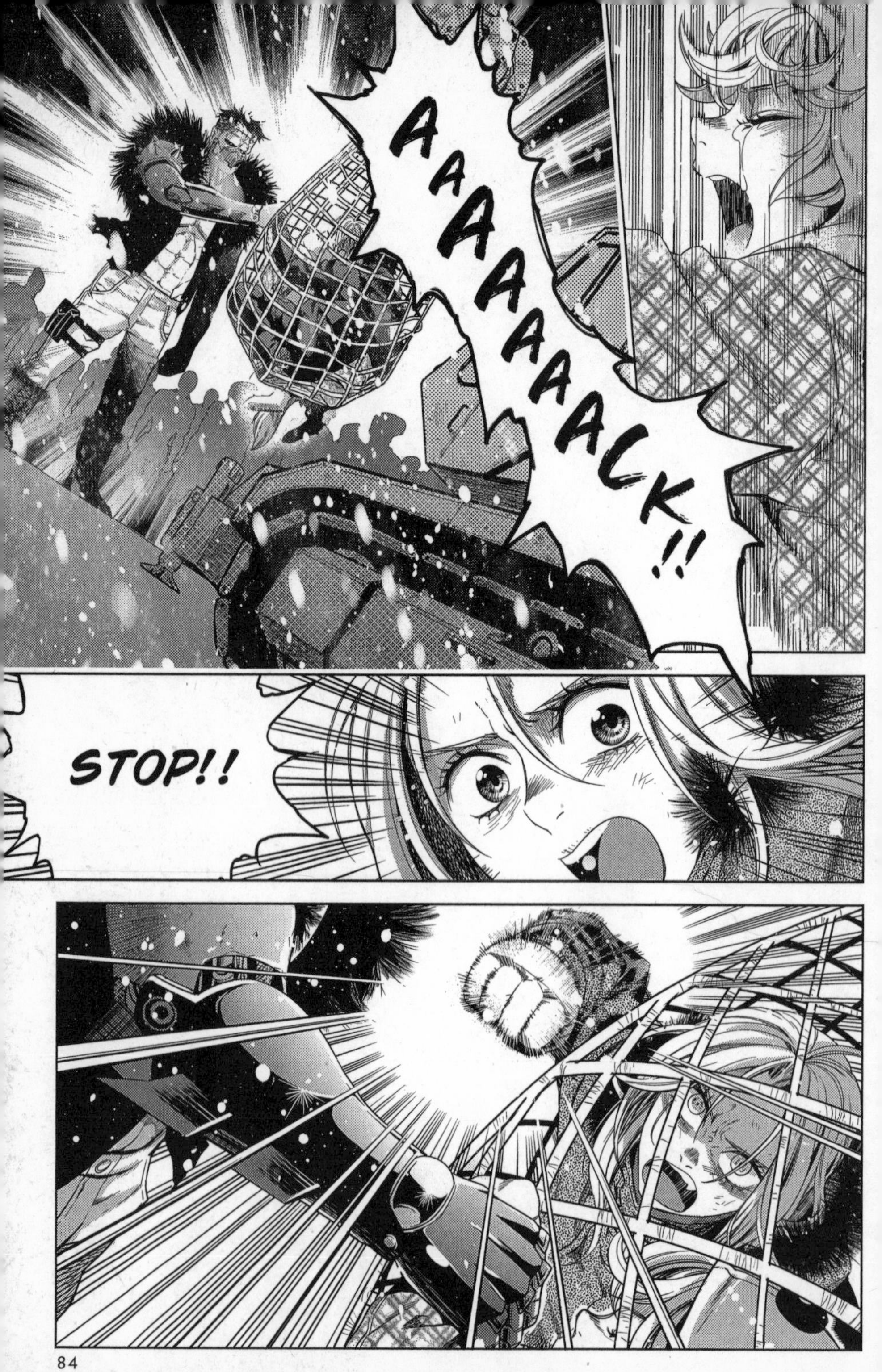
AAAAAAAAAACK!!
STOP!!

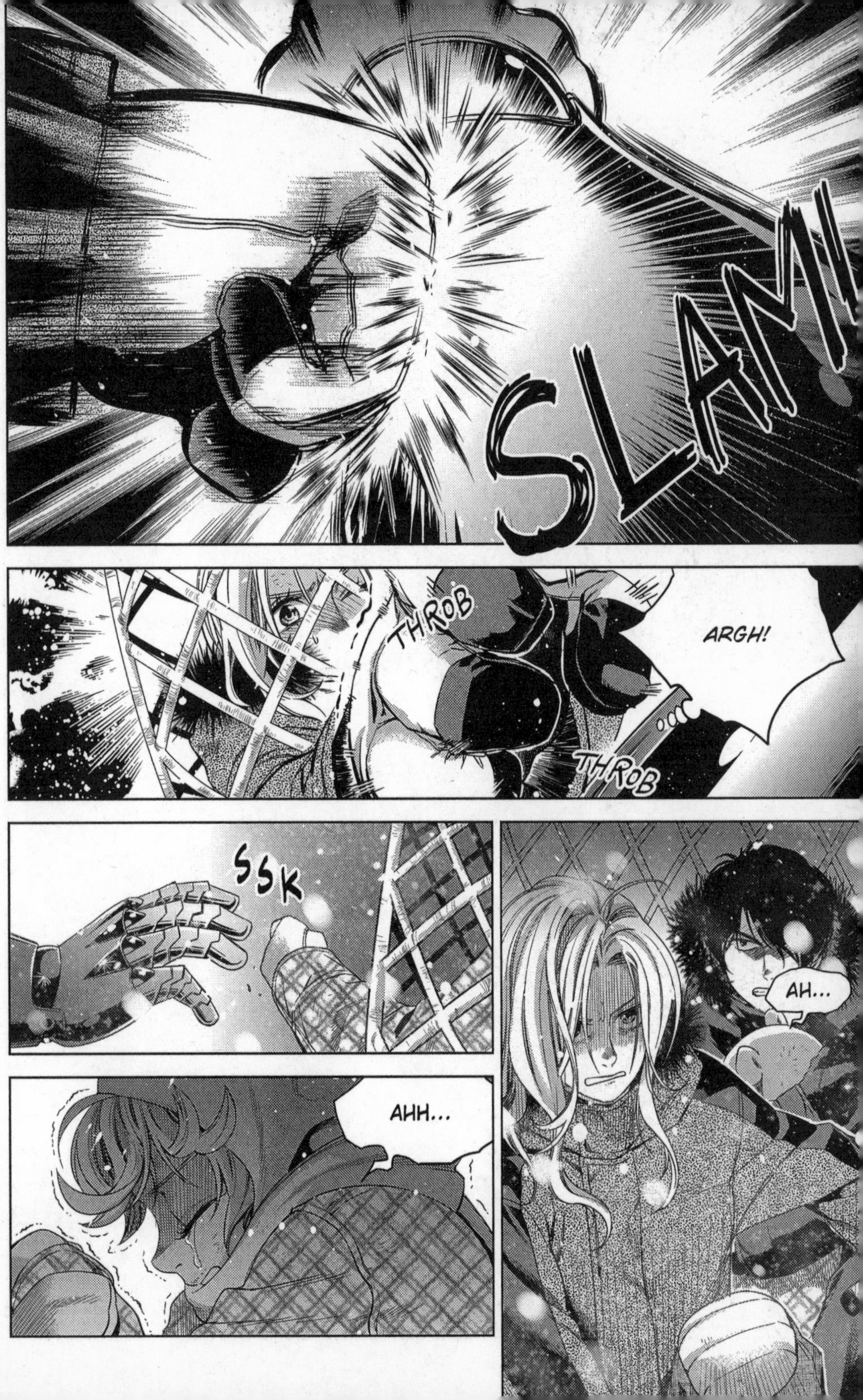
SLAM!!
THROB
ARGH!
THROB
SSK
AH...
AHH...

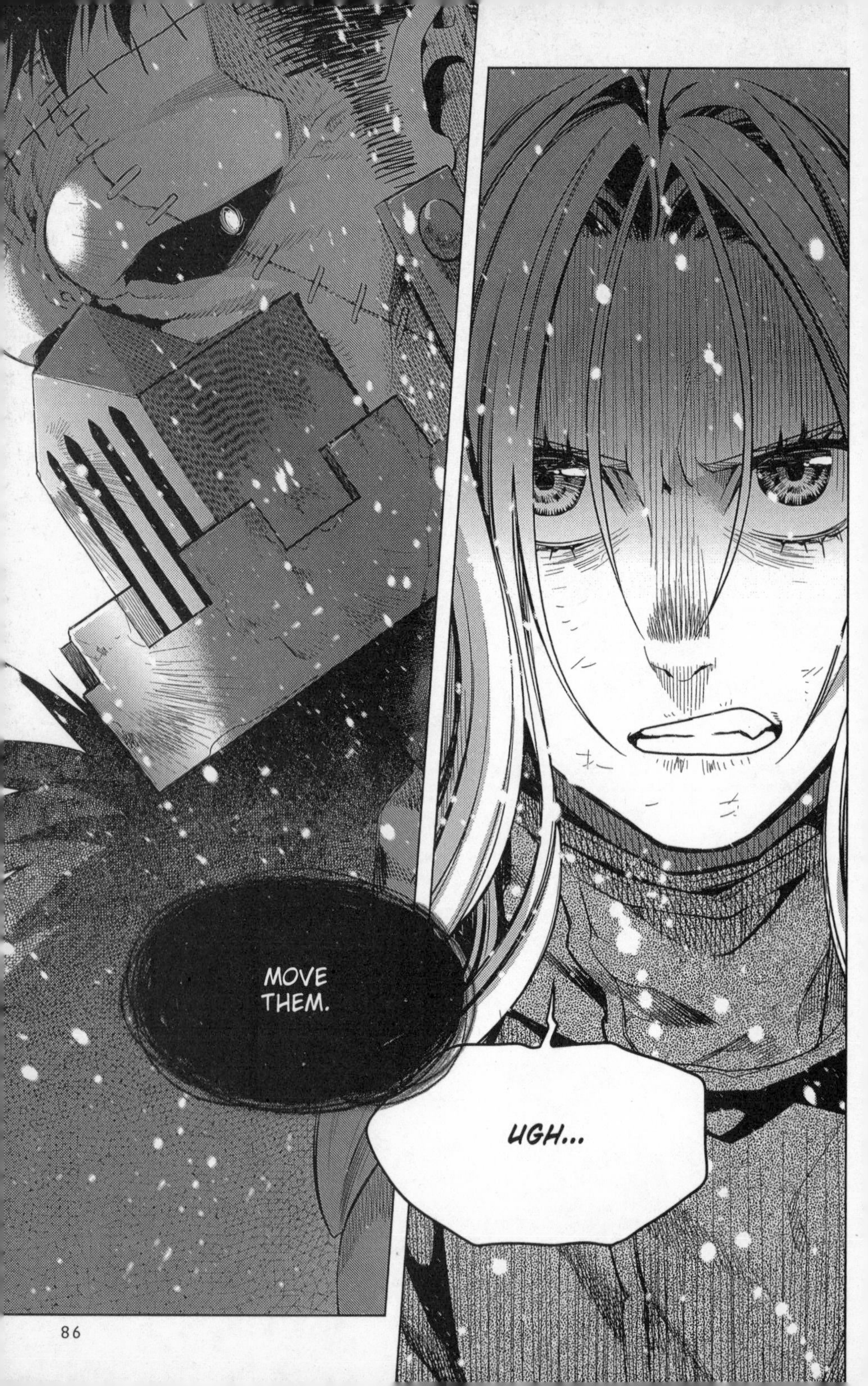
MOVE THEM.
UGH...

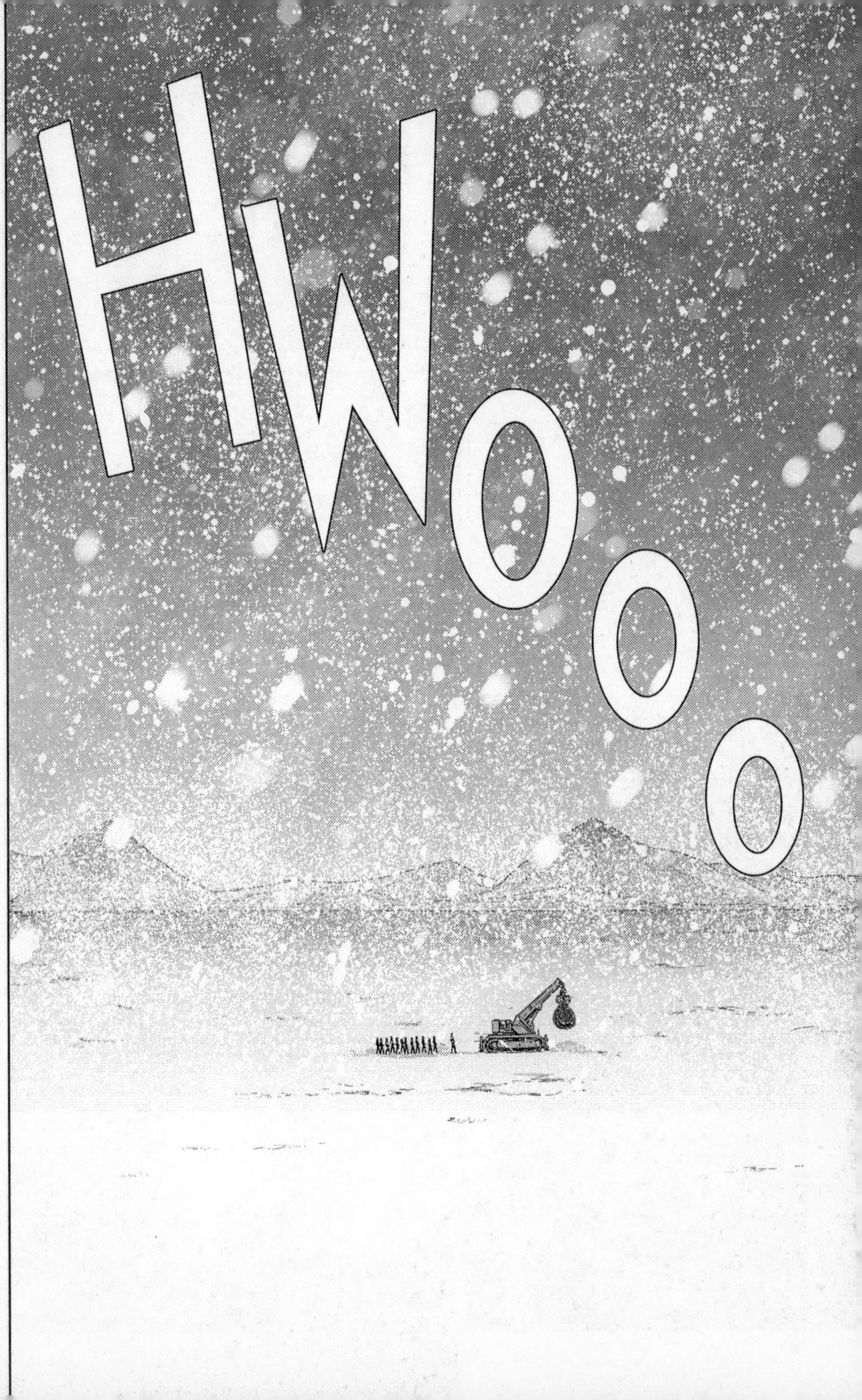
HIWOOO

HWOOOOO

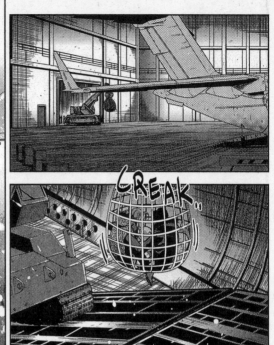

CREAK...

THUD

ACK!

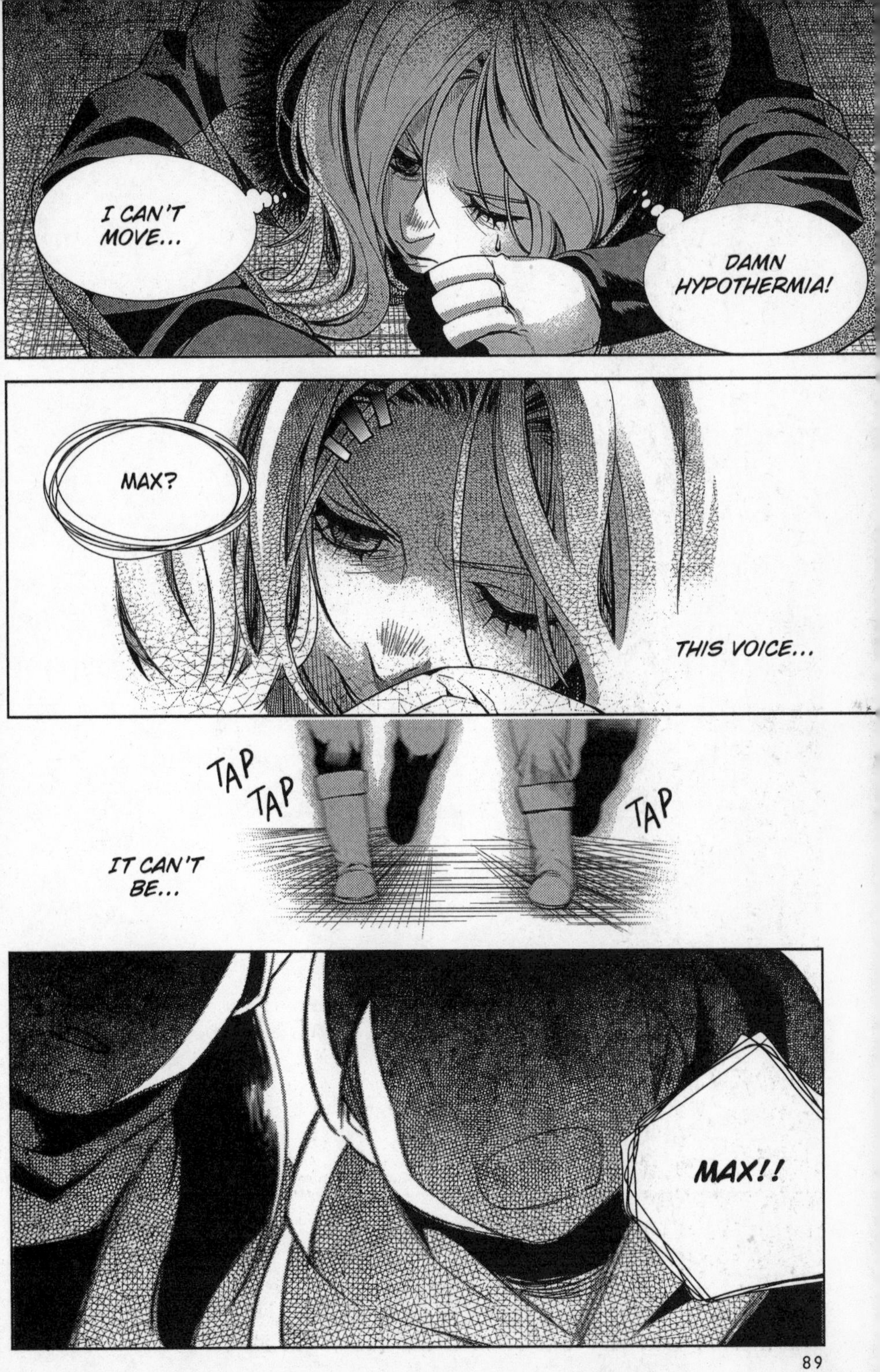
I CAN'T MOVE...
DAMN HYPOTHERMIA!
MAX?
THIS VOICE...
TAP TAP
TAP
IT CAN'T BE...
MAX!!

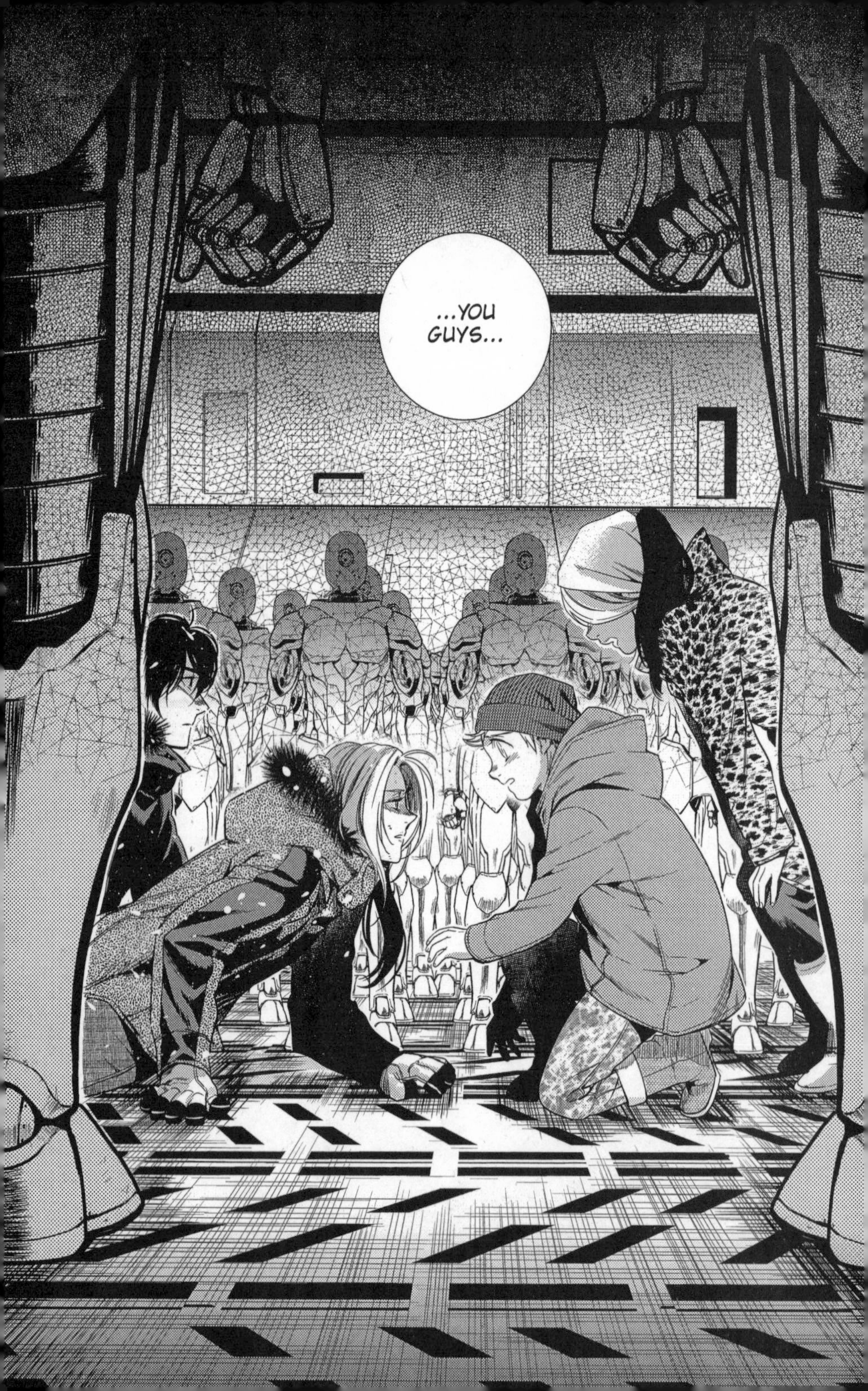
...YOU
GUYS...

MAXIMUM RIDE

CHAPTER 49

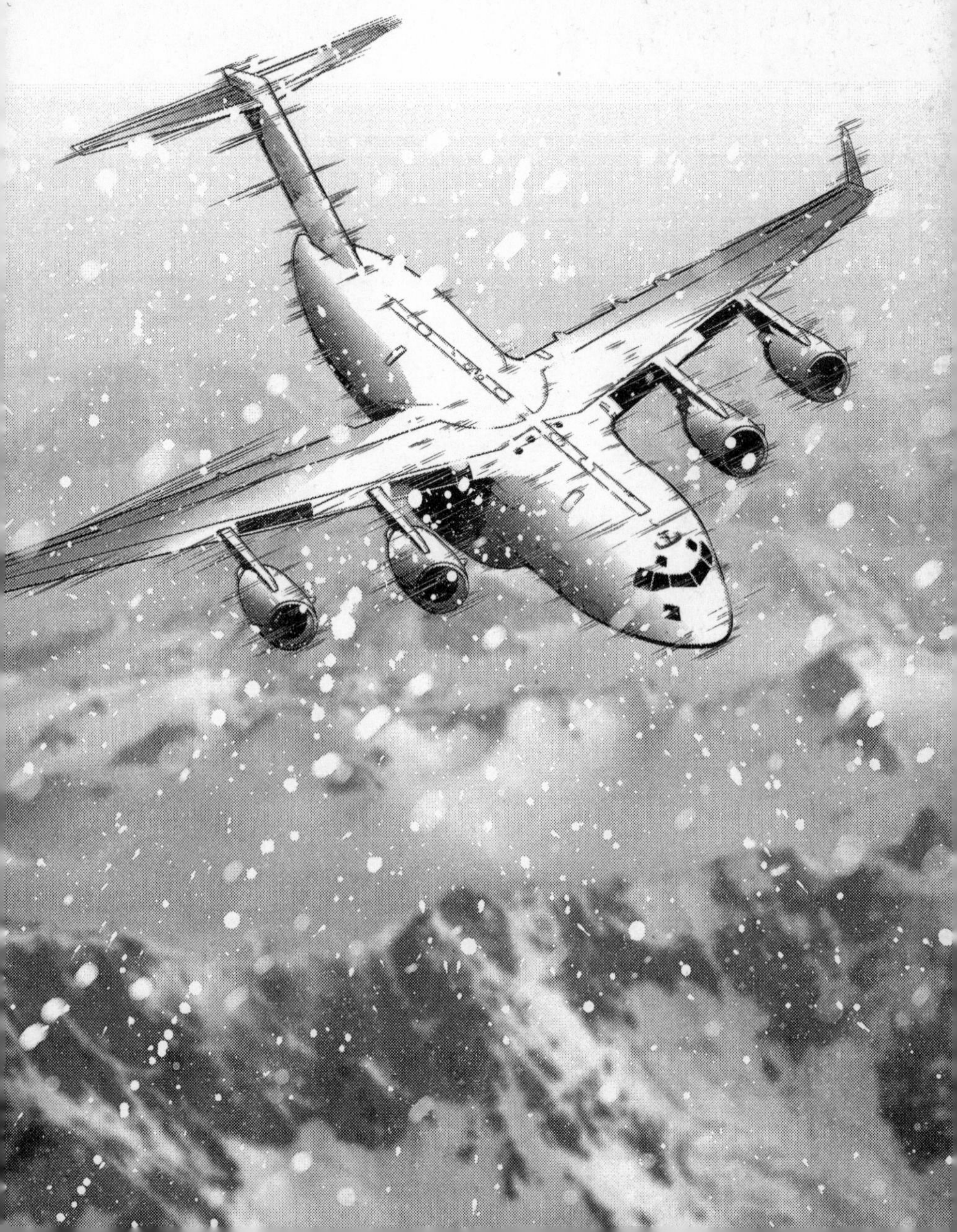

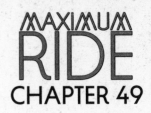

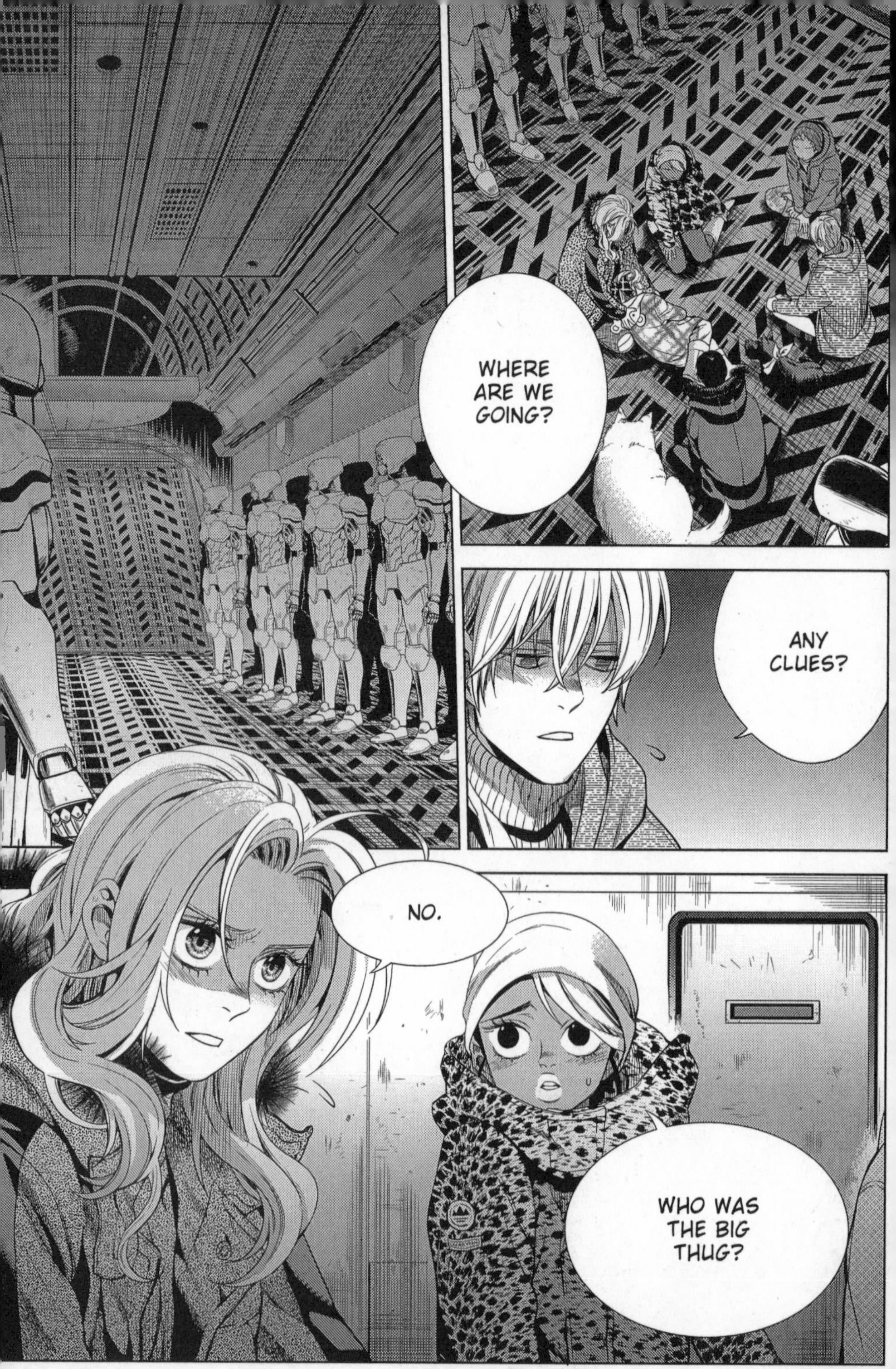
WHERE ARE WE GOING?
ANY CLUES?
NO.
WHO WAS THE BIG THUG?

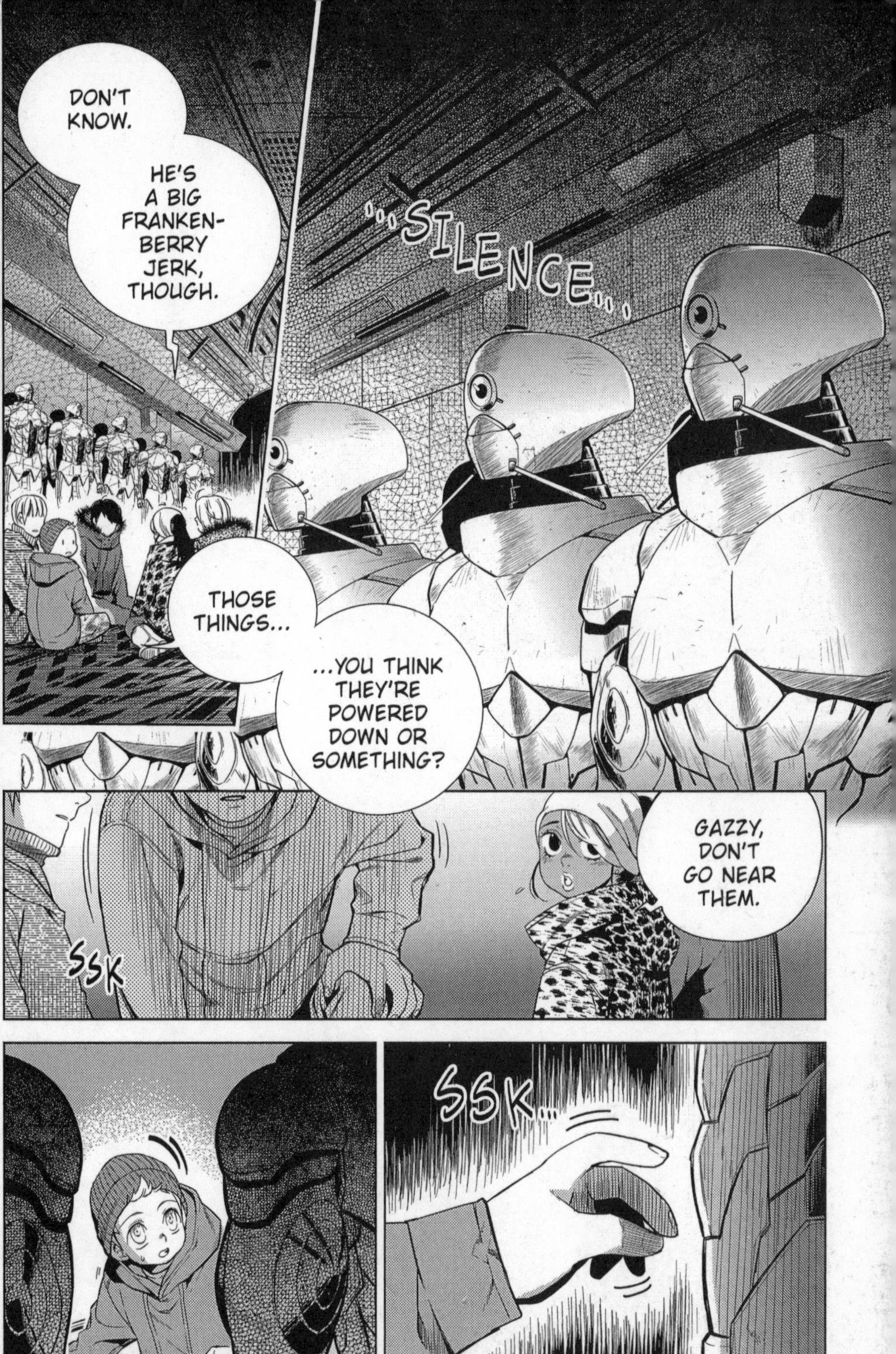
DON'T KNOW.
HE'S A BIG FRANKEN-BERRY JERK, THOUGH.
...SILENCE...
THOSE THINGS...
...YOU THINK THEY'RE POWERED DOWN OR SOMETHING?
SSK
GAZZY, DON'T GO NEAR THEM.
SSK...

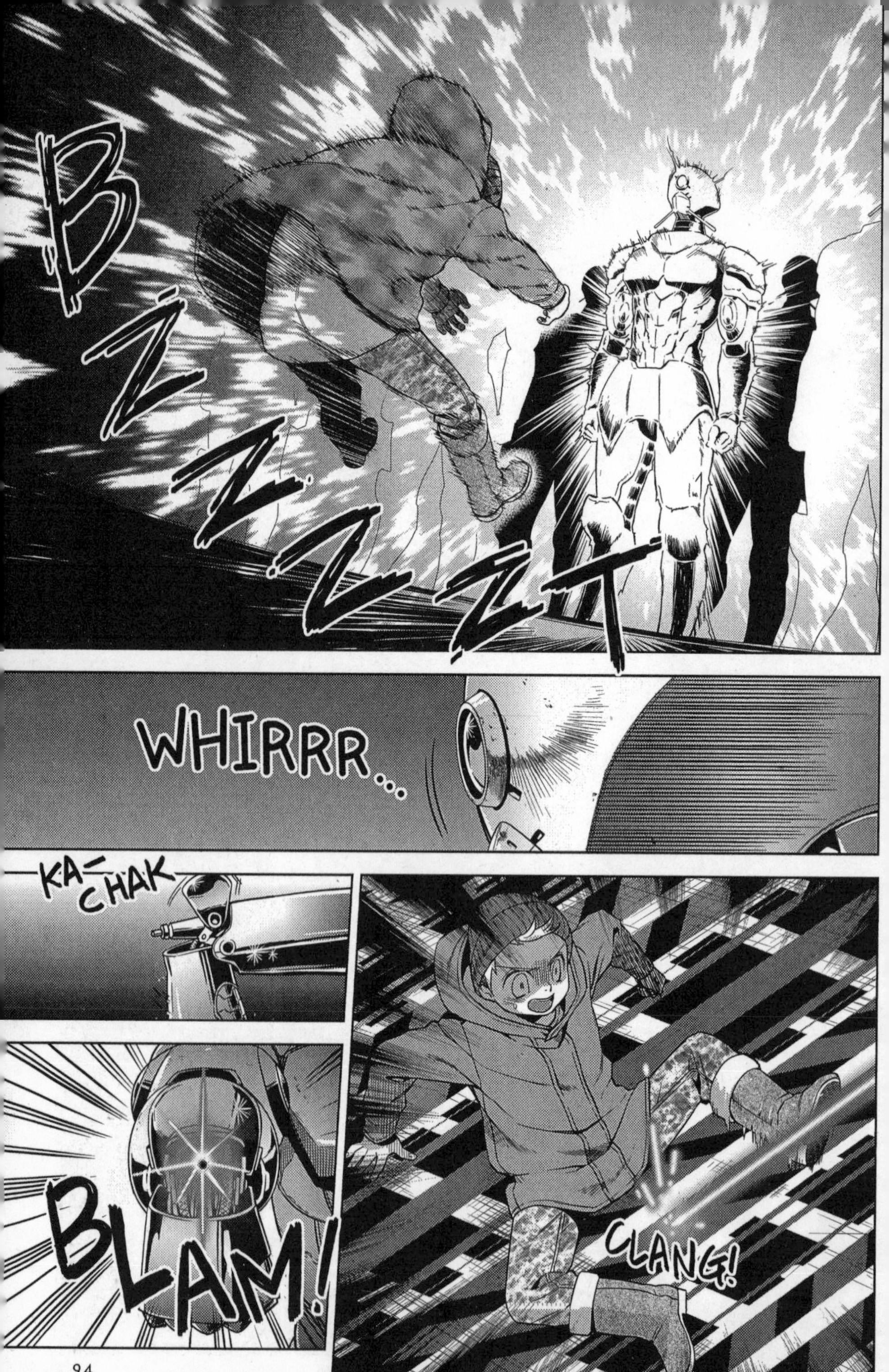
BZZZZZT
WHIRRR...
KA-CHAK
BLAM!
CLANG!

WHOA, THAT SCARED ME!

I almost wet my pants...

ARE YOU OKAY?

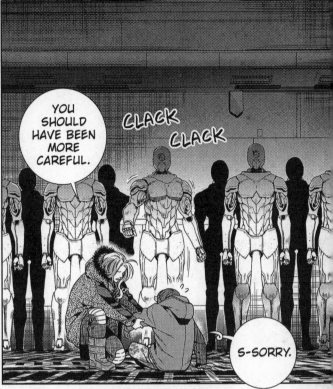

YOU SHOULD HAVE BEEN MORE CAREFUL.

CLACK CLACK

S-SORRY.

UD167B
1 E X 3 6 O N A Y O O N L

SHOO...

IS IT OFF NOW?

THESE THINGS ARE CLEARLY HAIR-TRIGGER.

LET'S JUST STAY STILL.

CLICK

?!

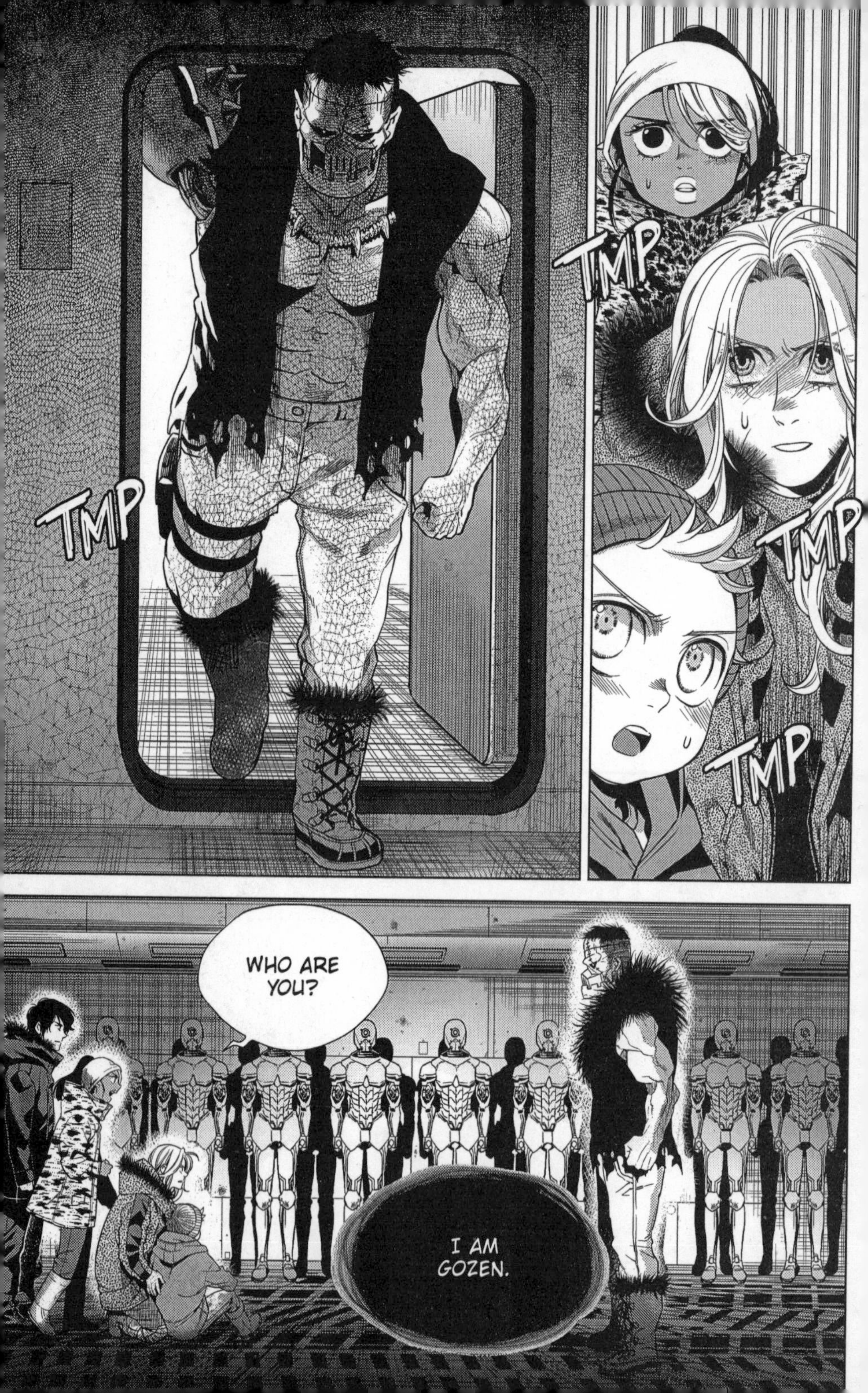
TMP
TMP
TMP
TMP
WHO ARE YOU?
I AM GOZEN.

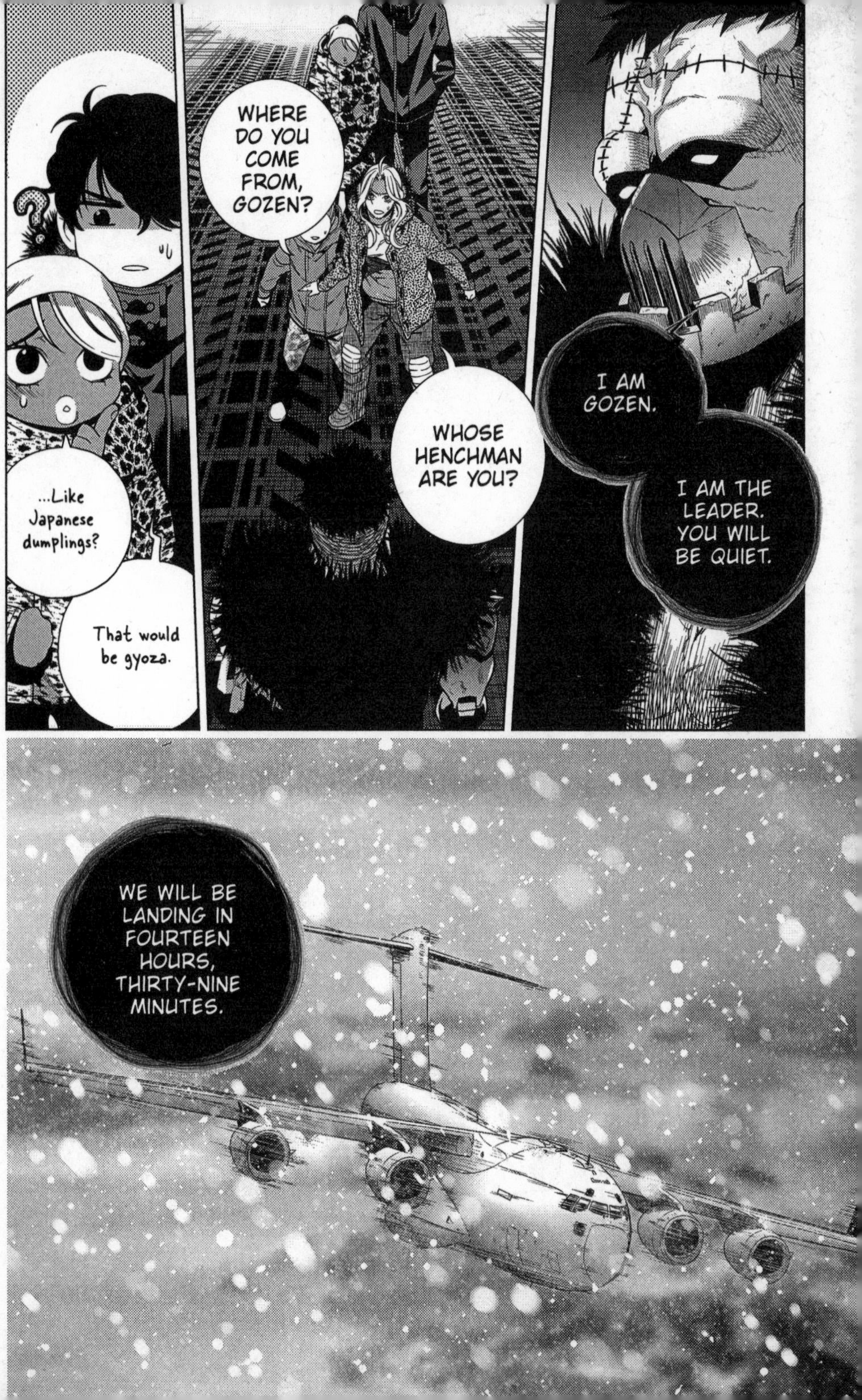
...Like Japanese dumplings?
That would be gyoza.
WHERE DO YOU COME FROM, GOZEN?
WHOSE HENCHMAN ARE YOU?
I AM GOZEN.
I AM THE LEADER. YOU WILL BE QUIET.
WE WILL BE LANDING IN FOURTEEN HOURS, THIRTY-NINE MINUTES.

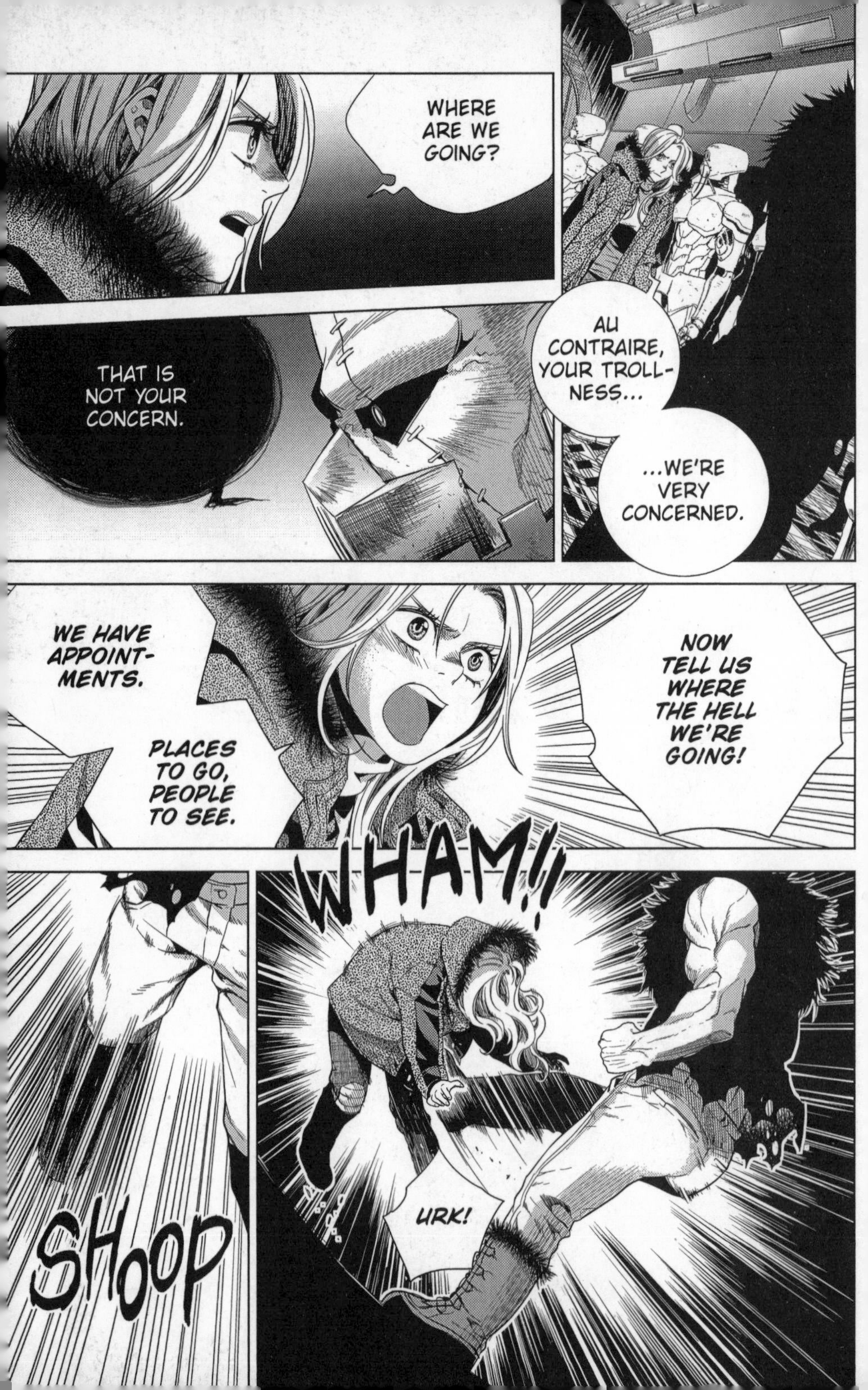
WHERE ARE WE GOING?
THAT IS NOT YOUR CONCERN.
AU CONTRAIRE, YOUR TROLL-NESS...
...WE'RE VERY CONCERNED.
WE HAVE APPOINT-MENTS.
PLACES TO GO, PEOPLE TO SEE.
NOW TELL US WHERE THE HELL WE'RE GOING!
SHOOP
WHAM!!
URK!

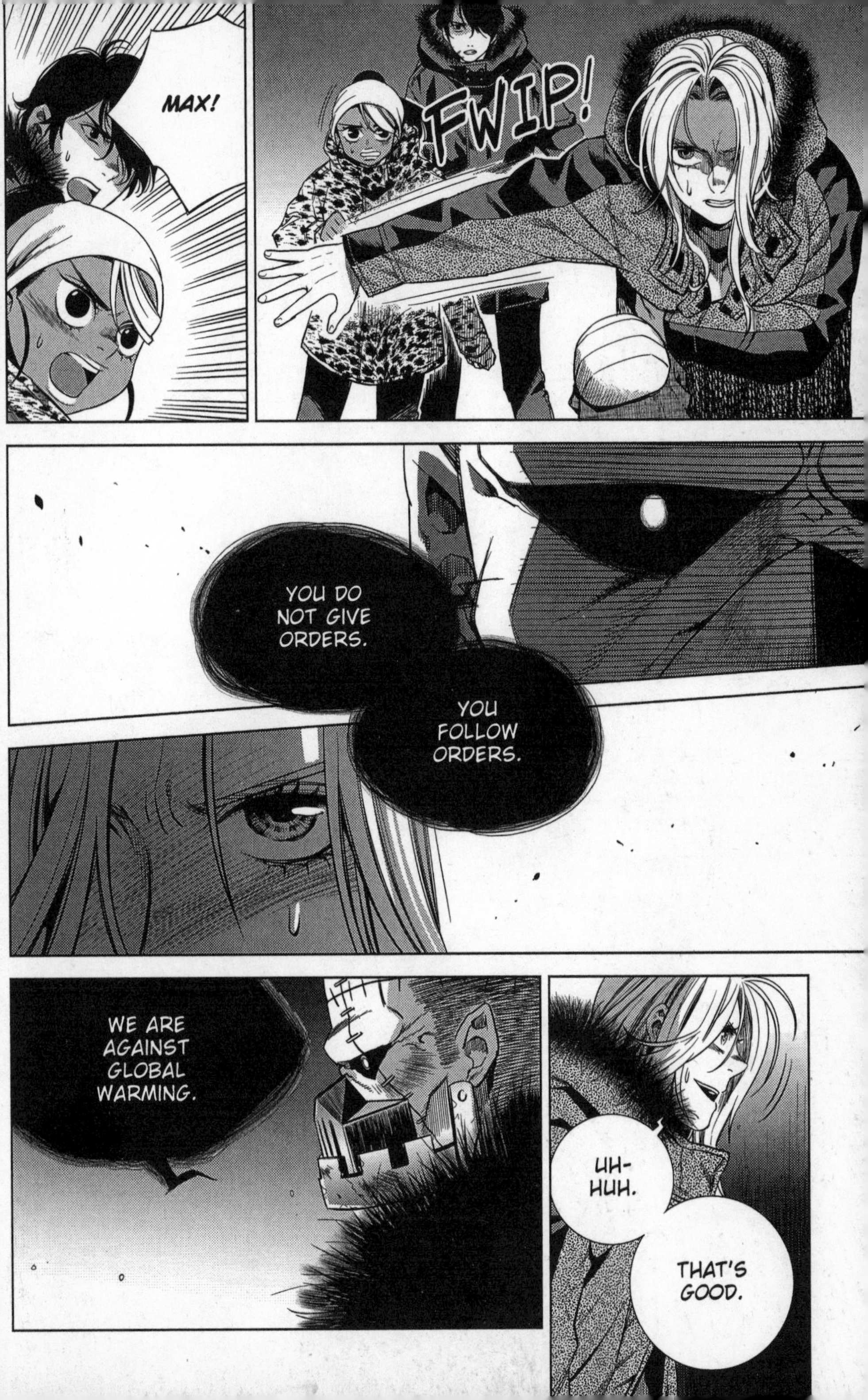
MAX!
FWIP!
YOU DO NOT GIVE ORDERS.
YOU FOLLOW ORDERS.
WE ARE AGAINST GLOBAL WARMING.
UH-HUH.
THAT'S GOOD.

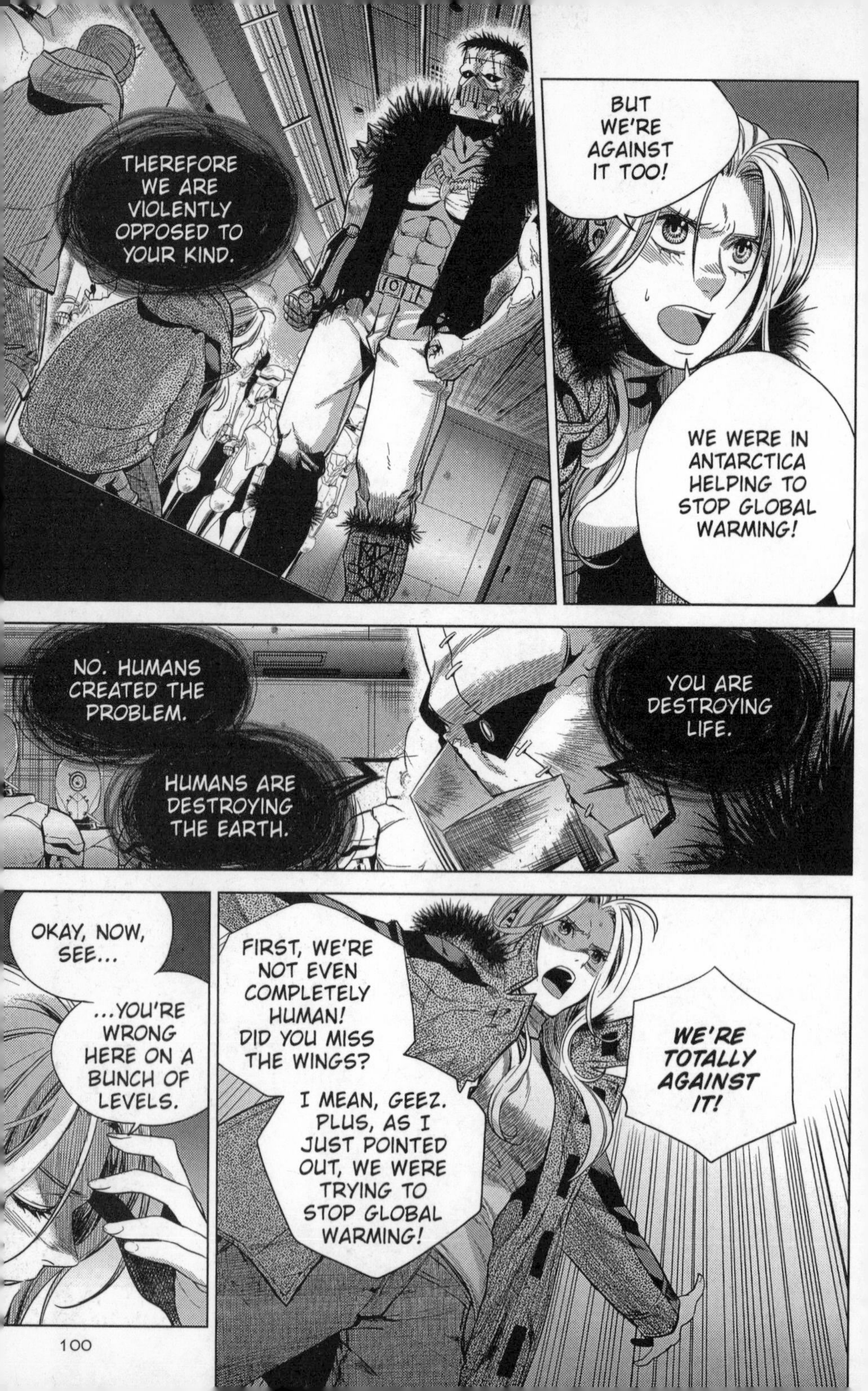
THEREFORE WE ARE VIOLENTLY OPPOSED TO YOUR KIND.
BUT WE'RE AGAINST IT TOO!
WE WERE IN ANTARCTICA HELPING TO STOP GLOBAL WARMING!
NO. HUMANS CREATED THE PROBLEM.
HUMANS ARE DESTROYING THE EARTH.
YOU ARE DESTROYING LIFE.
OKAY, NOW, SEE...
...YOU'RE WRONG HERE ON A BUNCH OF LEVELS.
FIRST, WE'RE NOT EVEN COMPLETELY HUMAN! DID YOU MISS THE WINGS?
I MEAN, GEEZ. PLUS, AS I JUST POINTED OUT, WE WERE TRYING TO STOP GLOBAL WARMING!
WE'RE TOTALLY AGAINST IT!

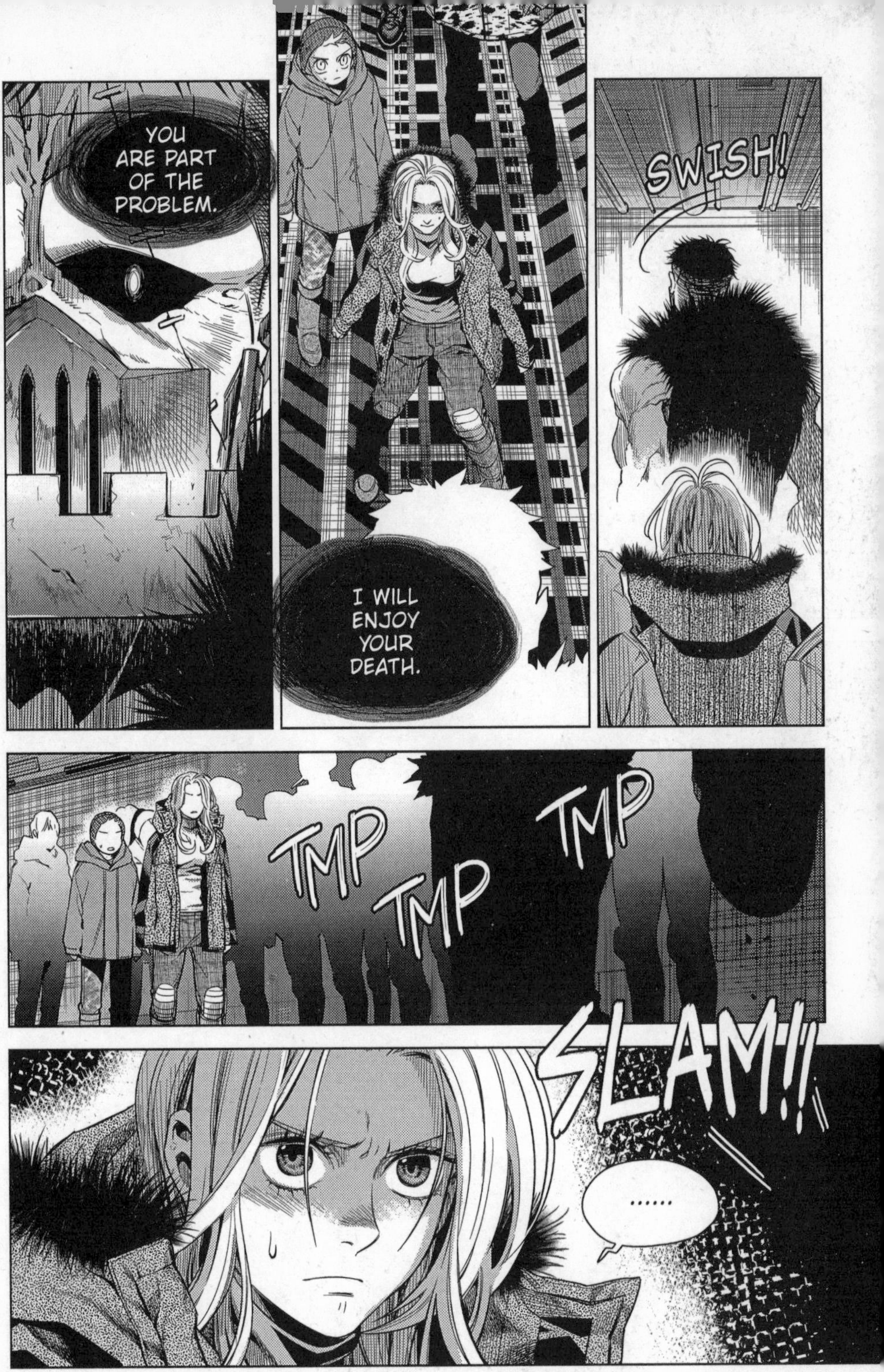
YOU ARE PART OF THE PROBLEM.
I WILL ENJOY YOUR DEATH.
SWISH!
TMP
TMP
TMP
SLAM!!
......

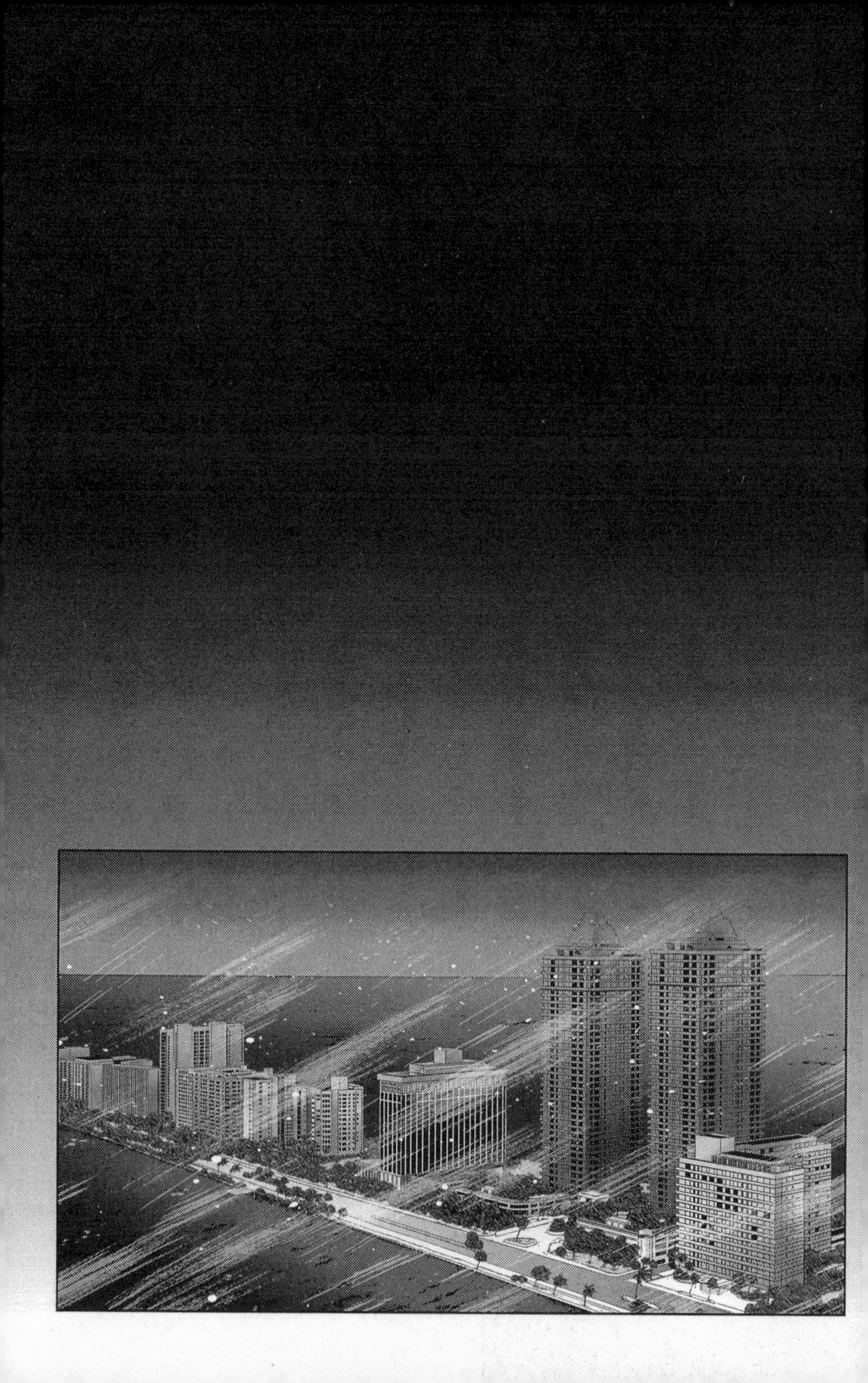

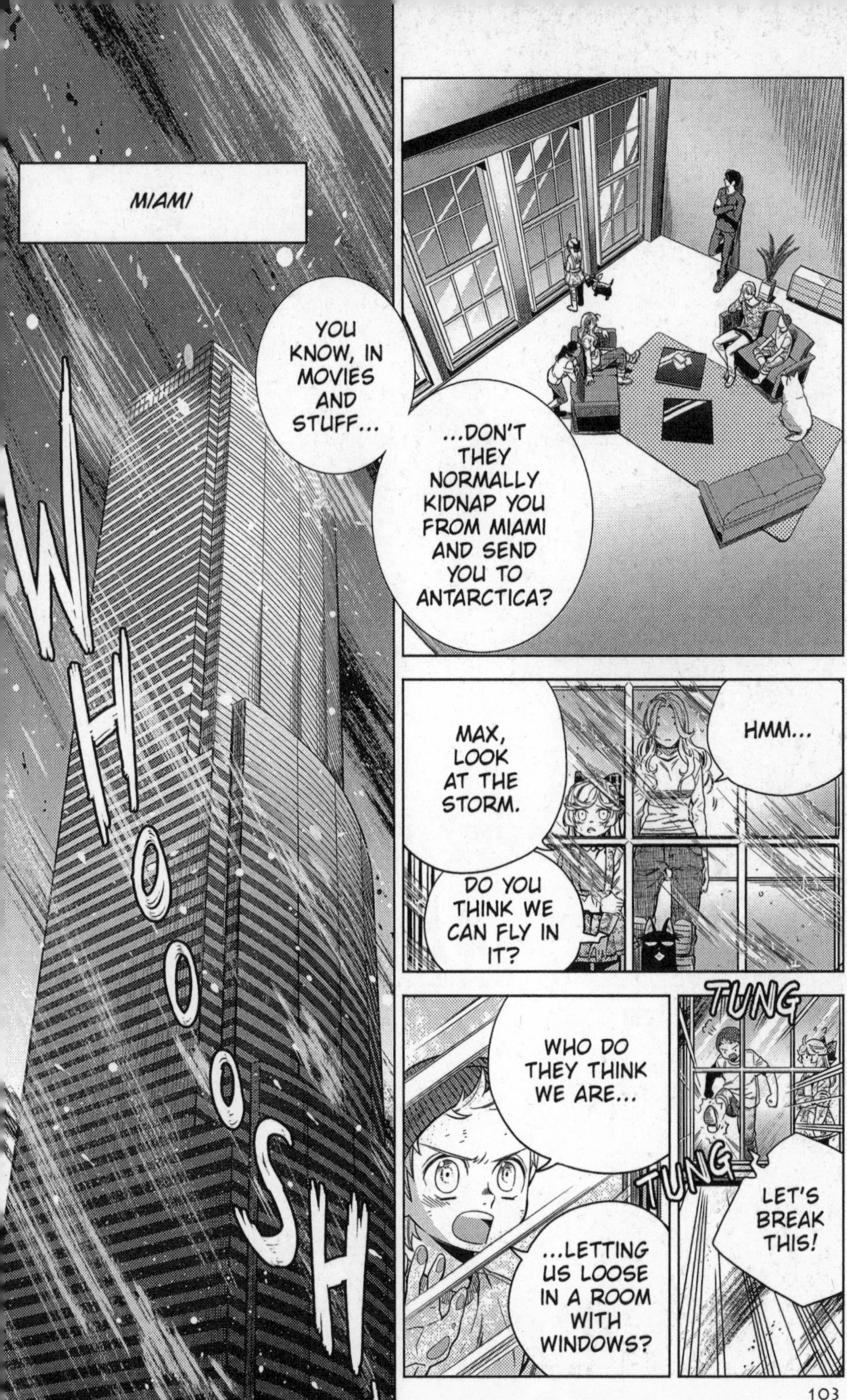
MIAMI
WHOOOOSH!
YOU KNOW, IN MOVIES AND STUFF...
...DON'T THEY NORMALLY KIDNAP YOU FROM MIAMI AND SEND YOU TO ANTARCTICA?
MAX, LOOK AT THE STORM.
HMM...
DO YOU THINK WE CAN FLY IN IT?
WHO DO THEY THINK WE ARE...
...LETTING US LOOSE IN A ROOM WITH WINDOWS?
TUNG
TUNG
LET'S BREAK THIS!

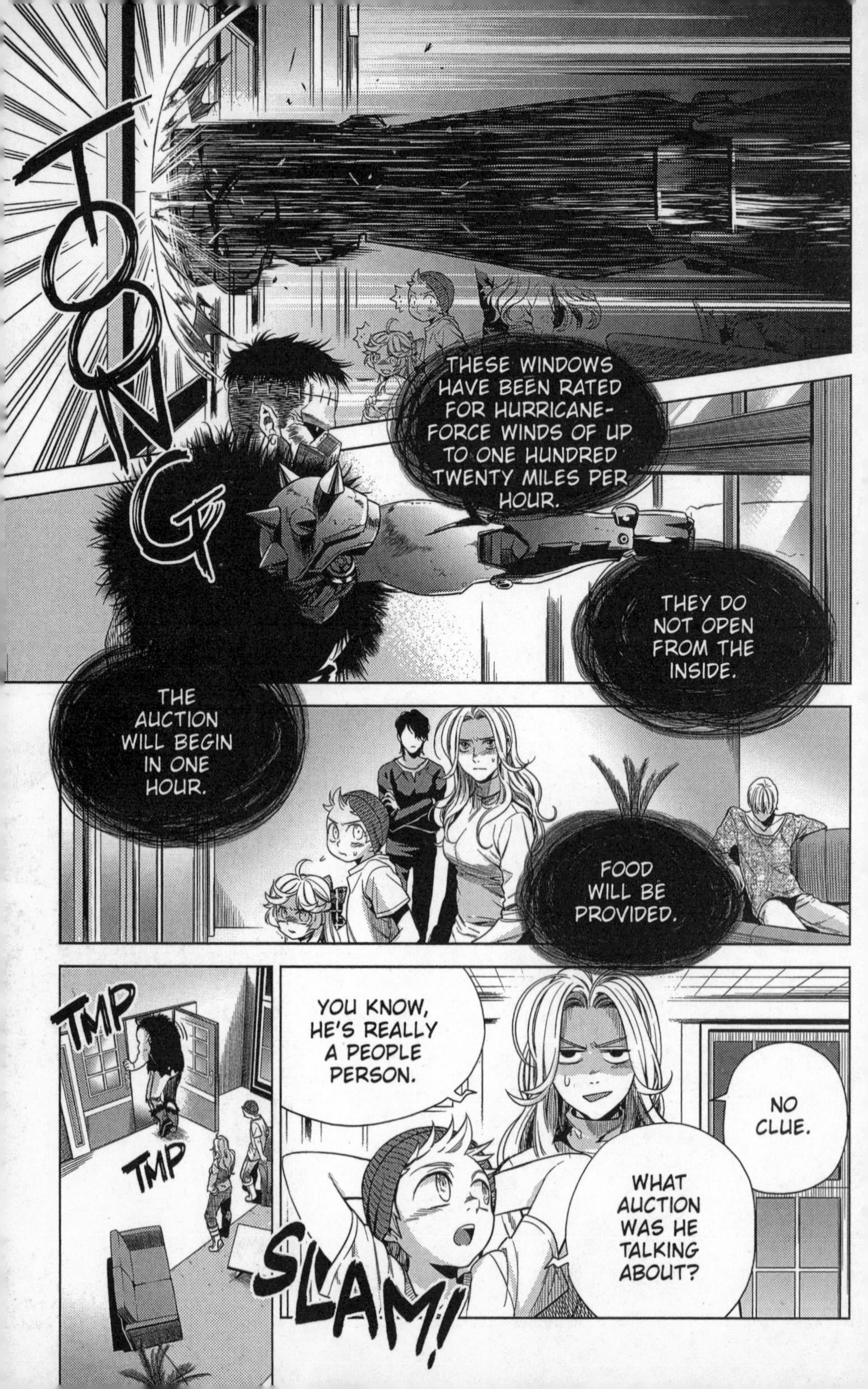

TOONG
THESE WINDOWS HAVE BEEN RATED FOR HURRICANE-FORCE WINDS OF UP TO ONE HUNDRED TWENTY MILES PER HOUR.
THEY DO NOT OPEN FROM THE INSIDE.
THE AUCTION WILL BEGIN IN ONE HOUR.
FOOD WILL BE PROVIDED.
TMP
TMP
SLAM!
YOU KNOW, HE'S REALLY A PEOPLE PERSON.
WHAT AUCTION WAS HE TALKING ABOUT?
NO CLUE.

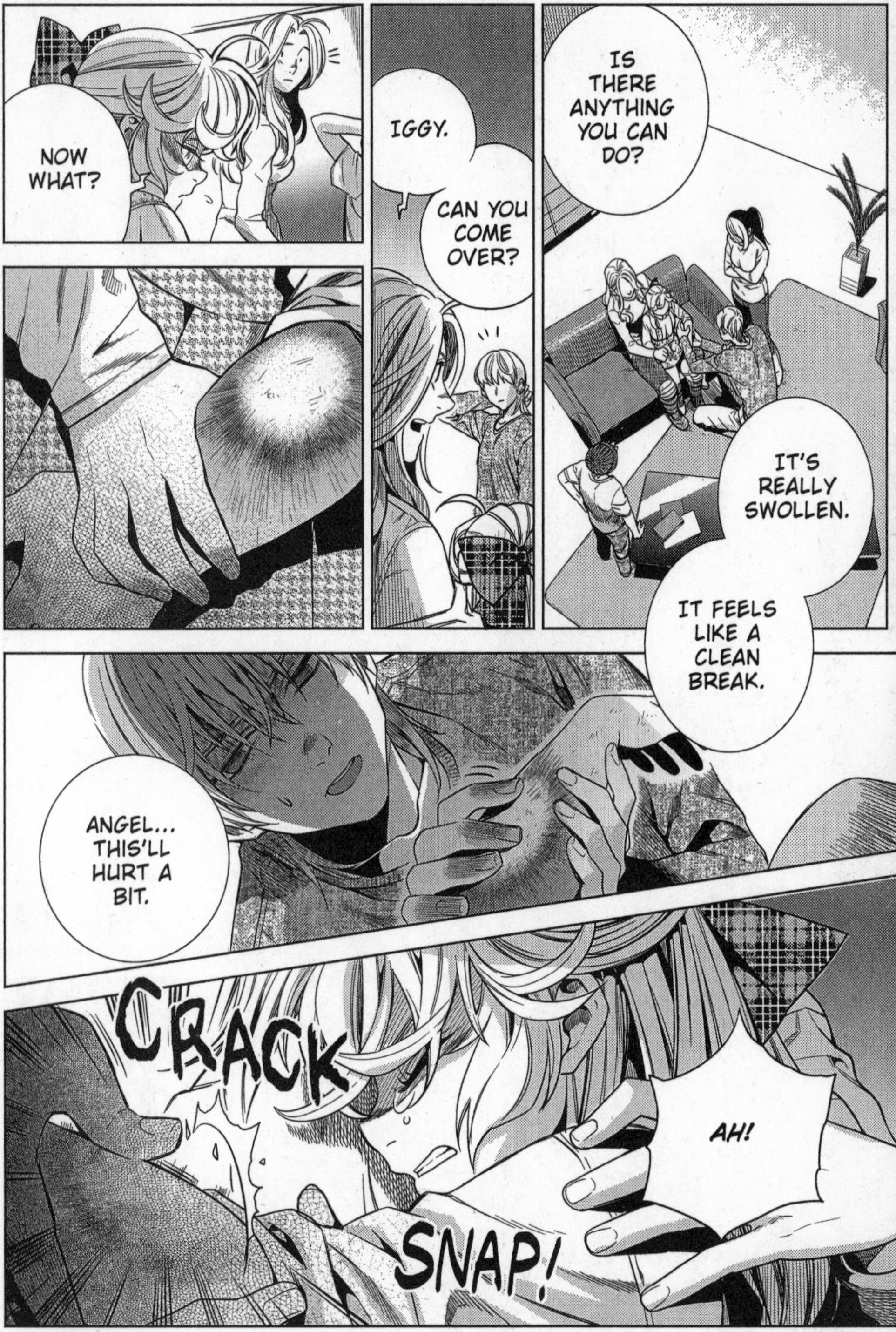
NOW WHAT?
IGGY.
CAN YOU COME OVER?
IS THERE ANYTHING YOU CAN DO?
IT'S REALLY SWOLLEN.
IT FEELS LIKE A CLEAN BREAK.
ANGEL... THIS'LL HURT A BIT.
CRACK
AH!
SNAP!

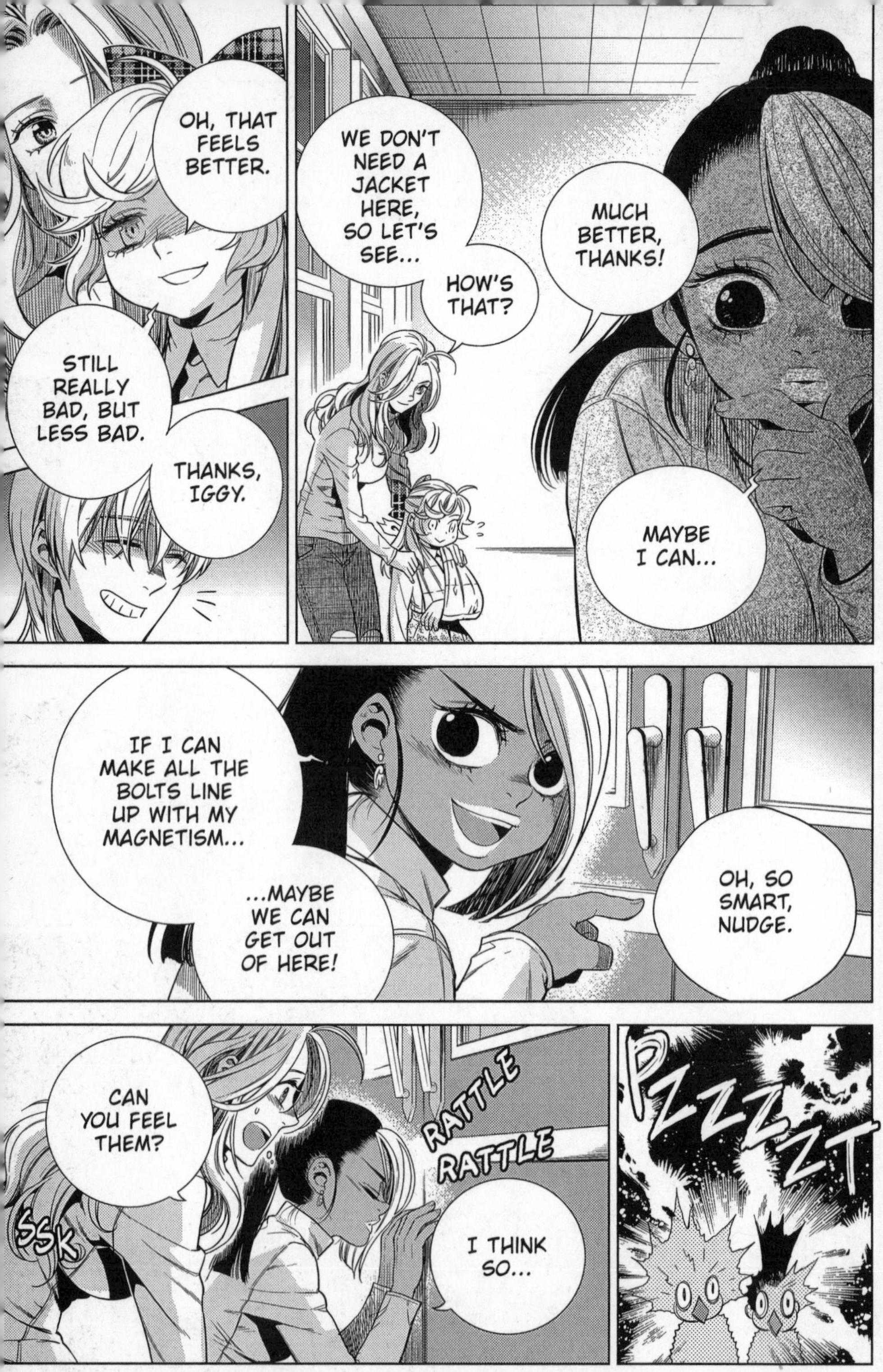
OH, THAT FEELS BETTER.
STILL REALLY BAD, BUT LESS BAD.
THANKS, IGGY.
WE DON'T NEED A JACKET HERE, SO LET'S SEE...
HOW'S THAT?
MUCH BETTER, THANKS!
MAYBE I CAN...
IF I CAN MAKE ALL THE BOLTS LINE UP WITH MY MAGNETISM...
...MAYBE WE CAN GET OUT OF HERE!
OH, SO SMART, NUDGE.
CAN YOU FEEL THEM?
SSK
RATTLE
RATTLE
I THINK SO...
PZZZZZT

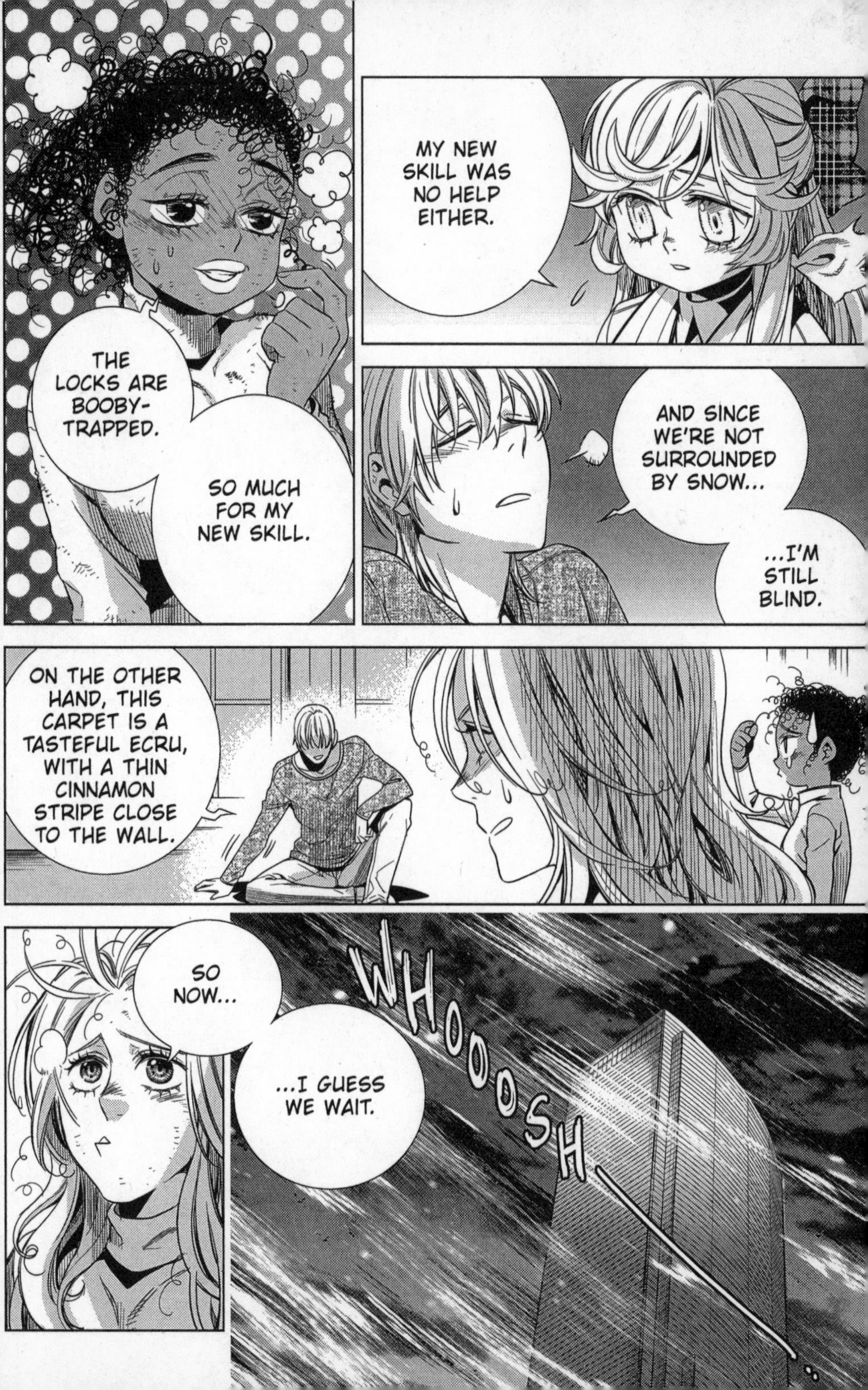
THE LOCKS ARE BOOBY-TRAPPED.
SO MUCH FOR MY NEW SKILL.
MY NEW SKILL WAS NO HELP EITHER.
AND SINCE WE'RE NOT SURROUNDED BY SNOW...
...I'M STILL BLIND.
ON THE OTHER HAND, THIS CARPET IS A TASTEFUL ECRU, WITH A THIN CINNAMON STRIPE CLOSE TO THE WALL.
SO NOW...
...I GUESS WE WAIT.
WHOOOSH

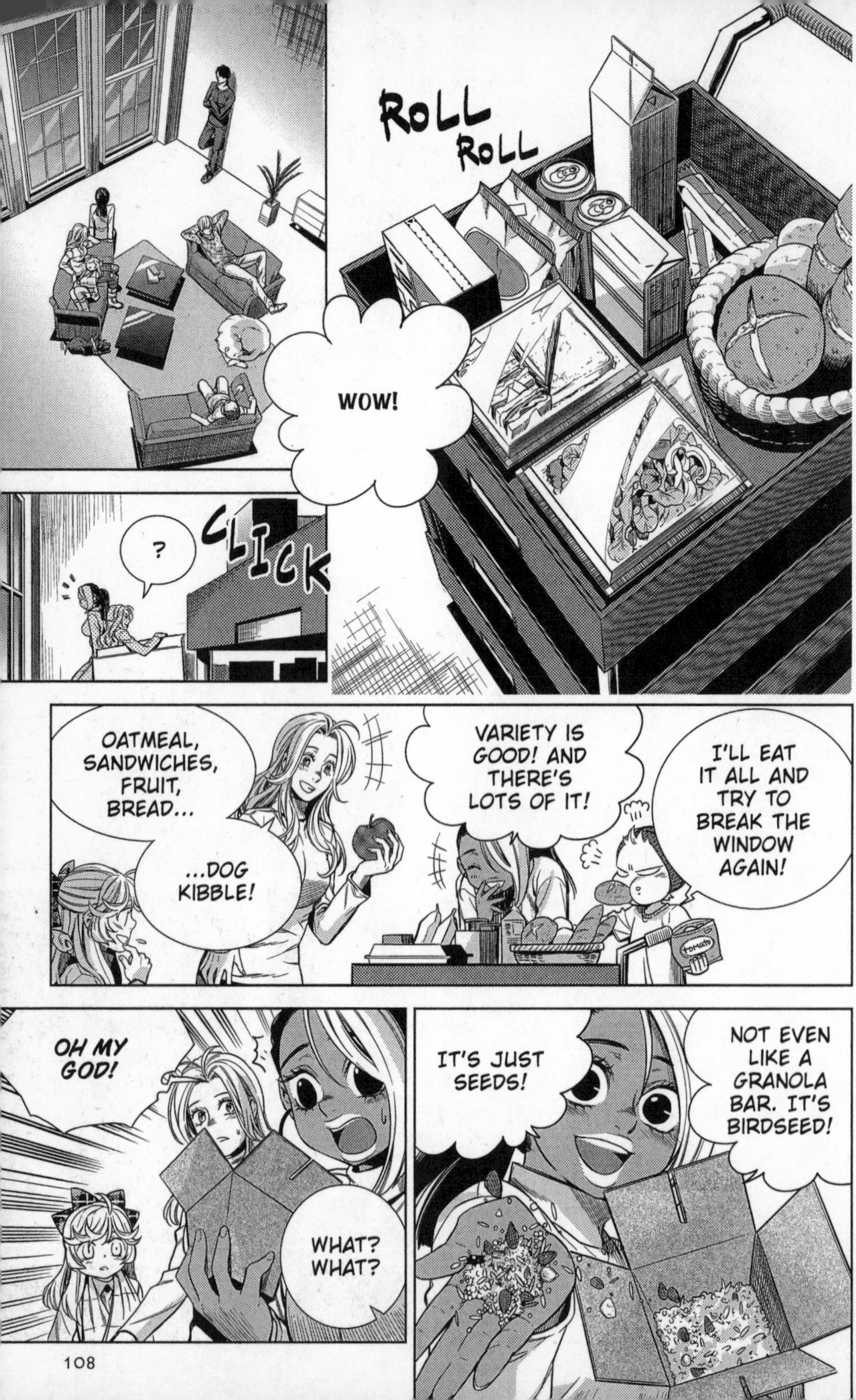

ROLL ROLL
WOW!
?
CLICK
OATMEAL, SANDWICHES, FRUIT, BREAD...
...DOG KIBBLE!
VARIETY IS GOOD! AND THERE'S LOTS OF IT!
I'LL EAT IT ALL AND TRY TO BREAK THE WINDOW AGAIN!
OH MY GOD!
WHAT? WHAT?
IT'S JUST SEEDS!
NOT EVEN LIKE A GRANOLA BAR. IT'S BIRDSEED!

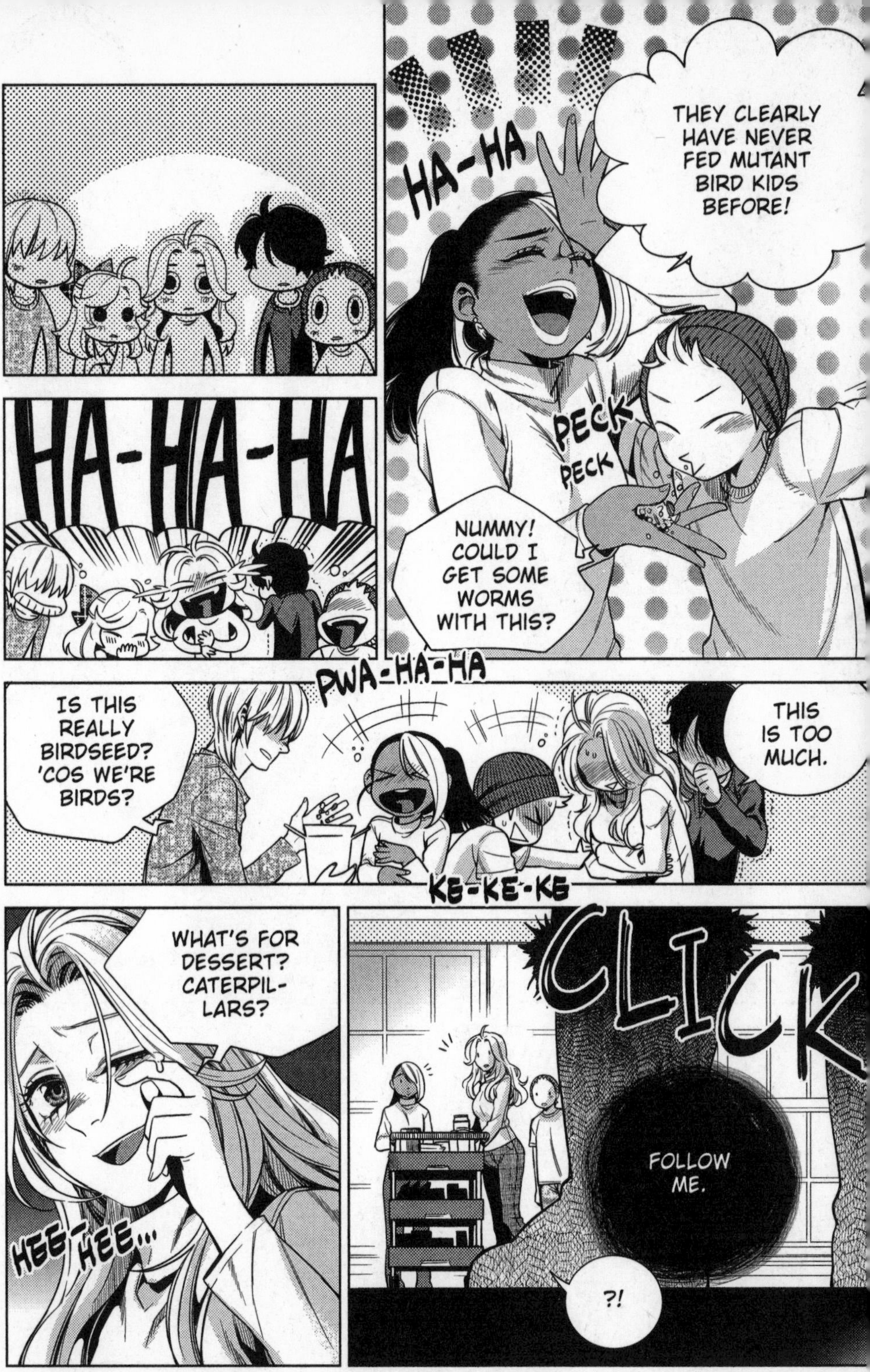
HA-HA-HA
HA-HA
THEY CLEARLY HAVE NEVER FED MUTANT BIRD KIDS BEFORE!
PECK PECK
NUMMY! COULD I GET SOME WORMS WITH THIS?
PWA-HA-HA
IS THIS REALLY BIRDSEED? 'COS WE'RE BIRDS?
THIS IS TOO MUCH.
KE-KE-KE
WHAT'S FOR DESSERT? CATERPIL-LARS?
HEE-HEE...
CLICK
FOLLOW ME.
?!

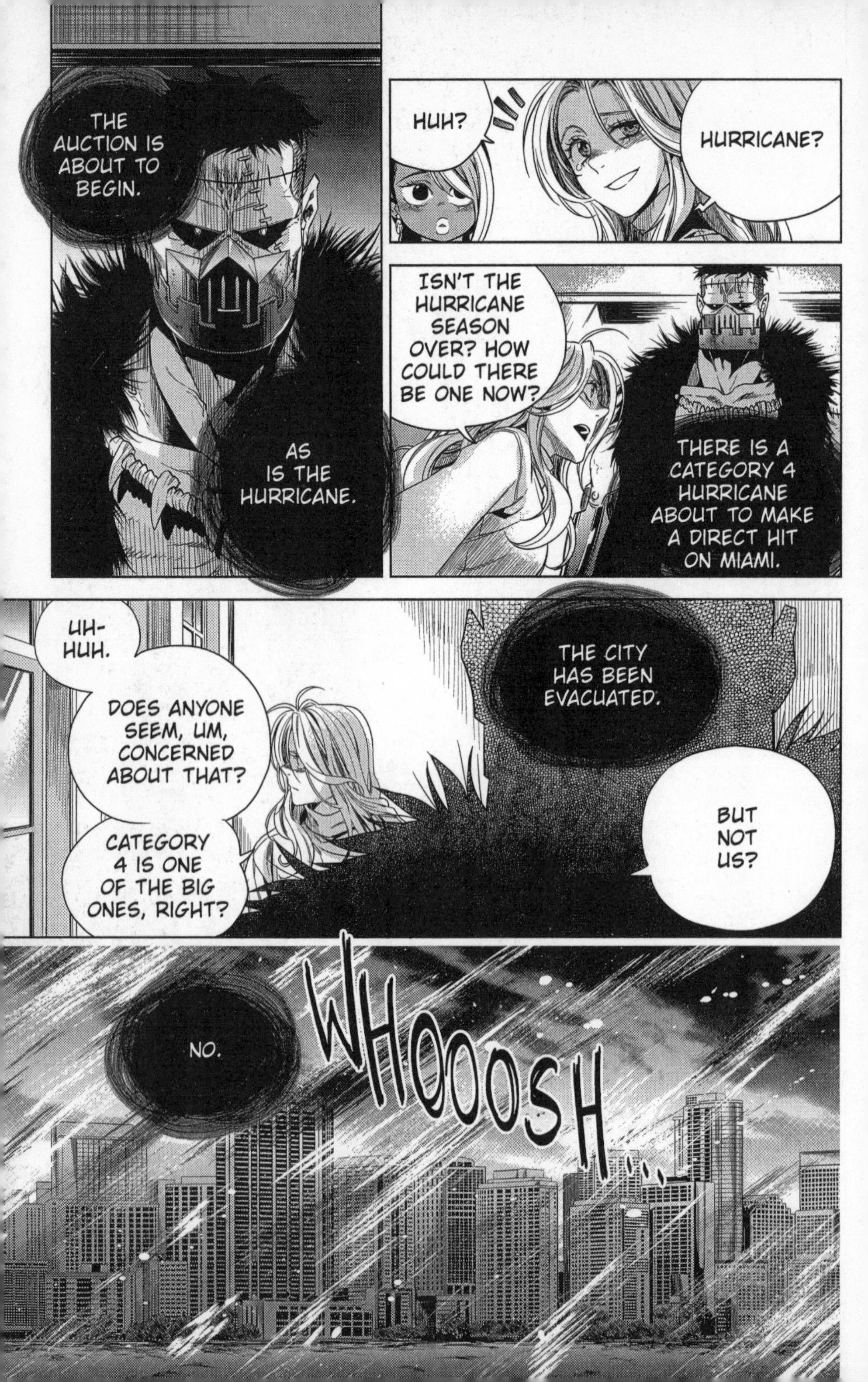
THE AUCTION IS ABOUT TO BEGIN.
AS IS THE HURRICANE.
HUH?
HURRICANE?
ISN'T THE HURRICANE SEASON OVER? HOW COULD THERE BE ONE NOW?
THERE IS A CATEGORY 4 HURRICANE ABOUT TO MAKE A DIRECT HIT ON MIAMI.
UH-HUH.
DOES ANYONE SEEM, UM, CONCERNED ABOUT THAT?
CATEGORY 4 IS ONE OF THE BIG ONES, RIGHT?
THE CITY HAS BEEN EVACUATED.
BUT NOT US?
NO.
WHOOOSH...

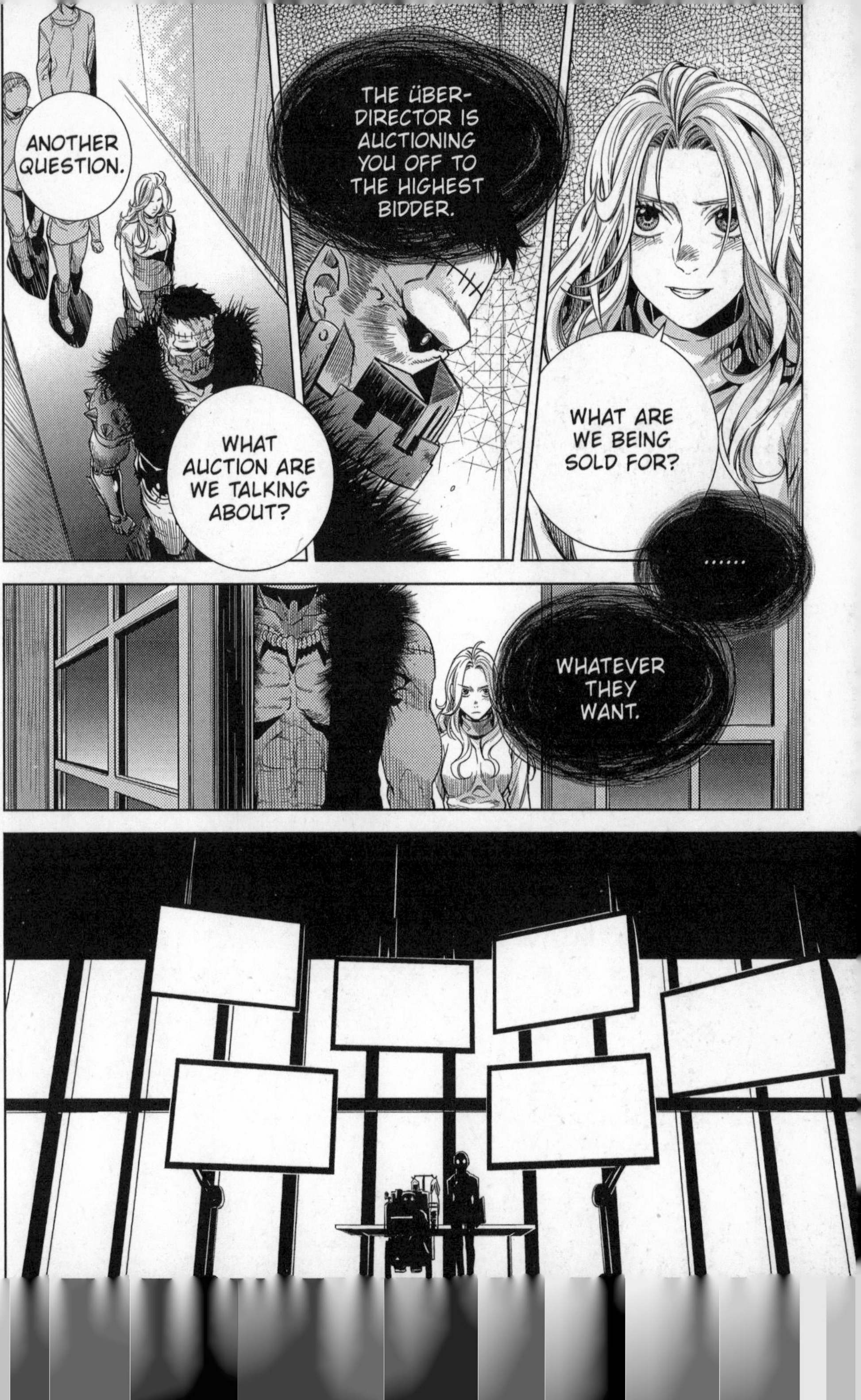
ANOTHER QUESTION.
WHAT AUCTION ARE WE TALKING ABOUT?
THE ÜBER-DIRECTOR IS AUCTIONING YOU OFF TO THE HIGHEST BIDDER.
WHAT ARE WE BEING SOLD FOR?
......
WHATEVER THEY WANT.

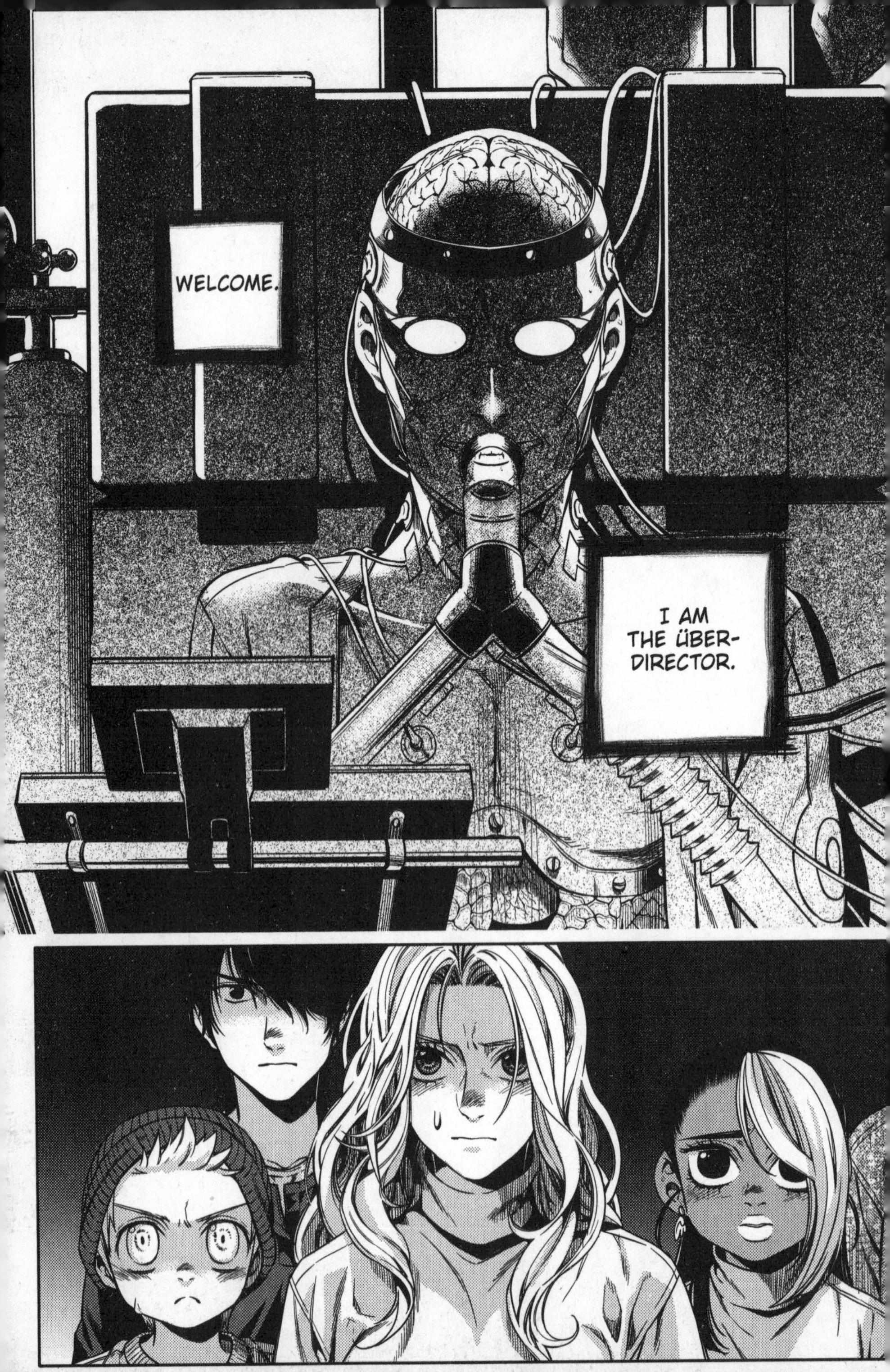
WELCOME.
I AM THE ÜBER-DIRECTOR.

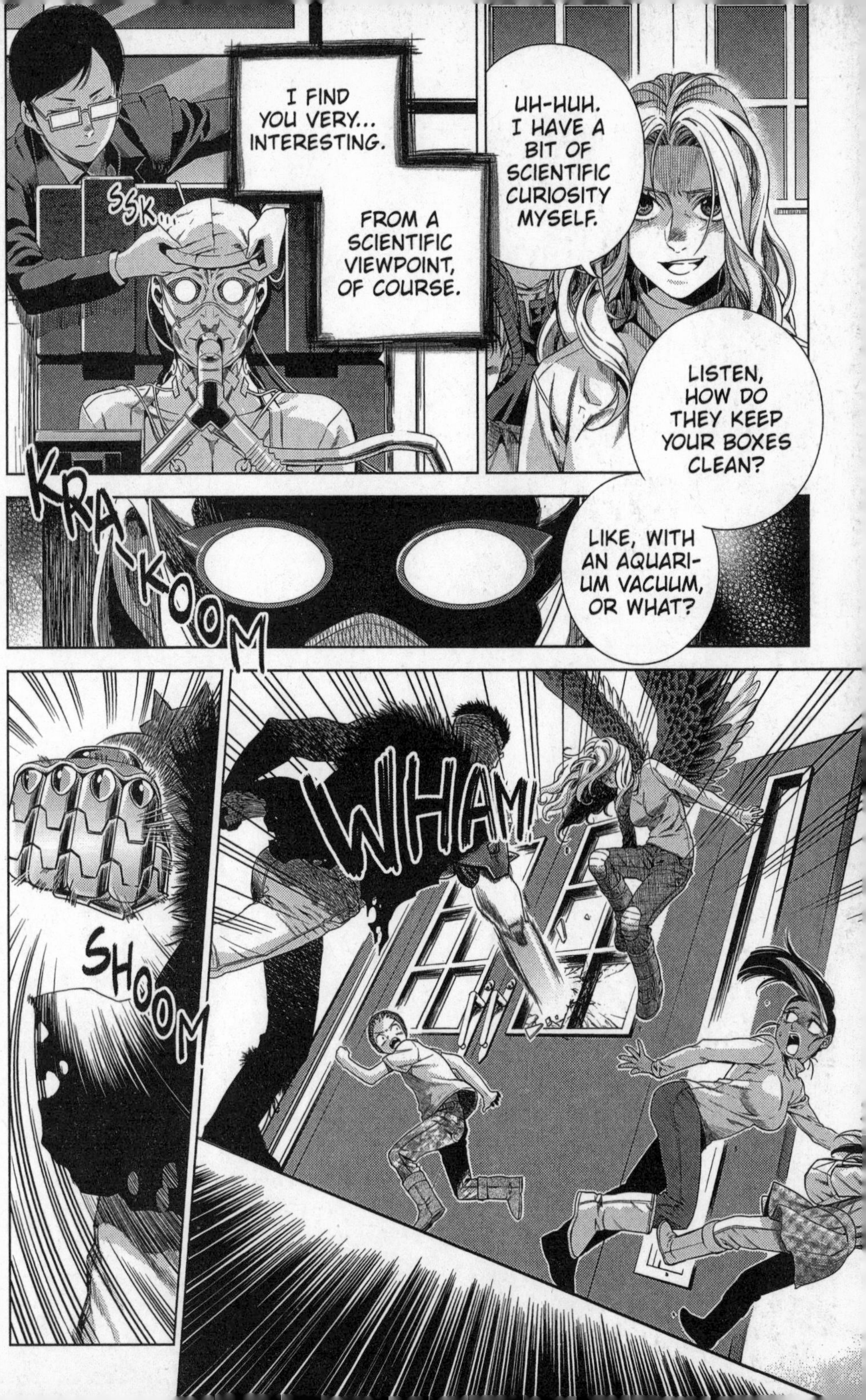
UH-HUH. I HAVE A BIT OF SCIENTIFIC CURIOSITY MYSELF.
I FIND YOU VERY... INTERESTING.
FROM A SCIENTIFIC VIEWPOINT, OF COURSE.
SSK...
LISTEN, HOW DO THEY KEEP YOUR BOXES CLEAN?
LIKE, WITH AN AQUARI-UM VACUUM, OR WHAT?
KRA-KOOM
WHAM
SHOOM

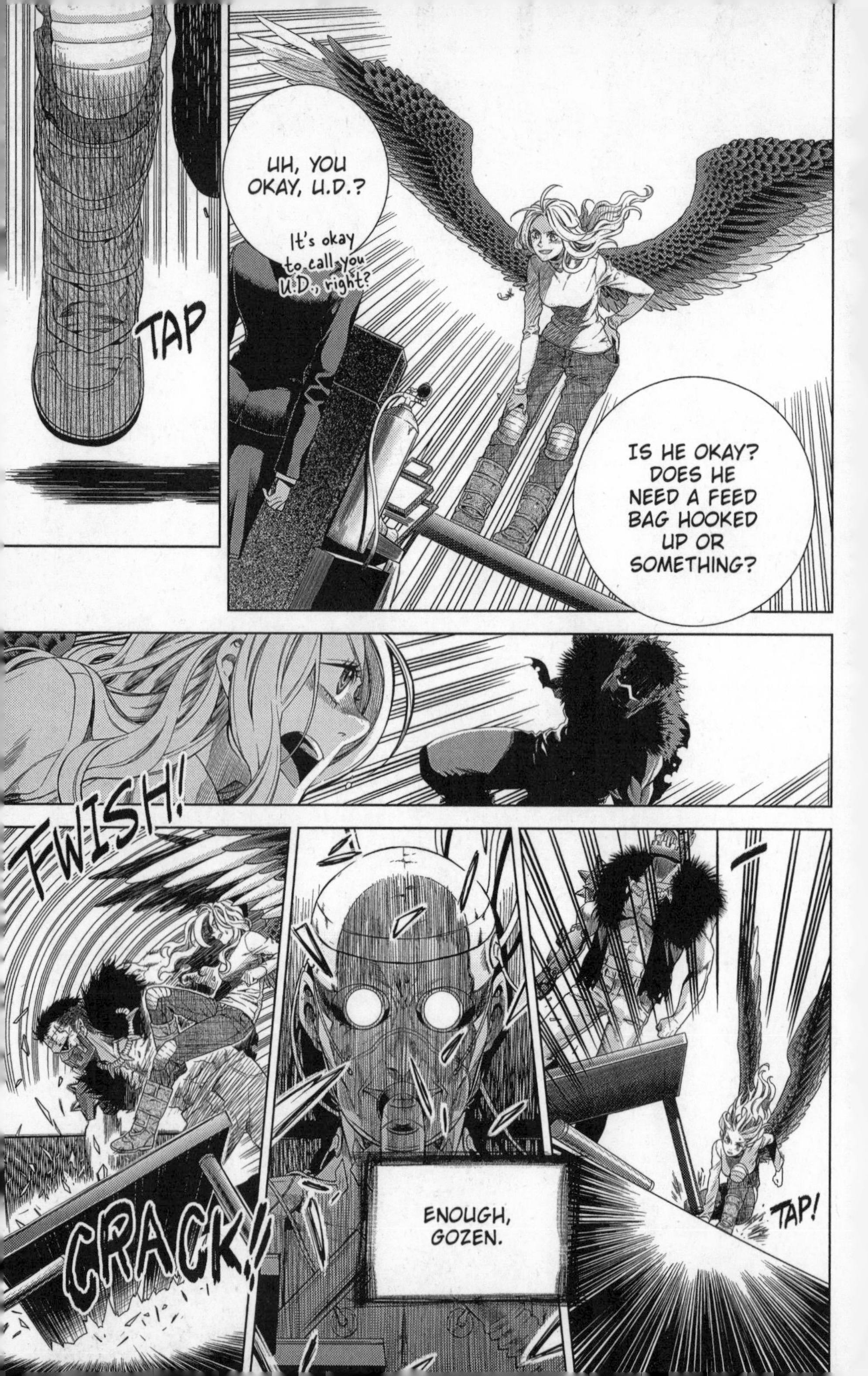
TAP
UH, YOU OKAY, U.D.?
It's okay to call you U.D., right?
IS HE OKAY? DOES HE NEED A FEED BAG HOOKED UP OR SOMETHING?
FWISH!
CRACK!
ENOUGH, GOZEN.
TAP!

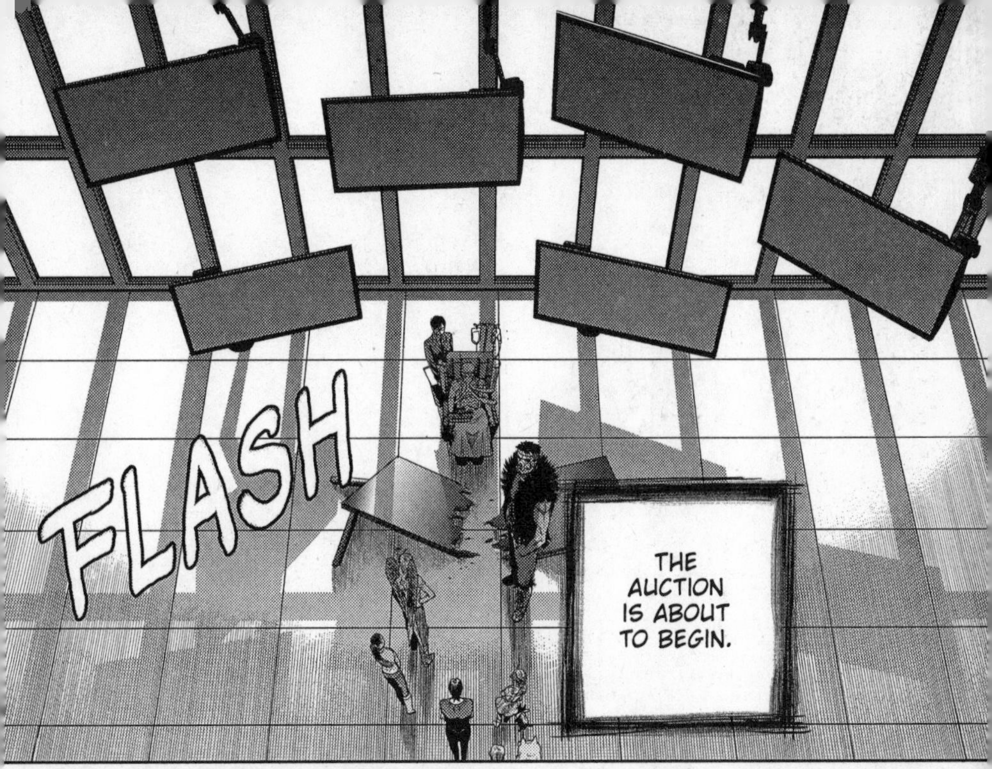
FLASH
THE AUCTION IS ABOUT TO BEGIN.
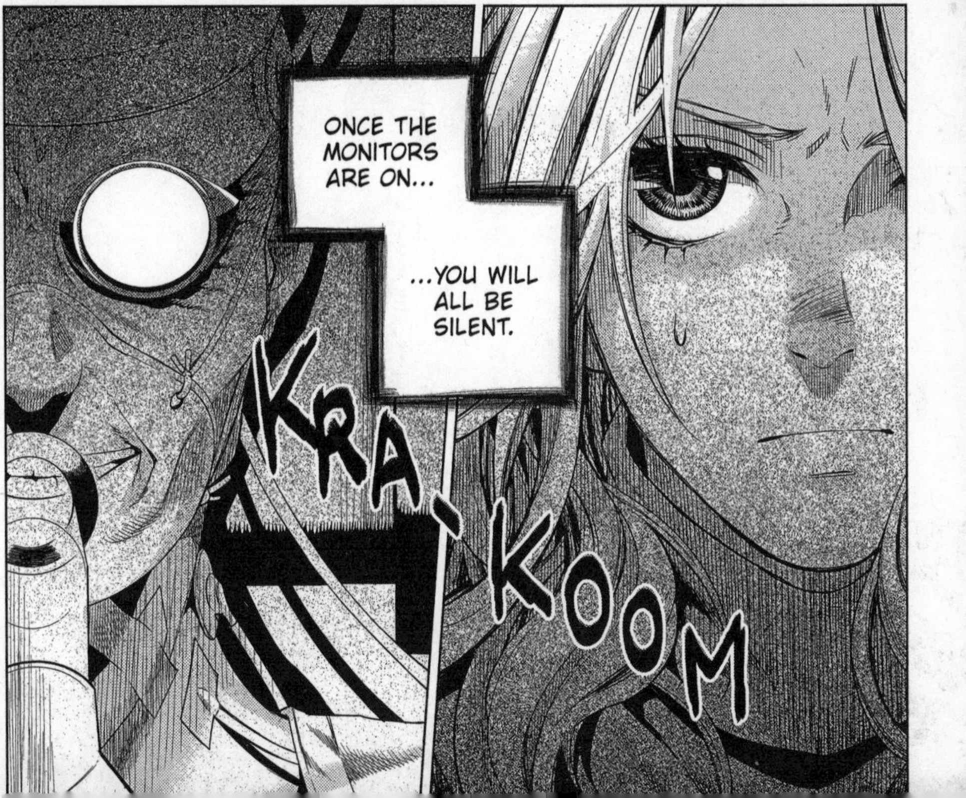
ONCE THE MONITORS ARE ON...
...YOU WILL ALL BE SILENT.
KRA-KOOM

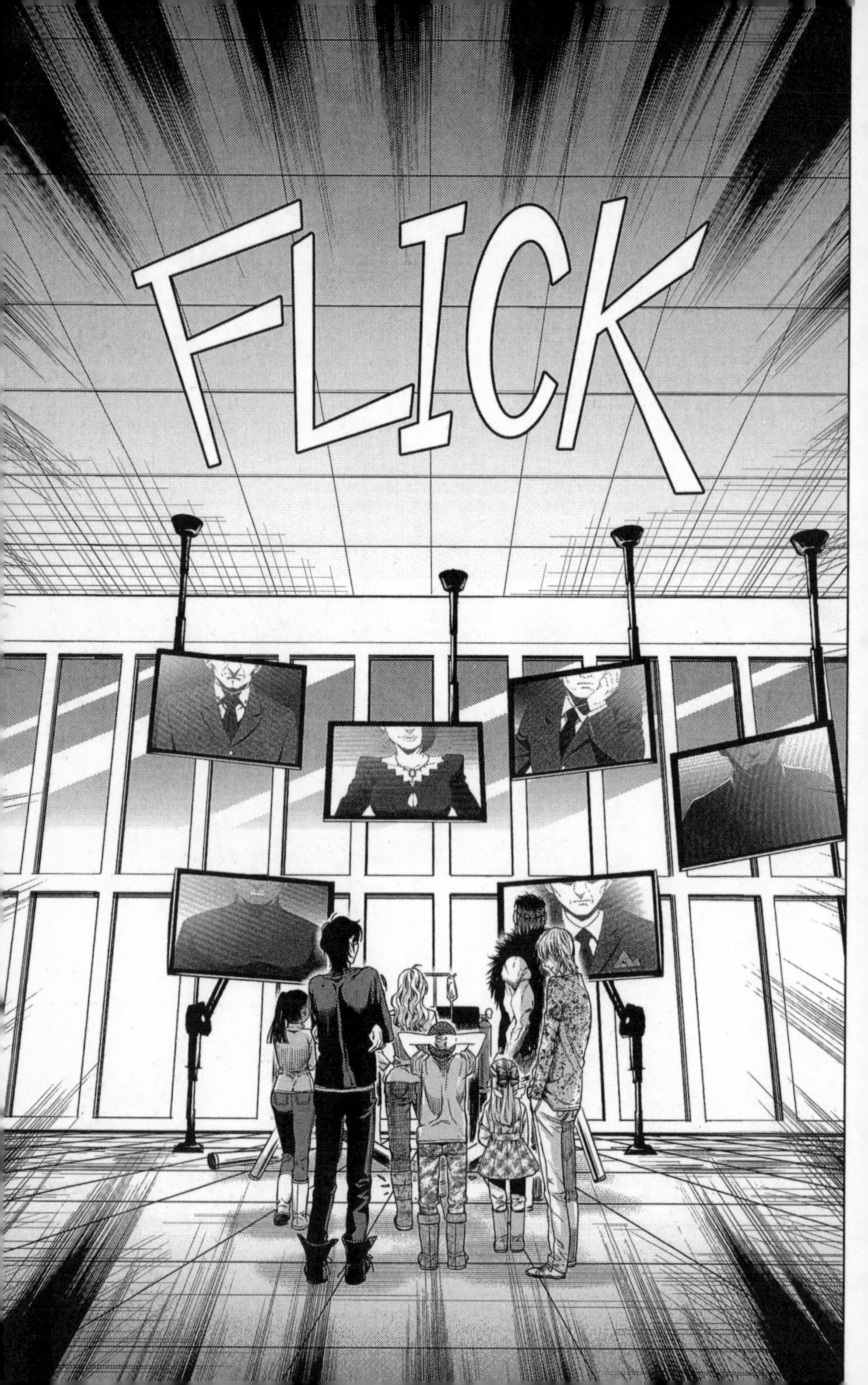
FLICK

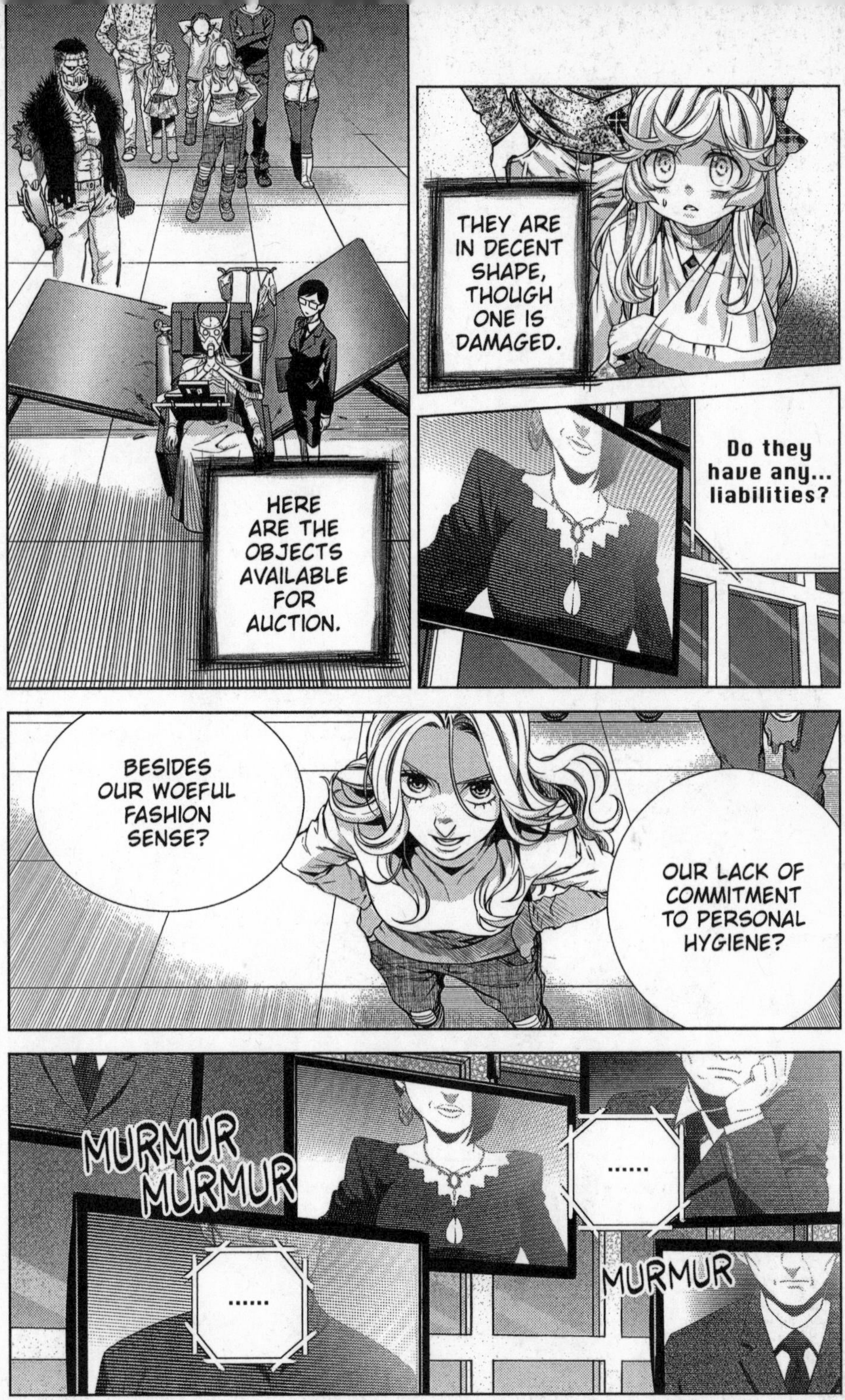
HERE ARE THE OBJECTS AVAILABLE FOR AUCTION.
THEY ARE IN DECENT SHAPE, THOUGH ONE IS DAMAGED.
Do they have any... liabilities?
BESIDES OUR WOEFUL FASHION SENSE?
OUR LACK OF COMMITMENT TO PERSONAL HYGIENE?
MURMUR MURMUR
......
......
MURMUR

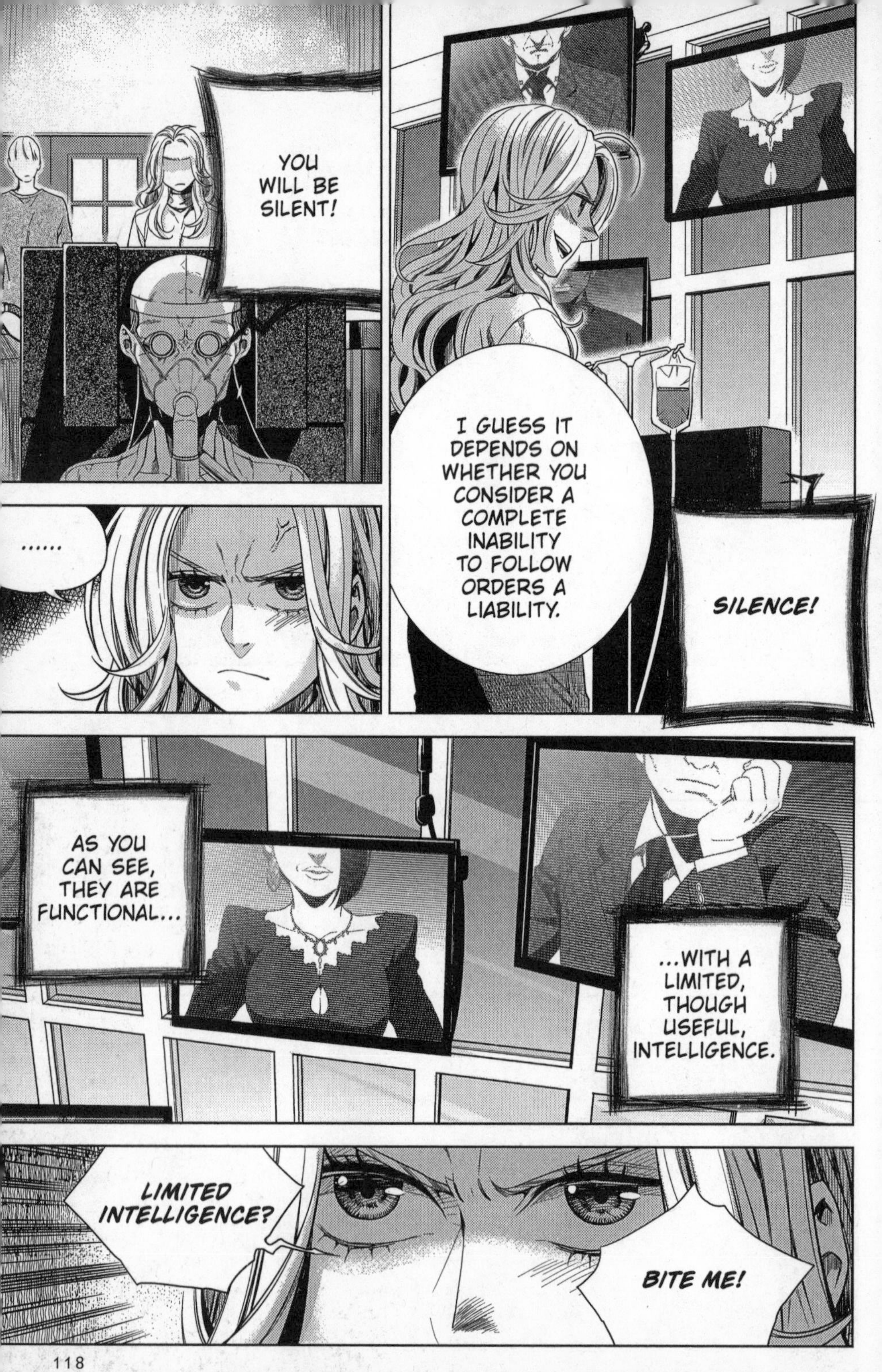
YOU WILL BE SILENT!
I GUESS IT DEPENDS ON WHETHER YOU CONSIDER A COMPLETE INABILITY TO FOLLOW ORDERS A LIABILITY.
......
SILENCE!
AS YOU CAN SEE, THEY ARE FUNCTIONAL...
...WITH A LIMITED, THOUGH USEFUL, INTELLIGENCE.
LIMITED INTELLIGENCE?
BITE ME!

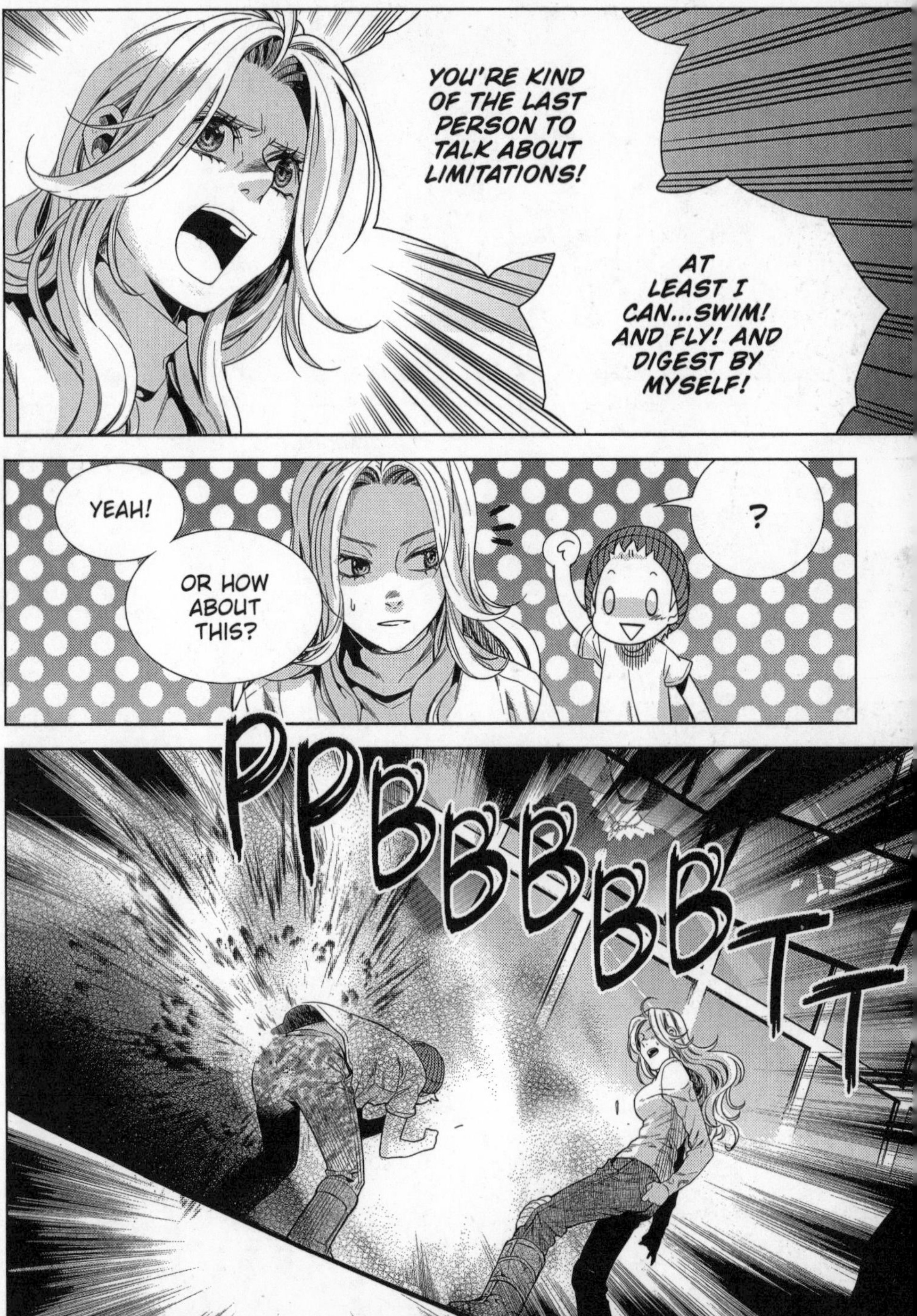
YOU'RE KIND OF THE LAST PERSON TO TALK ABOUT LIMITATIONS!
AT LEAST I CAN...SWIM! AND FLY! AND DIGEST BY MYSELF!
YEAH!
OR HOW ABOUT THIS?
?
PPBBBBBBTTT

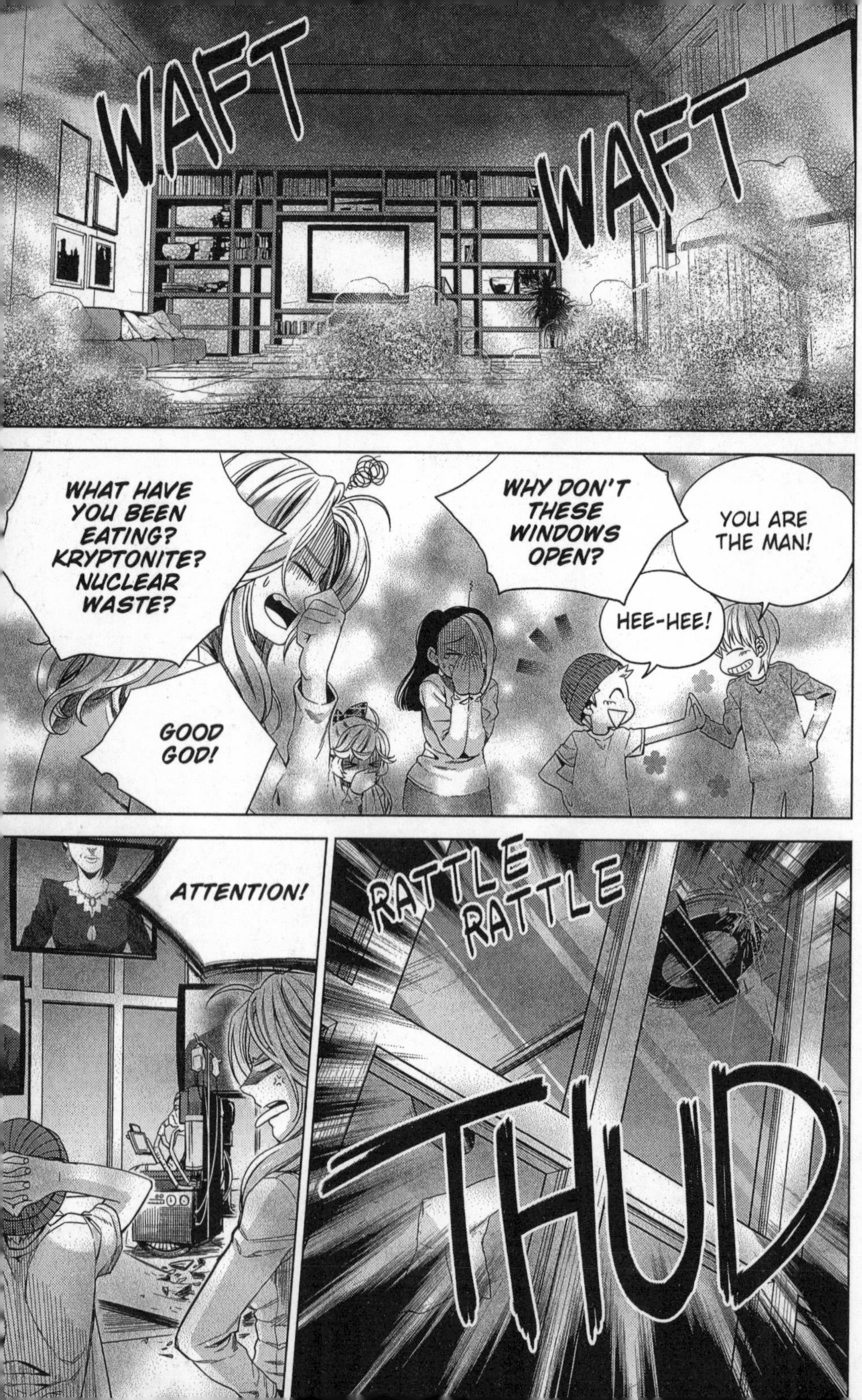
WAFT
WAFT
WHAT HAVE YOU BEEN EATING? KRYPTONITE? NUCLEAR WASTE?
GOOD GOD!
WHY DON'T THESE WINDOWS OPEN?
HEE-HEE!
YOU ARE THE MAN!
ATTENTION!
RATTLE RATTLE
THUD

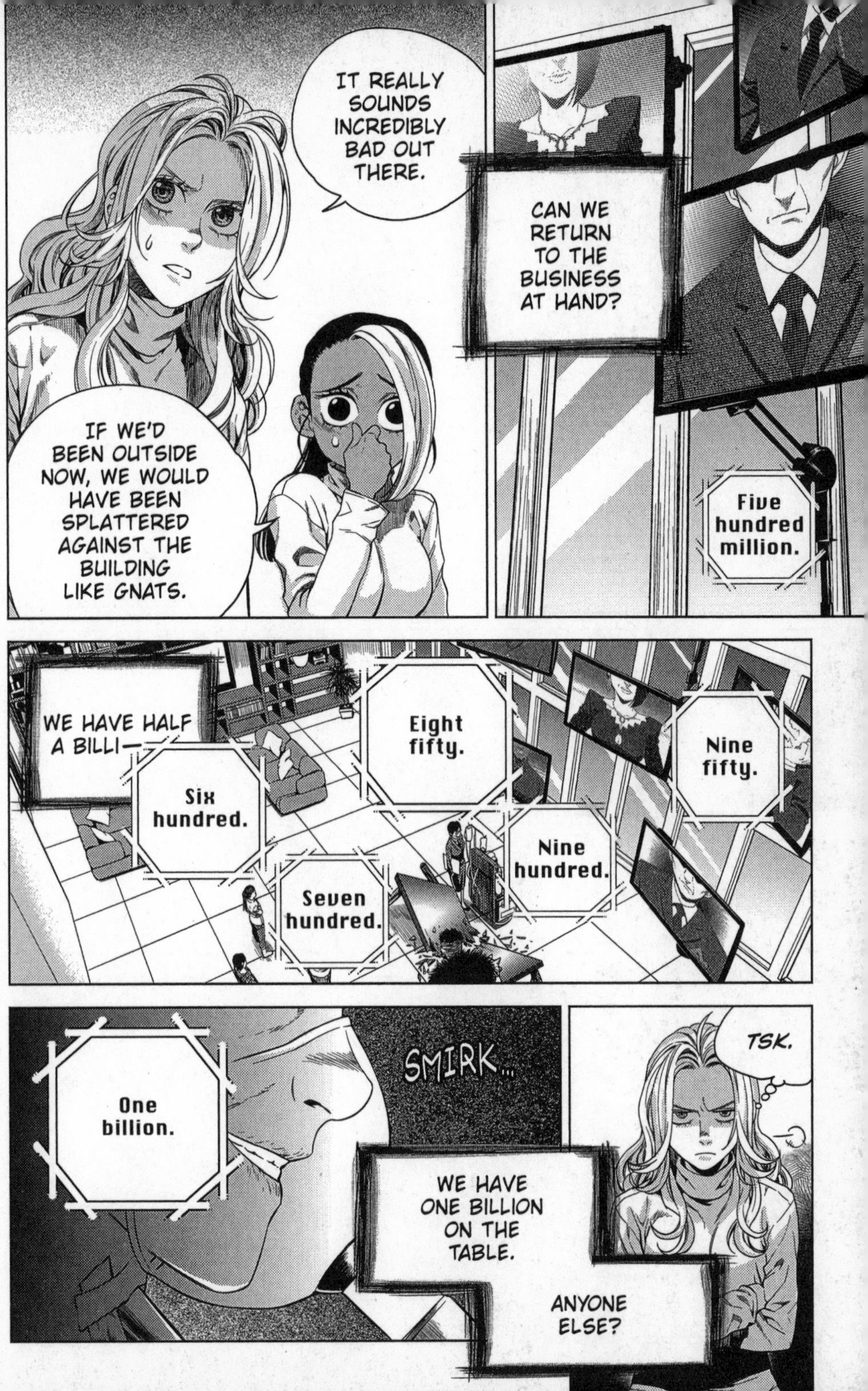
IT REALLY SOUNDS INCREDIBLY BAD OUT THERE.
IF WE'D BEEN OUTSIDE NOW, WE WOULD HAVE BEEN SPLATTERED AGAINST THE BUILDING LIKE GNATS.
CAN WE RETURN TO THE BUSINESS AT HAND?
Five hundred million.
WE HAVE HALF A BILLI—
Six hundred.
Seven hundred.
Eight fifty.
Nine hundred.
Nine fifty.
One billion.
SMIRK...
WE HAVE ONE BILLION ON THE TABLE.
ANYONE ELSE?
TSK.

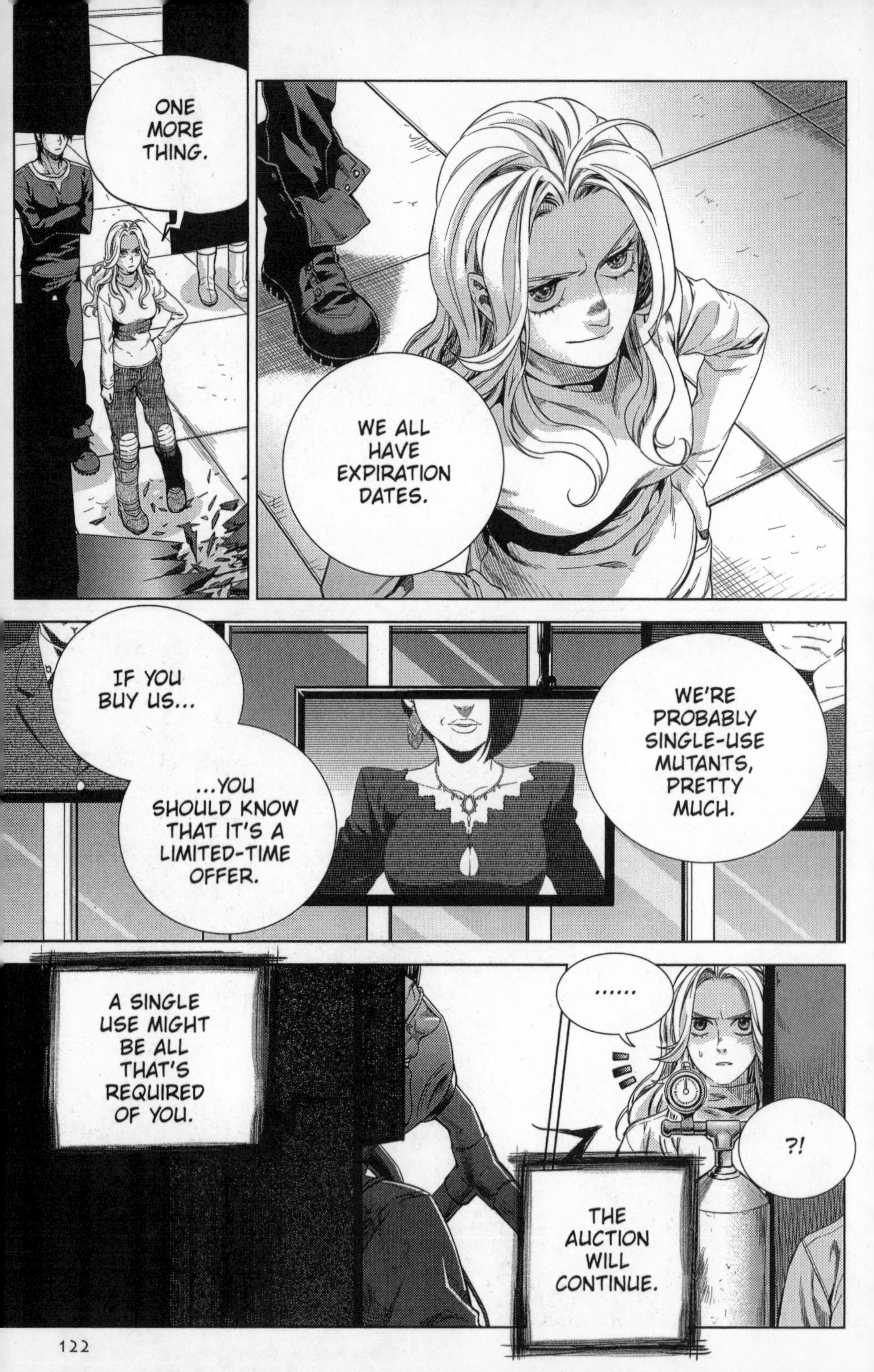
ONE MORE THING.
WE ALL HAVE EXPIRATION DATES.
IF YOU BUY US...
...YOU SHOULD KNOW THAT IT'S A LIMITED-TIME OFFER.
WE'RE PROBABLY SINGLE-USE MUTANTS, PRETTY MUCH.
A SINGLE USE MIGHT BE ALL THAT'S REQUIRED OF YOU.
......
THE AUCTION WILL CONTINUE.
?!

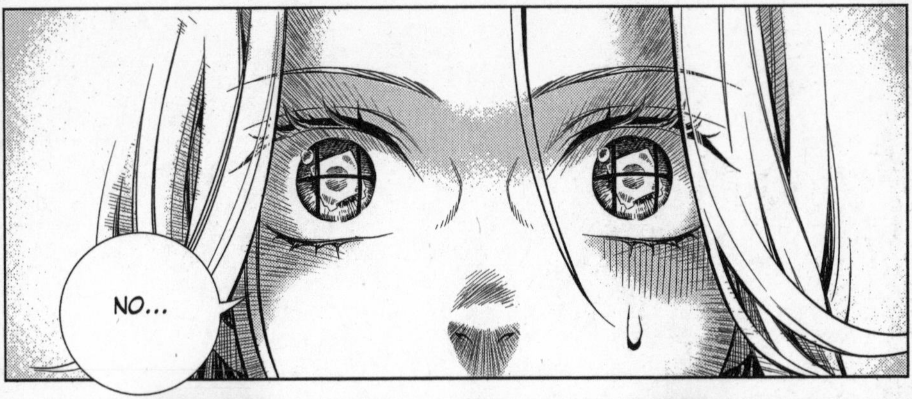
NO...

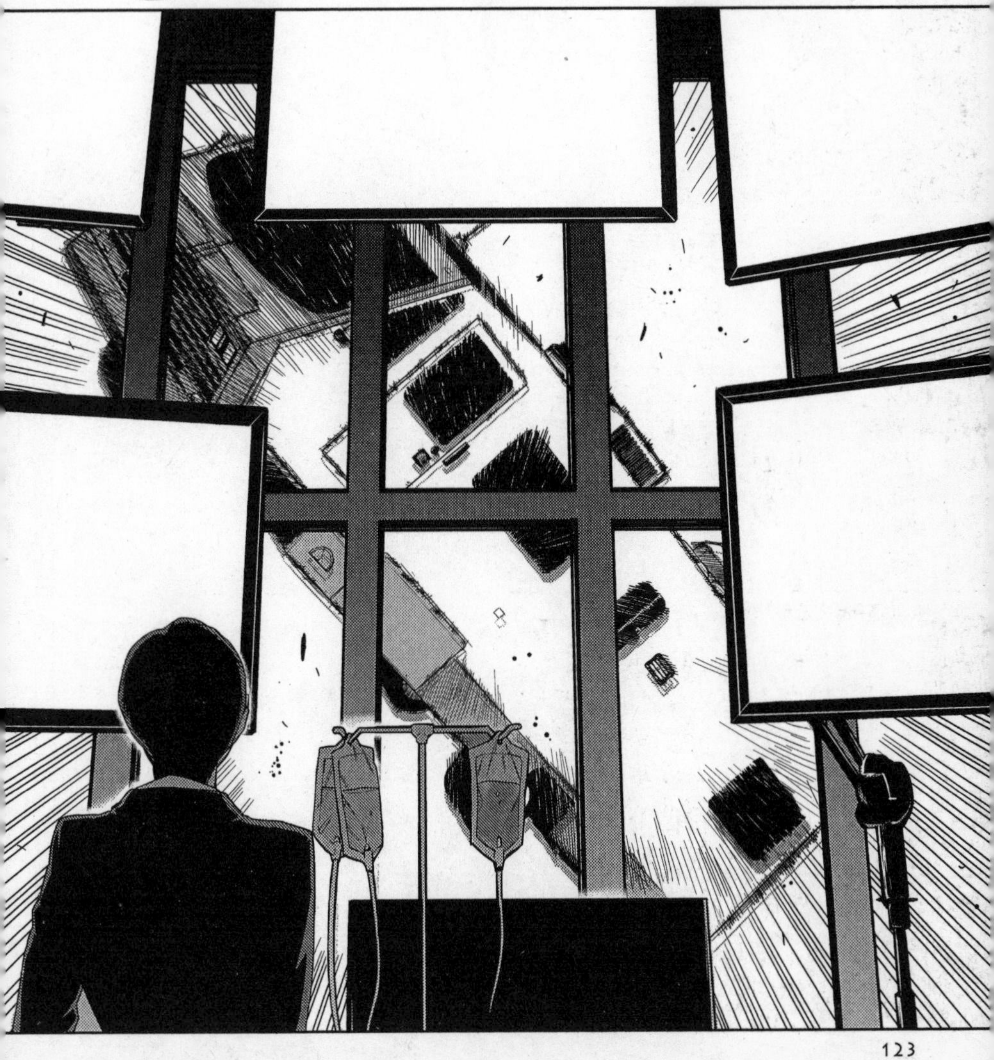

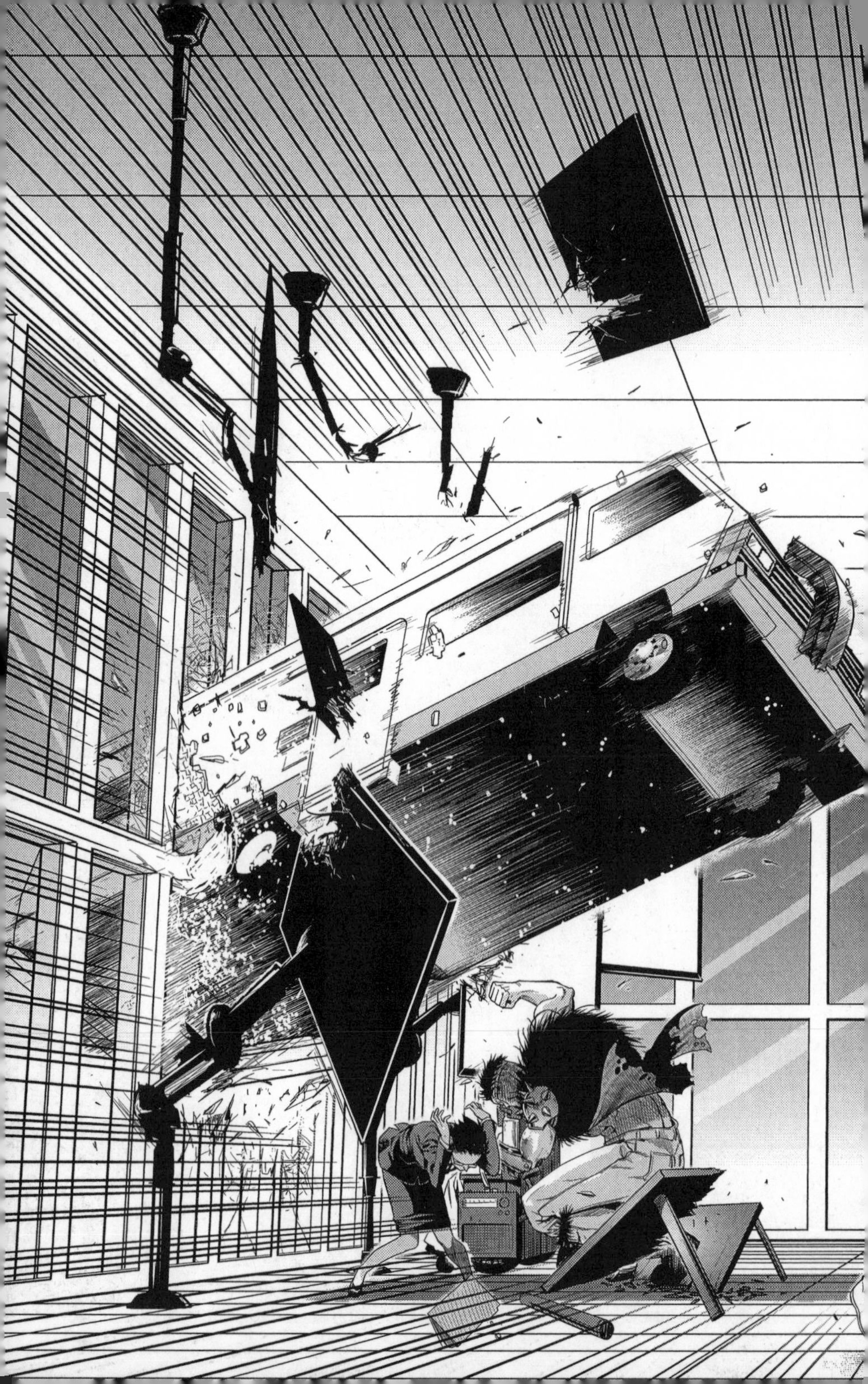

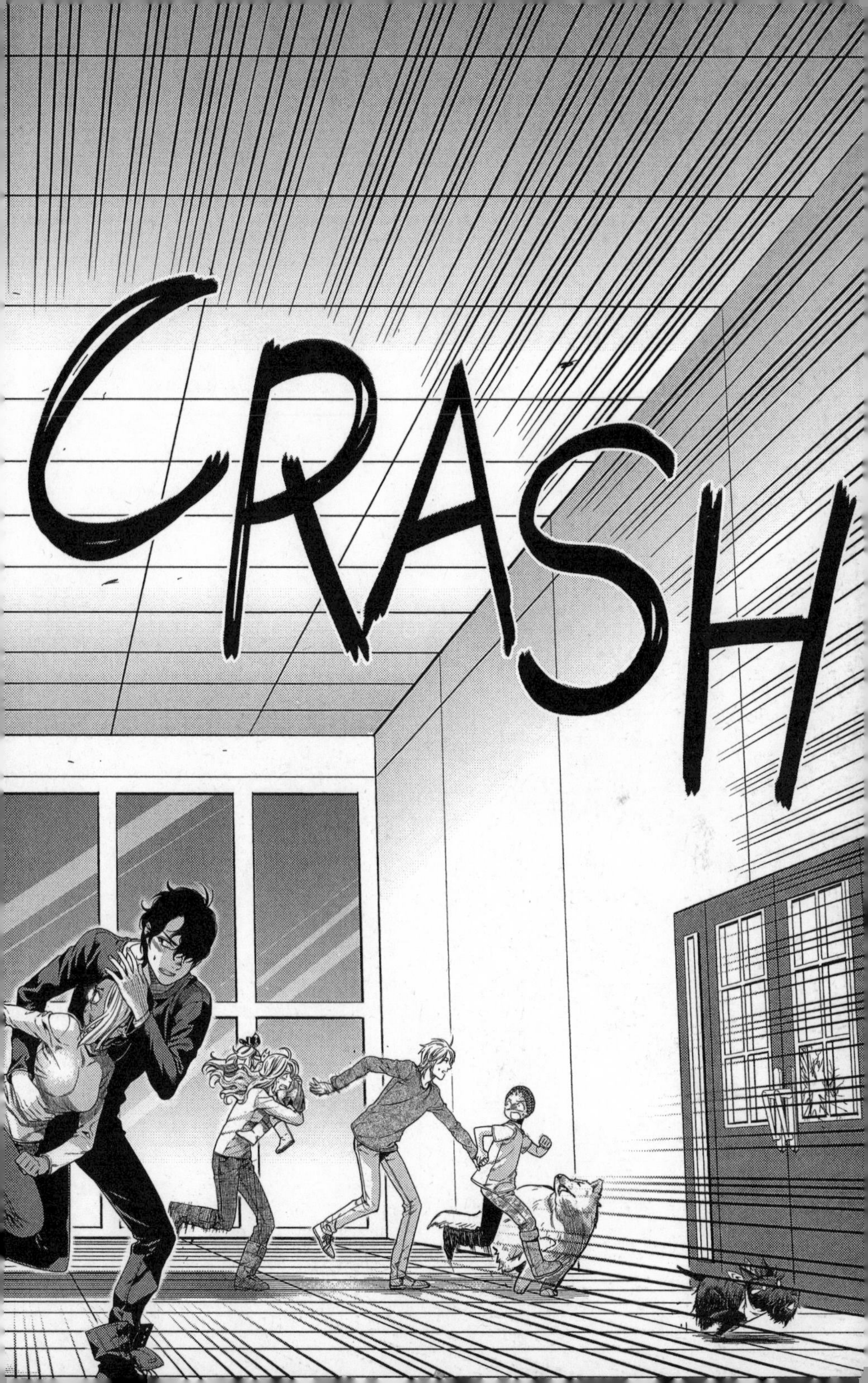
CRASH

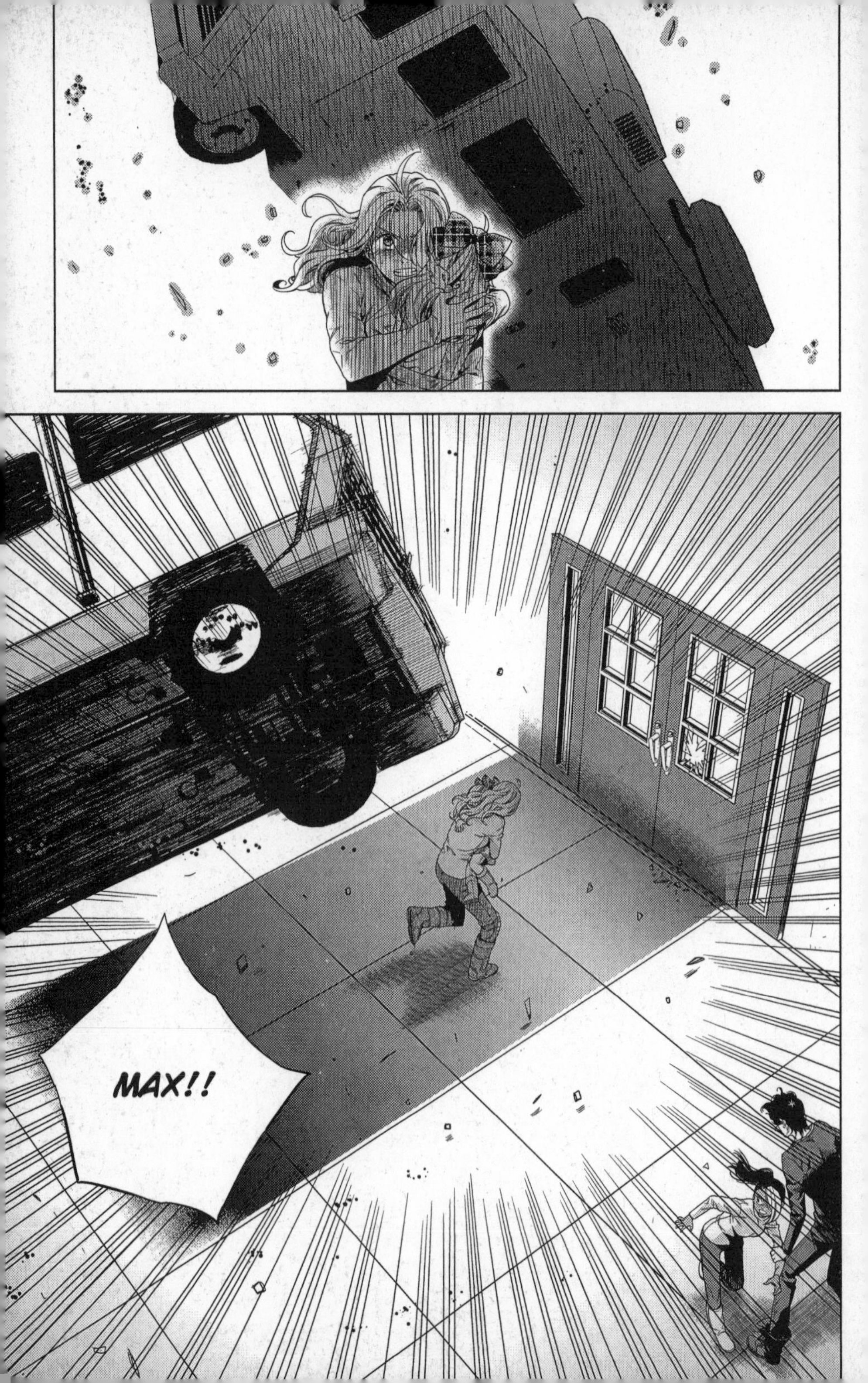
MAX!!

MAXIMUM
RIDE

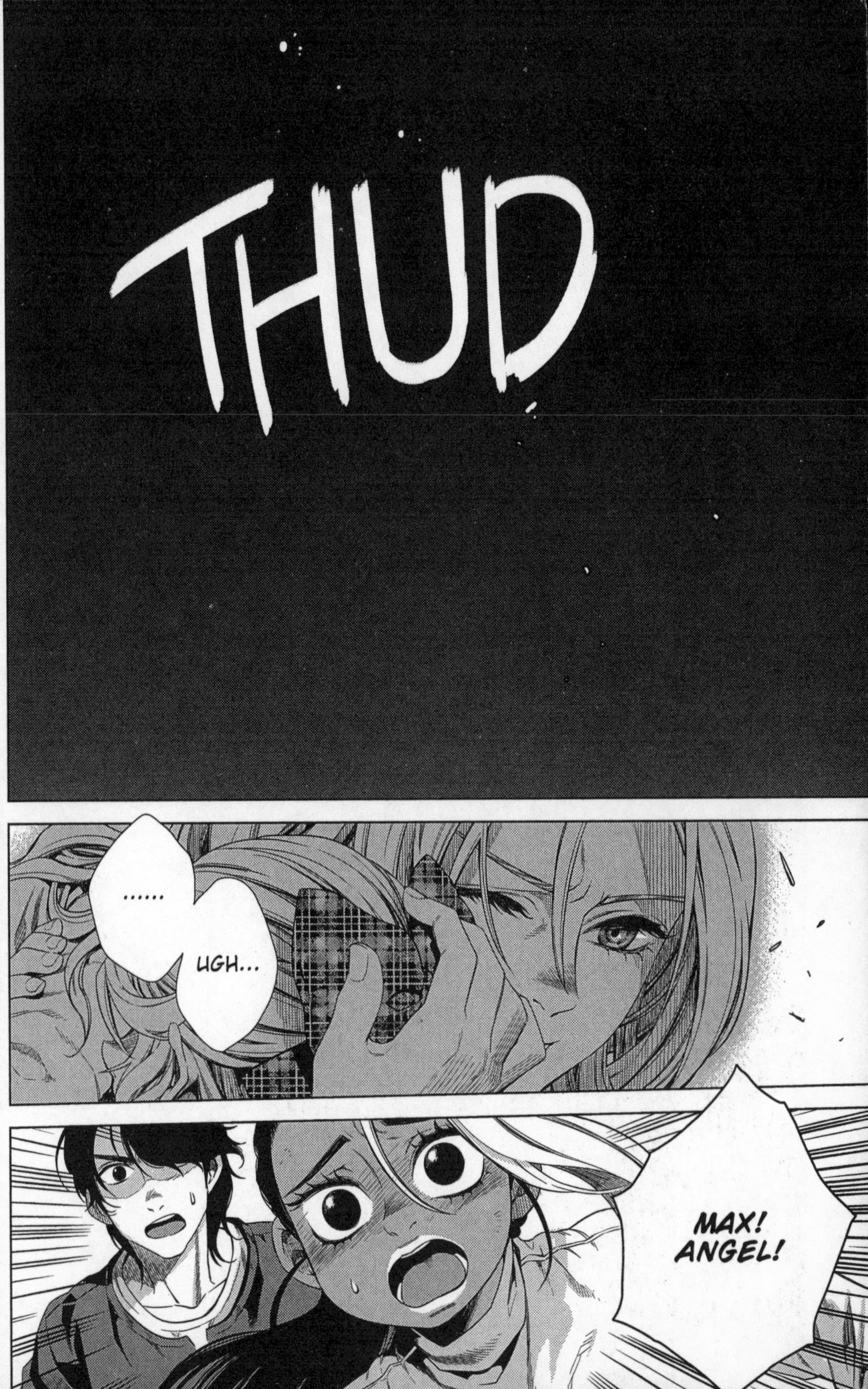
THUD
......
UGH...
MAX!
ANGEL!

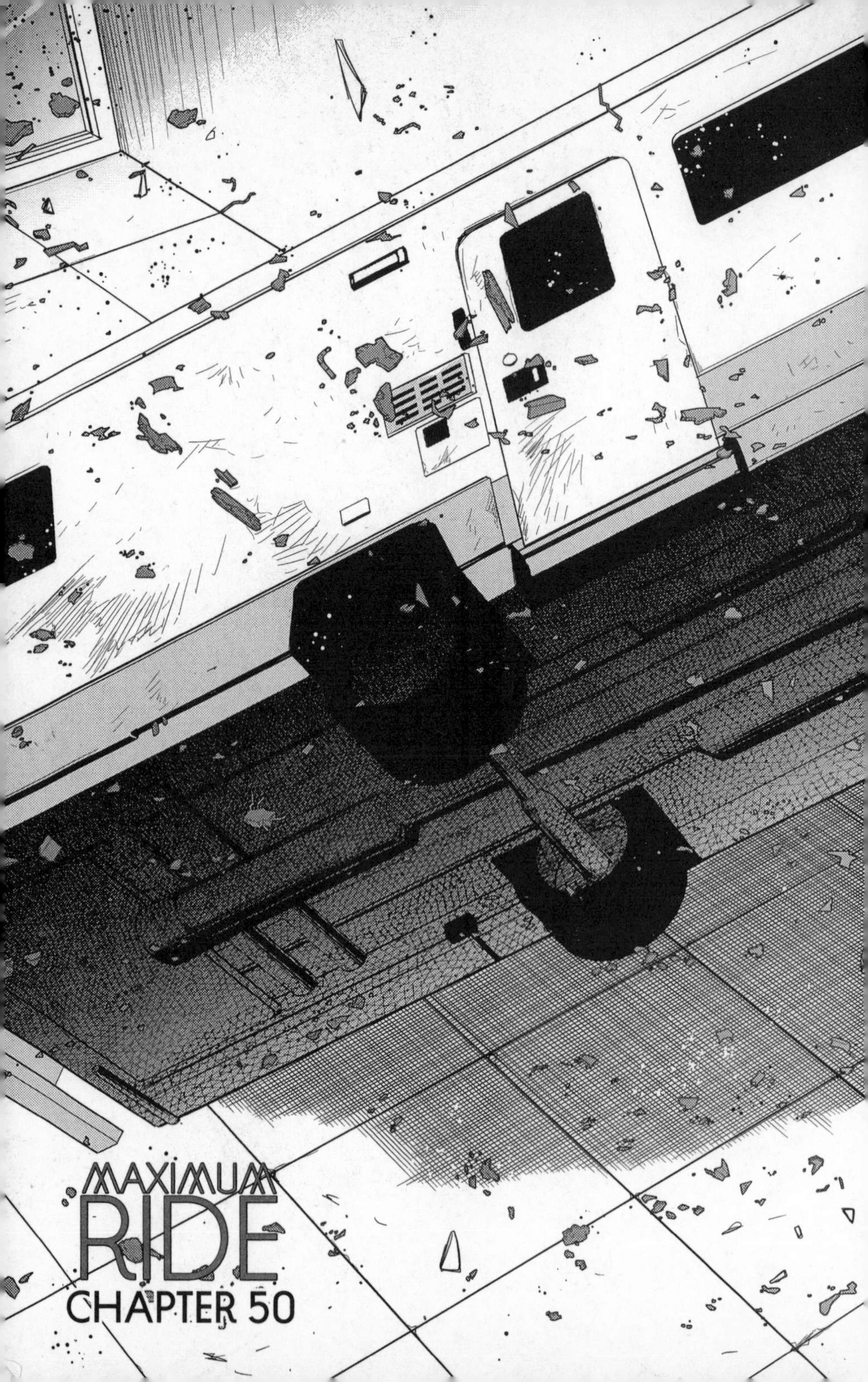
MAXIMUM RIDE
CHAPTER 50

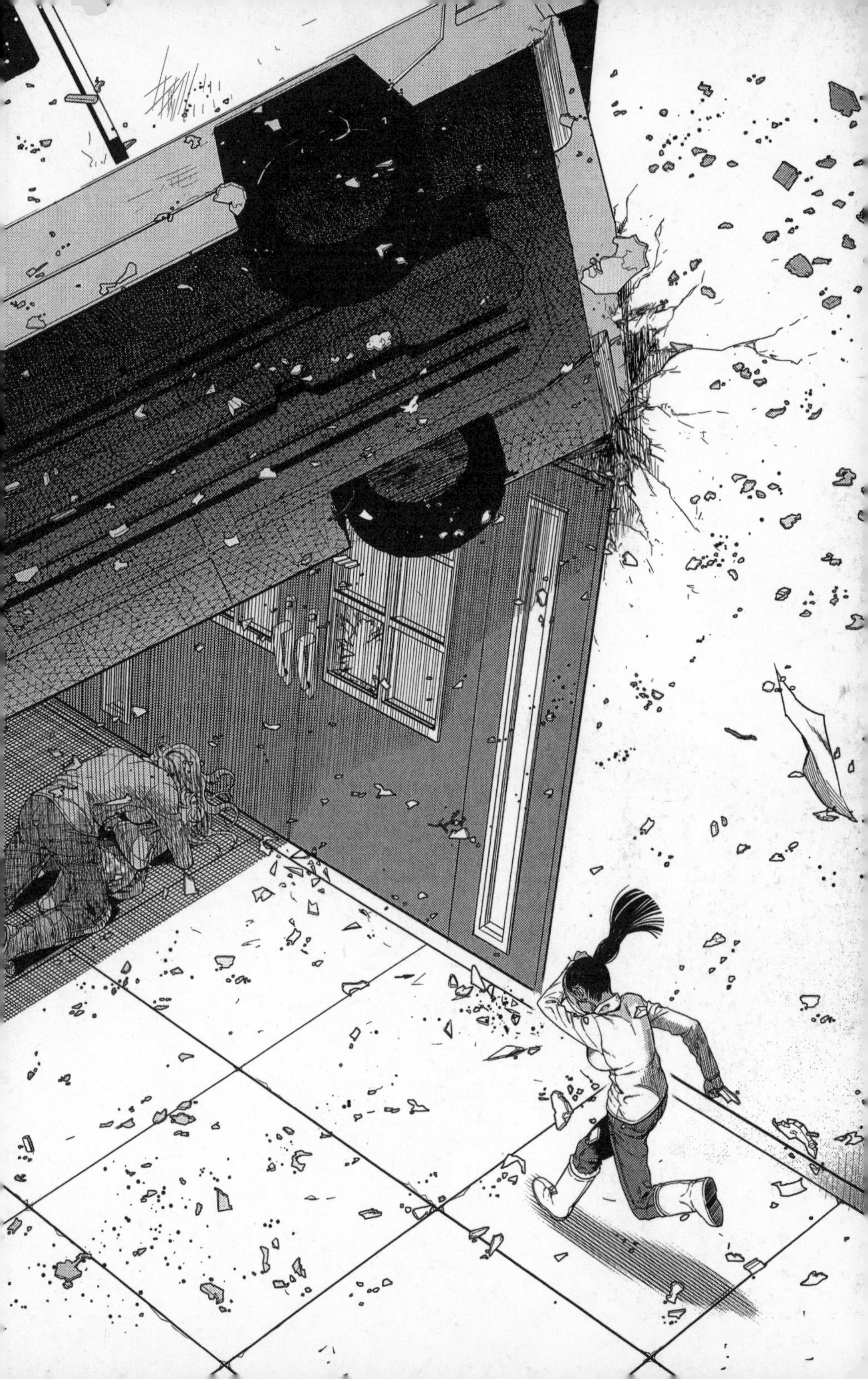

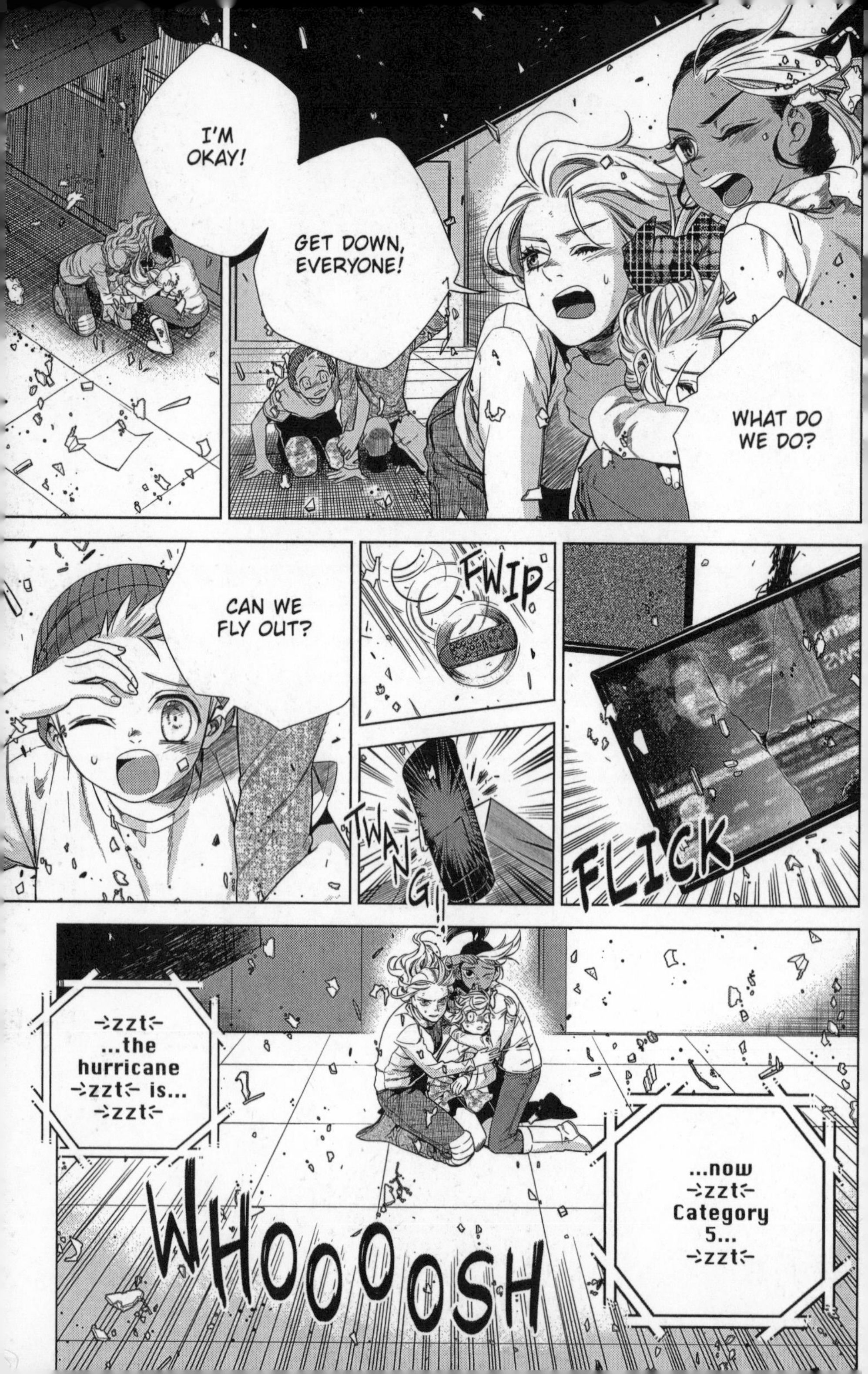

I'M OKAY!
GET DOWN, EVERYONE!
WHAT DO WE DO?
CAN WE FLY OUT?
FWIP
TWANG
FLICK
→zzt← ...the hurricane →zzt← is... →zzt←
WHOOOOSH
...now →zzt← Category 5... →zzt←

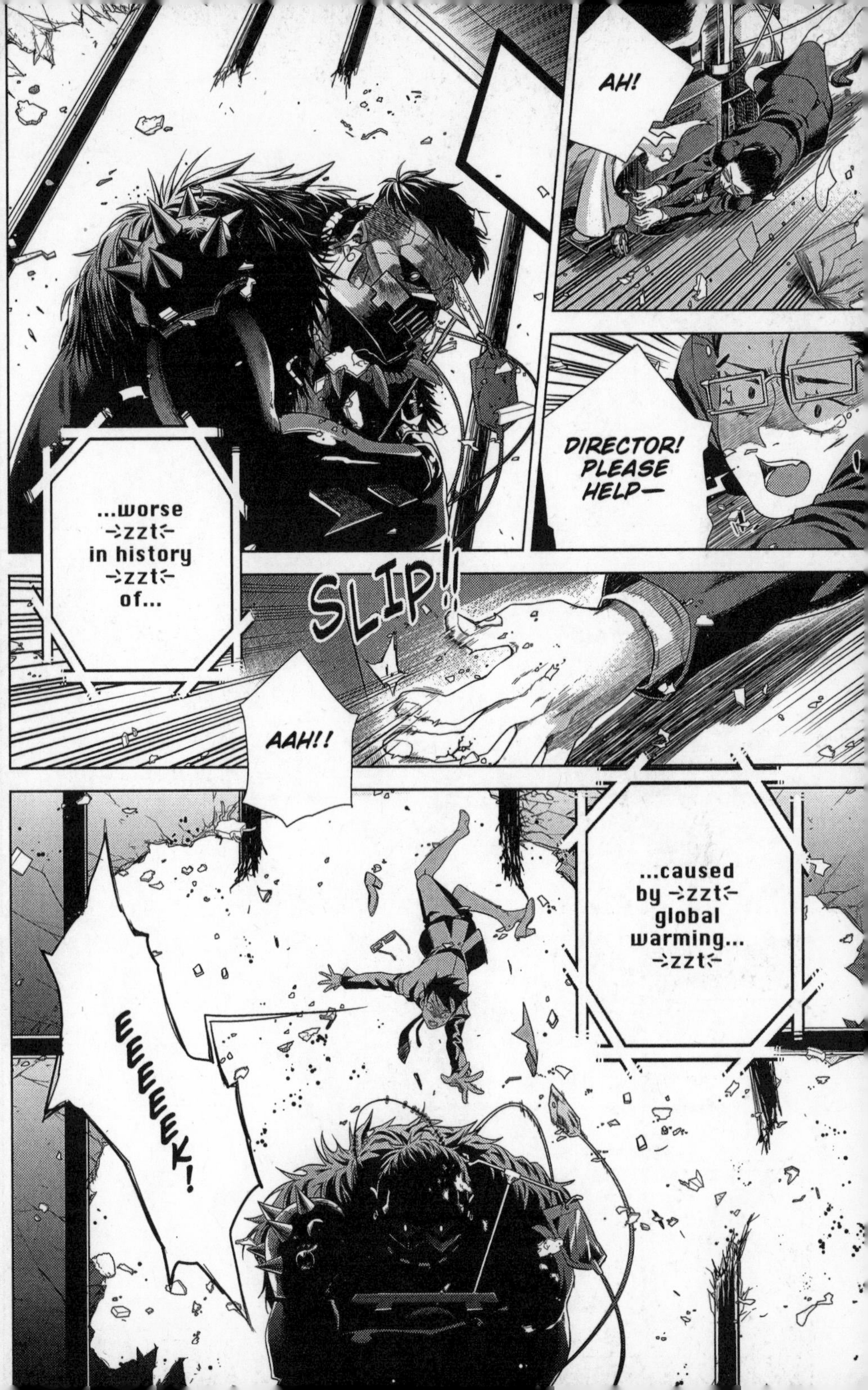
...worse ->zzt<- in history ->zzt<- of...
AH!
DIRECTOR! PLEASE HELP—
SLIP!!
AAH!!
EEEEEEK!
...caused by ->zzt<- global warming... ->zzt<-

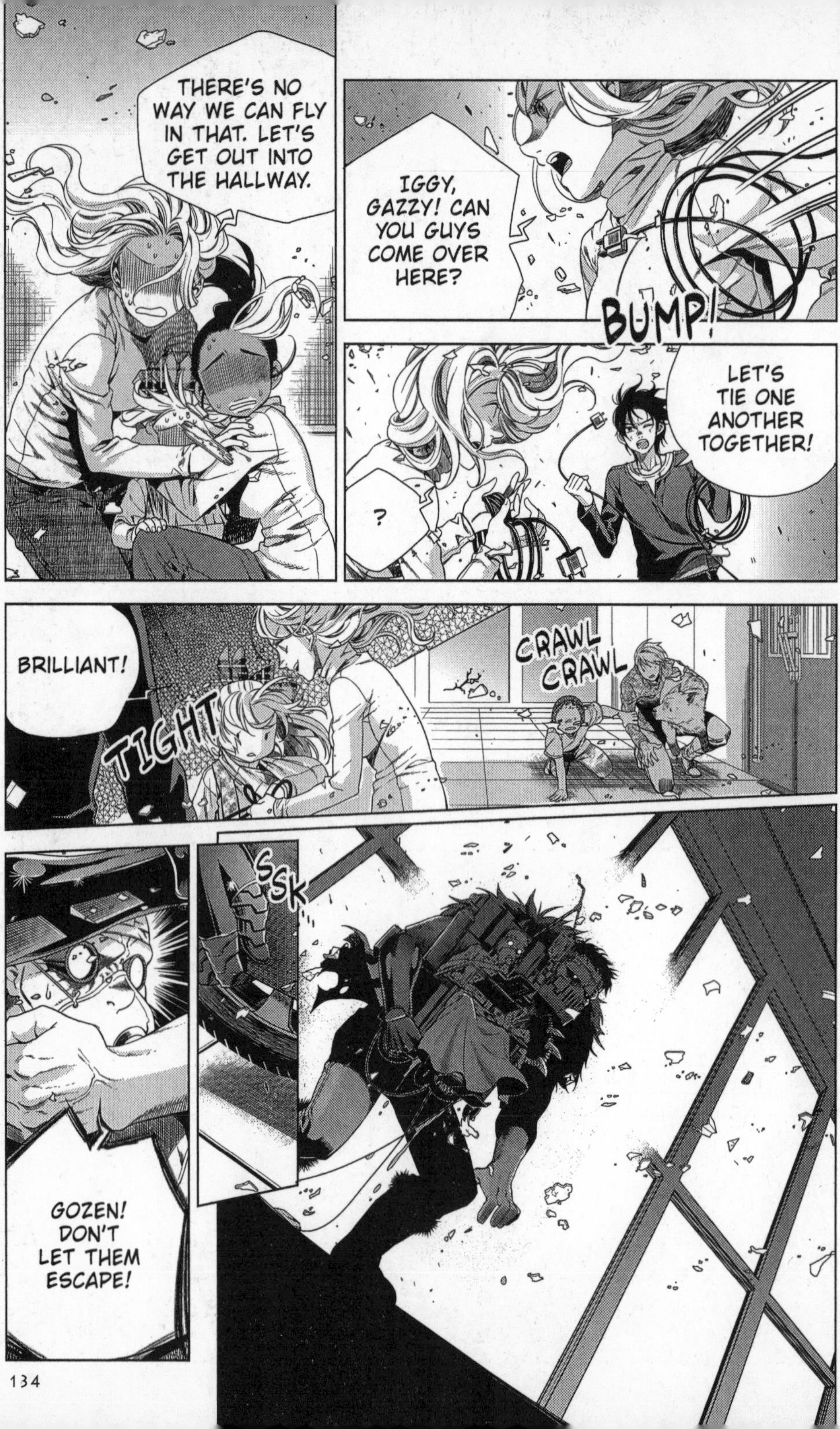
THERE'S NO WAY WE CAN FLY IN THAT. LET'S GET OUT INTO THE HALLWAY.
IGGY, GAZZY! CAN YOU GUYS COME OVER HERE?
BUMP!
?
LET'S TIE ONE ANOTHER TOGETHER!
BRILLIANT!
TIGHT
CRAWL CRAWL
SSK
GOZEN! DON'T LET THEM ESCAPE!

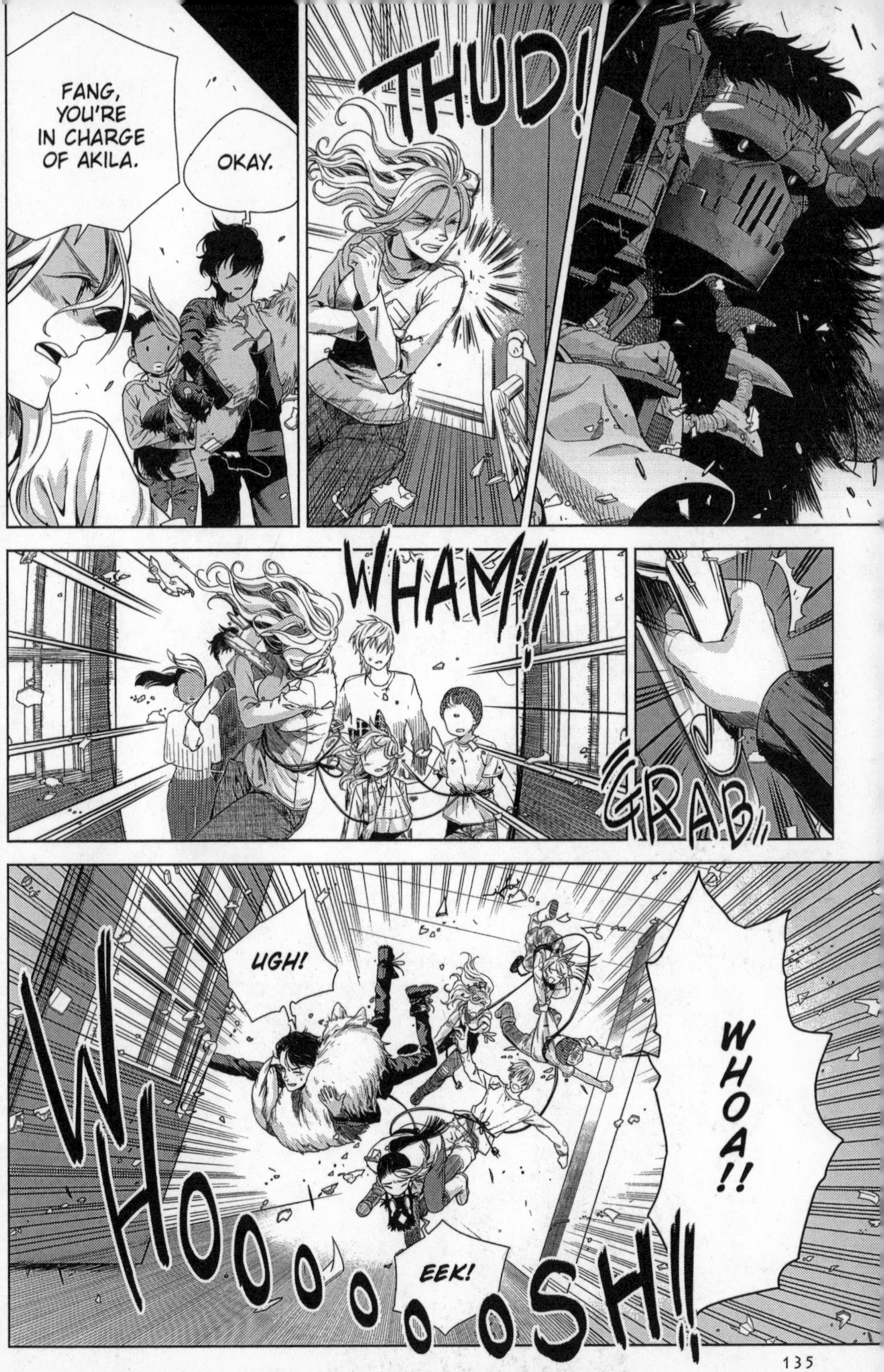
FANG, YOU'RE IN CHARGE OF AKILA.
OKAY.
THUD!
WHAM!!
GRAB
UGH!
WHOOOOOOSH!!
WHOA!!
EEK!

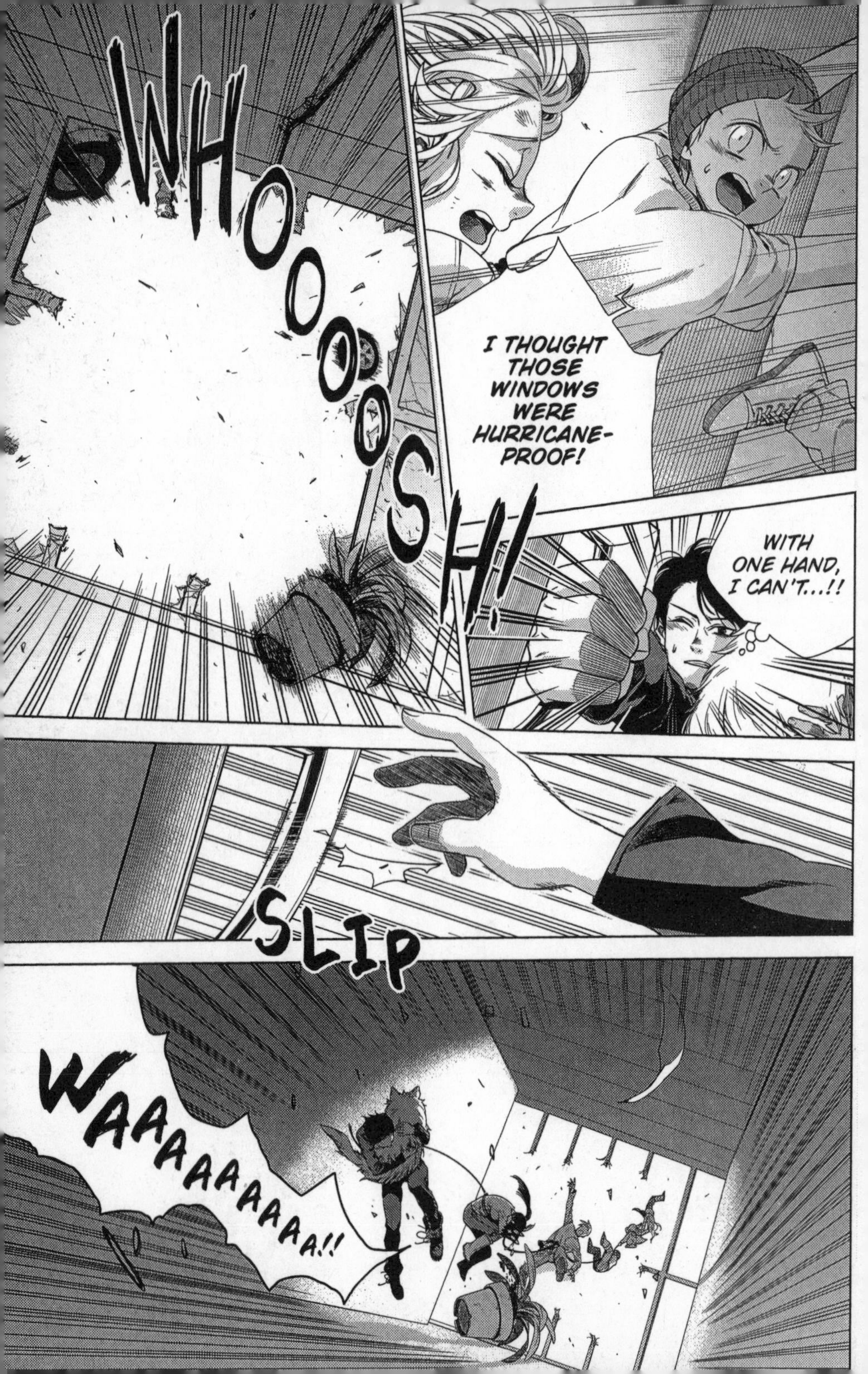
WHOOOOOSH!!
I THOUGHT THOSE WINDOWS WERE HURRICANE-PROOF!
WITH ONE HAND, I CAN'T...!!
SLIP
WAAAAAAAAAA!!

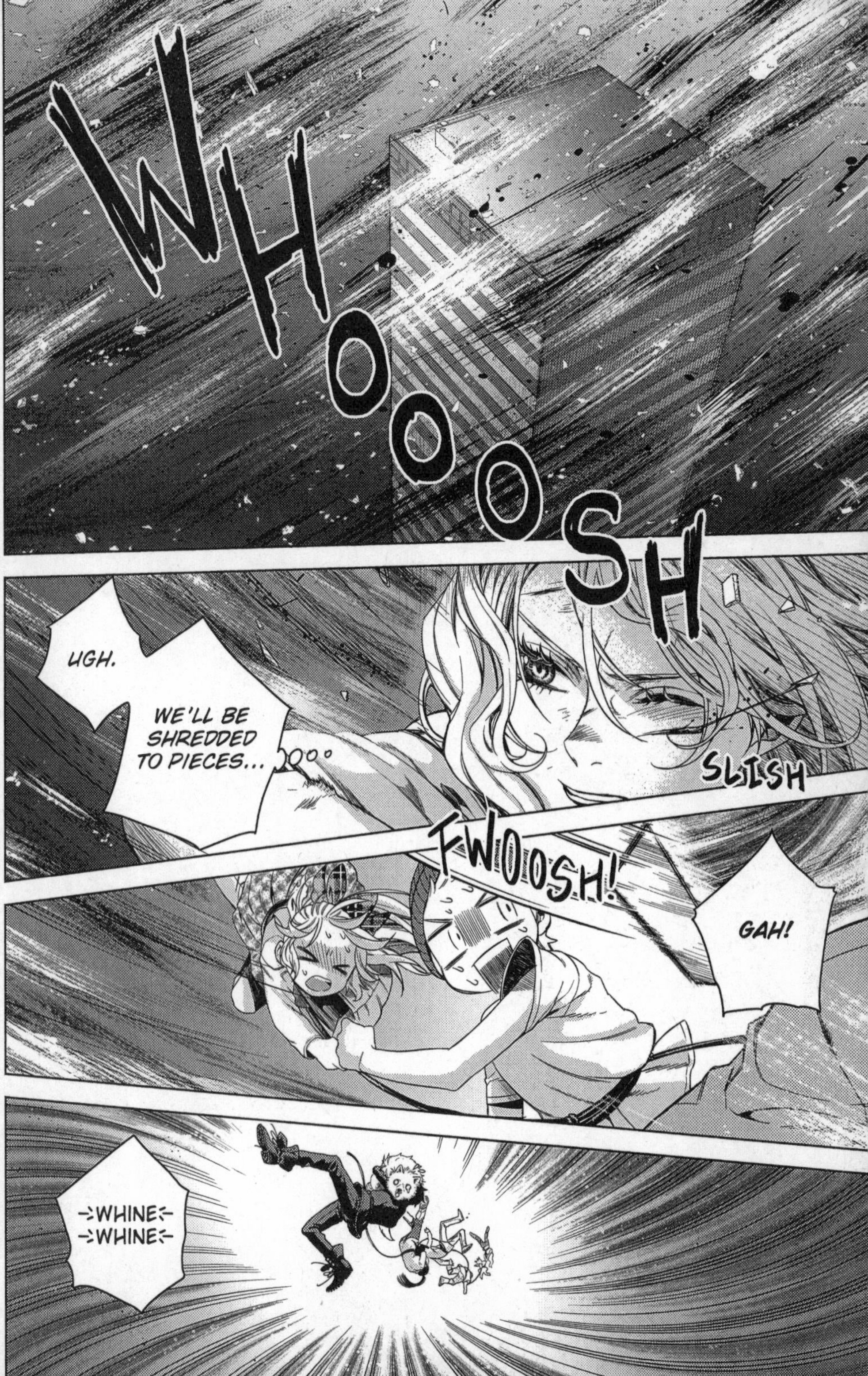
WHOOOOSH
UGH.
WE'LL BE SHREDDED TO PIECES...
SLISH
FWOOSH!
GAH!
WHINE
WHINE

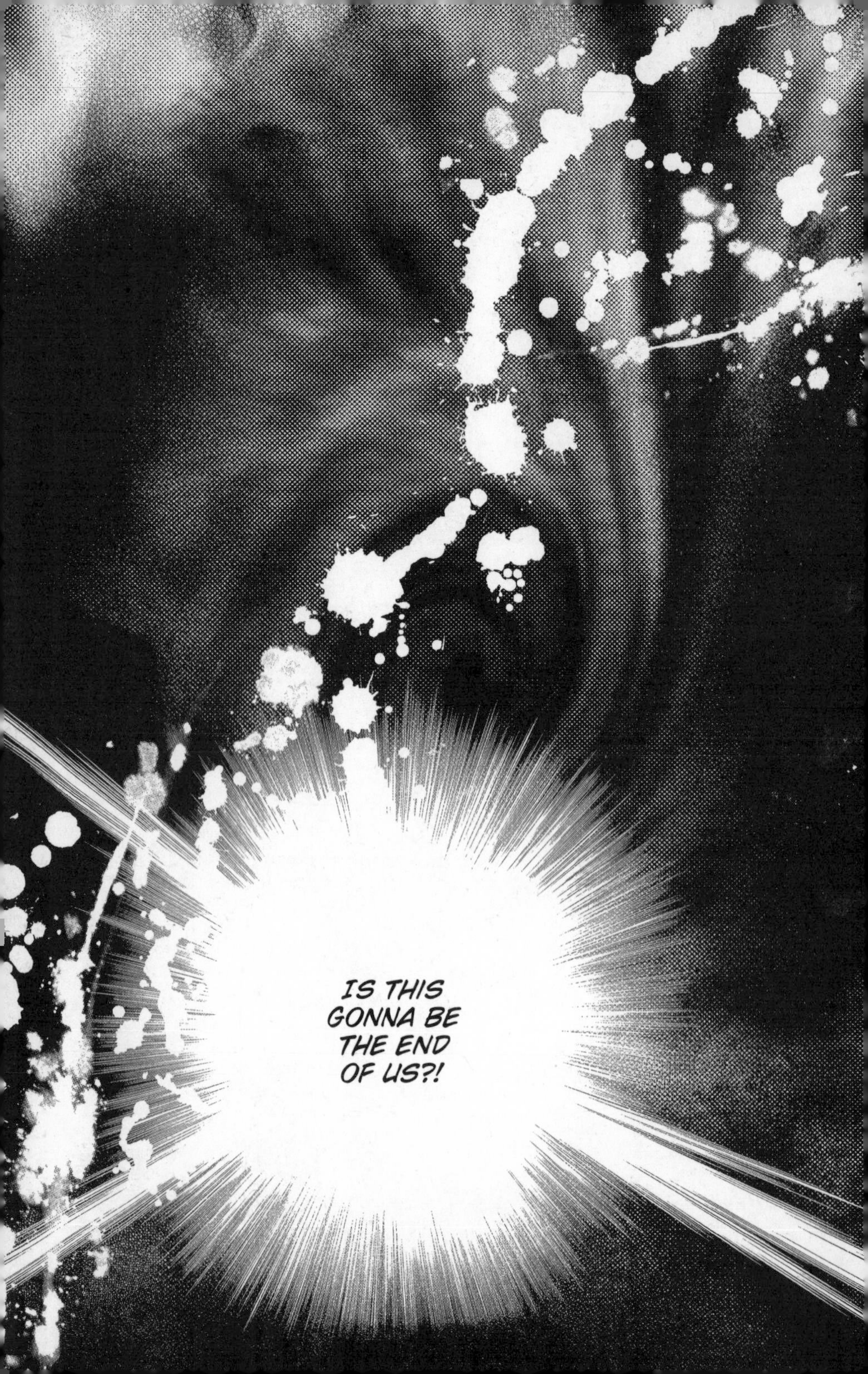
IS THIS GONNA BE THE END OF US?!

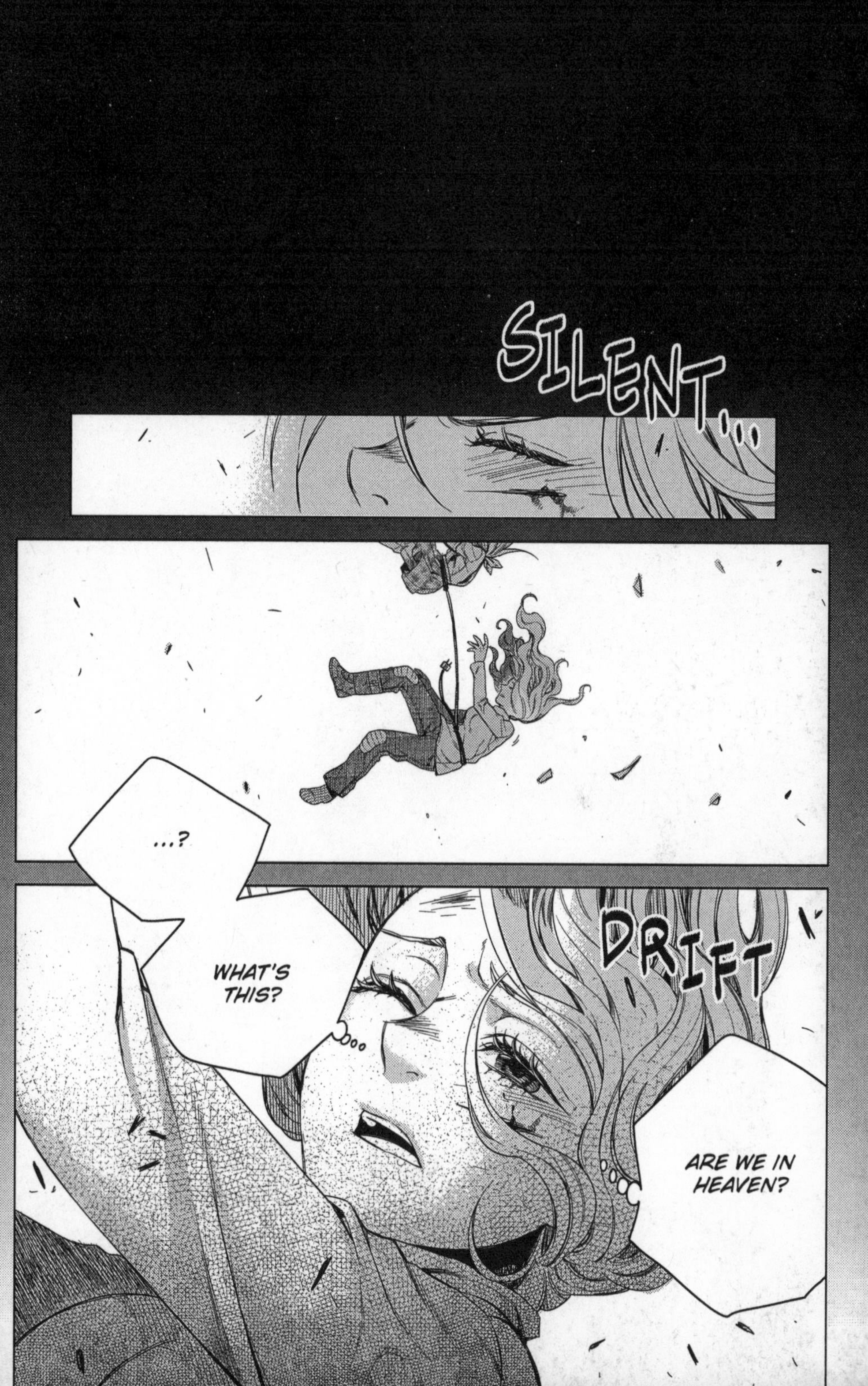
SILENT...
...?
DRIFT
WHAT'S THIS?
ARE WE IN HEAVEN?

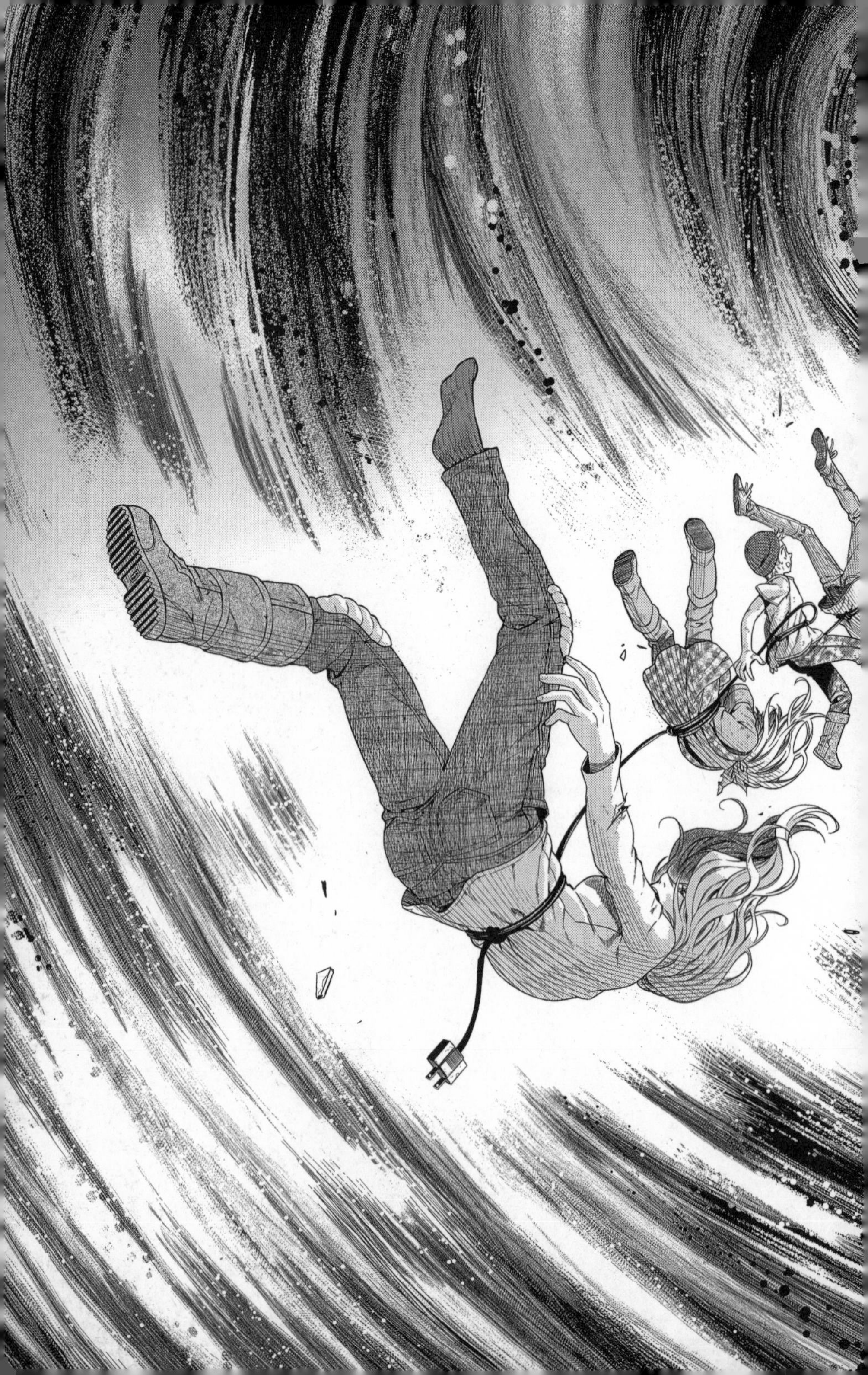

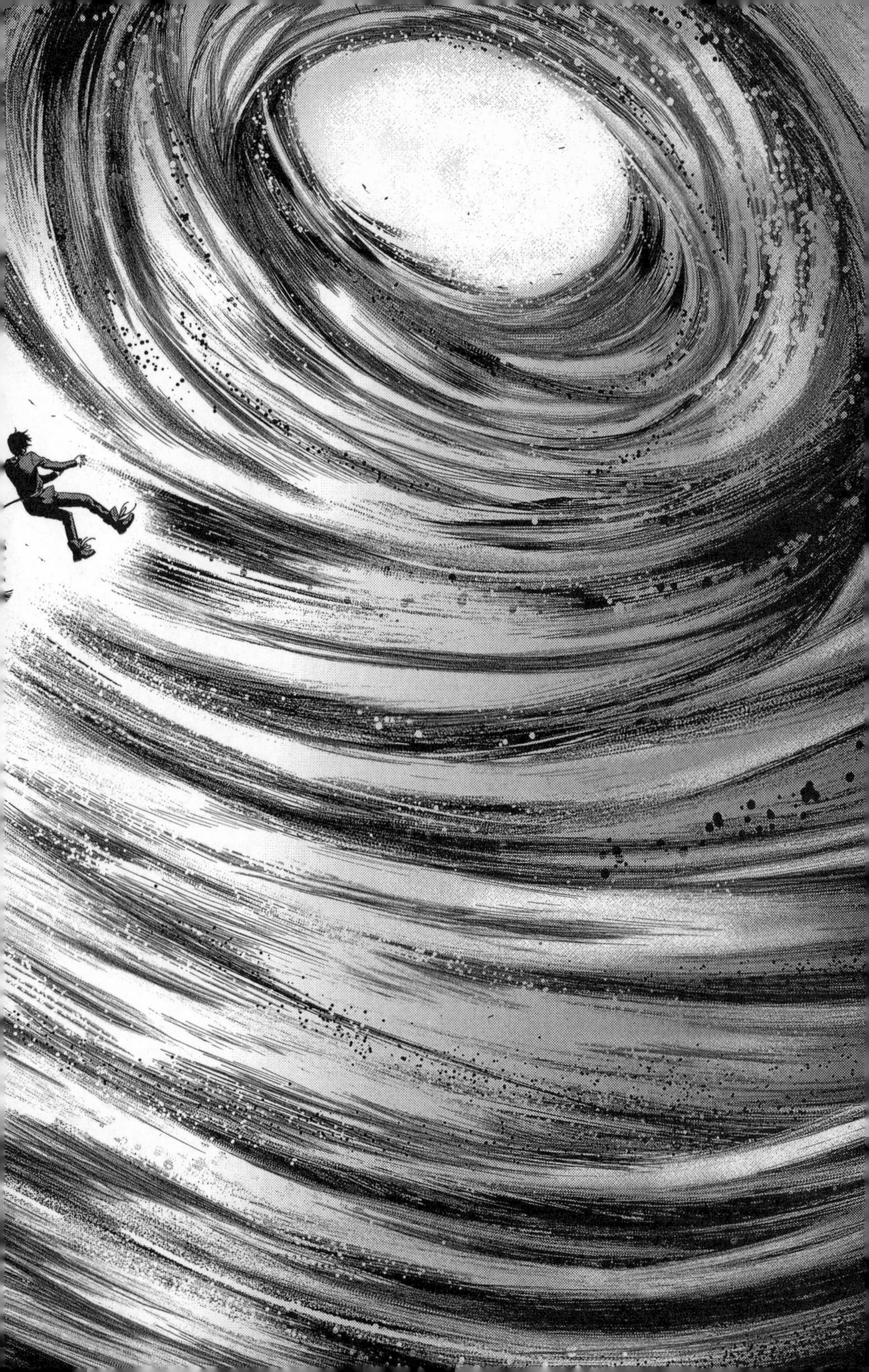

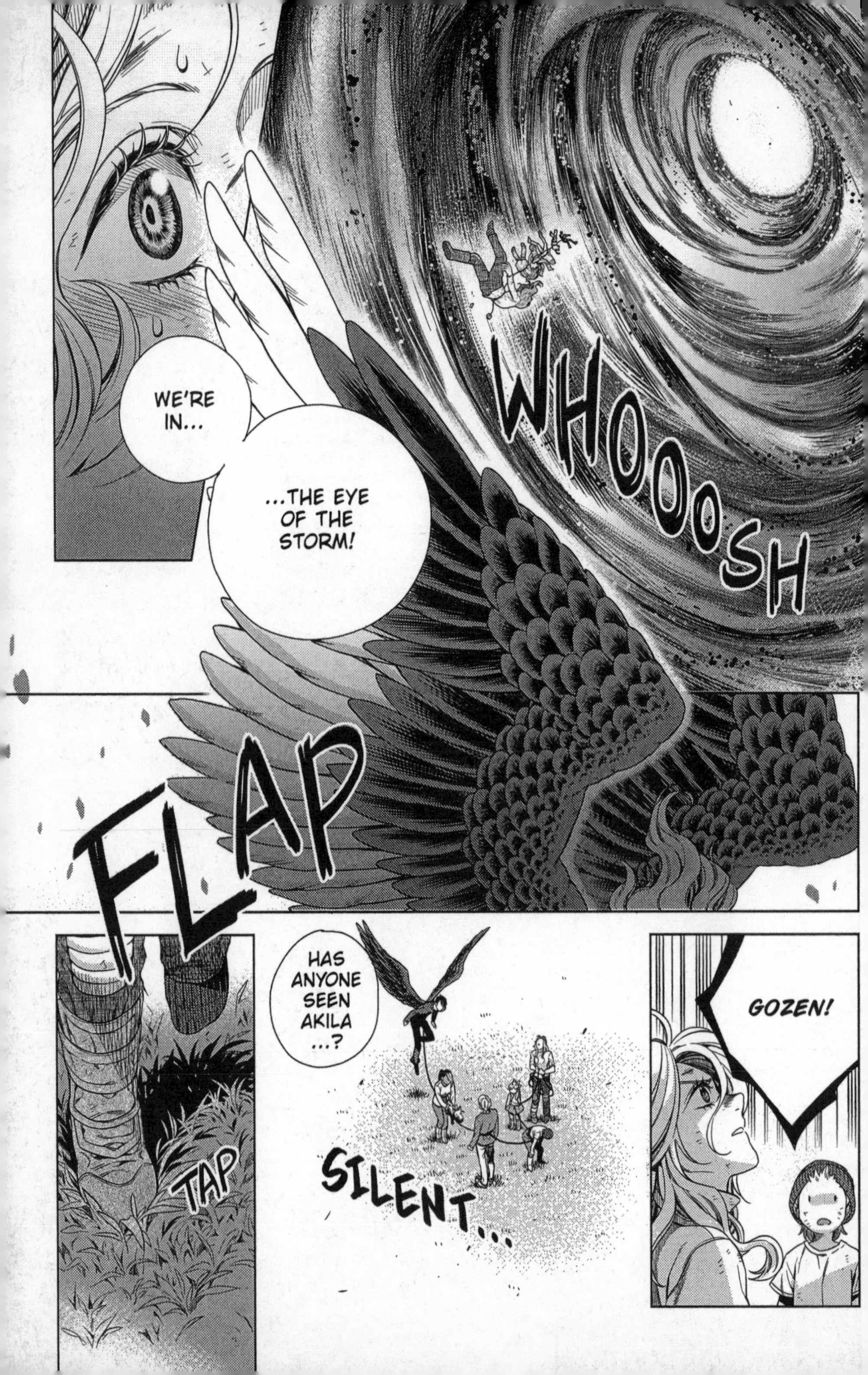
WE'RE IN...
...THE EYE OF THE STORM!
WHOOOSH
FLAP
TAP
HAS ANYONE SEEN AKILA ...?
SILENT...
GOZEN!

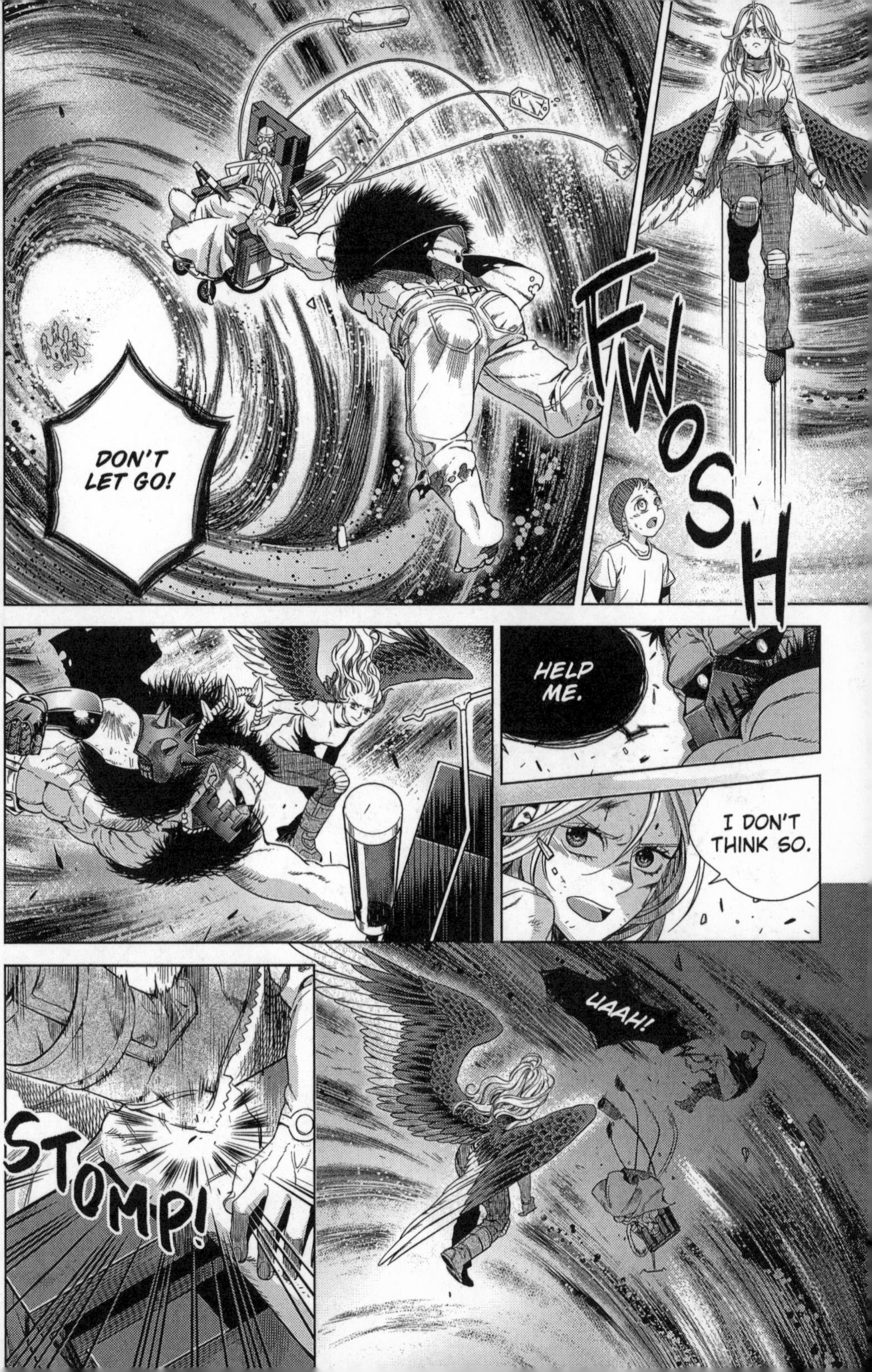
DON'T LET GO!
FWOSH
HELP ME.
I DON'T THINK SO.
STOMP!
UAAH!

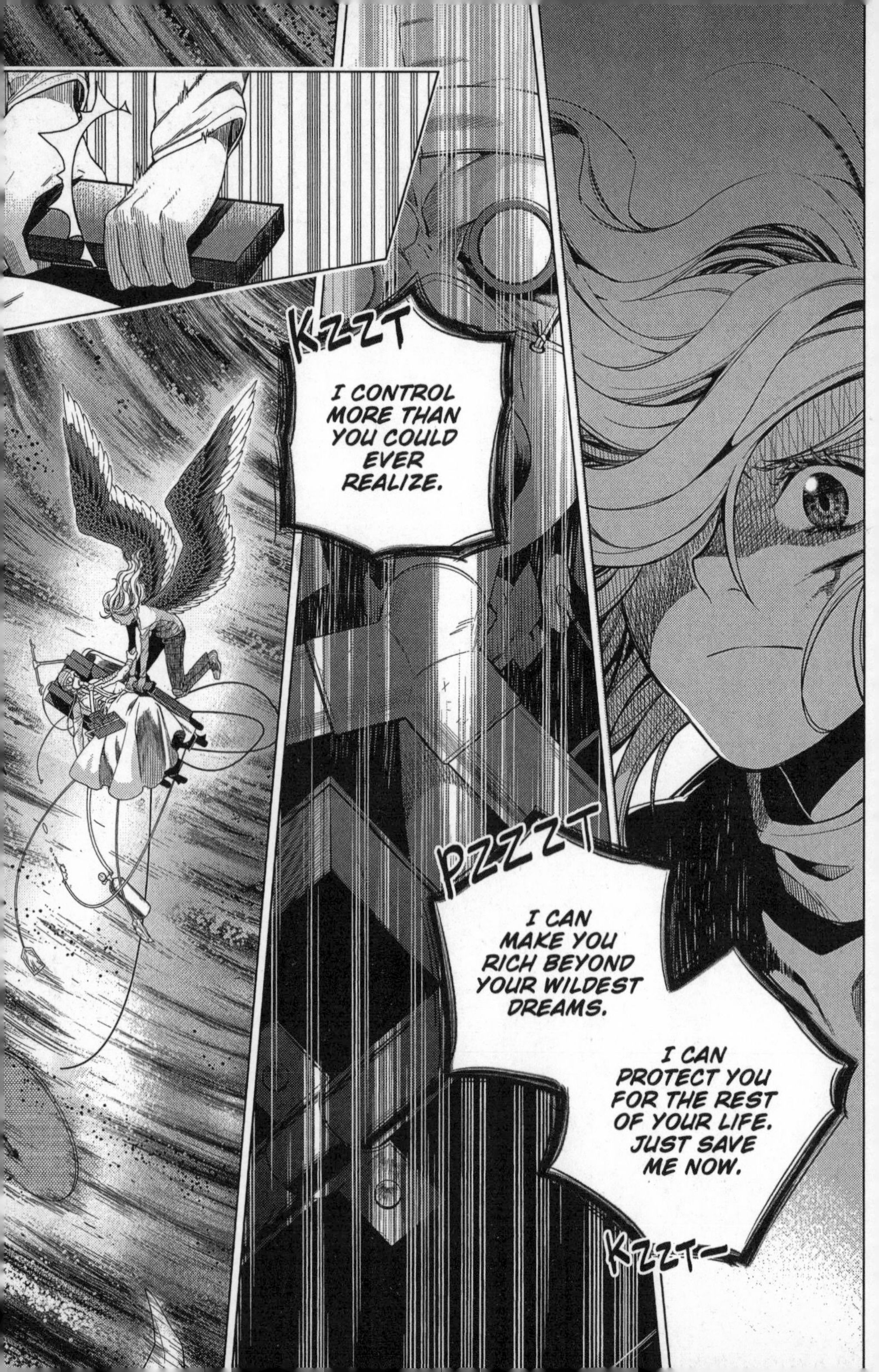
KZZZT
I CONTROL MORE THAN YOU COULD EVER REALIZE.
PZZZZT
I CAN MAKE YOU RICH BEYOND YOUR WILDEST DREAMS.
I CAN PROTECT YOU FOR THE REST OF YOUR LIFE. JUST SAVE ME NOW.
KZZZT—

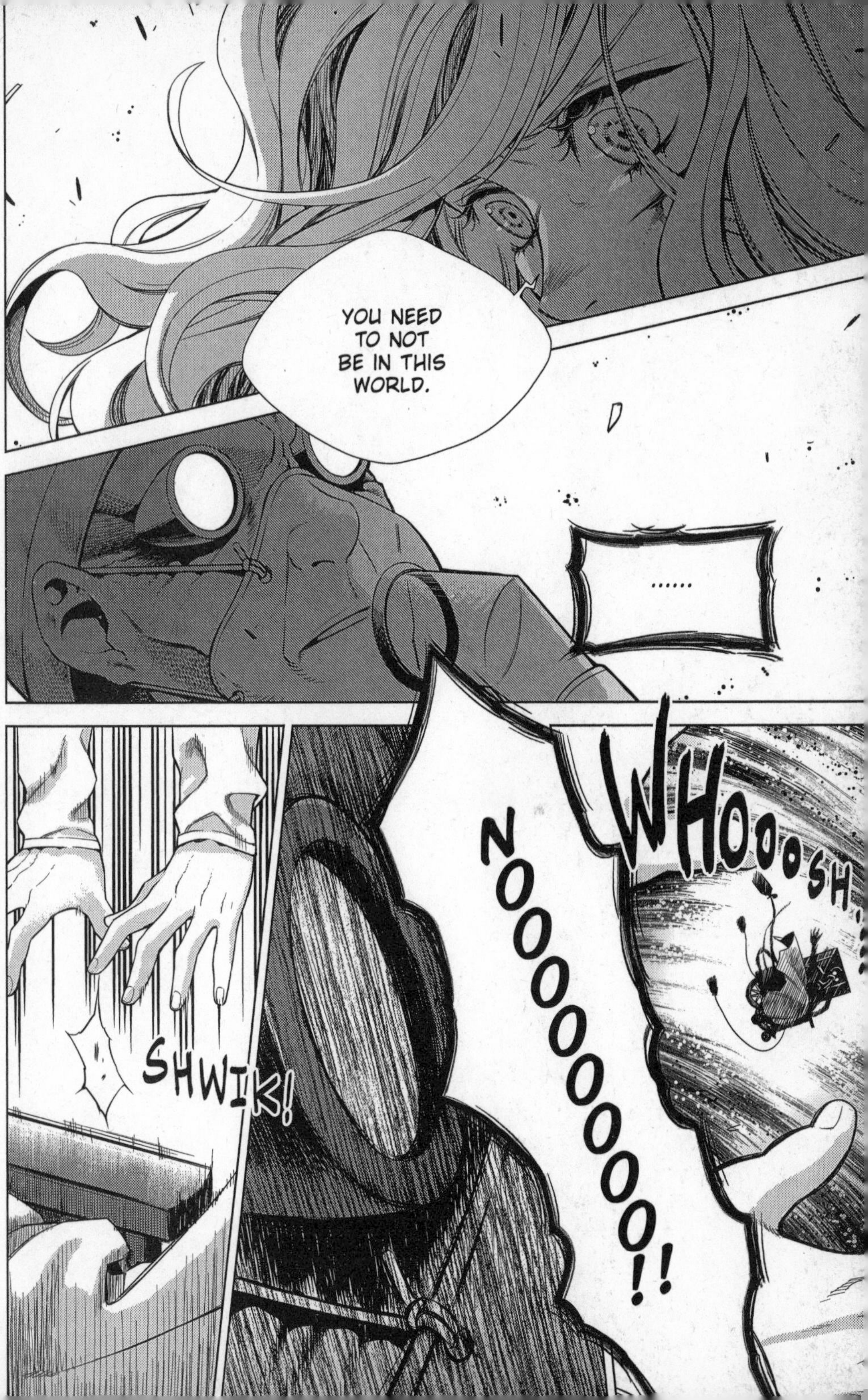
YOU NEED TO NOT BE IN THIS WORLD.
......
SHWIK!
NOOOOOOOOOO!!
WHOOOSH...

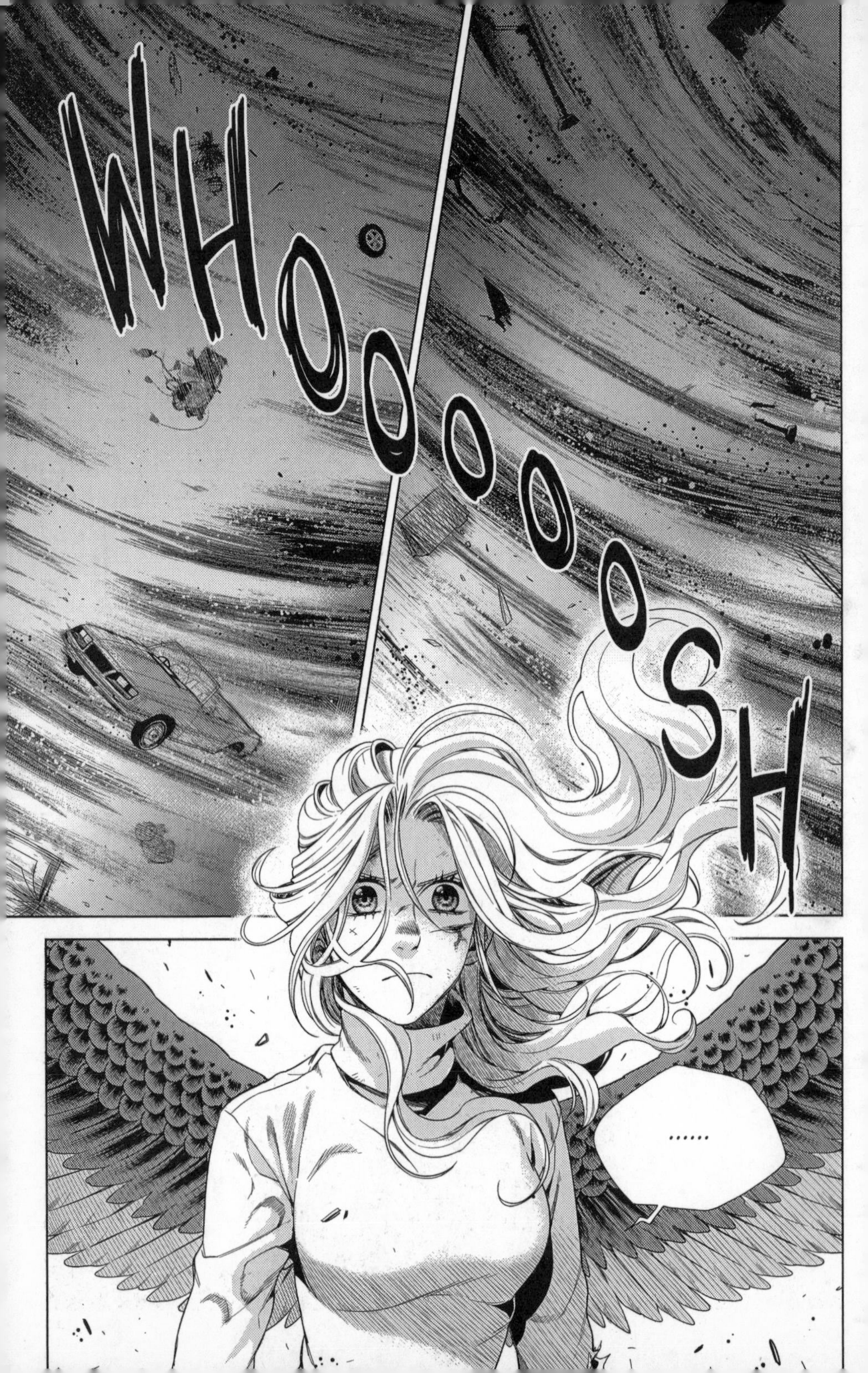
WHOOOOOOOSH
......

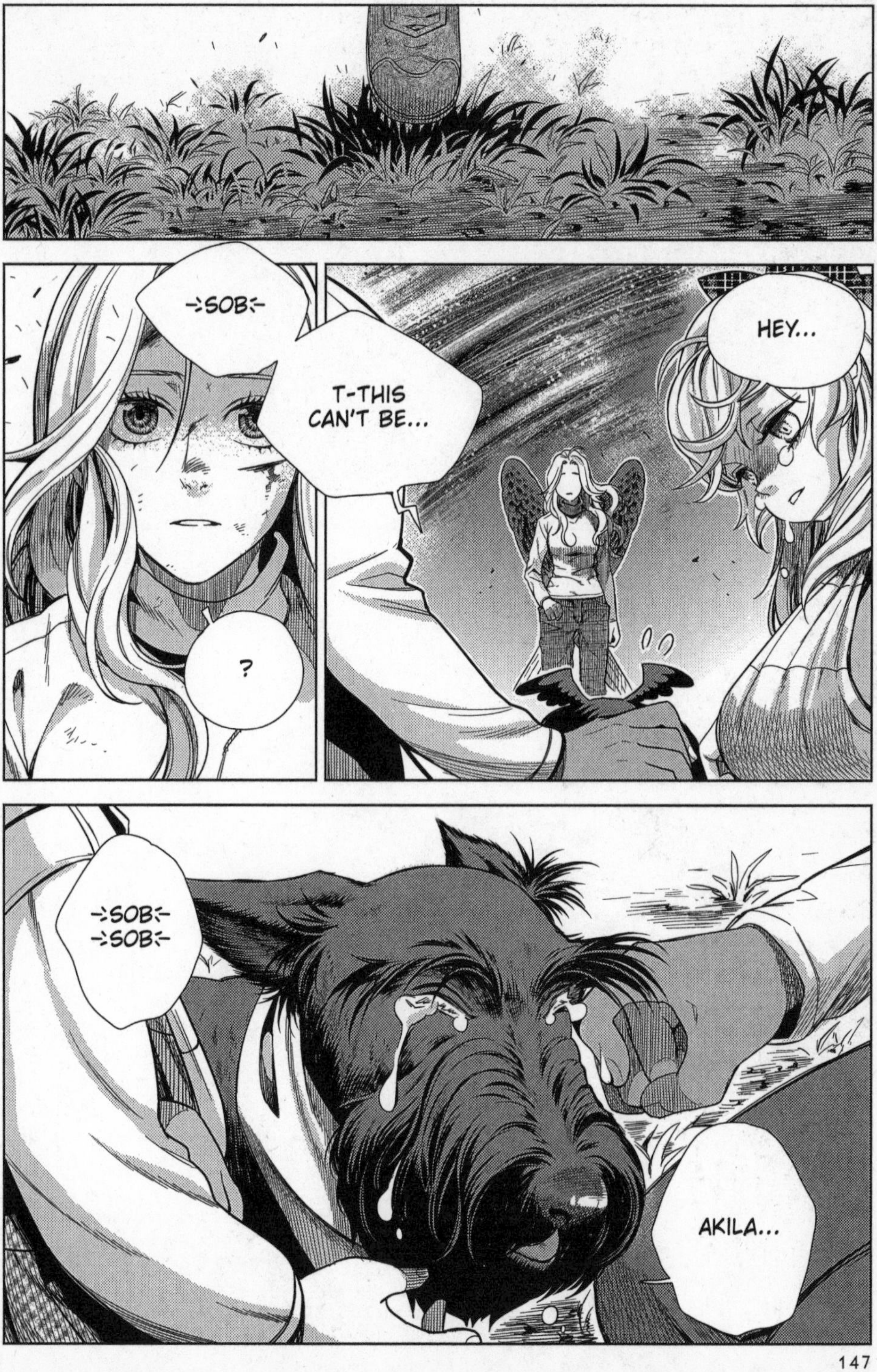

-SOB-
T-THIS CAN'T BE...
?
HEY...
-SOB-
-SOB-
AKILA...

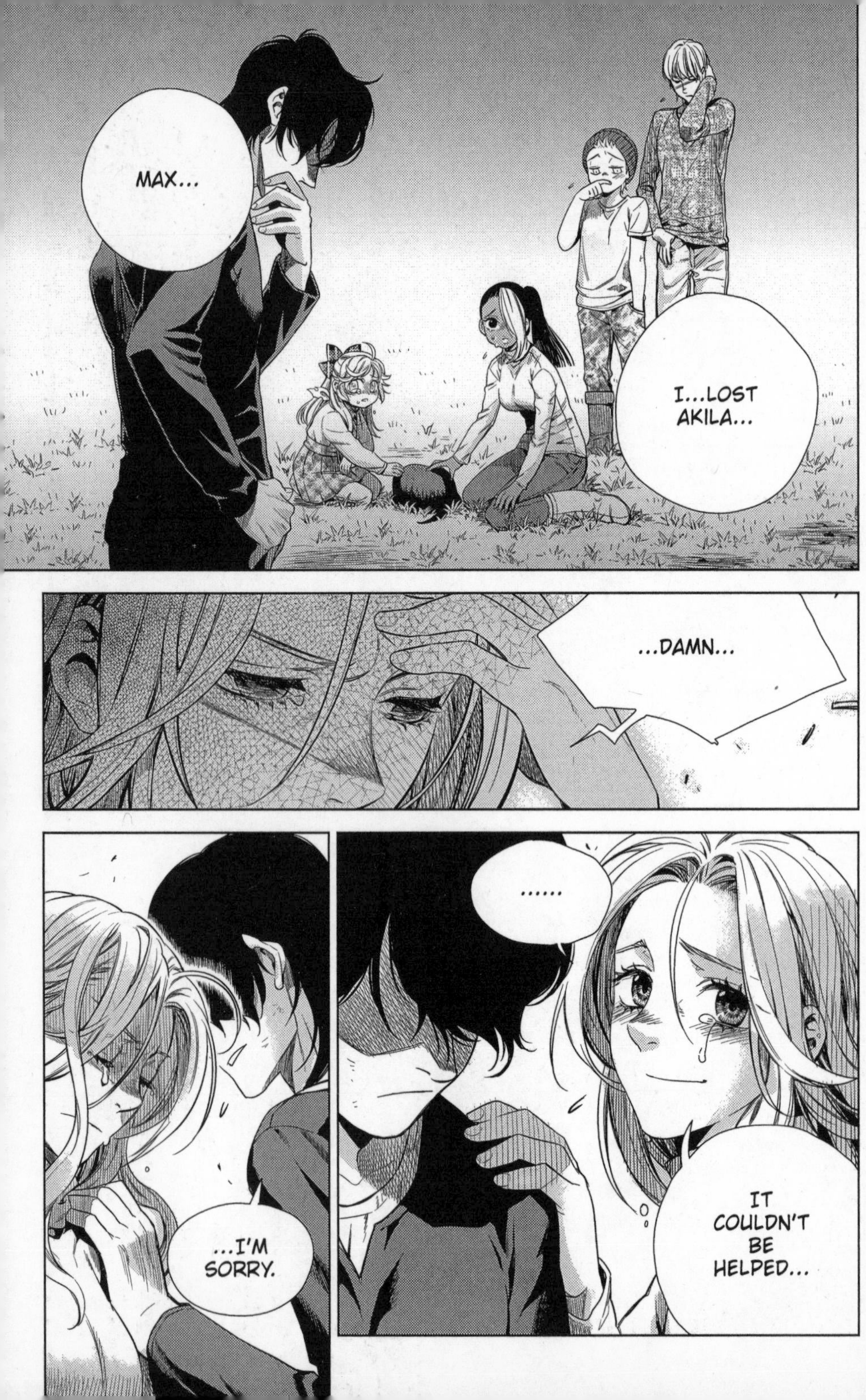
MAX...
I...LOST AKILA...
...DAMN...
...I'M SORRY.
......
IT COULDN'T BE HELPED...

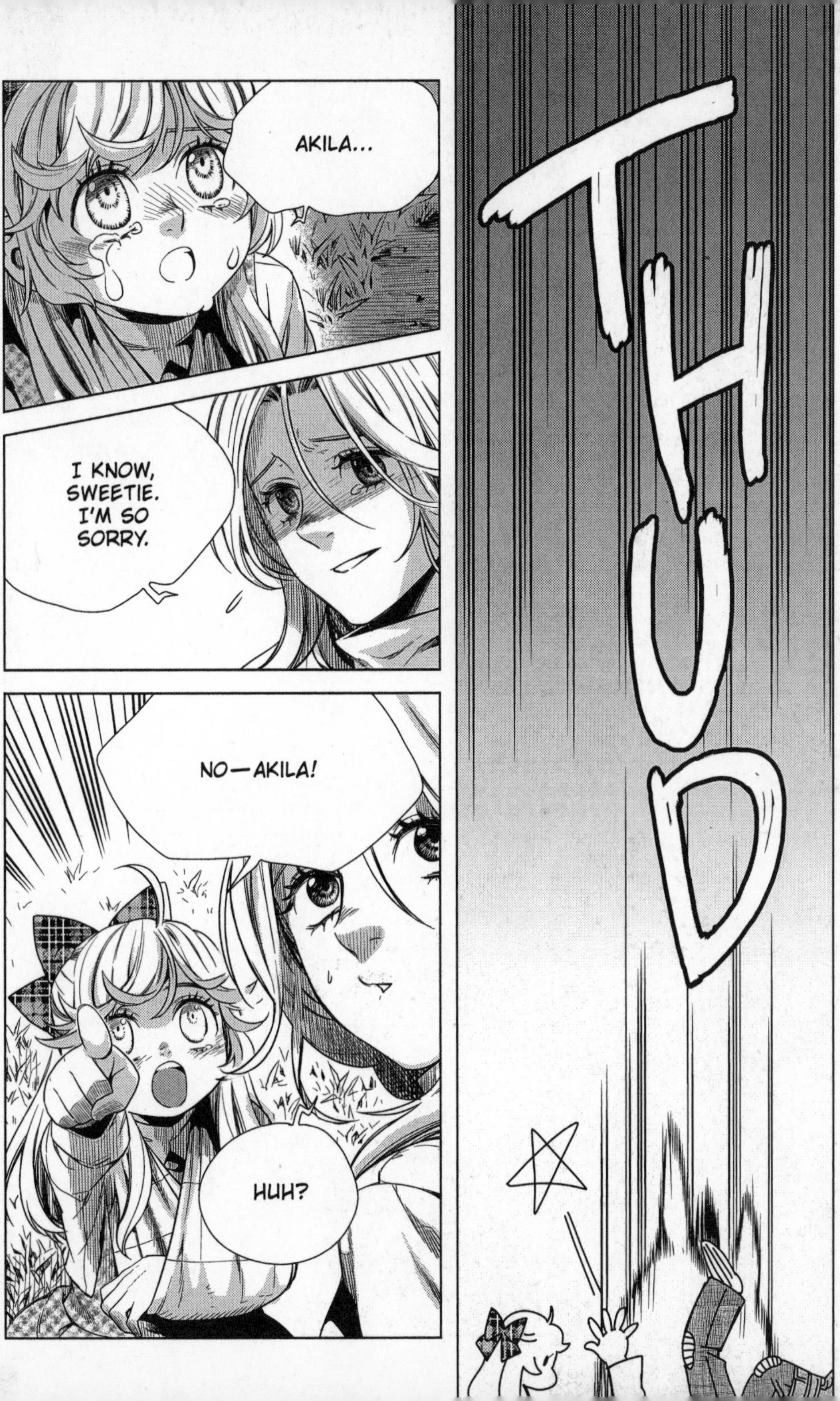
AKILA...
I KNOW, SWEETIE. I'M SO SORRY.
NO—AKILA!
HUH?
THUD

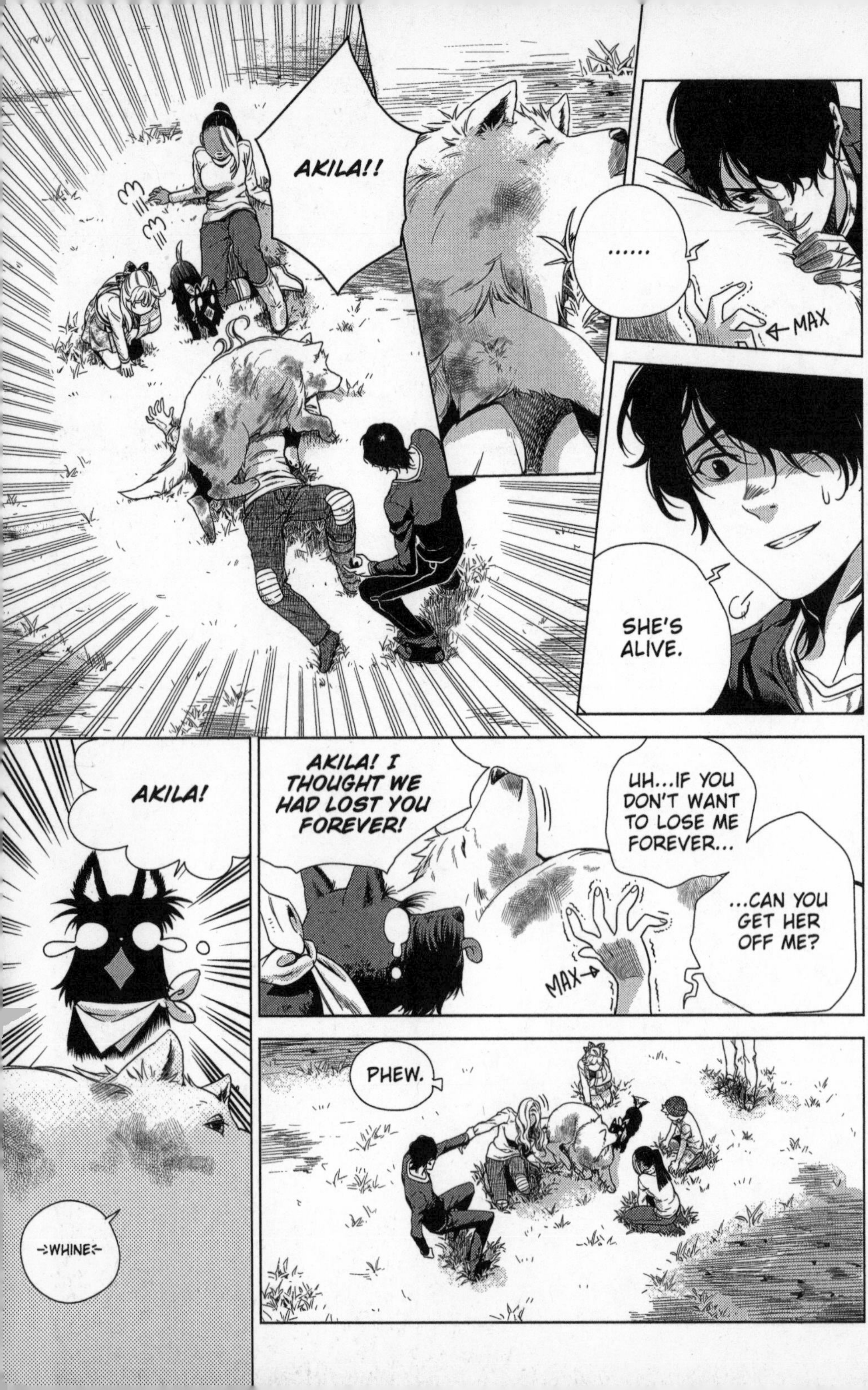
AKILA!!
......
MAX
SHE'S ALIVE.
AKILA!
-WHINE-
AKILA! I THOUGHT WE HAD LOST YOU FOREVER!
UH...IF YOU DON'T WANT TO LOSE ME FOREVER...
...CAN YOU GET HER OFF ME?
MAX
PHEW.

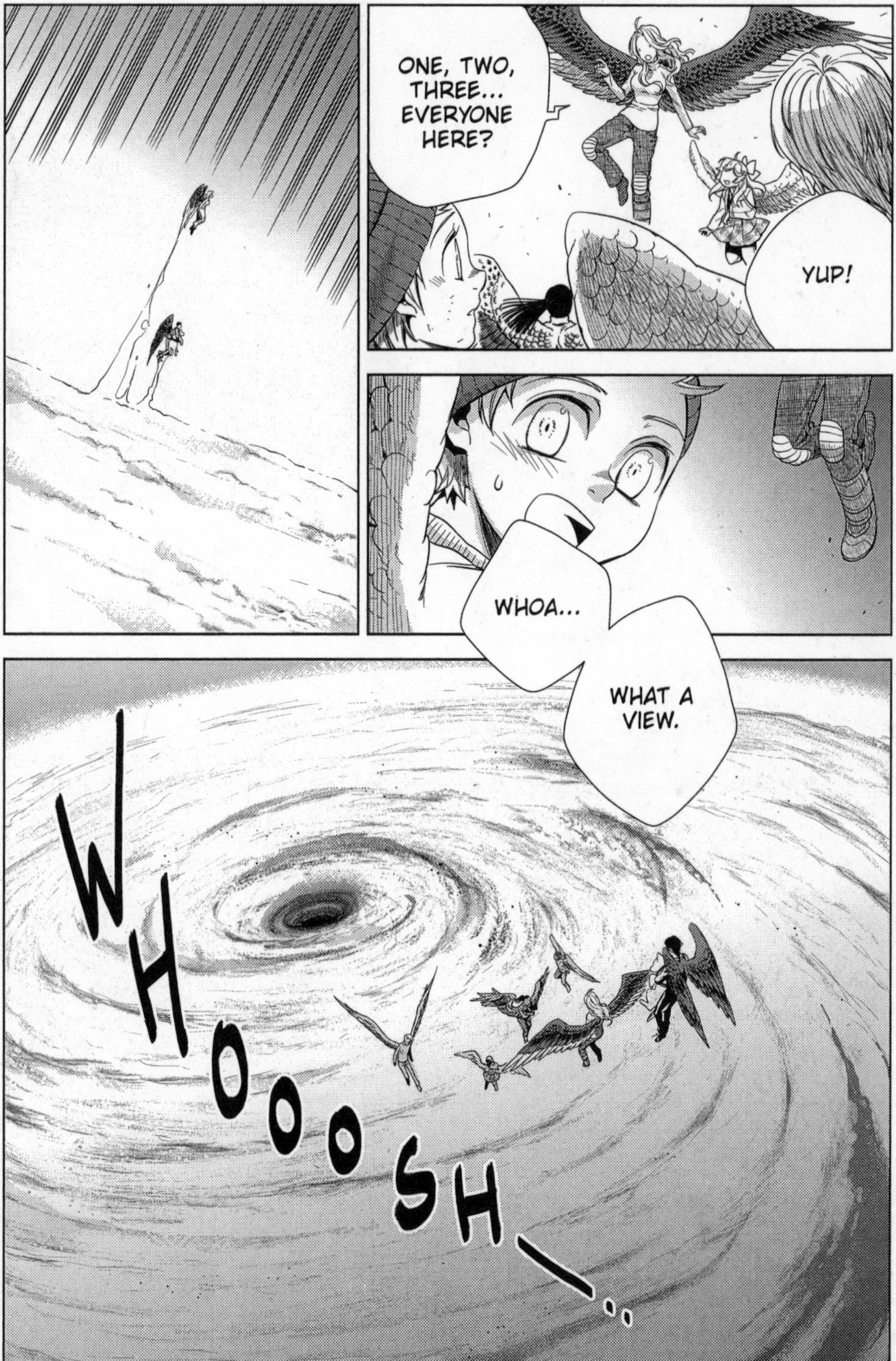
ONE, TWO, THREE... EVERYONE HERE?
YUP!
WHOA...
WHAT A VIEW.
WHOOOSH...

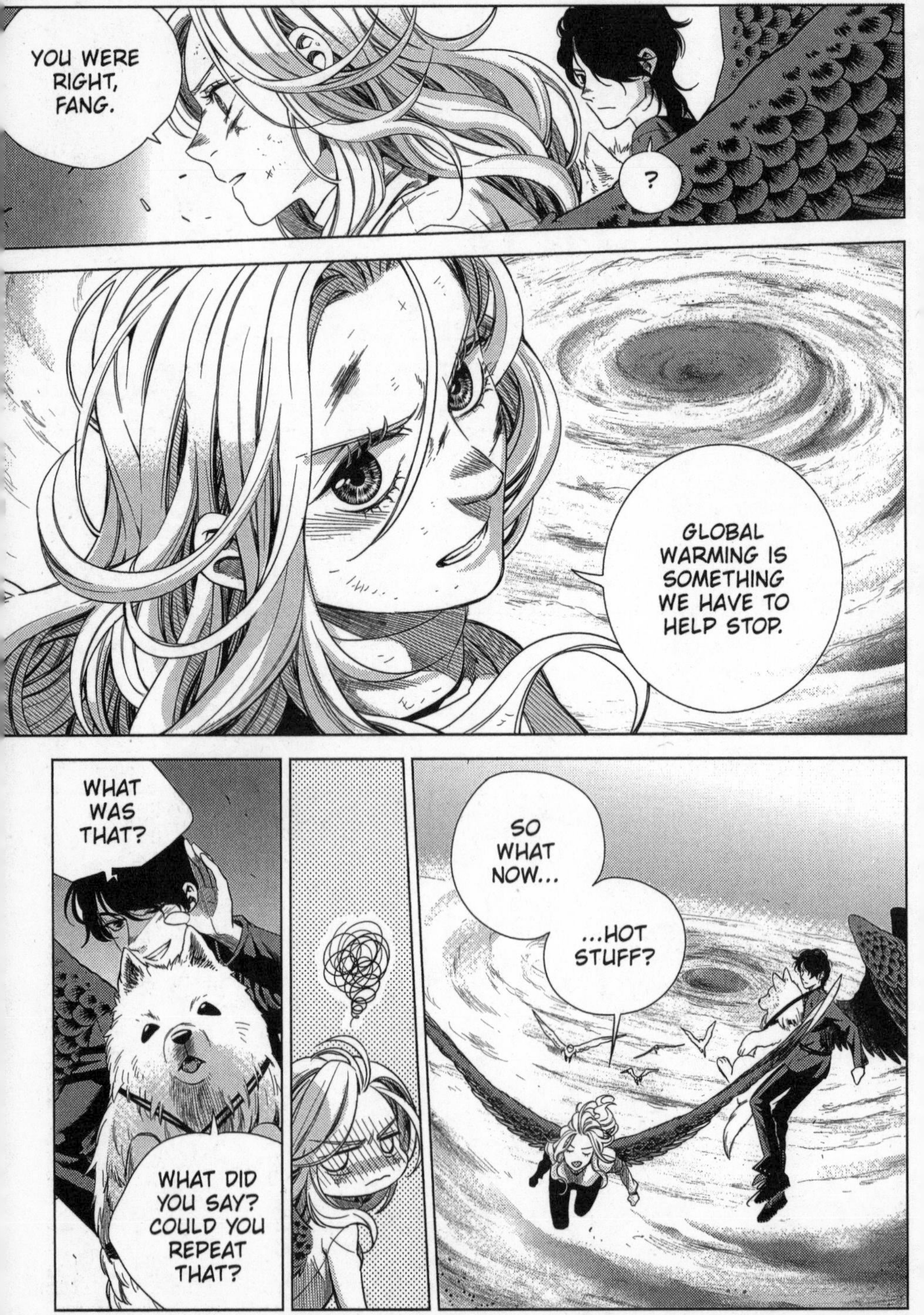
YOU WERE RIGHT, FANG.
?
GLOBAL WARMING IS SOMETHING WE HAVE TO HELP STOP.
WHAT WAS THAT?
WHAT DID YOU SAY? COULD YOU REPEAT THAT?
SO WHAT NOW...
...HOT STUFF?

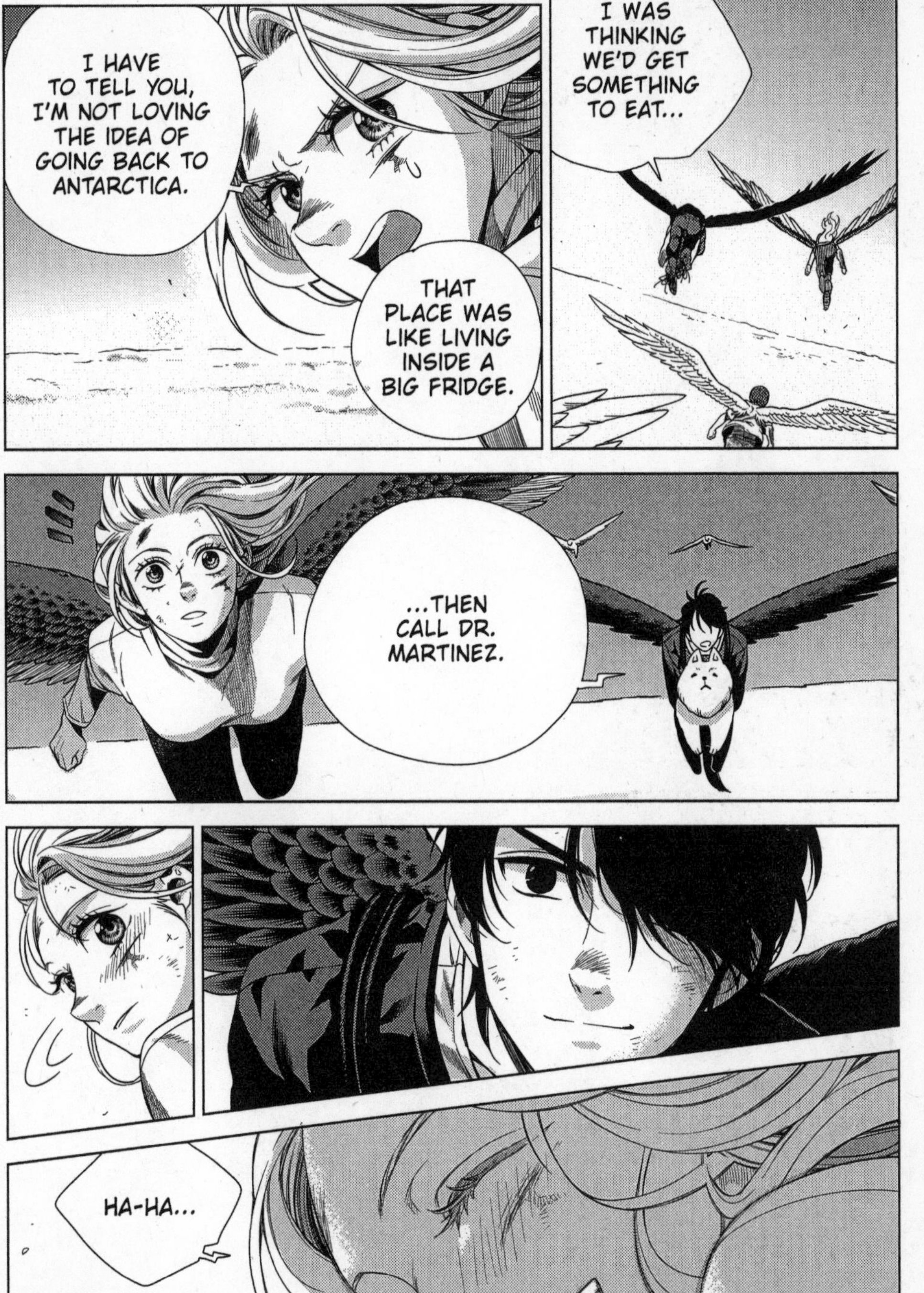
I HAVE TO TELL YOU, I'M NOT LOVING THE IDEA OF GOING BACK TO ANTARCTICA.
THAT PLACE WAS LIKE LIVING INSIDE A BIG FRIDGE.
I WAS THINKING WE'D GET SOMETHING TO EAT...
...THEN CALL DR. MARTINEZ.
HA-HA...

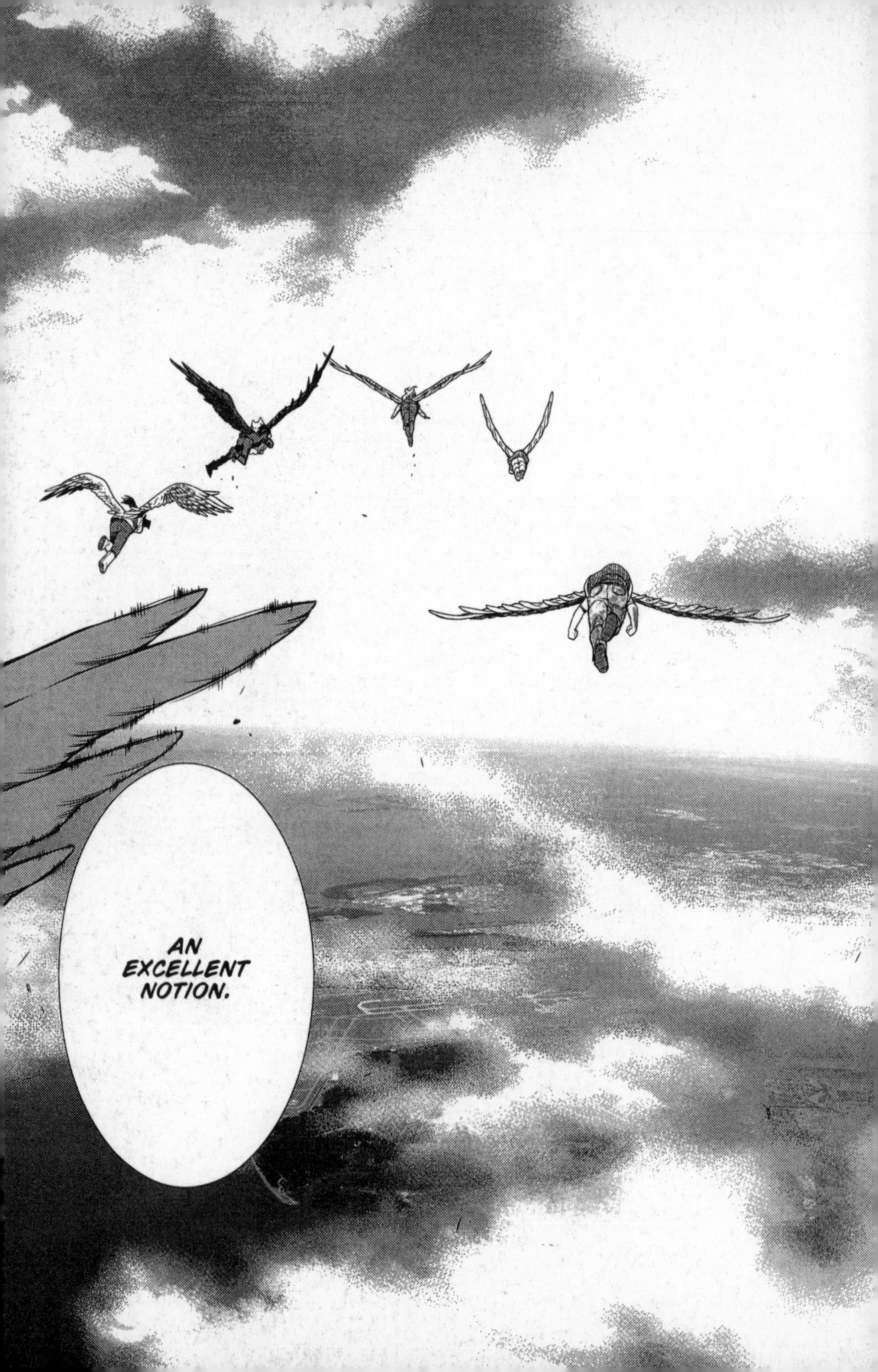
AN EXCELLENT NOTION.

MAXIMUM RIDE

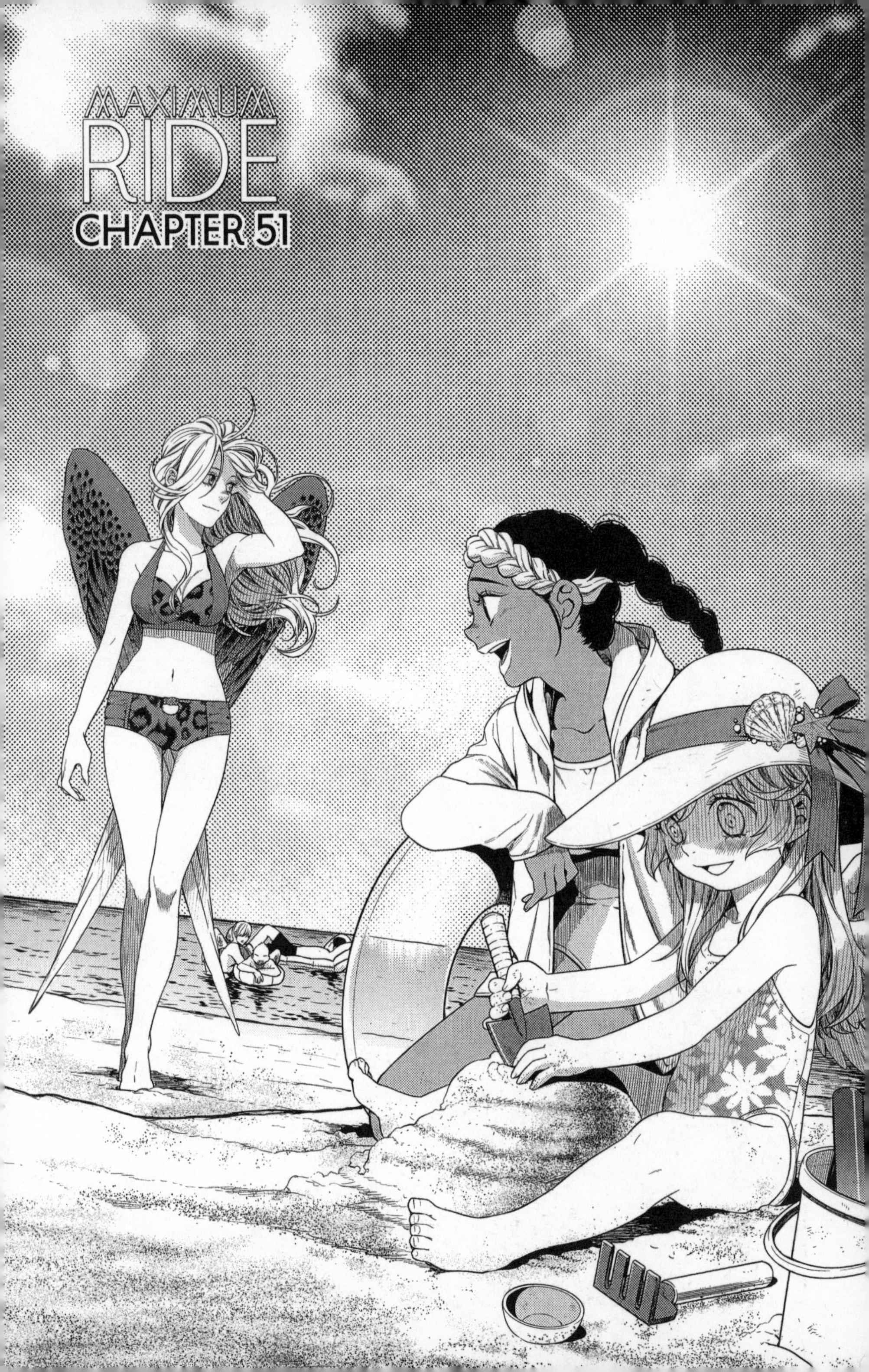
MAXIMUM
RIDE
CHAPTER 51

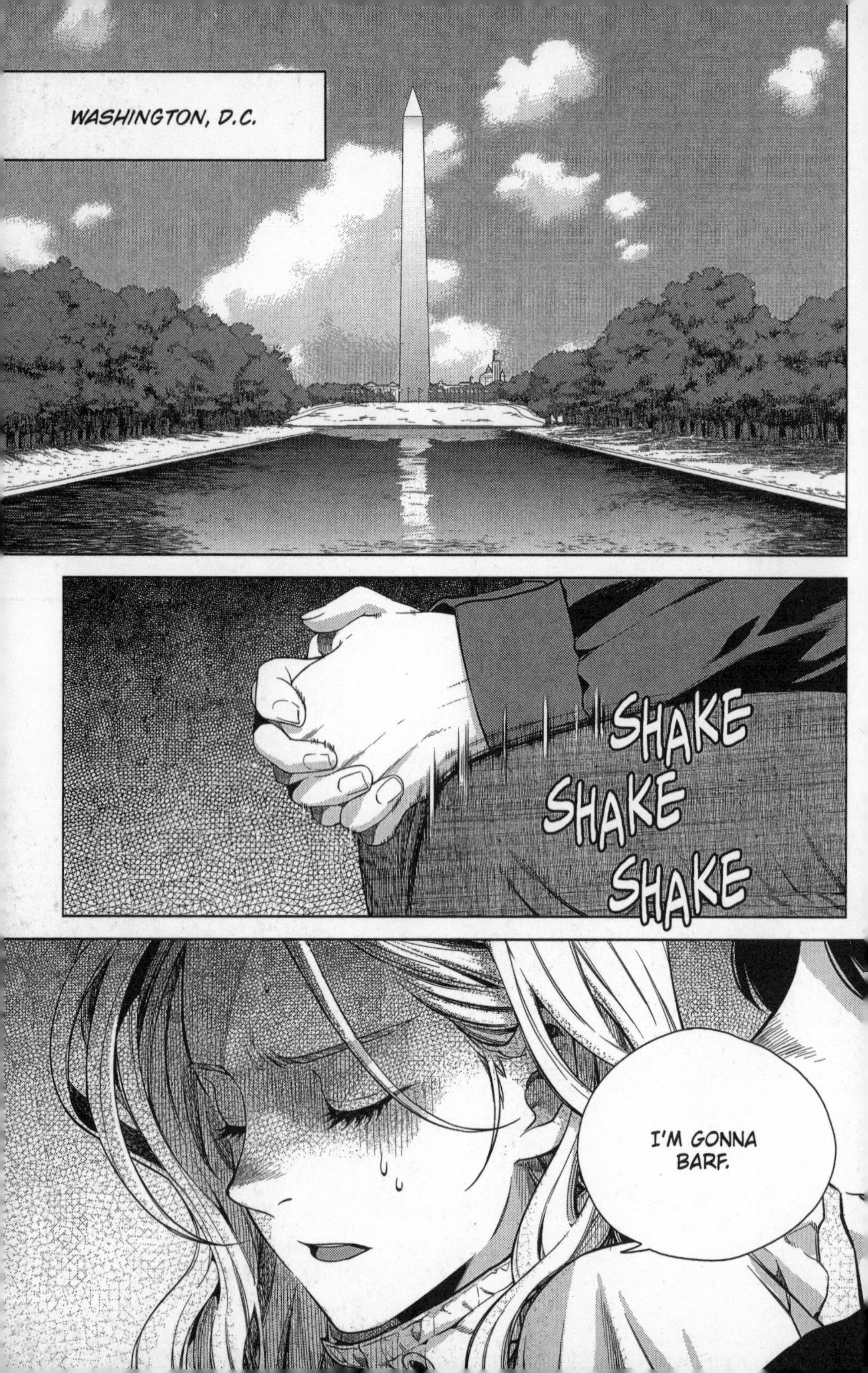
WASHINGTON, D.C.
SHAKE SHAKE SHAKE
I'M GONNA BARF.

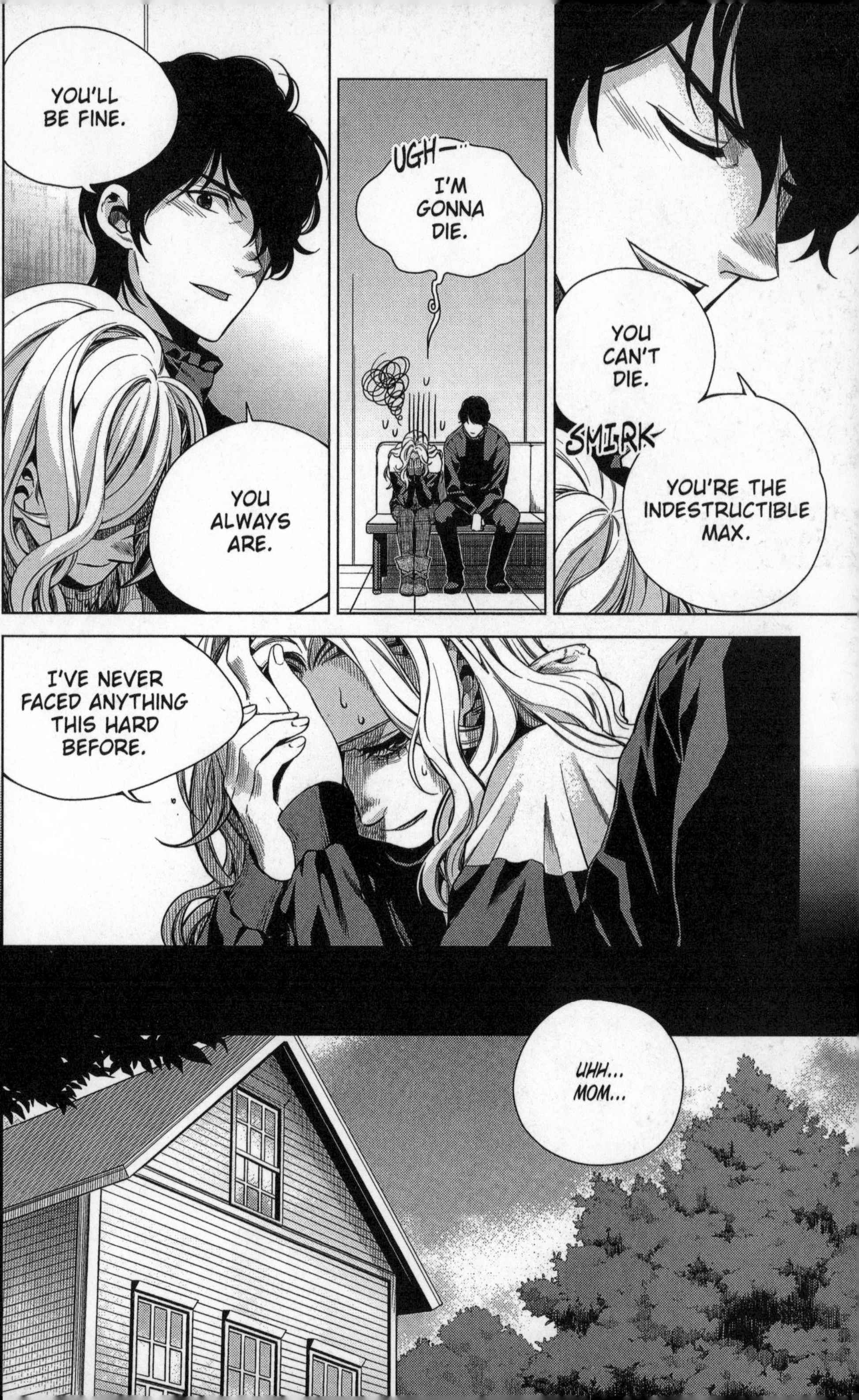
YOU'LL BE FINE.
YOU ALWAYS ARE.
UGH—..
I'M GONNA DIE.
YOU CAN'T DIE.
SMIRK
YOU'RE THE INDESTRUCTIBLE MAX.
I'VE NEVER FACED ANYTHING THIS HARD BEFORE.
UHH... MOM...

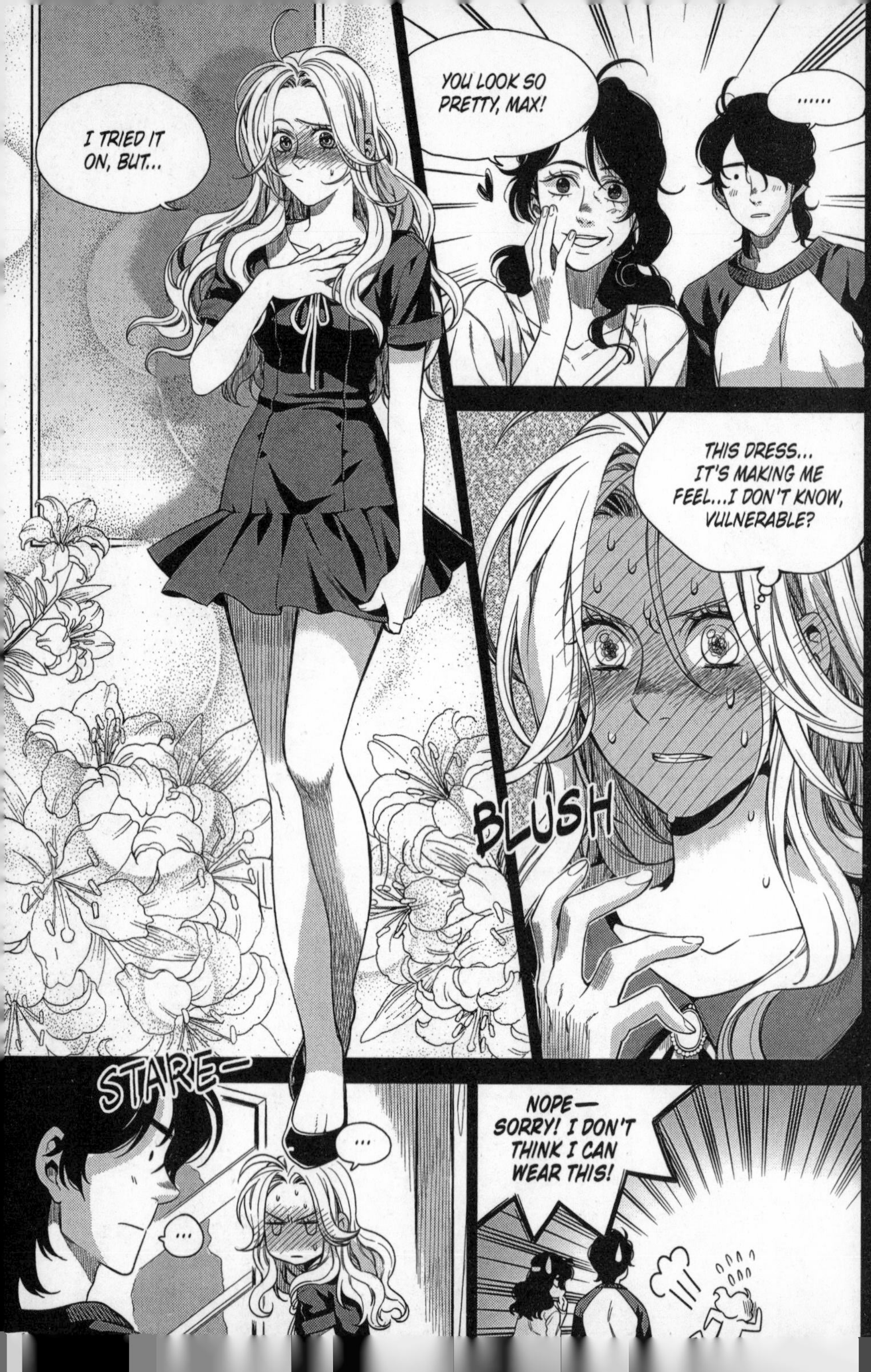
I TRIED IT ON, BUT...
YOU LOOK SO PRETTY, MAX!
......
THIS DRESS... IT'S MAKING ME FEEL...I DON'T KNOW, VULNERABLE?
BLUSH
STARE—
...
...
NOPE— SORRY! I DON'T THINK I CAN WEAR THIS!

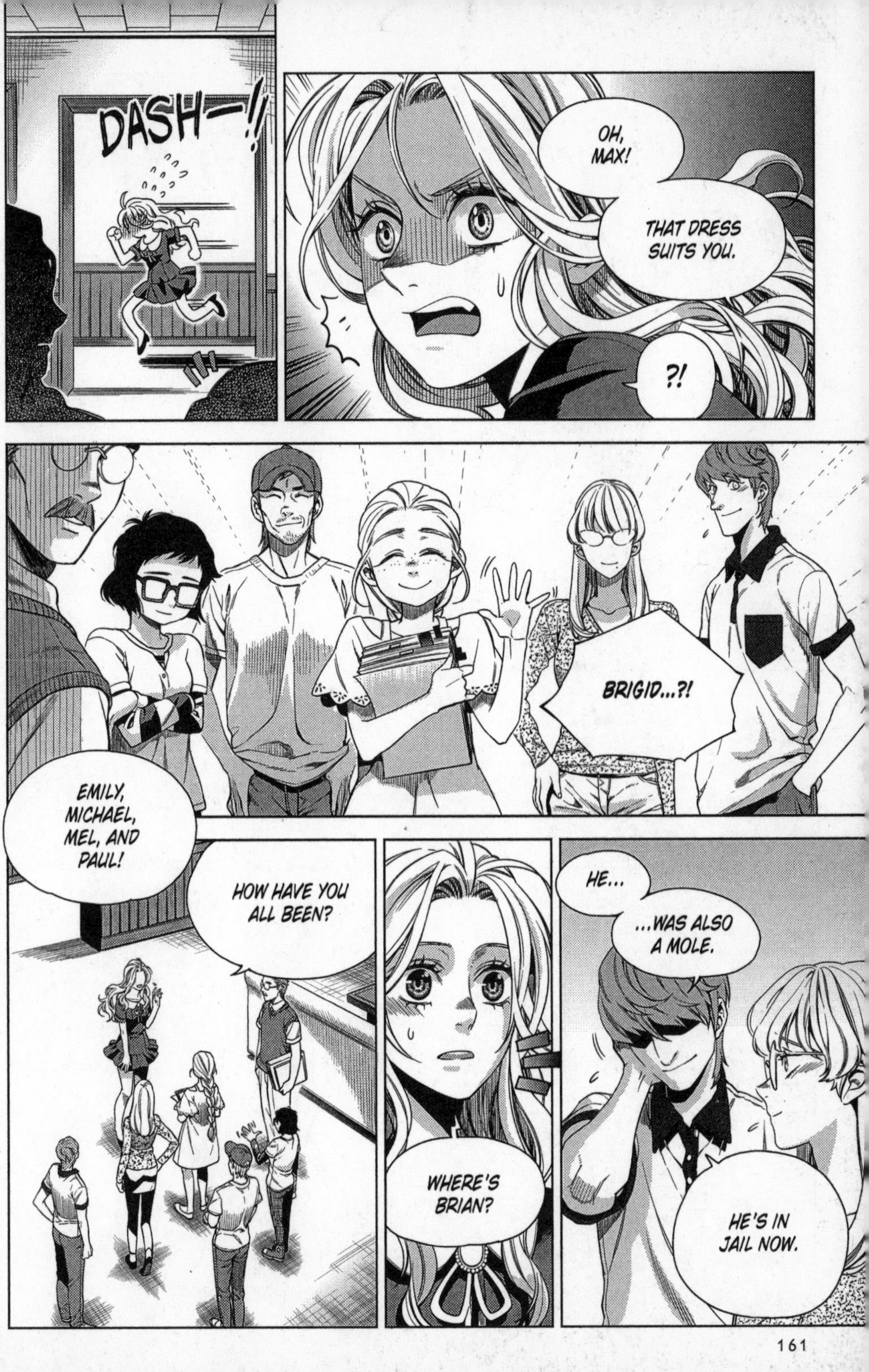
DASH—!!
OH, MAX!
THAT DRESS SUITS YOU.
?!
BRIGID...?!
EMILY, MICHAEL, MEL, AND PAUL!
HOW HAVE YOU ALL BEEN?
WHERE'S BRIAN?
HE...
...WAS ALSO A MOLE.
HE'S IN JAIL NOW.

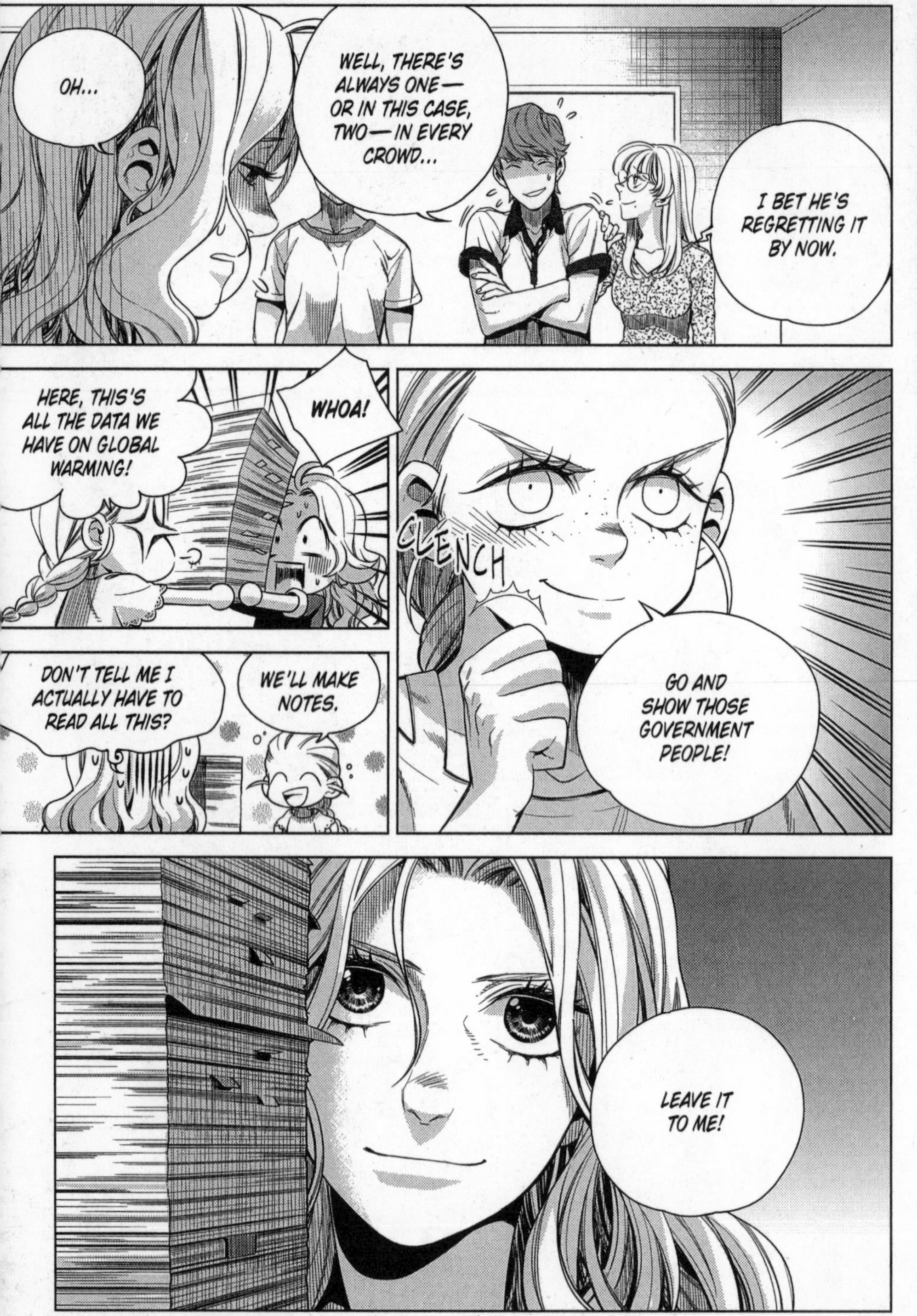
OH...
WELL, THERE'S ALWAYS ONE—OR IN THIS CASE, TWO—IN EVERY CROWD...
I BET HE'S REGRETTING IT BY NOW.
HERE, THIS'S ALL THE DATA WE HAVE ON GLOBAL WARMING!
WHOA!
DON'T TELL ME I ACTUALLY HAVE TO READ ALL THIS?
WE'LL MAKE NOTES.
CLENCH
GO AND SHOW THOSE GOVERNMENT PEOPLE!
LEAVE IT TO ME!

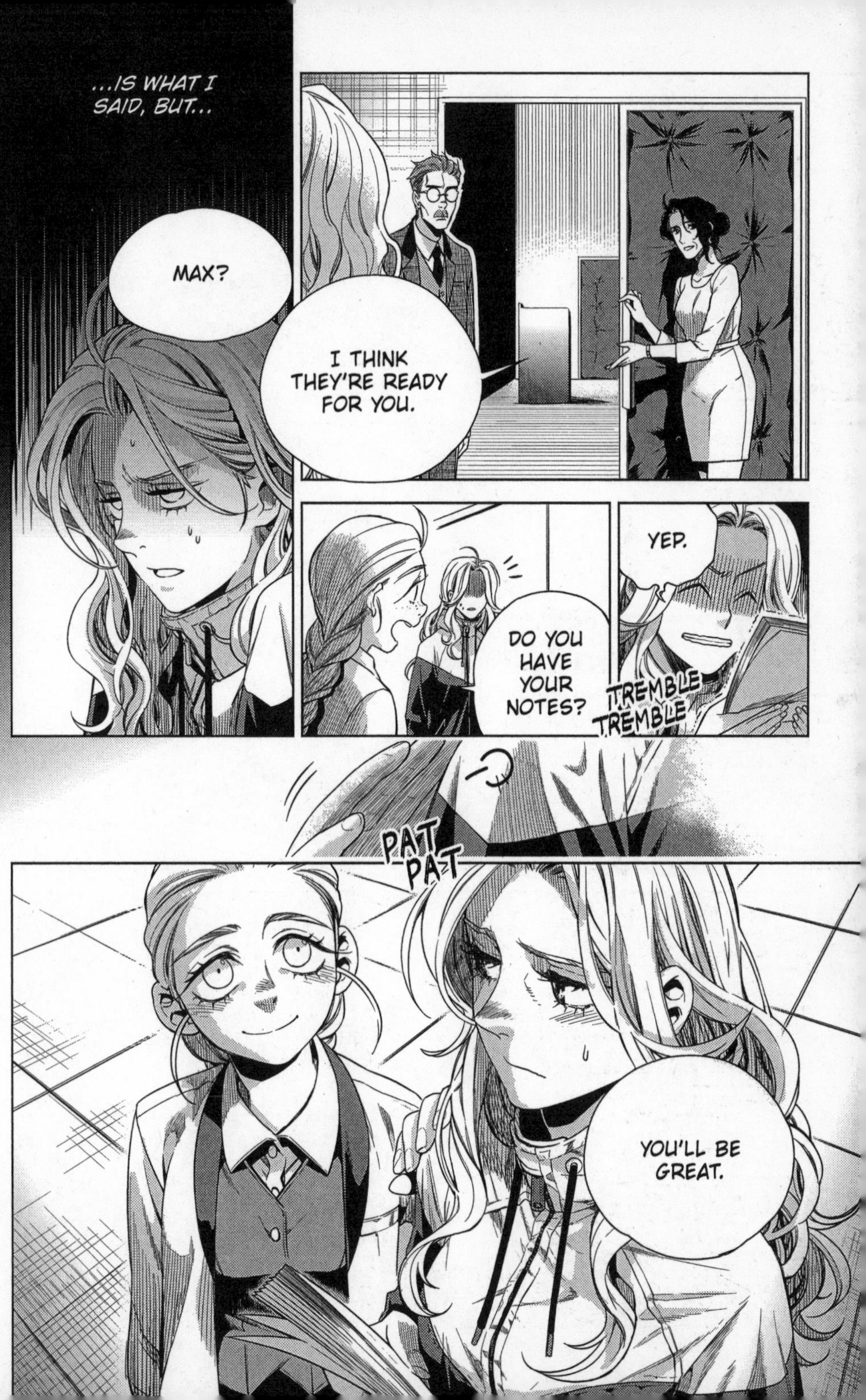

...IS WHAT I SAID, BUT...
MAX?
I THINK THEY'RE READY FOR YOU.
DO YOU HAVE YOUR NOTES?
YEP.
TREMBLE TREMBLE
PAT PAT
YOU'LL BE GREAT.

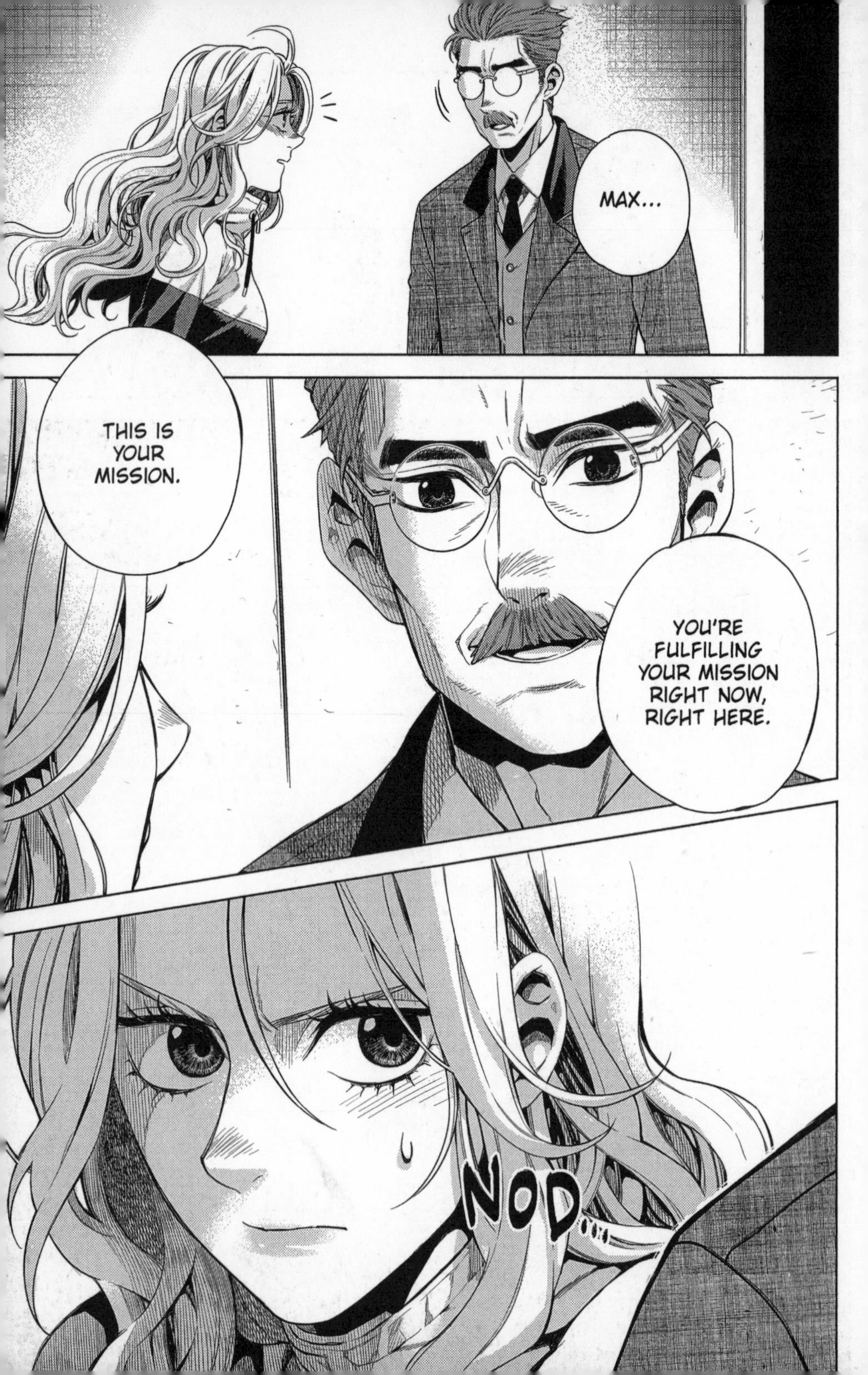
MAX...
THIS IS YOUR MISSION.
YOU'RE FULFILLING YOUR MISSION RIGHT NOW, RIGHT HERE.
NOD

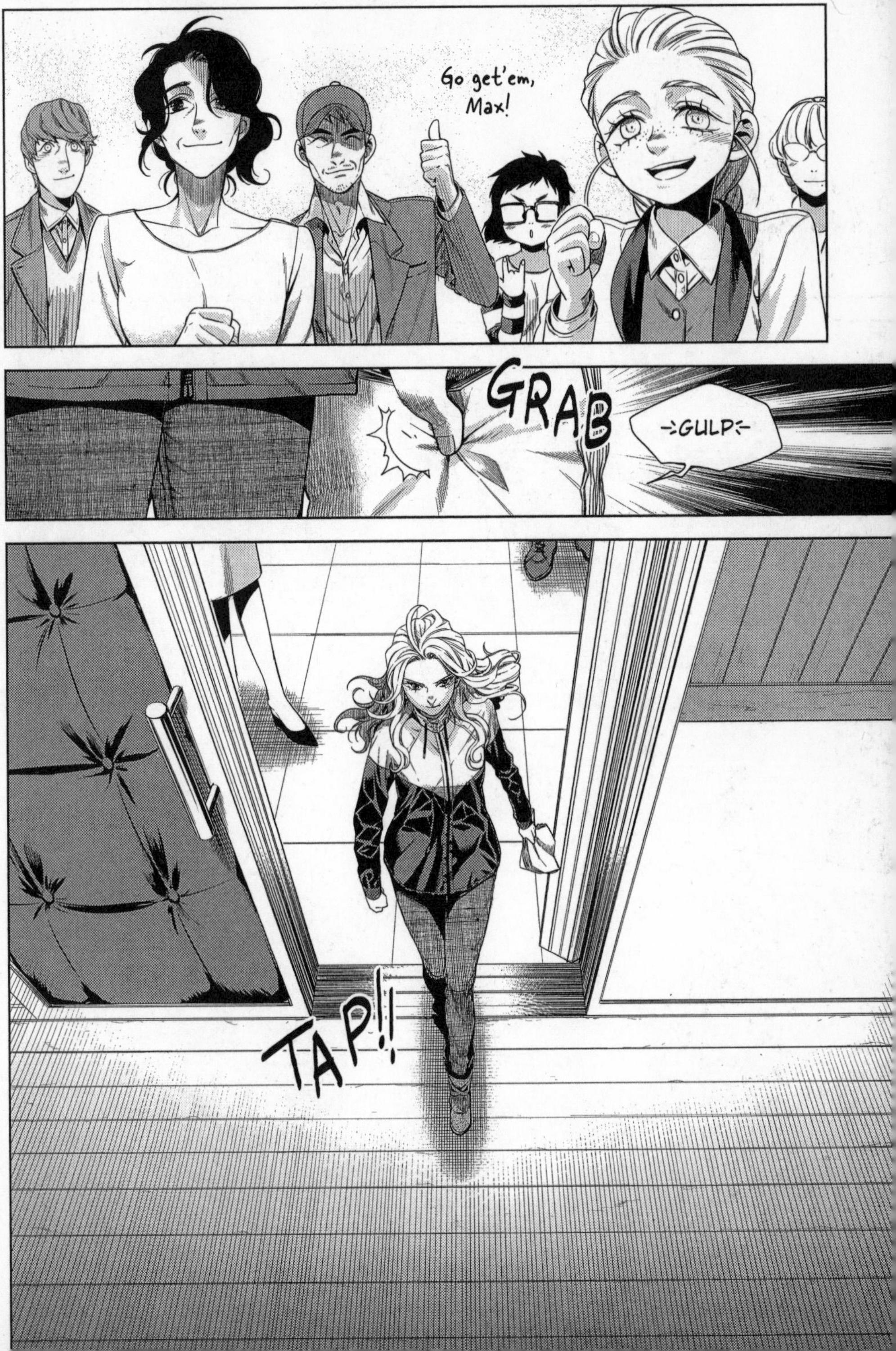
Go get'em, Max!
GRAB
-GULP-
TAP!!

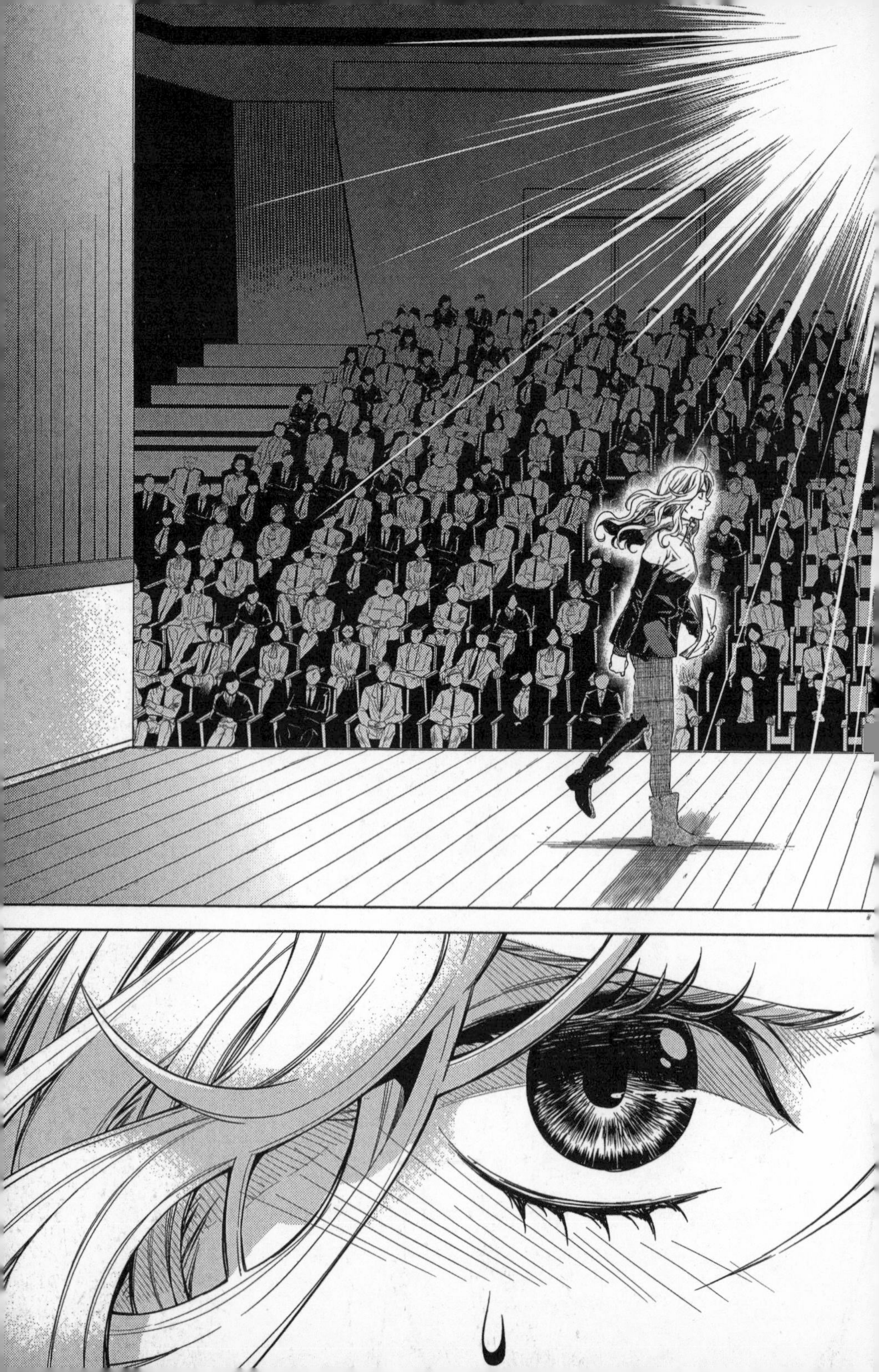

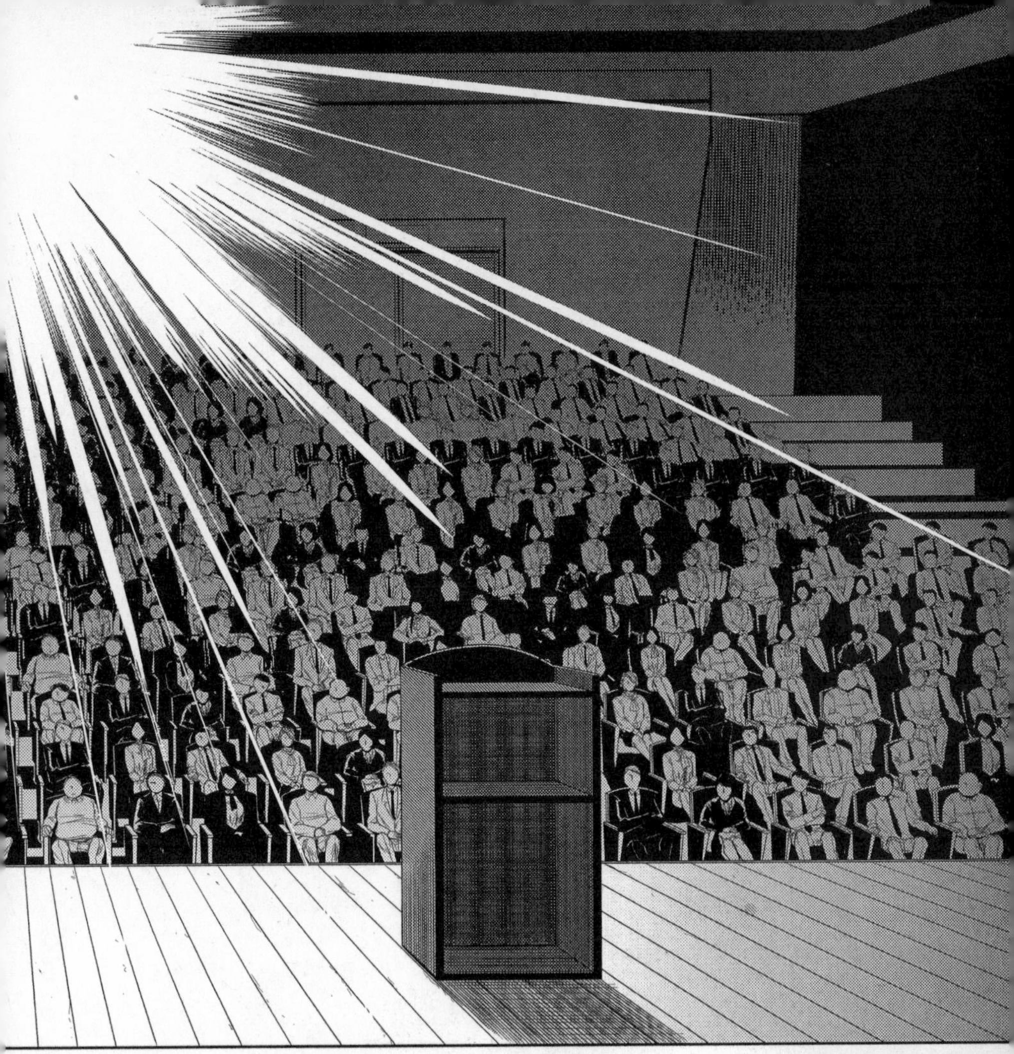
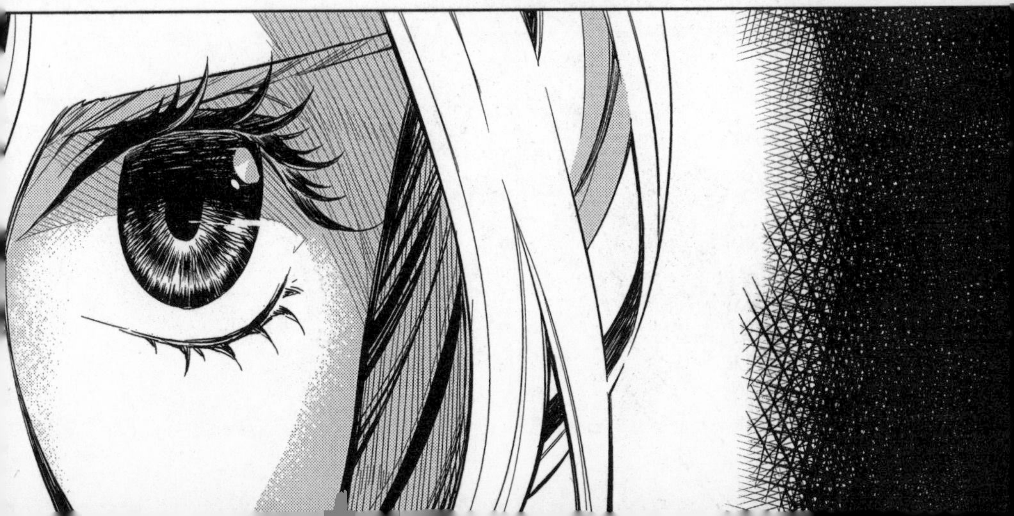

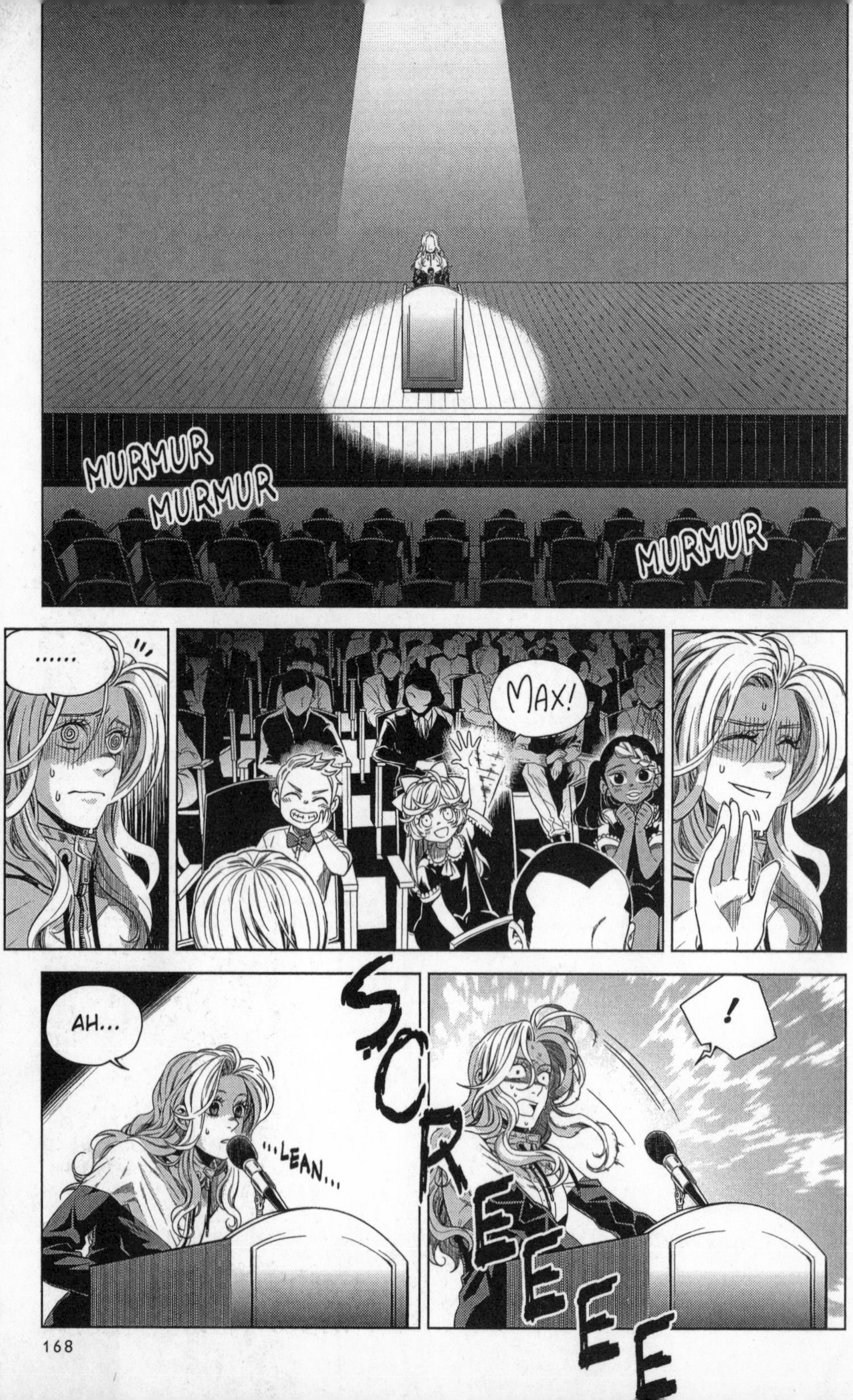
MURMUR
MURMUR
MURMUR
......
MAX!
AH...
...LEAN...
SCREEEEE
!

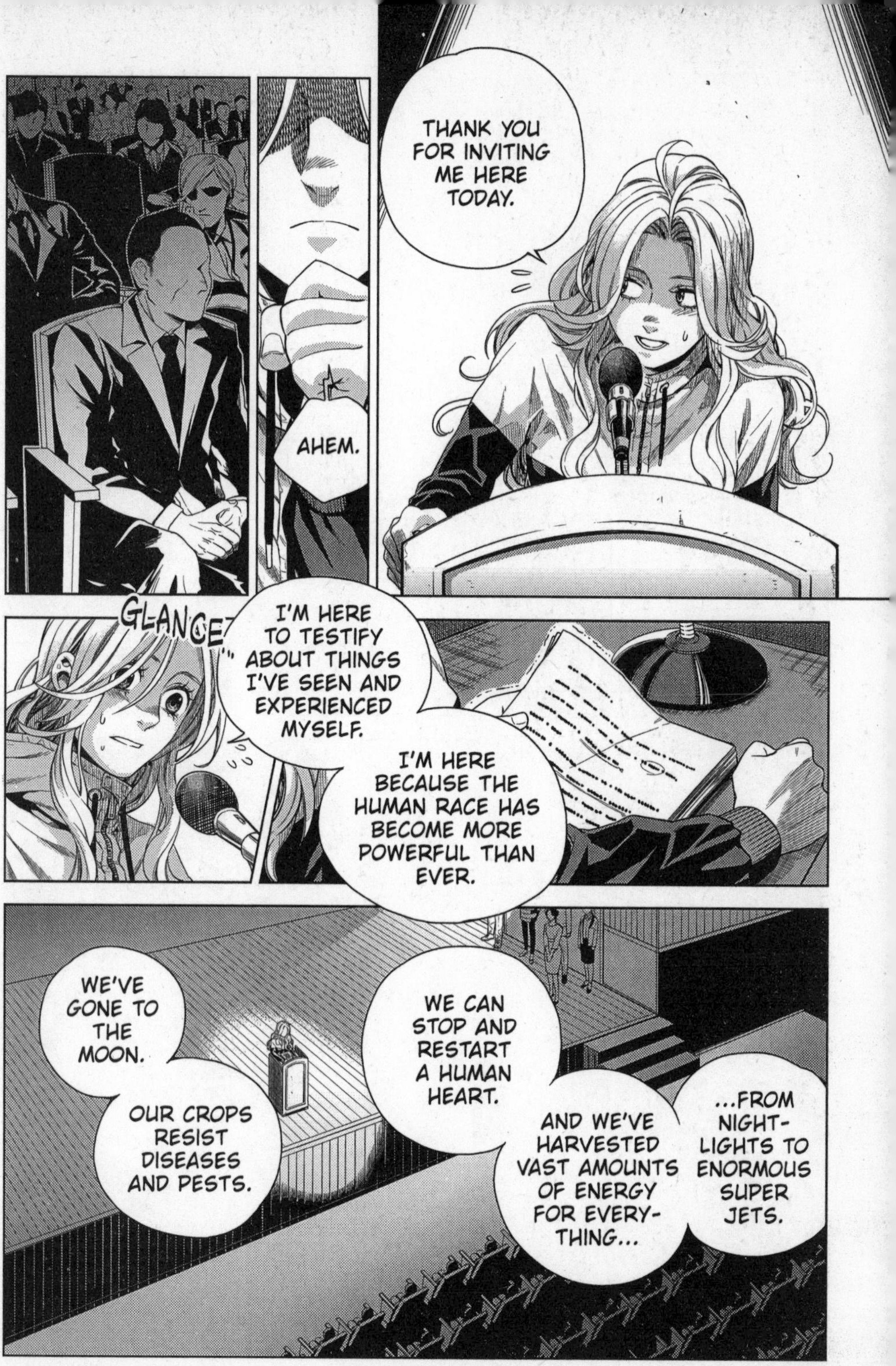
AHEM.
THANK YOU FOR INVITING ME HERE TODAY.
GLANCE
I'M HERE TO TESTIFY ABOUT THINGS I'VE SEEN AND EXPERIENCED MYSELF.
I'M HERE BECAUSE THE HUMAN RACE HAS BECOME MORE POWERFUL THAN EVER.
WE'VE GONE TO THE MOON.
OUR CROPS RESIST DISEASES AND PESTS.
WE CAN STOP AND RESTART A HUMAN HEART.
AND WE'VE HARVESTED VAST AMOUNTS OF ENERGY FOR EVERY-THING...
...FROM NIGHT-LIGHTS TO ENORMOUS SUPER JETS.

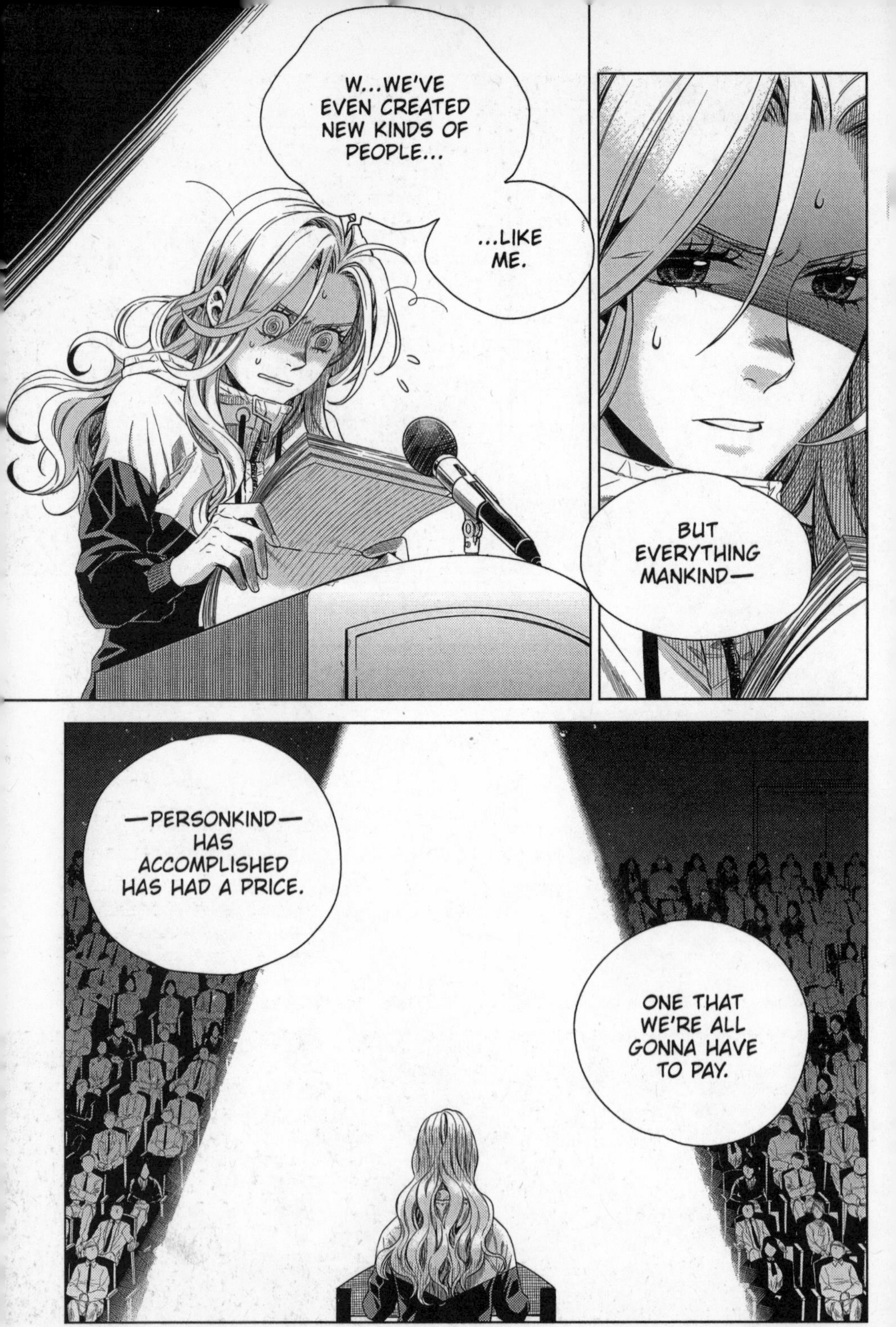
W...WE'VE EVEN CREATED NEW KINDS OF PEOPLE...
...LIKE ME.
BUT EVERYTHING MANKIND—
—PERSONKIND— HAS ACCOMPLISHED HAS HAD A PRICE.
ONE THAT WE'RE ALL GONNA HAVE TO PAY.

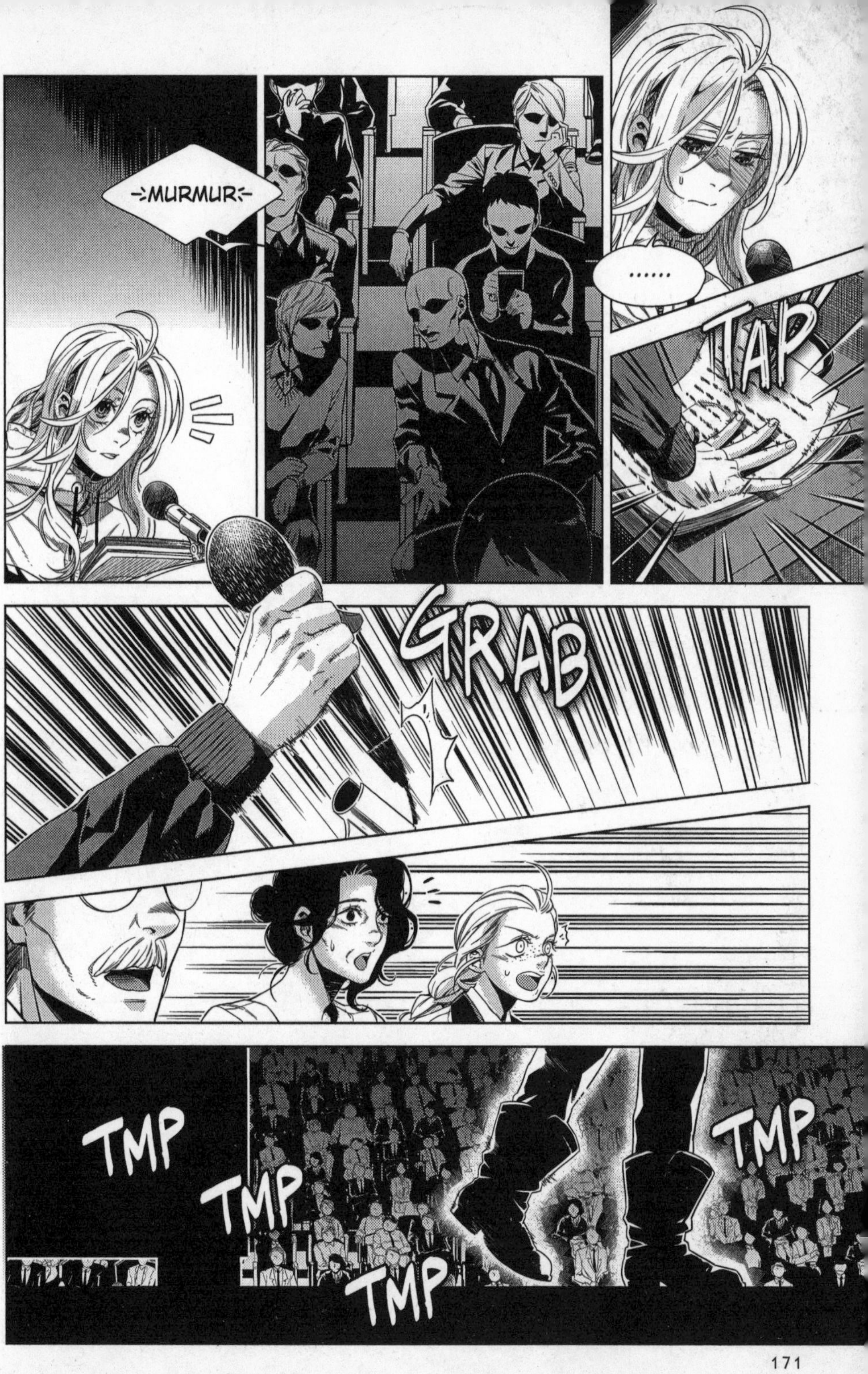
-MURMUR-
......
TAP
GRAB
TMP
TMP
TMP
TMP

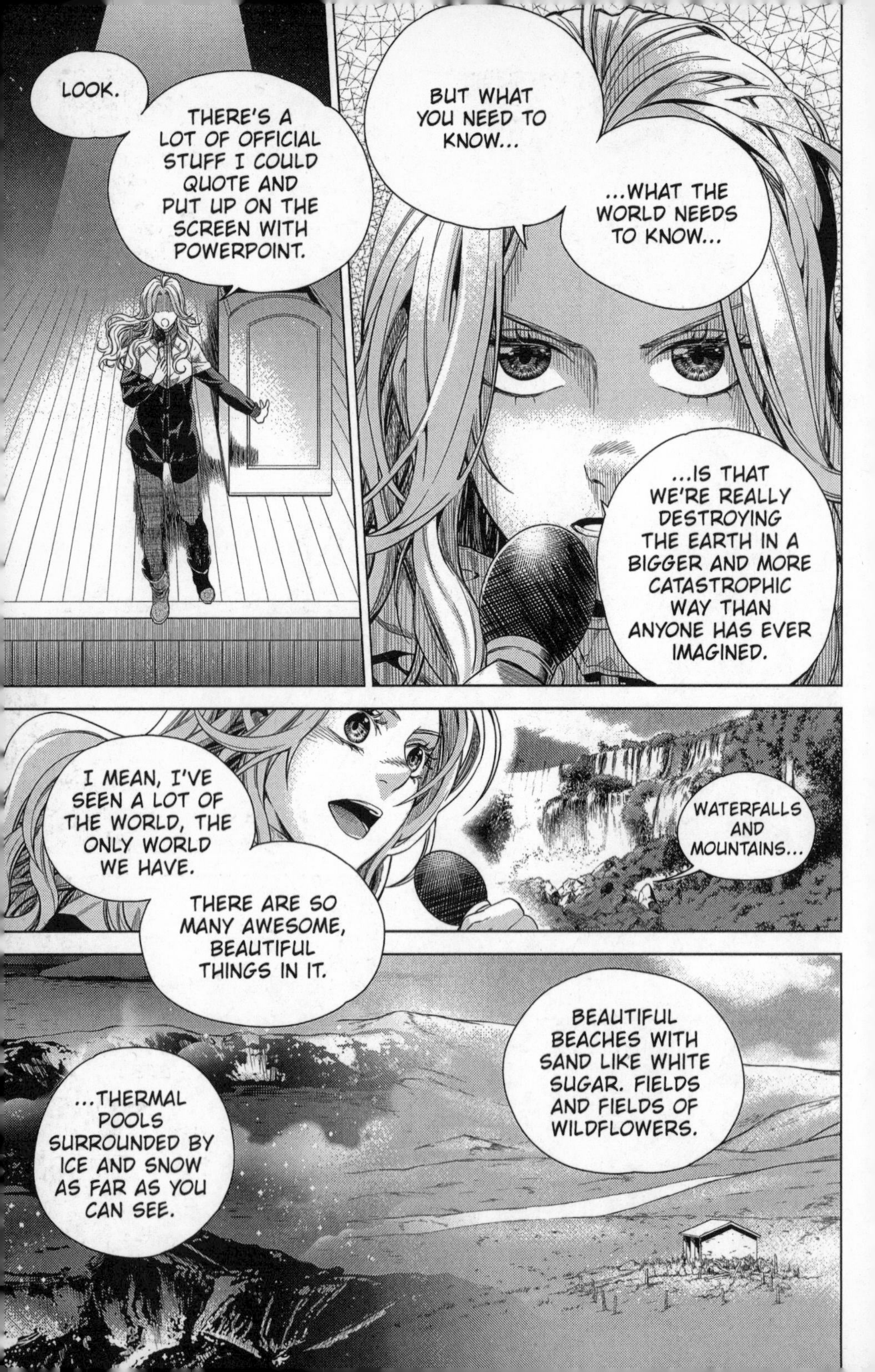
LOOK.
THERE'S A LOT OF OFFICIAL STUFF I COULD QUOTE AND PUT UP ON THE SCREEN WITH POWERPOINT.
BUT WHAT YOU NEED TO KNOW...
...WHAT THE WORLD NEEDS TO KNOW...
...IS THAT WE'RE REALLY DESTROYING THE EARTH IN A BIGGER AND MORE CATASTROPHIC WAY THAN ANYONE HAS EVER IMAGINED.
I MEAN, I'VE SEEN A LOT OF THE WORLD, THE ONLY WORLD WE HAVE.
THERE ARE SO MANY AWESOME, BEAUTIFUL THINGS IN IT.
WATERFALLS AND MOUNTAINS...
...THERMAL POOLS SURROUNDED BY ICE AND SNOW AS FAR AS YOU CAN SEE.
BEAUTIFUL BEACHES WITH SAND LIKE WHITE SUGAR. FIELDS AND FIELDS OF WILDFLOWERS.

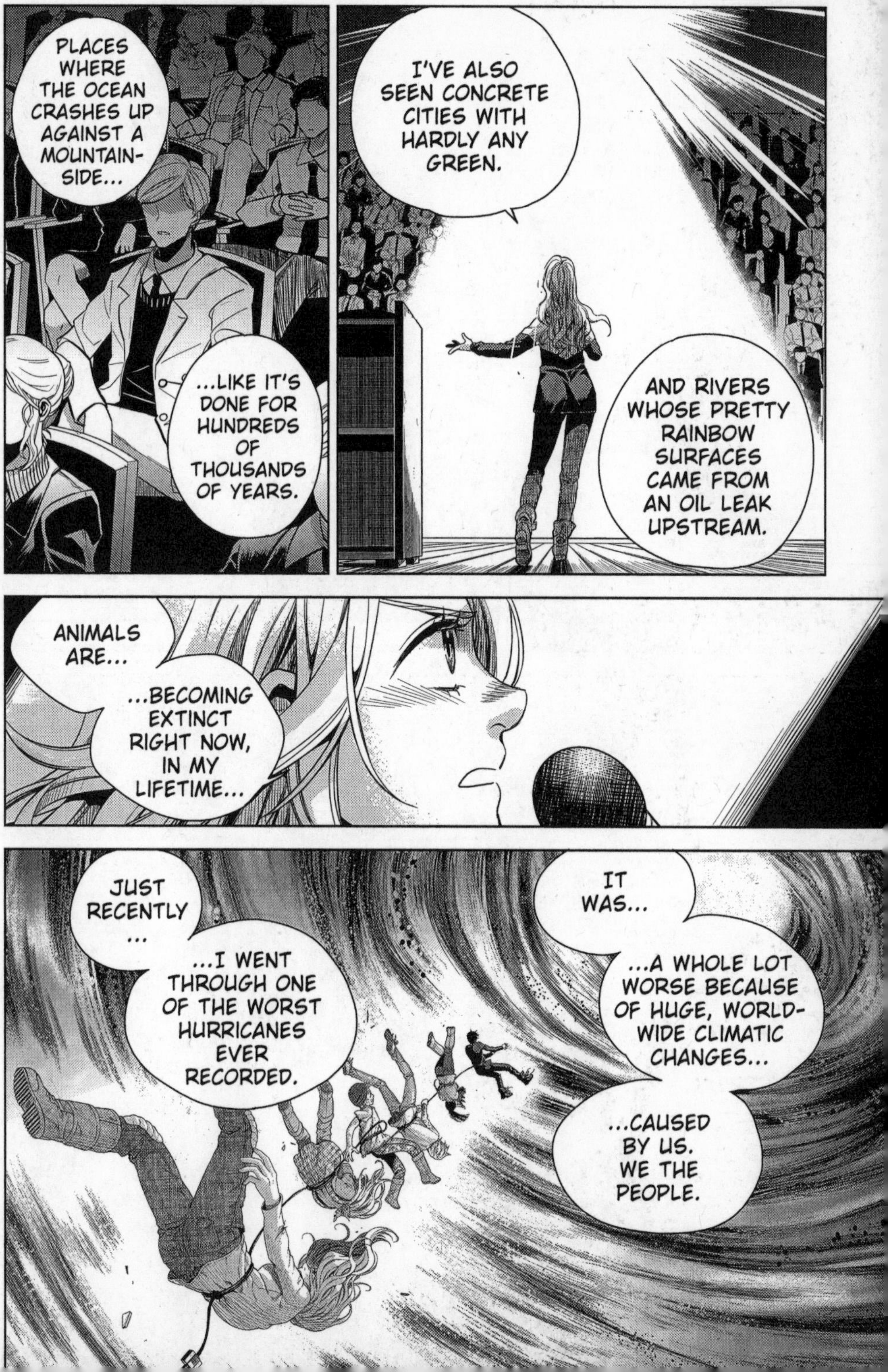
PLACES WHERE THE OCEAN CRASHES UP AGAINST A MOUNTAIN-SIDE...
...LIKE IT'S DONE FOR HUNDREDS OF THOUSANDS OF YEARS.
I'VE ALSO SEEN CONCRETE CITIES WITH HARDLY ANY GREEN.
AND RIVERS WHOSE PRETTY RAINBOW SURFACES CAME FROM AN OIL LEAK UPSTREAM.
ANIMALS ARE...
...BECOMING EXTINCT RIGHT NOW, IN MY LIFETIME...
JUST RECENTLY ...
...I WENT THROUGH ONE OF THE WORST HURRICANES EVER RECORDED.
IT WAS...
...A WHOLE LOT WORSE BECAUSE OF HUGE, WORLD-WIDE CLIMATIC CHANGES...
...CAUSED BY US. WE THE PEOPLE.

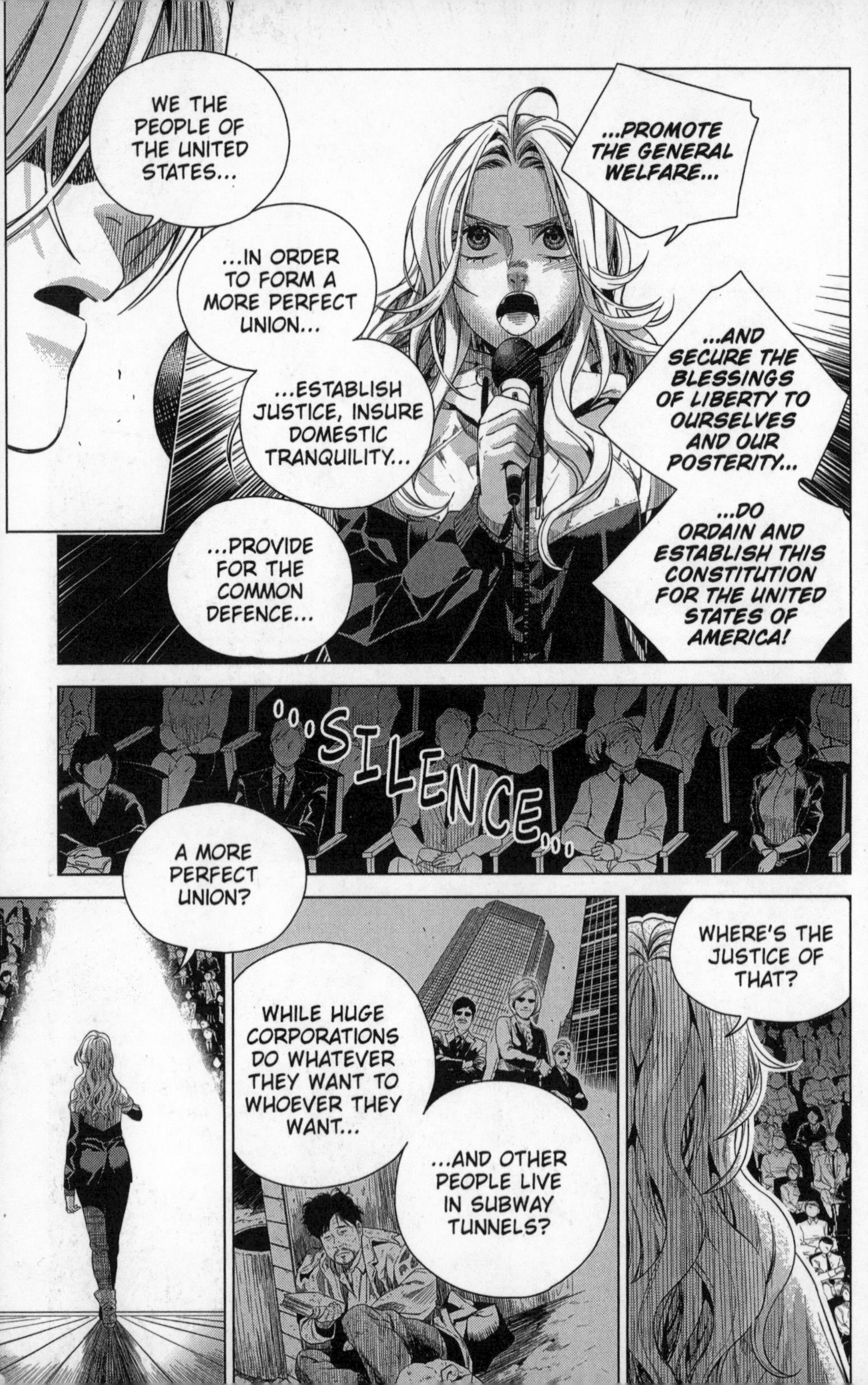
WE THE PEOPLE OF THE UNITED STATES...
...IN ORDER TO FORM A MORE PERFECT UNION...
...ESTABLISH JUSTICE, INSURE DOMESTIC TRANQUILITY...
...PROVIDE FOR THE COMMON DEFENCE...
...PROMOTE THE GENERAL WELFARE...
...AND SECURE THE BLESSINGS OF LIBERTY TO OURSELVES AND OUR POSTERITY...
...DO ORDAIN AND ESTABLISH THIS CONSTITUTION FOR THE UNITED STATES OF AMERICA!
SILENCE
A MORE PERFECT UNION?
WHILE HUGE CORPORATIONS DO WHATEVER THEY WANT TO WHOEVER THEY WANT...
...AND OTHER PEOPLE LIVE IN SUBWAY TUNNELS?
WHERE'S THE JUSTICE OF THAT?

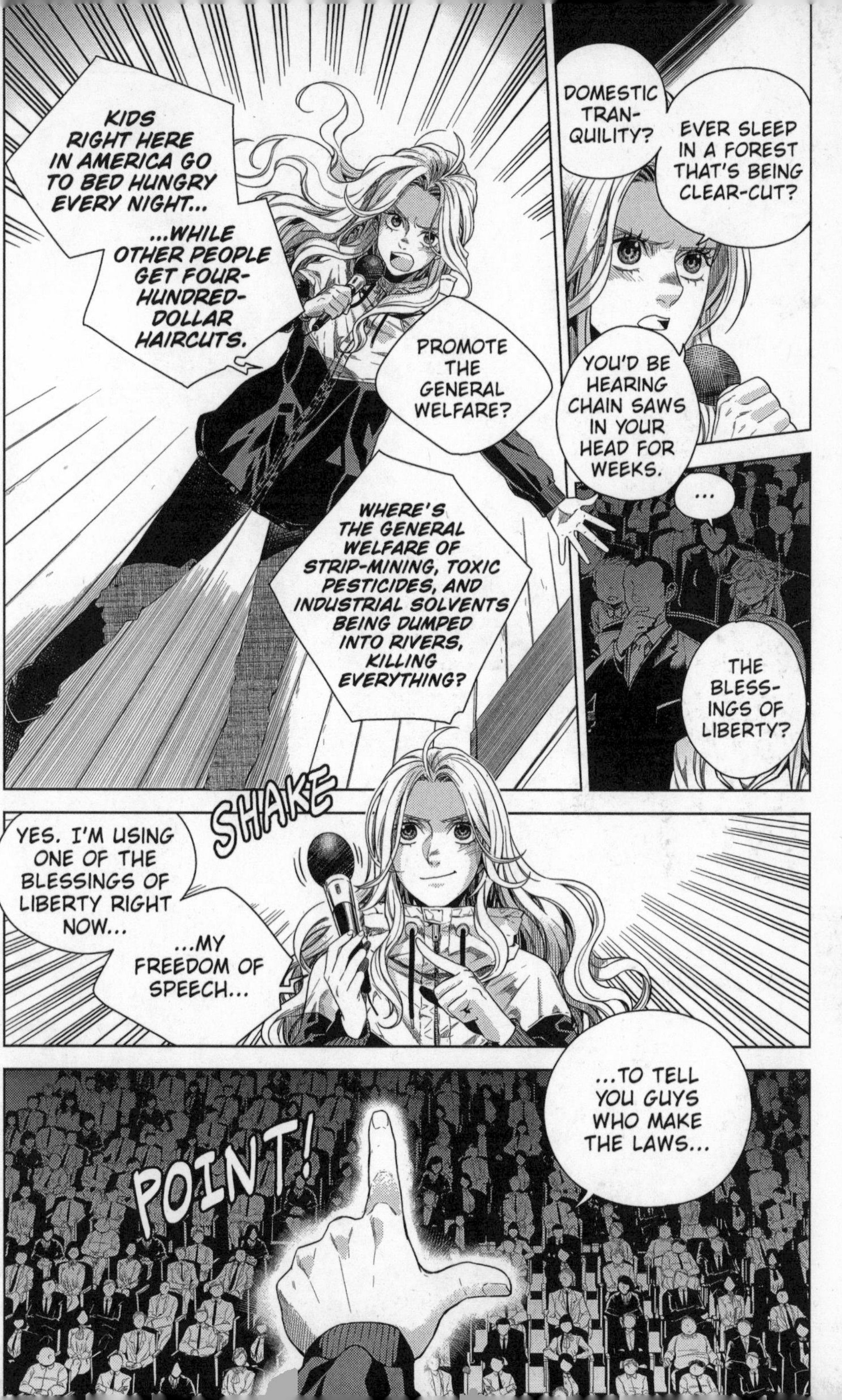
KIDS RIGHT HERE IN AMERICA GO TO BED HUNGRY EVERY NIGHT...
...WHILE OTHER PEOPLE GET FOUR-HUNDRED-DOLLAR HAIRCUTS.
PROMOTE THE GENERAL WELFARE?
WHERE'S THE GENERAL WELFARE OF STRIP-MINING, TOXIC PESTICIDES, AND INDUSTRIAL SOLVENTS BEING DUMPED INTO RIVERS, KILLING EVERYTHING?
DOMESTIC TRAN-QUILITY?
EVER SLEEP IN A FOREST THAT'S BEING CLEAR-CUT?
YOU'D BE HEARING CHAIN SAWS IN YOUR HEAD FOR WEEKS.
...
THE BLESS-INGS OF LIBERTY?
SHAKE
YES. I'M USING ONE OF THE BLESSINGS OF LIBERTY RIGHT NOW...
...MY FREEDOM OF SPEECH...
POINT!
...TO TELL YOU GUYS WHO MAKE THE LAWS...

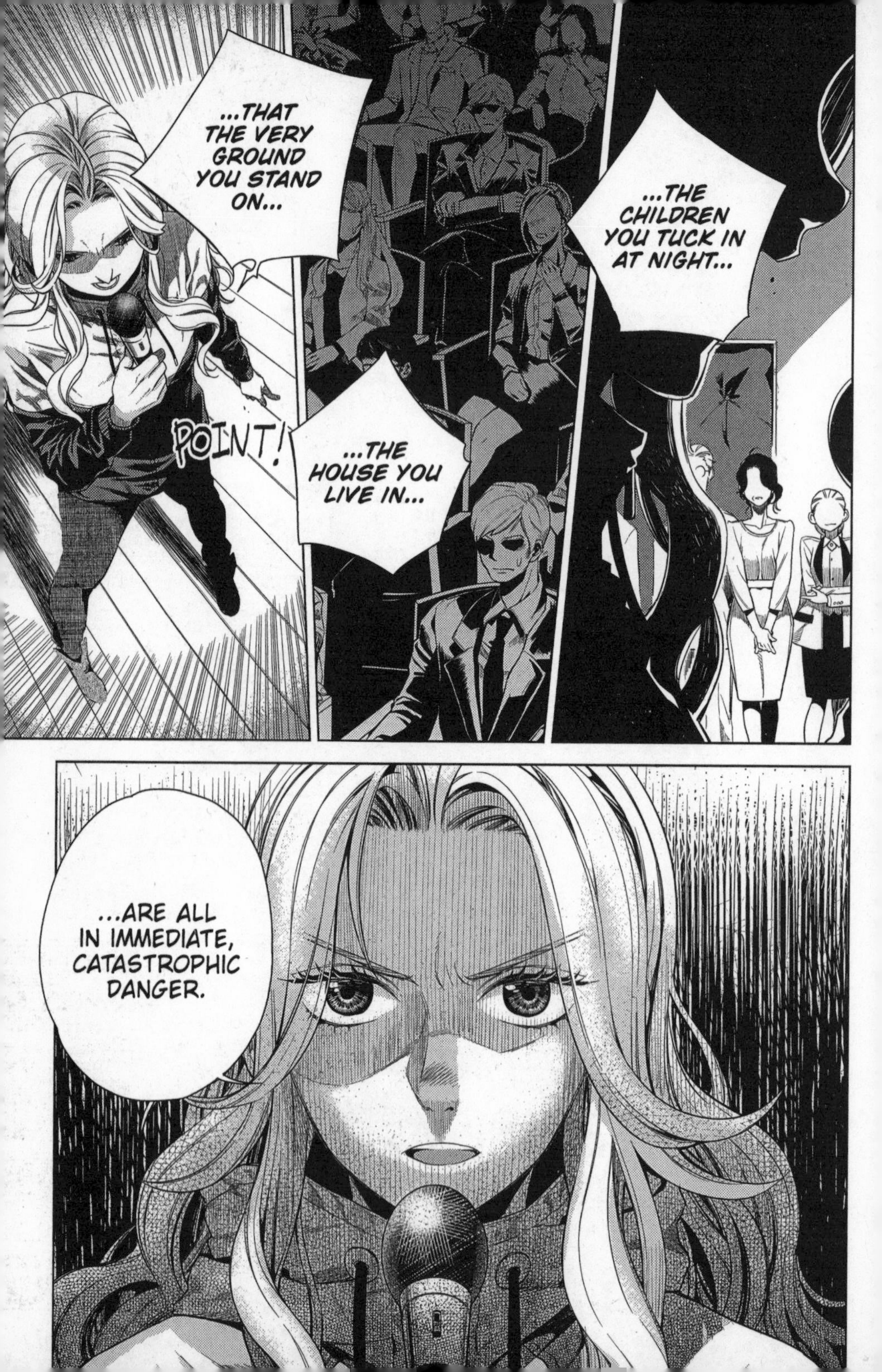
...THAT THE VERY GROUND YOU STAND ON...
POINT!
...THE HOUSE YOU LIVE IN...
...THE CHILDREN YOU TUCK IN AT NIGHT...
...ARE ALL IN IMMEDIATE, CATASTROPHIC DANGER.

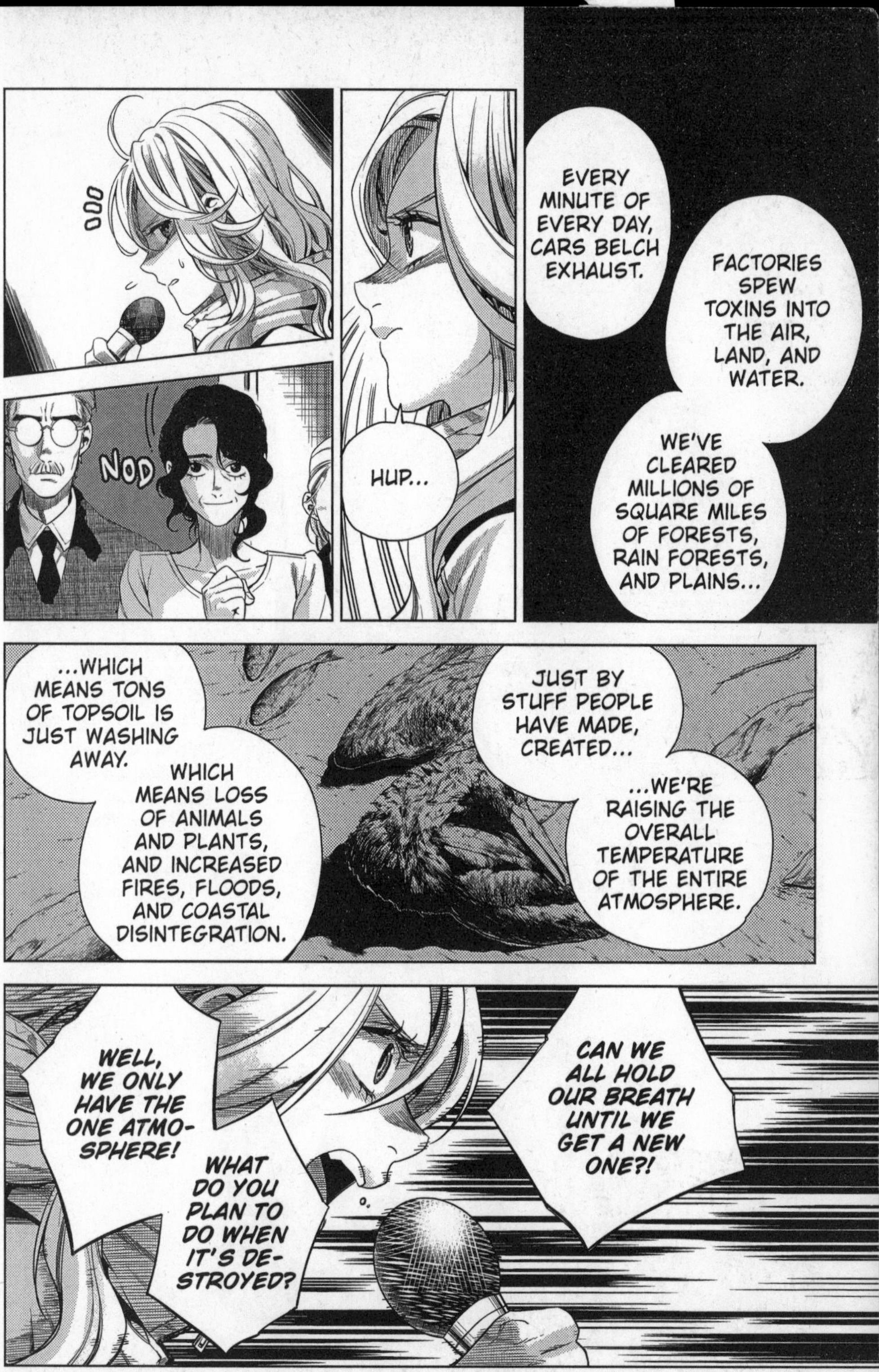

Ooo
NOD
HUP...
EVERY MINUTE OF EVERY DAY, CARS BELCH EXHAUST.
FACTORIES SPEW TOXINS INTO THE AIR, LAND, AND WATER.
WE'VE CLEARED MILLIONS OF SQUARE MILES OF FORESTS, RAIN FORESTS, AND PLAINS...
...WHICH MEANS TONS OF TOPSOIL IS JUST WASHING AWAY.
WHICH MEANS LOSS OF ANIMALS AND PLANTS, AND INCREASED FIRES, FLOODS, AND COASTAL DISINTEGRATION.
JUST BY STUFF PEOPLE HAVE MADE, CREATED...
...WE'RE RAISING THE OVERALL TEMPERATURE OF THE ENTIRE ATMOSPHERE.
WELL, WE ONLY HAVE THE ONE ATMOSPHERE!
WHAT DO YOU PLAN TO DO WHEN IT'S DESTROYED?
CAN WE ALL HOLD OUR BREATH UNTIL WE GET A NEW ONE?!

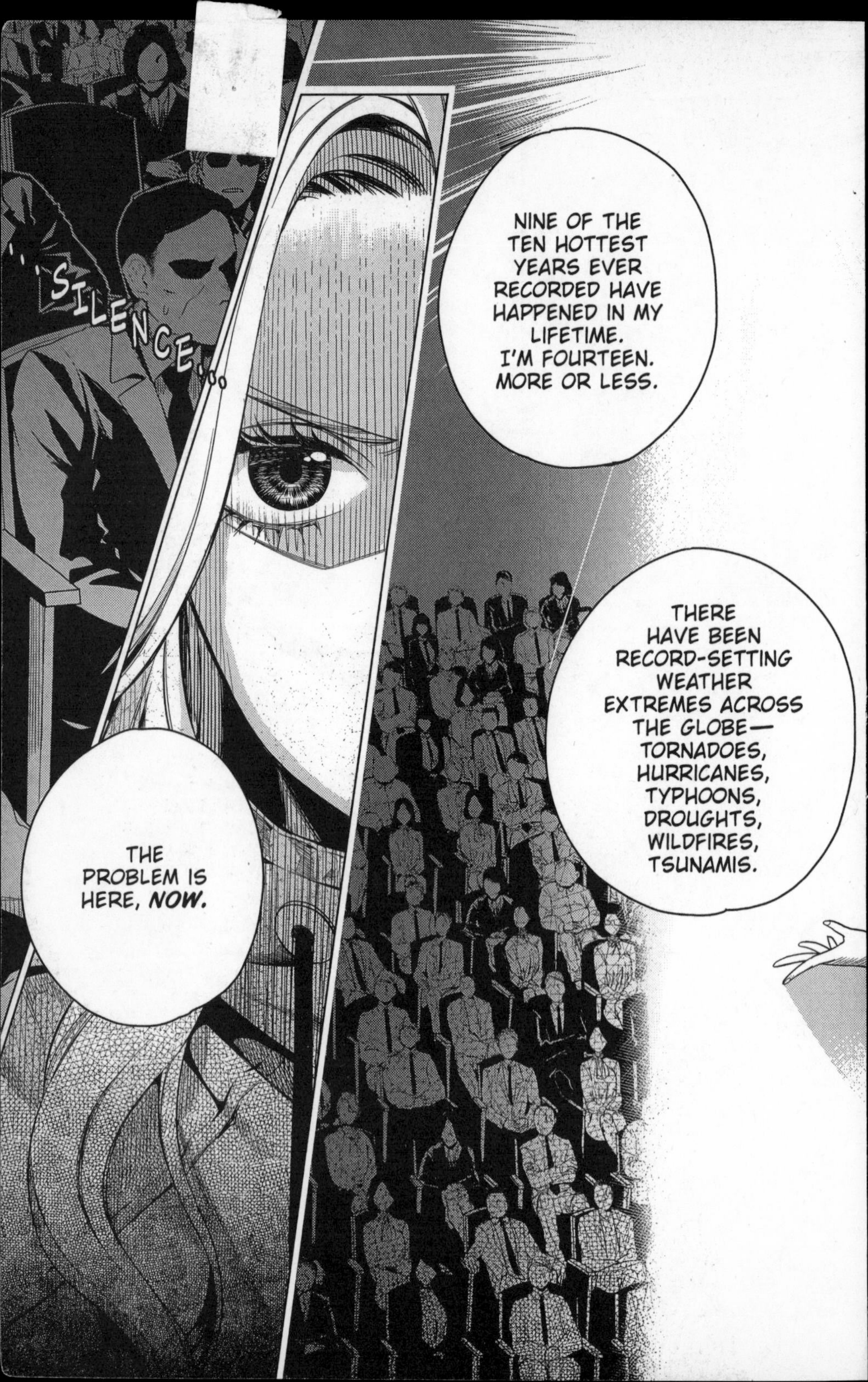
...SILENCE...
NINE OF THE TEN HOTTEST YEARS EVER RECORDED HAVE HAPPENED IN MY LIFETIME. I'M FOURTEEN. MORE OR LESS.
THERE HAVE BEEN RECORD-SETTING WEATHER EXTREMES ACROSS THE GLOBE—TORNADOES, HURRICANES, TYPHOONS, DROUGHTS, WILDFIRES, TSUNAMIS.
THE PROBLEM IS HERE, NOW.

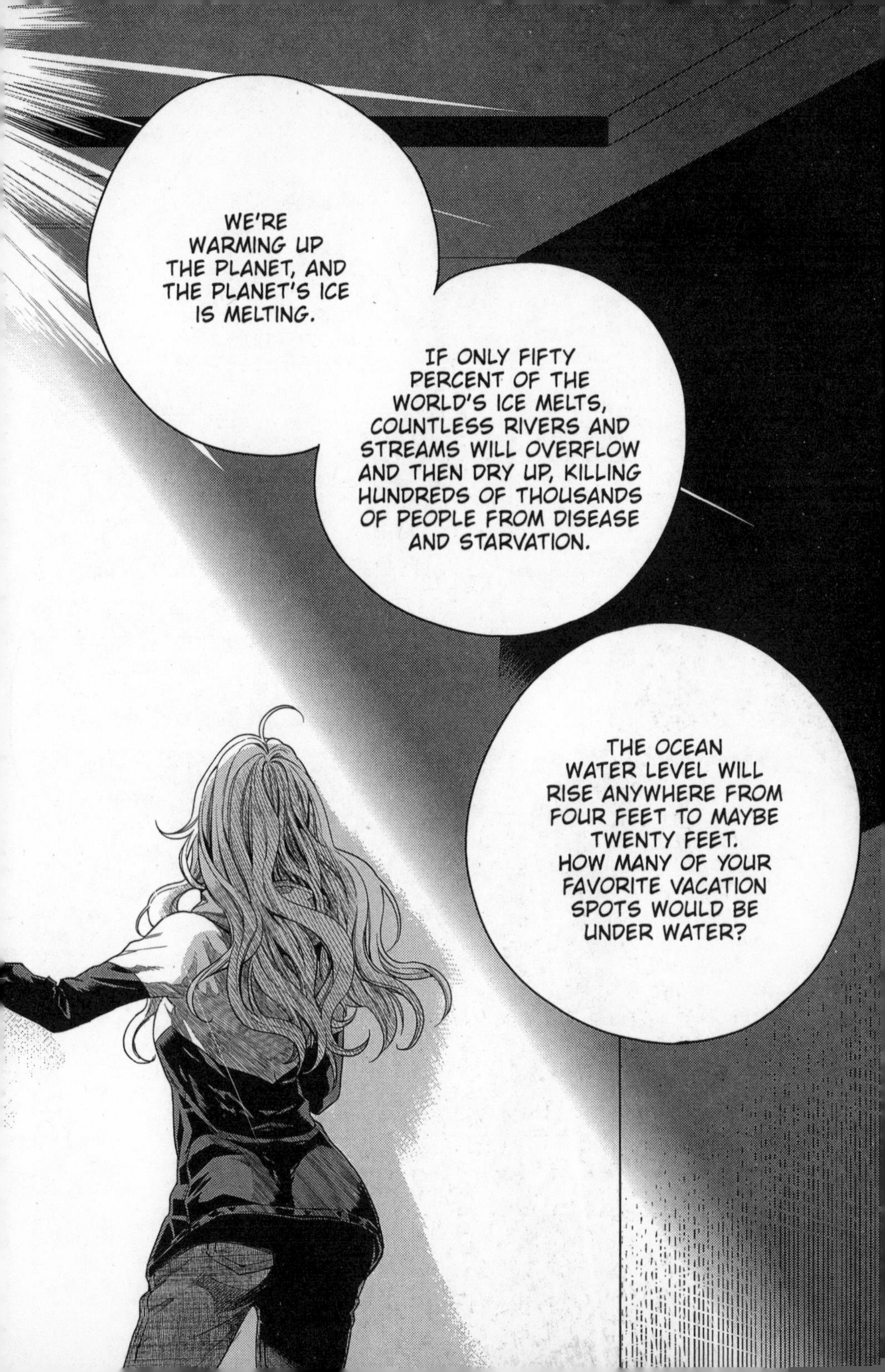
WE'RE WARMING UP THE PLANET, AND THE PLANET'S ICE IS MELTING.
IF ONLY FIFTY PERCENT OF THE WORLD'S ICE MELTS, COUNTLESS RIVERS AND STREAMS WILL OVERFLOW AND THEN DRY UP, KILLING HUNDREDS OF THOUSANDS OF PEOPLE FROM DISEASE AND STARVATION.
THE OCEAN WATER LEVEL WILL RISE ANYWHERE FROM FOUR FEET TO MAYBE TWENTY FEET. HOW MANY OF YOUR FAVORITE VACATION SPOTS WOULD BE UNDER WATER?

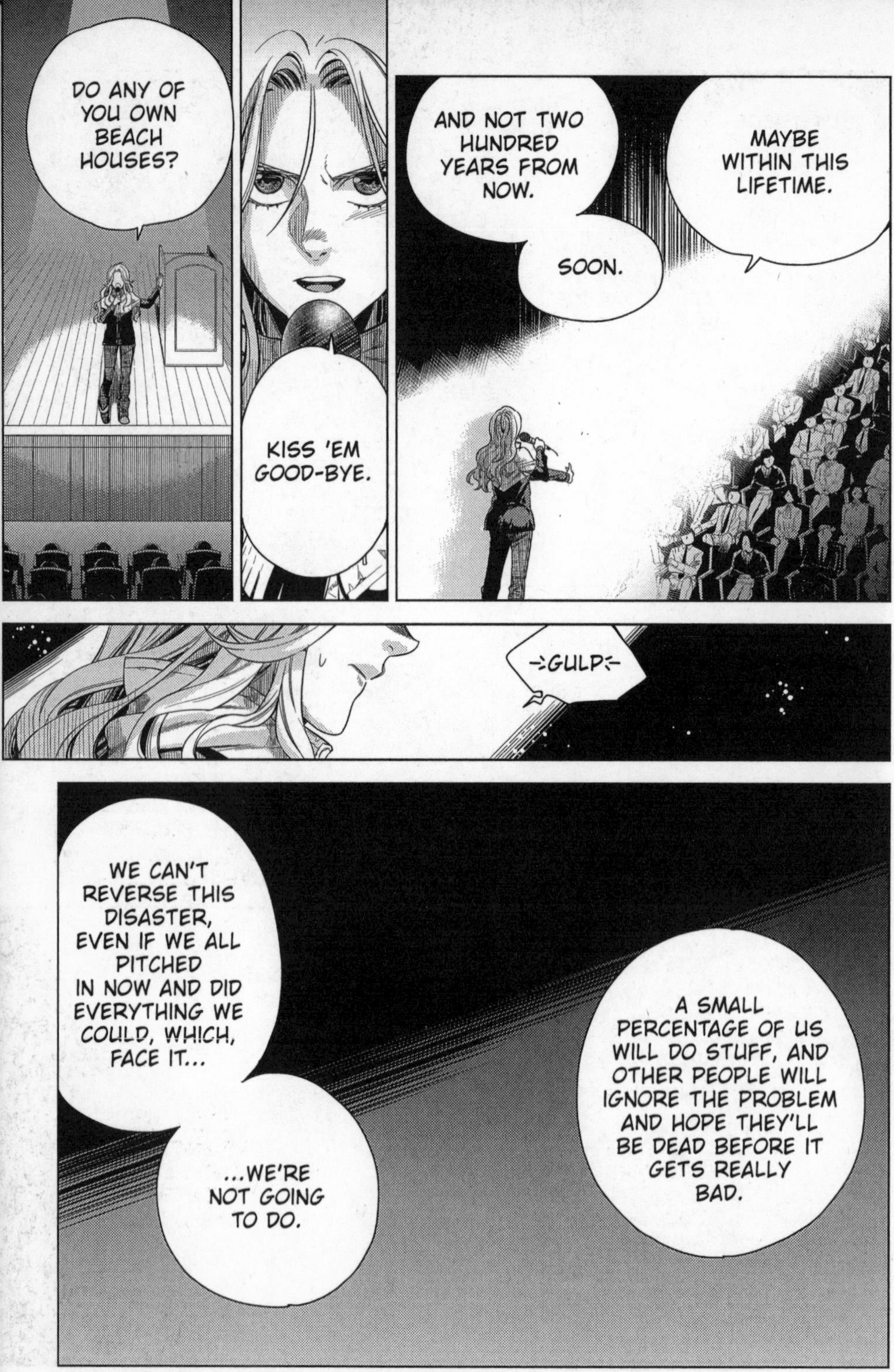
DO ANY OF YOU OWN BEACH HOUSES?
KISS 'EM GOOD-BYE.
AND NOT TWO HUNDRED YEARS FROM NOW.
SOON.
MAYBE WITHIN THIS LIFETIME.
-GULP-
WE CAN'T REVERSE THIS DISASTER, EVEN IF WE ALL PITCHED IN NOW AND DID EVERYTHING WE COULD, WHICH, FACE IT...
...WE'RE NOT GOING TO DO.
A SMALL PERCENTAGE OF US WILL DO STUFF, AND OTHER PEOPLE WILL IGNORE THE PROBLEM AND HOPE THEY'LL BE DEAD BEFORE IT GETS REALLY BAD.

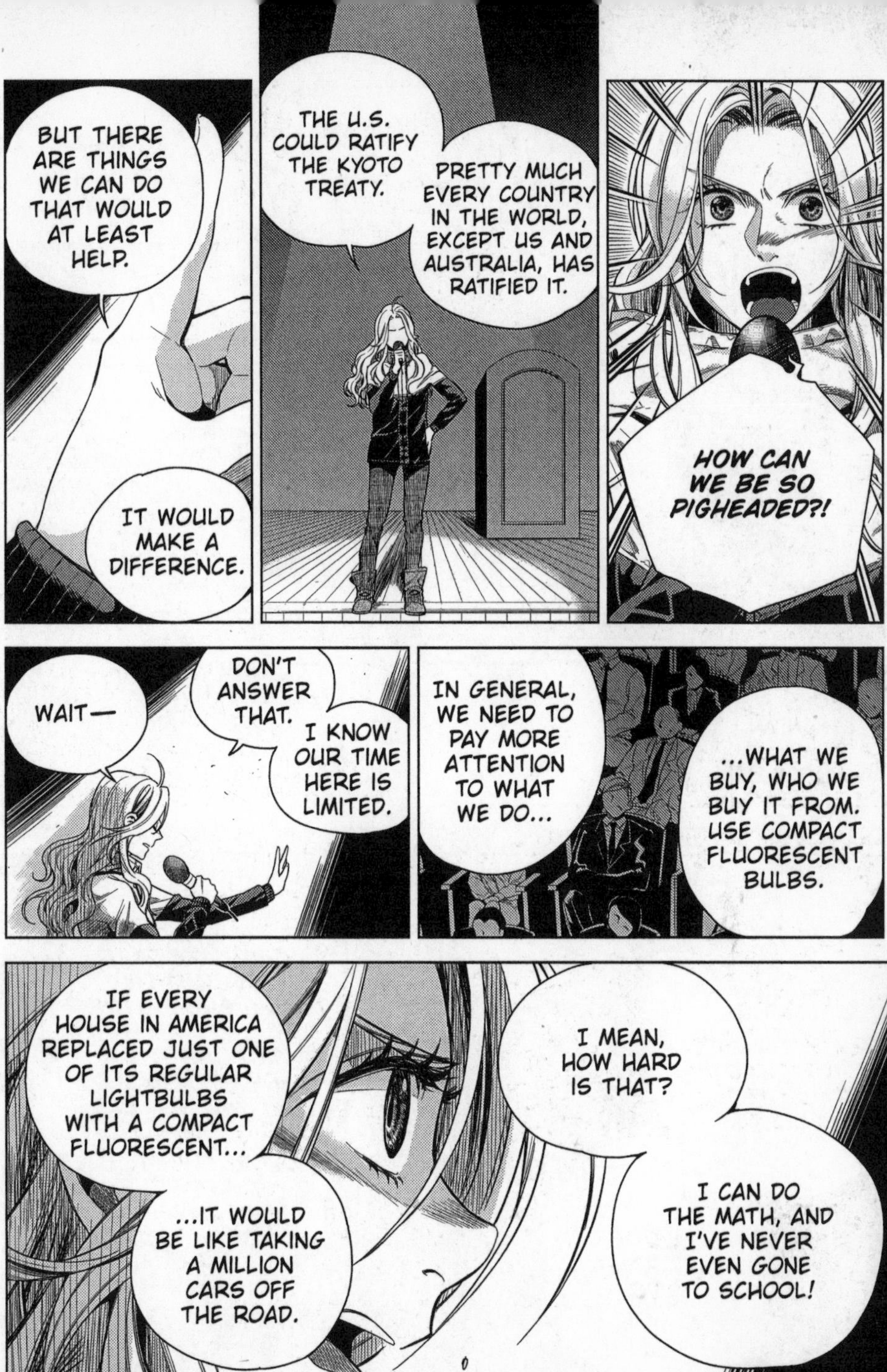
BUT THERE ARE THINGS WE CAN DO THAT WOULD AT LEAST HELP.
IT WOULD MAKE A DIFFERENCE.
THE U.S. COULD RATIFY THE KYOTO TREATY.
PRETTY MUCH EVERY COUNTRY IN THE WORLD, EXCEPT US AND AUSTRALIA, HAS RATIFIED IT.
HOW CAN WE BE SO PIGHEADED?!
WAIT—
DON'T ANSWER THAT.
I KNOW OUR TIME HERE IS LIMITED.
IN GENERAL, WE NEED TO PAY MORE ATTENTION TO WHAT WE DO...
...WHAT WE BUY, WHO WE BUY IT FROM. USE COMPACT FLUORESCENT BULBS.
IF EVERY HOUSE IN AMERICA REPLACED JUST ONE OF ITS REGULAR LIGHTBULBS WITH A COMPACT FLUORESCENT...
...IT WOULD BE LIKE TAKING A MILLION CARS OFF THE ROAD.
I MEAN, HOW HARD IS THAT?
I CAN DO THE MATH, AND I'VE NEVER EVEN GONE TO SCHOOL!

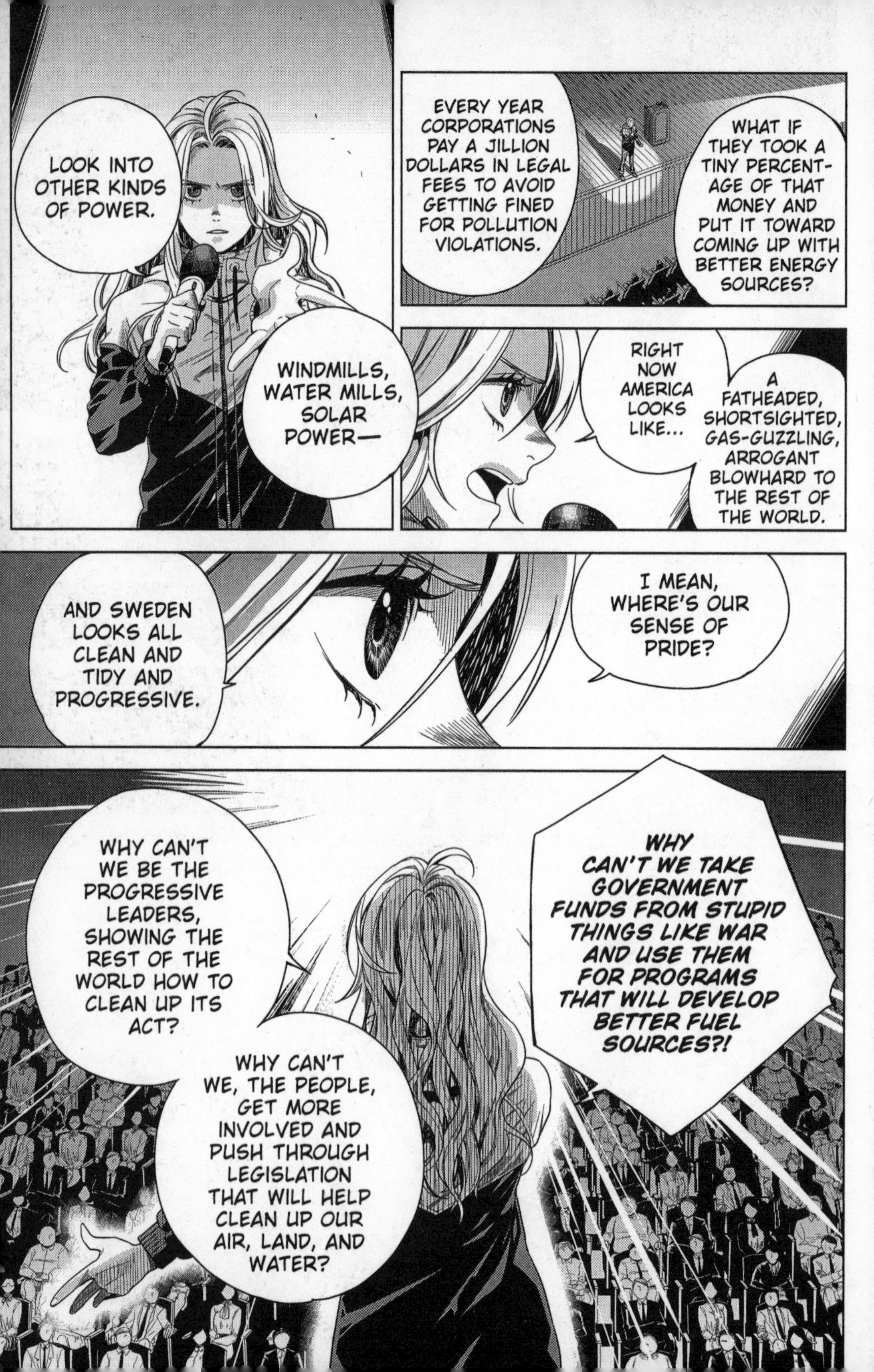
LOOK INTO OTHER KINDS OF POWER.
WINDMILLS, WATER MILLS, SOLAR POWER—
EVERY YEAR CORPORATIONS PAY A JILLION DOLLARS IN LEGAL FEES TO AVOID GETTING FINED FOR POLLUTION VIOLATIONS.
WHAT IF THEY TOOK A TINY PERCENTAGE OF THAT MONEY AND PUT IT TOWARD COMING UP WITH BETTER ENERGY SOURCES?
RIGHT NOW AMERICA LOOKS LIKE...
A FATHEADED, SHORTSIGHTED, GAS-GUZZLING, ARROGANT BLOWHARD TO THE REST OF THE WORLD.
AND SWEDEN LOOKS ALL CLEAN AND TIDY AND PROGRESSIVE.
I MEAN, WHERE'S OUR SENSE OF PRIDE?
WHY CAN'T WE BE THE PROGRESSIVE LEADERS, SHOWING THE REST OF THE WORLD HOW TO CLEAN UP ITS ACT?
WHY CAN'T WE, THE PEOPLE, GET MORE INVOLVED AND PUSH THROUGH LEGISLATION THAT WILL HELP CLEAN UP OUR AIR, LAND, AND WATER?
WHY CAN'T WE TAKE GOVERNMENT FUNDS FROM STUPID THINGS LIKE WAR AND USE THEM FOR PROGRAMS THAT WILL DEVELOP BETTER FUEL SOURCES?!

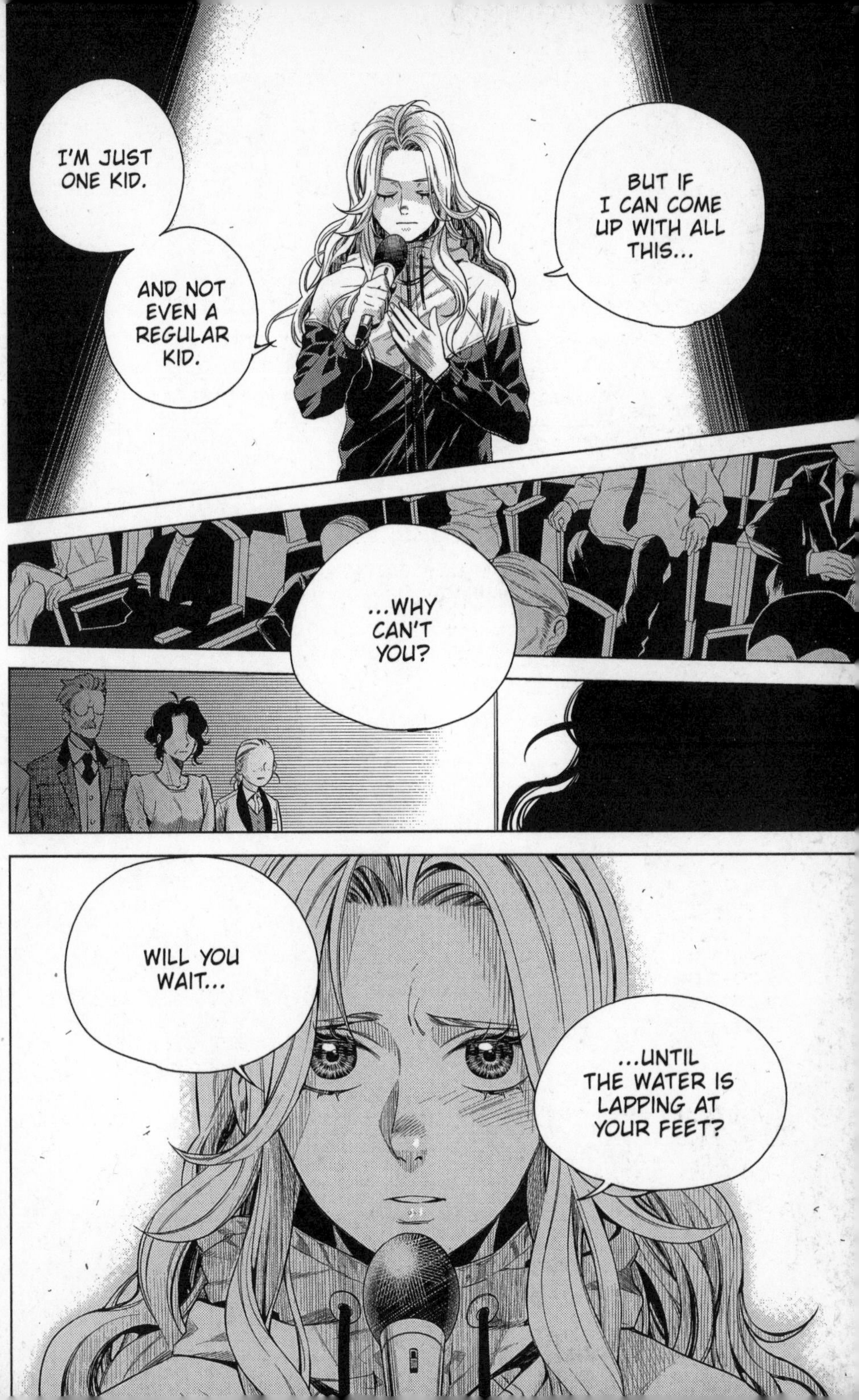
I'M JUST ONE KID.
AND NOT EVEN A REGULAR KID.
BUT IF I CAN COME UP WITH ALL THIS...
...WHY CAN'T YOU?
WILL YOU WAIT...
...UNTIL THE WATER IS LAPPING AT YOUR FEET?

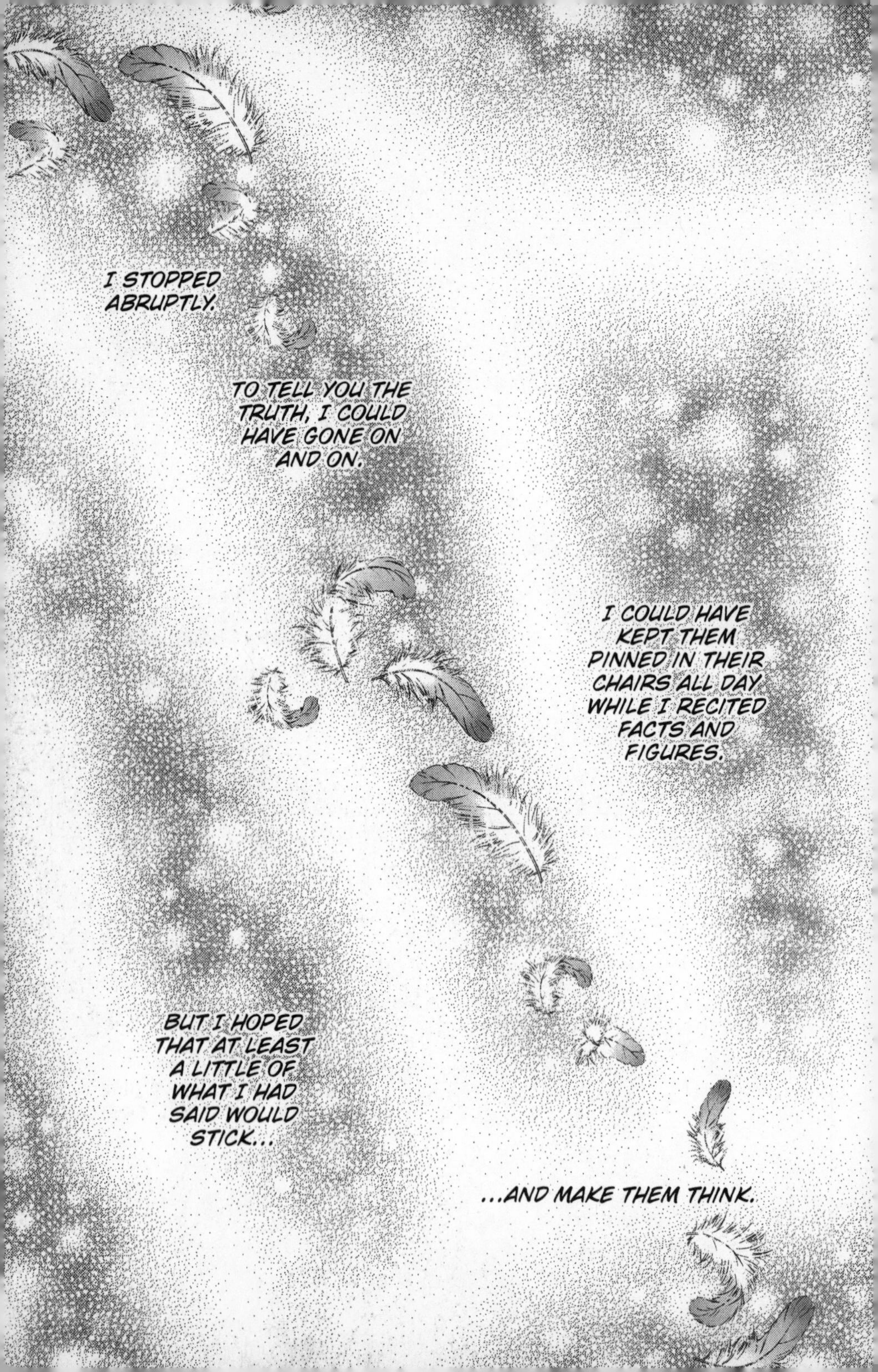
I STOPPED ABRUPTLY.
TO TELL YOU THE TRUTH, I COULD HAVE GONE ON AND ON.
I COULD HAVE KEPT THEM PINNED IN THEIR CHAIRS ALL DAY WHILE I RECITED FACTS AND FIGURES.
BUT I HOPED THAT AT LEAST A LITTLE OF WHAT I HAD SAID WOULD STICK...
...AND MAKE THEM THINK.

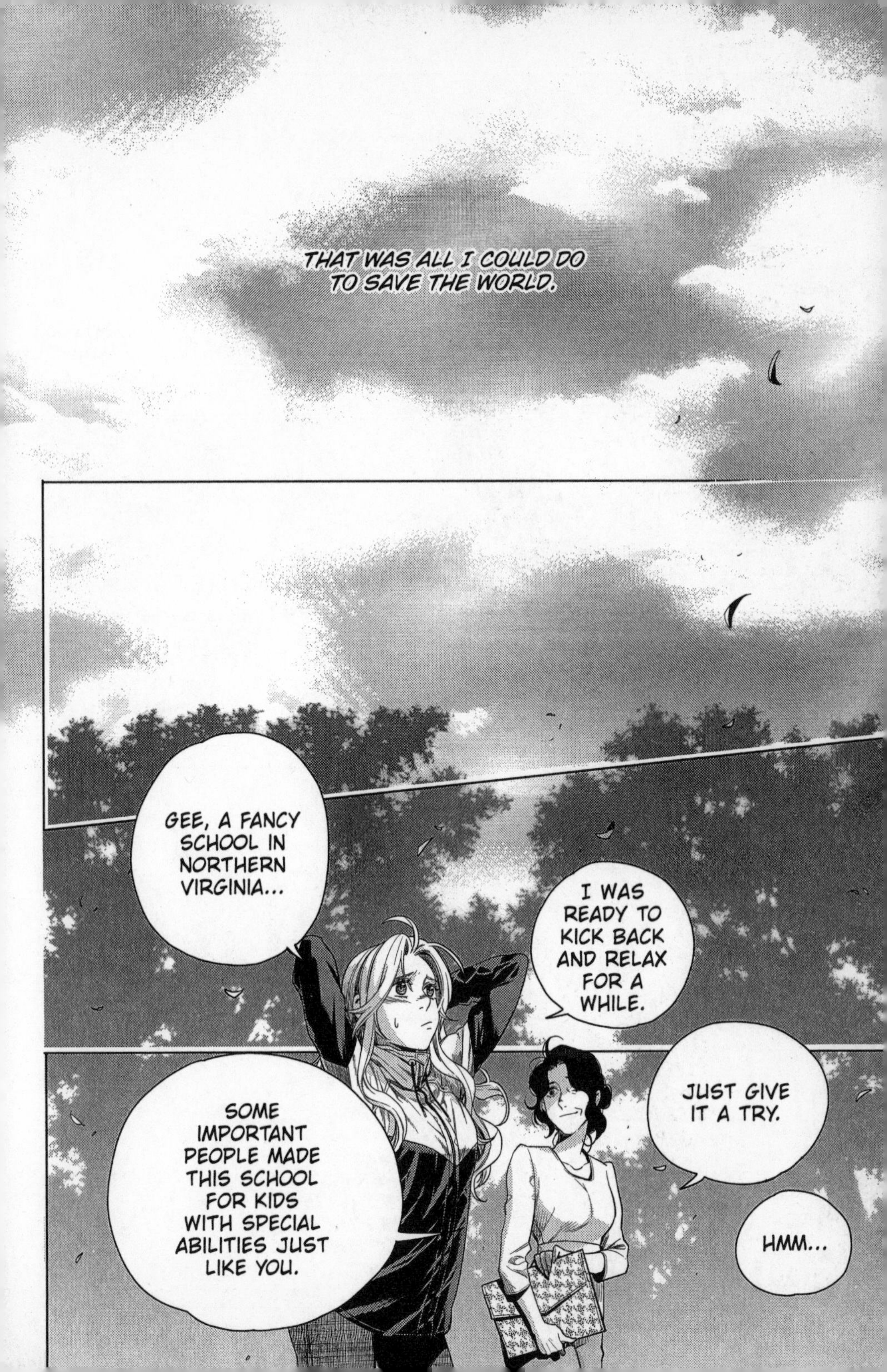
THAT WAS ALL I COULD DO TO SAVE THE WORLD.
GEE, A FANCY SCHOOL IN NORTHERN VIRGINIA...
I WAS READY TO KICK BACK AND RELAX FOR A WHILE.
SOME IMPORTANT PEOPLE MADE THIS SCHOOL FOR KIDS WITH SPECIAL ABILITIES JUST LIKE YOU.
JUST GIVE IT A TRY.
HMM...

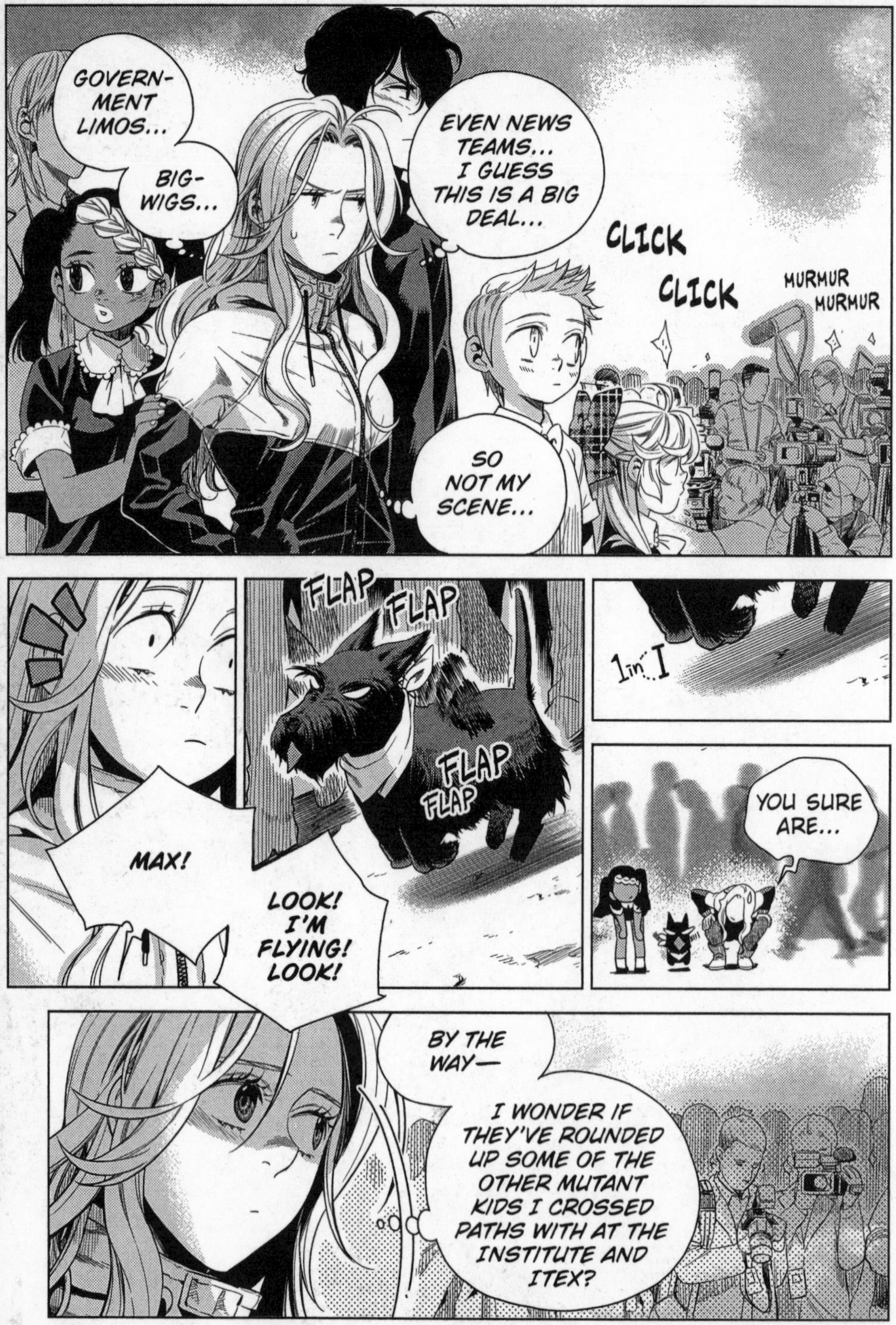
GOVERNMENT LIMOS...
BIG-WIGS...
EVEN NEWS TEAMS... I GUESS THIS IS A BIG DEAL...
CLICK
CLICK
MURMUR MURMUR
SO NOT MY SCENE...
MAX!
FLAP FLAP
FLAP FLAP
LOOK! I'M FLYING! LOOK!
YOU SURE ARE...
BY THE WAY—
I WONDER IF THEY'VE ROUNDED UP SOME OF THE OTHER MUTANT KIDS I CROSSED PATHS WITH AT THE INSTITUTE AND ITEX?

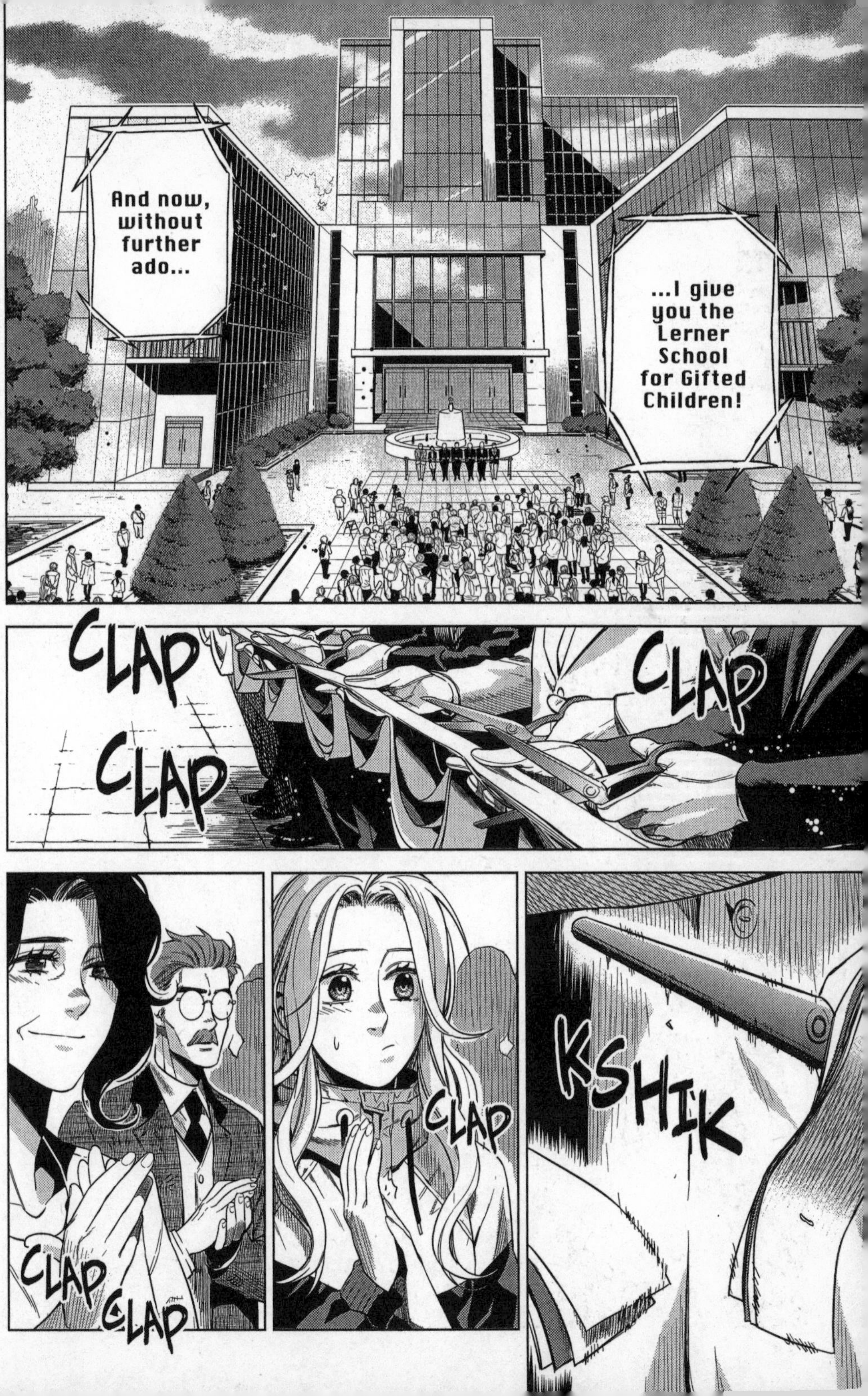
And now, without further ado...
...I give you the Lerner School for Gifted Children!
CLAP
CLAP
CLAP
CLAP
CLAP
CLAP
CLAP
KSHIK

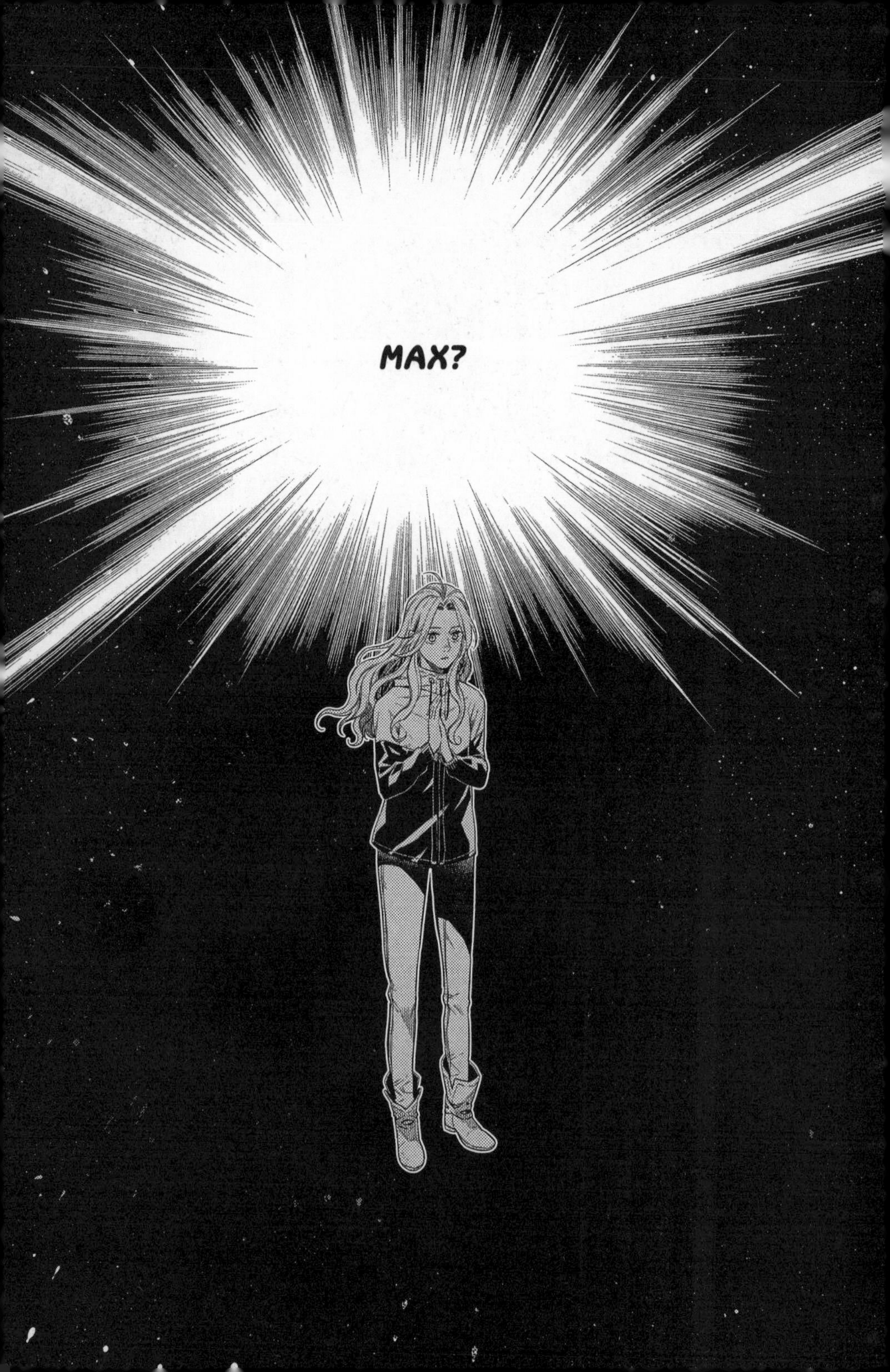
MAX?

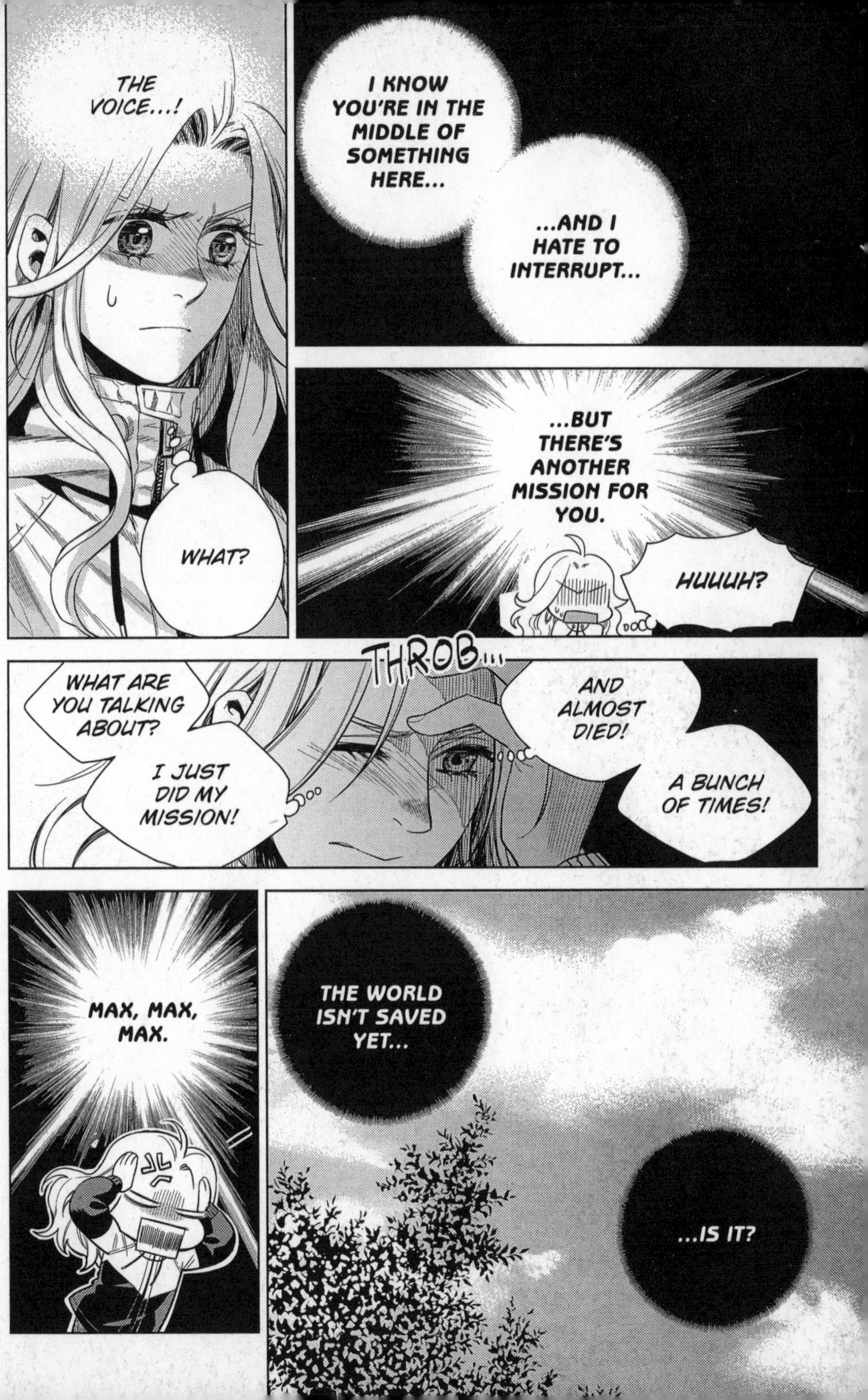
THE VOICE...!
WHAT?
I KNOW YOU'RE IN THE MIDDLE OF SOMETHING HERE...
...AND I HATE TO INTERRUPT...
...BUT THERE'S ANOTHER MISSION FOR YOU.
HUUUH?
THROB...
WHAT ARE YOU TALKING ABOUT?
I JUST DID MY MISSION!
AND ALMOST DIED!
A BUNCH OF TIMES!
MAX, MAX, MAX.
THE WORLD ISN'T SAVED YET...
...IS IT?

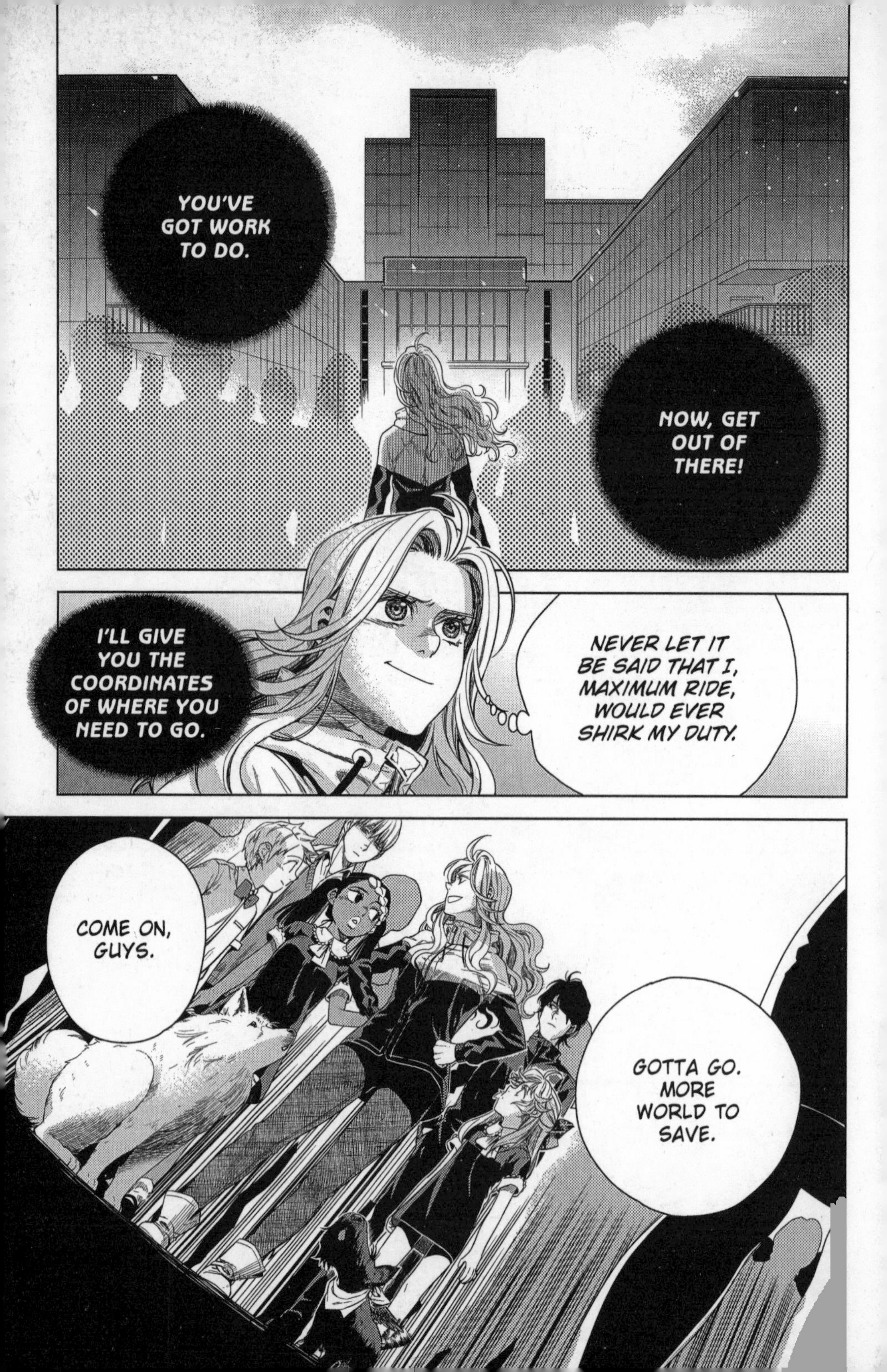
YOU'VE GOT WORK TO DO.
NOW, GET OUT OF THERE!
I'LL GIVE YOU THE COORDINATES OF WHERE YOU NEED TO GO.
NEVER LET IT BE SAID THAT I, MAXIMUM RIDE, WOULD EVER SHIRK MY DUTY.
COME ON, GUYS.
GOTTA GO. MORE WORLD TO SAVE.

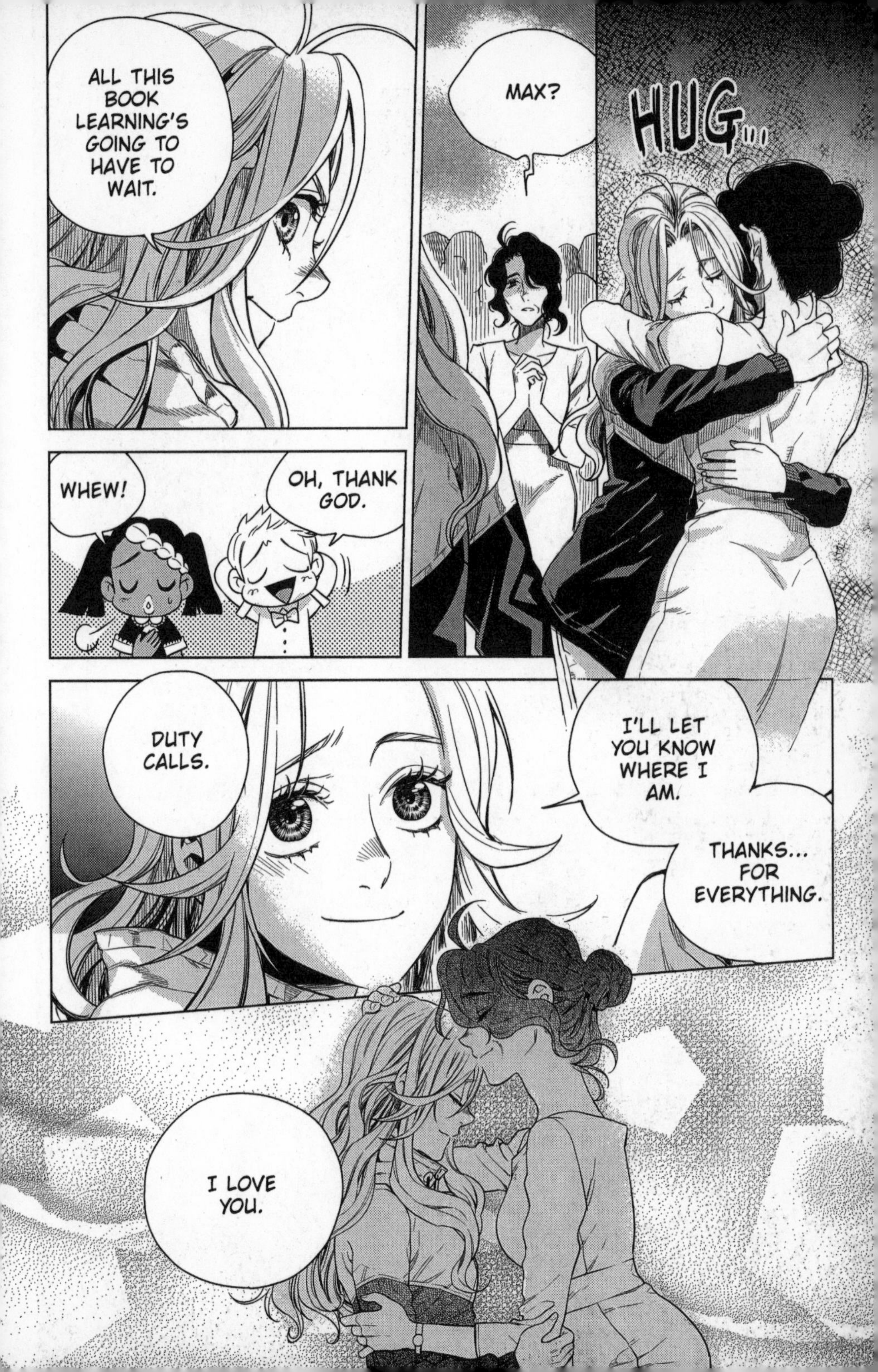
ALL THIS BOOK LEARNING'S GOING TO HAVE TO WAIT.
MAX?
HUG...
WHEW!
OH, THANK GOD.
DUTY CALLS.
I'LL LET YOU KNOW WHERE I AM.
THANKS... FOR EVERYTHING.
I LOVE YOU.

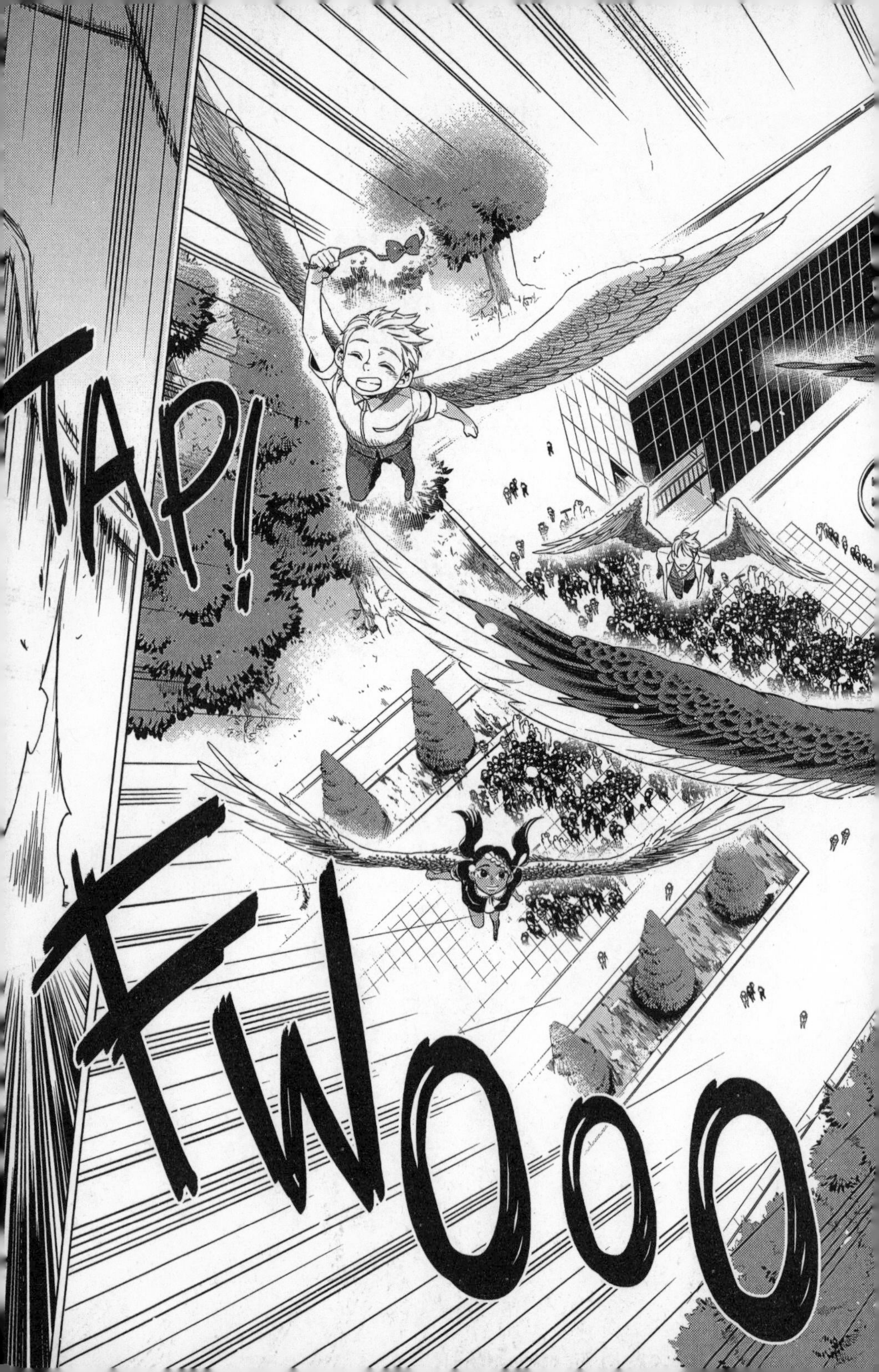
TAP!!
FWOOO

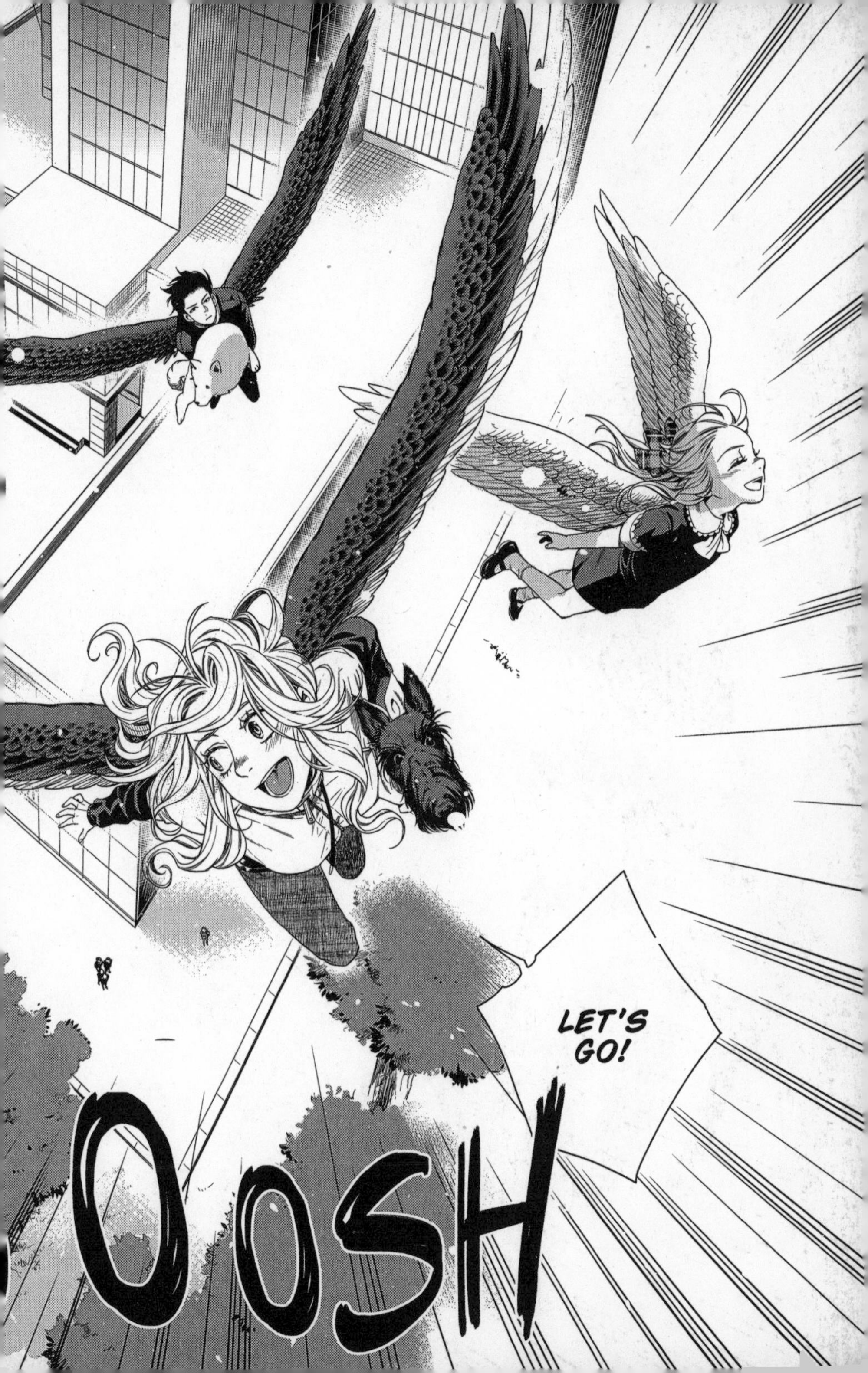
LET'S GO!
OOSH

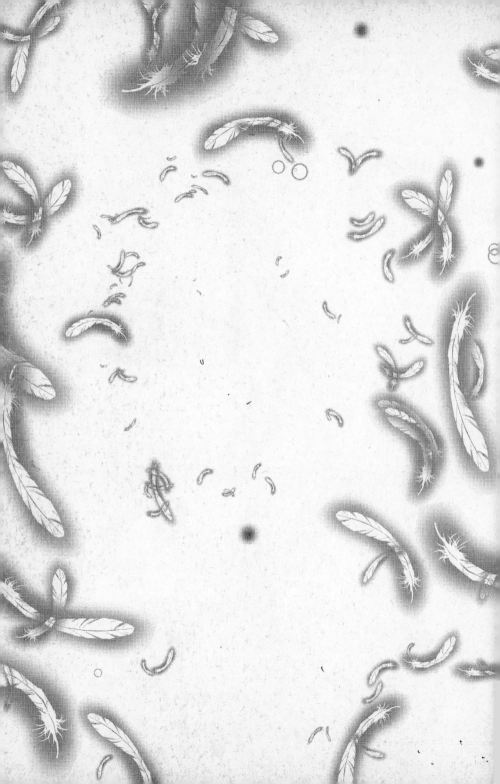

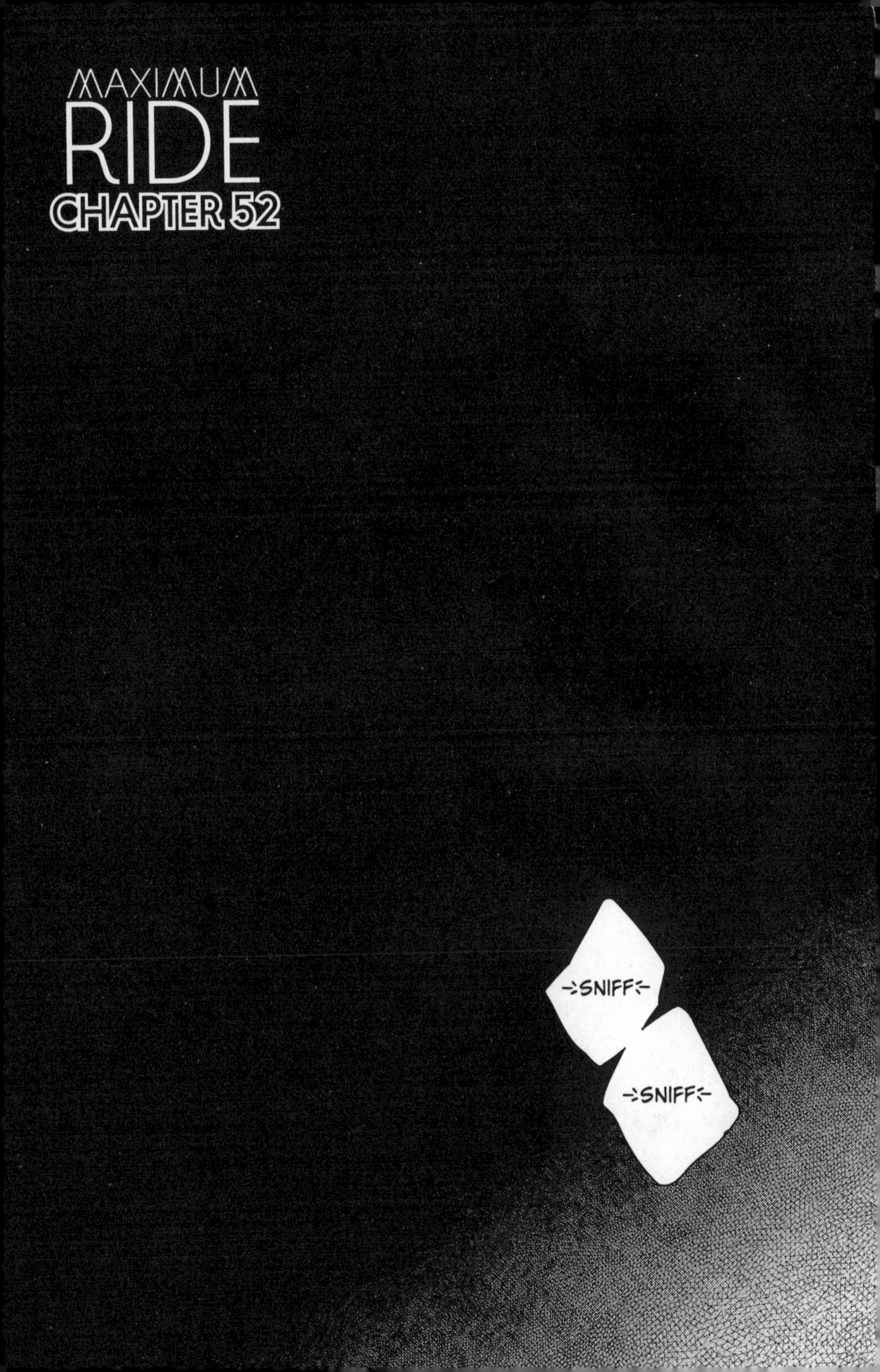
MAXIMUM RIDE
CHAPTER 52
SNIFF
SNIFF

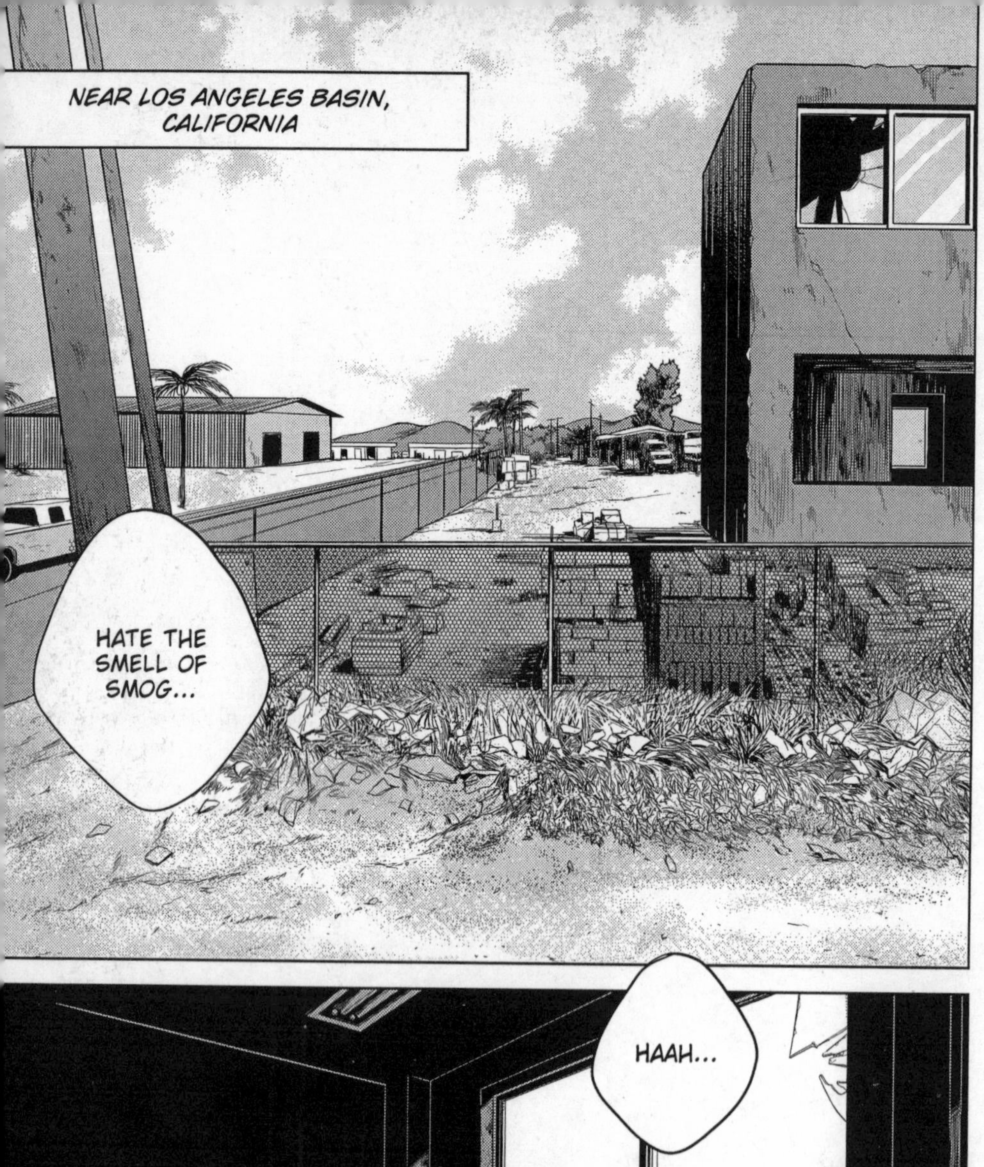
NEAR LOS ANGELES BASIN, CALIFORNIA
HATE THE SMELL OF SMOG...

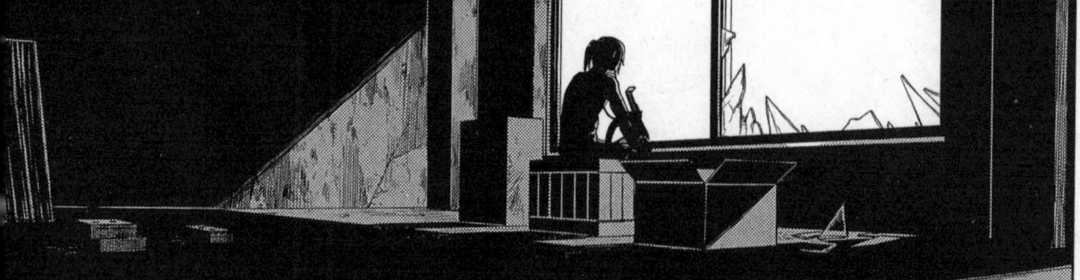
HAAH...

HAAH...
HAAH ...
ONE...
TWO...
THREE ...
FOUR...
FIVE...
SIX...
SEVEN...
SEVEN?

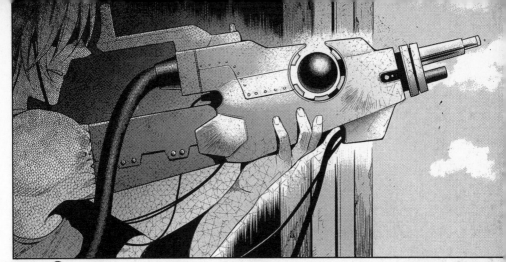

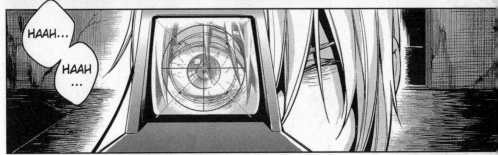

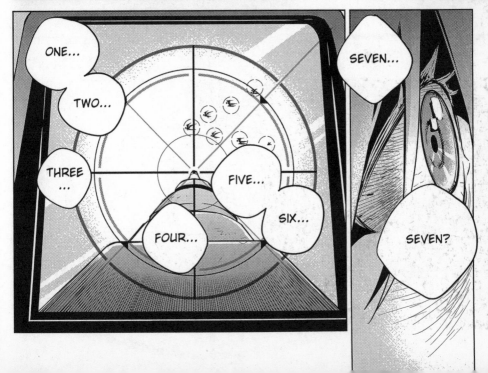

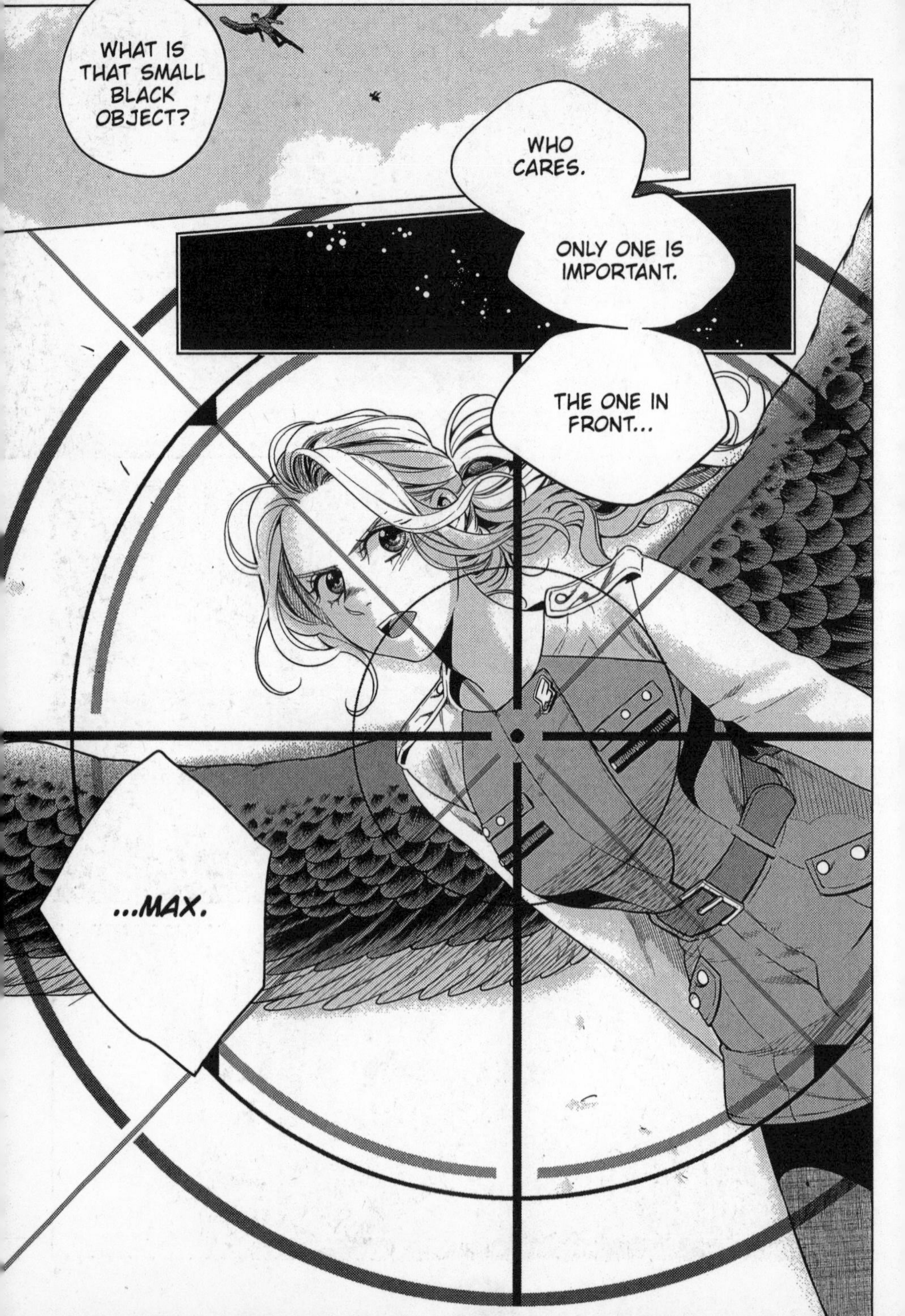
WHAT IS THAT SMALL BLACK OBJECT?
WHO CARES.
ONLY ONE IS IMPORTANT.
THE ONE IN FRONT...
...MAX.

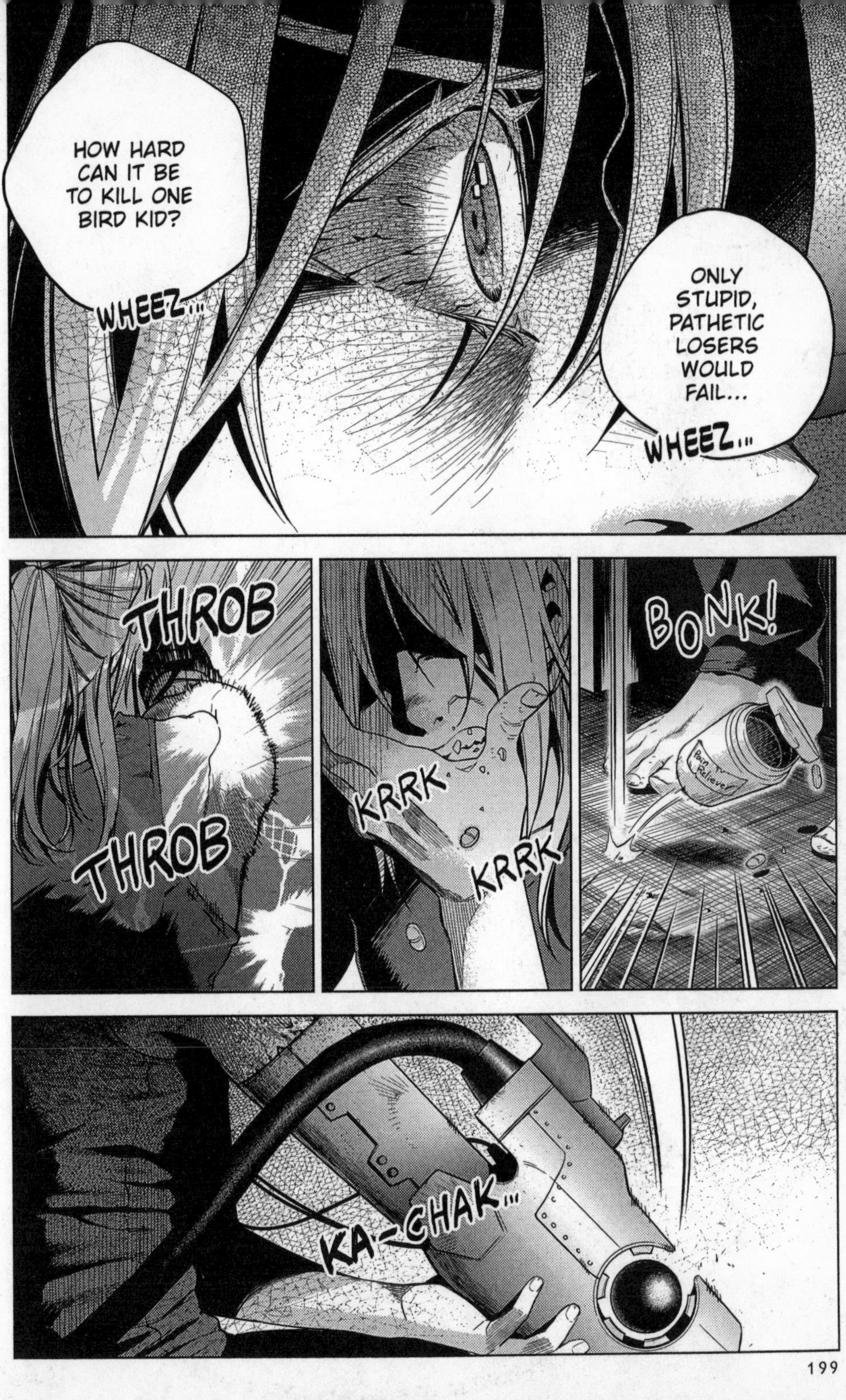
HOW HARD CAN IT BE TO KILL ONE BIRD KID?
WHEEZ...
ONLY STUPID, PATHETIC LOSERS WOULD FAIL...
WHEEZ...
THROB
THROB
KRRK
KRRK
BONK!
Pain Reliever
KA-CHAK...

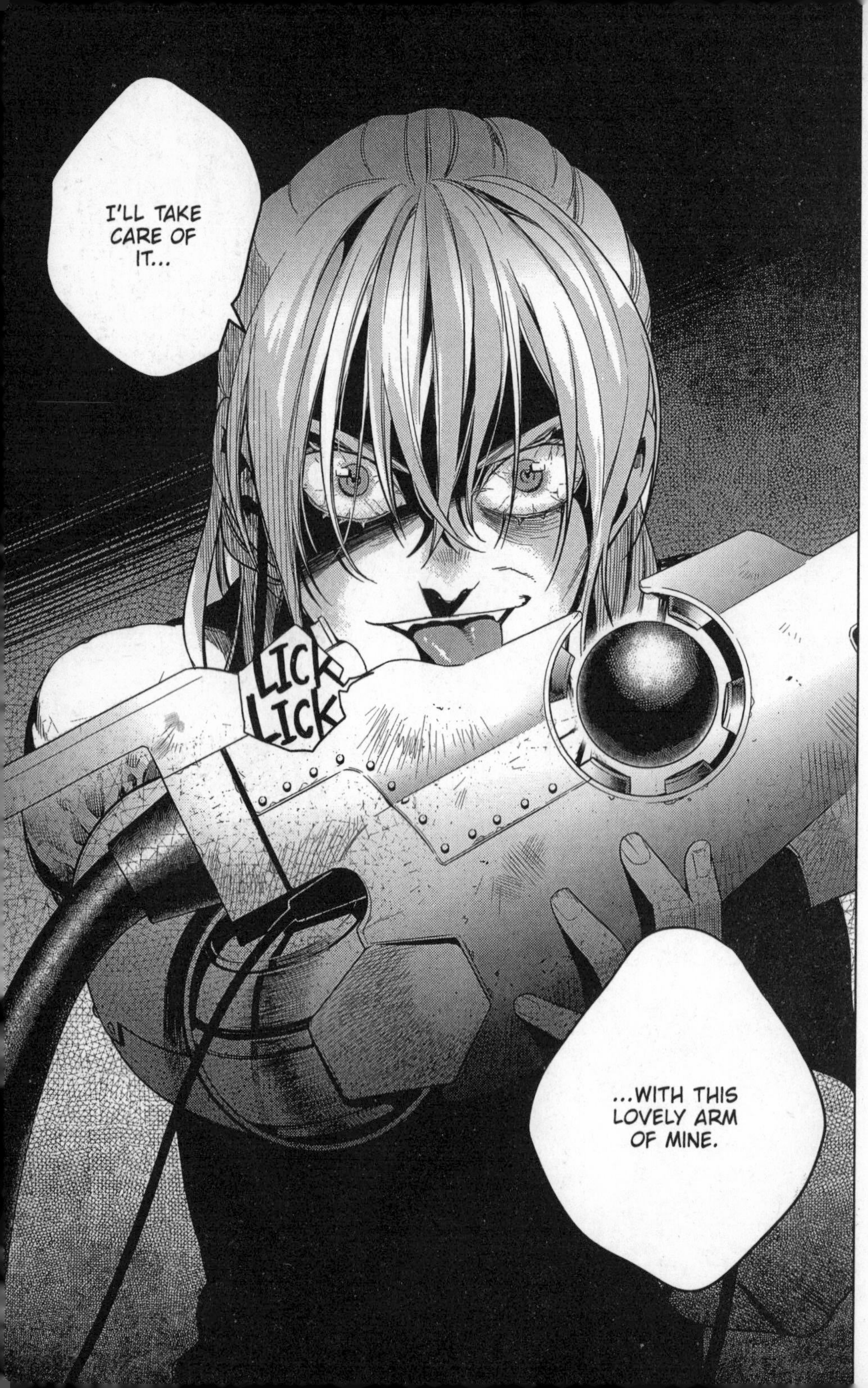
I'LL TAKE CARE OF IT...
LICK LICK
...WITH THIS LOVELY ARM OF MINE.

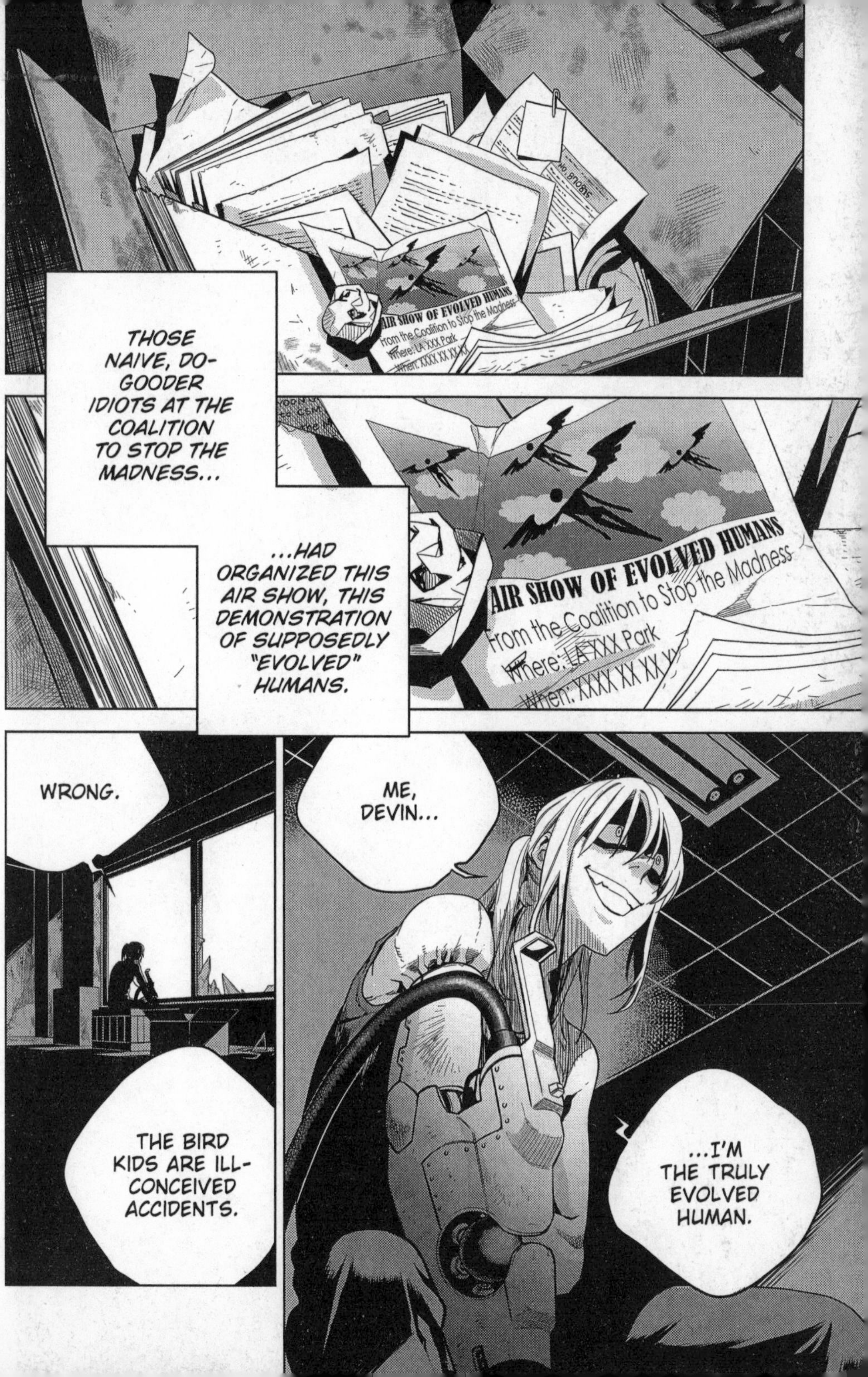
AIR SHOW OF EVOLVED HUMANS
From the Coalition to Stop the Madness
Where: LA XXX Park
THOSE NAIVE, DO-GOODER IDIOTS AT THE COALITION TO STOP THE MADNESS...
...HAD ORGANIZED THIS AIR SHOW, THIS DEMONSTRATION OF SUPPOSEDLY "EVOLVED" HUMANS.
AIR SHOW OF EVOLVED HUMANS
From the Coalition to Stop the Madness
Where: LA XXX Park
When: XXXX XX XX
WRONG.
THE BIRD KIDS ARE ILL-CONCEIVED ACCIDENTS.
ME, DEVIN...
...I'M THE TRULY EVOLVED HUMAN.

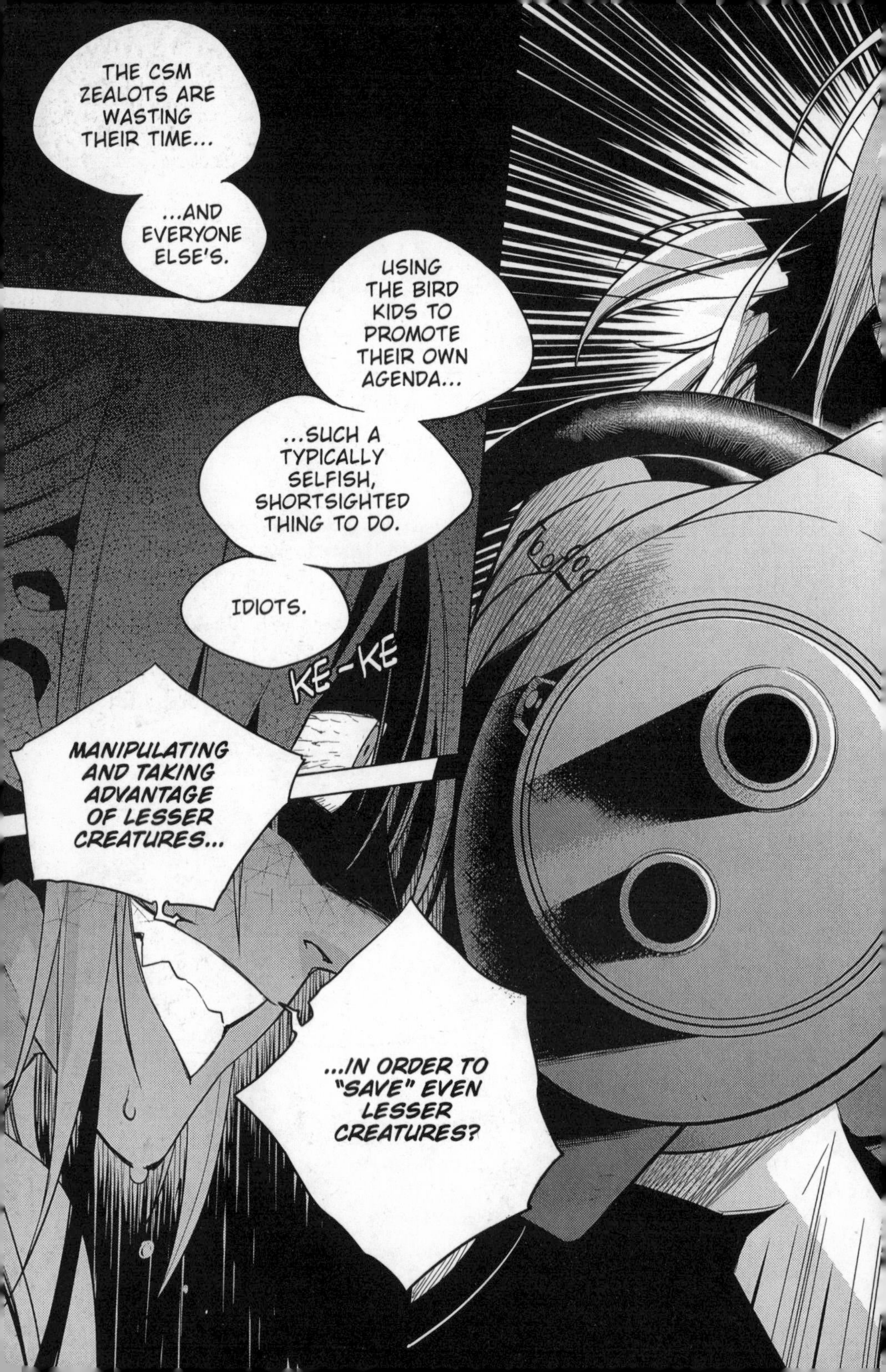
THE CSM ZEALOTS ARE WASTING THEIR TIME...
...AND EVERYONE ELSE'S.
USING THE BIRD KIDS TO PROMOTE THEIR OWN AGENDA...
...SUCH A TYPICALLY SELFISH, SHORTSIGHTED THING TO DO.
IDIOTS.
KE-KE
MANIPULATING AND TAKING ADVANTAGE OF LESSER CREATURES...
...IN ORDER TO "SAVE" EVEN LESSER CREATURES?

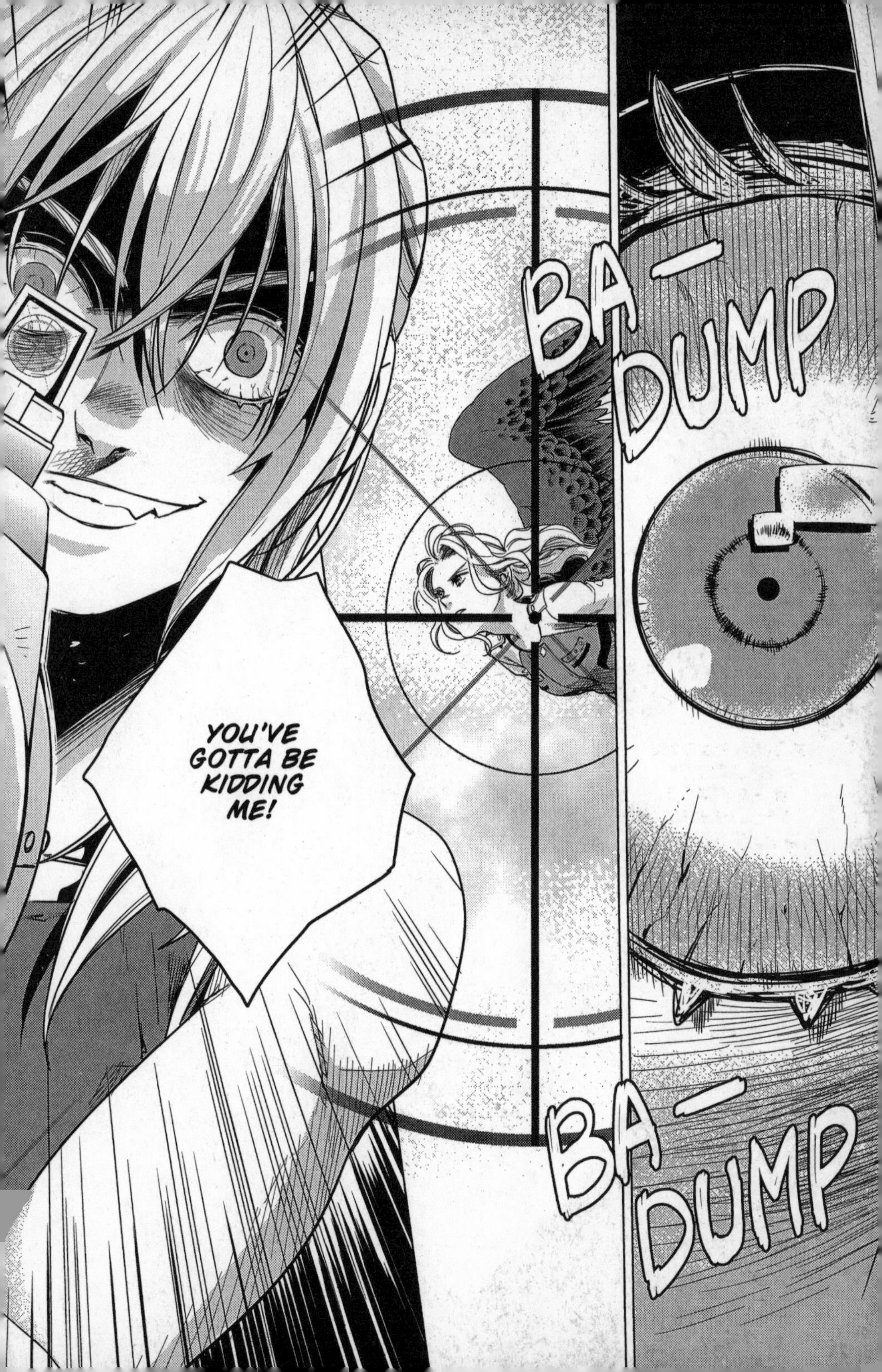
YOU'VE GOTTA BE KIDDING ME!
BA-DUMP
BA-DUMP

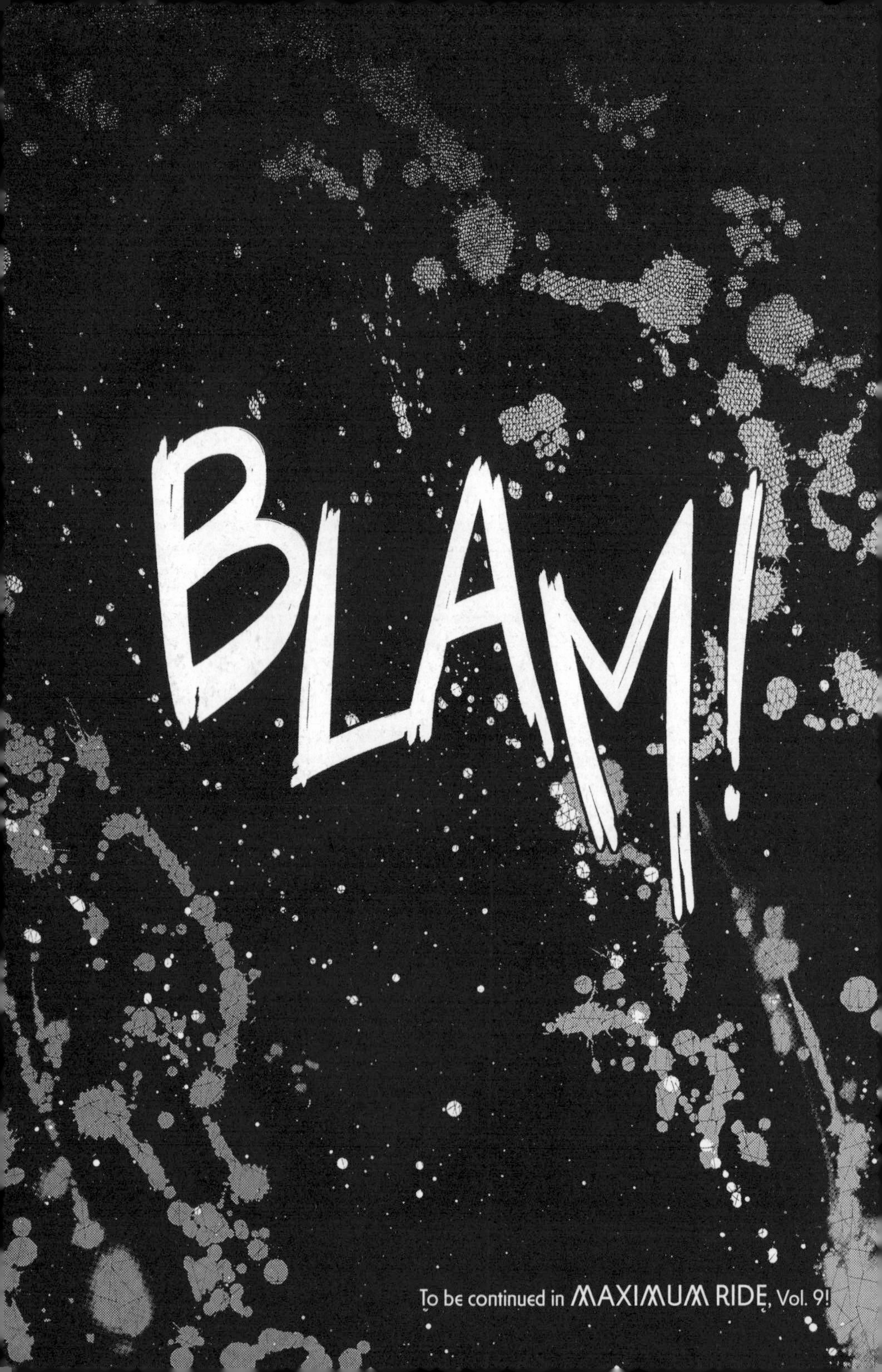
BLAM!
To be continued in MAXIMUM RIDE, Vol. 9!

MAXIMUM
RIDE

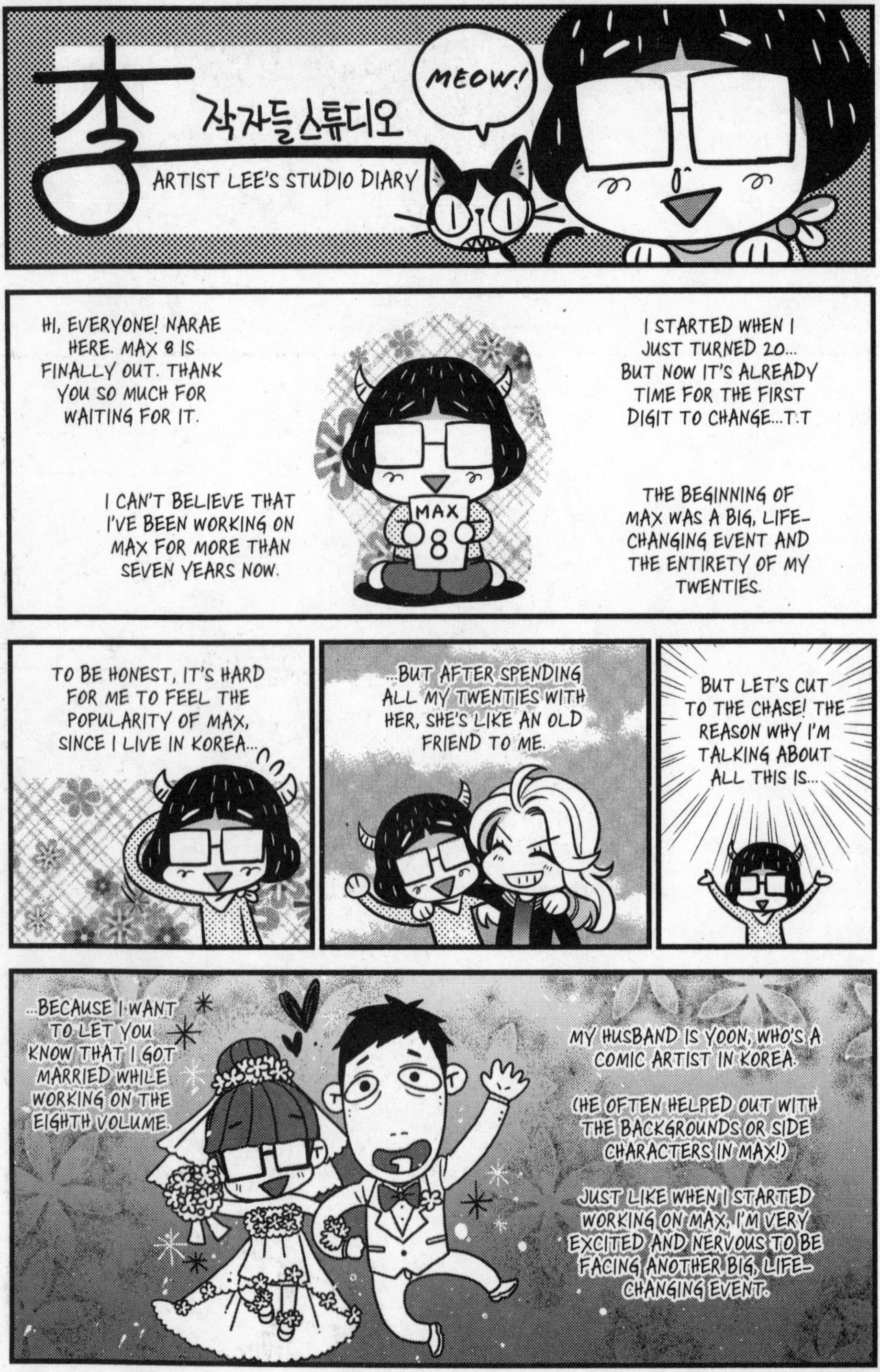
李
작자들 스튜디오
ARTIST LEE'S STUDIO DIARY
MEOW!
HI, EVERYONE! NARAE HERE. MAX 8 IS FINALLY OUT. THANK YOU SO MUCH FOR WAITING FOR IT.
I CAN'T BELIEVE THAT I'VE BEEN WORKING ON MAX FOR MORE THAN SEVEN YEARS NOW.
MAX 8
I STARTED WHEN I JUST TURNED 20... BUT NOW IT'S ALREADY TIME FOR THE FIRST DIGIT TO CHANGE...T.T
THE BEGINNING OF MAX WAS A BIG, LIFE-CHANGING EVENT AND THE ENTIRETY OF MY TWENTIES.
TO BE HONEST, IT'S HARD FOR ME TO FEEL THE POPULARITY OF MAX, SINCE I LIVE IN KOREA...
...BUT AFTER SPENDING ALL MY TWENTIES WITH HER, SHE'S LIKE AN OLD FRIEND TO ME.
BUT LET'S CUT TO THE CHASE! THE REASON WHY I'M TALKING ABOUT ALL THIS IS...
...BECAUSE I WANT TO LET YOU KNOW THAT I GOT MARRIED WHILE WORKING ON THE EIGHTH VOLUME.
MY HUSBAND IS YOON, WHO'S A COMIC ARTIST IN KOREA.
(HE OFTEN HELPED OUT WITH THE BACKGROUNDS OR SIDE CHARACTERS IN MAX!)
JUST LIKE WHEN I STARTED WORKING ON MAX, I'M VERY EXCITED AND NERVOUS TO BE FACING ANOTHER BIG, LIFE-CHANGING EVENT.

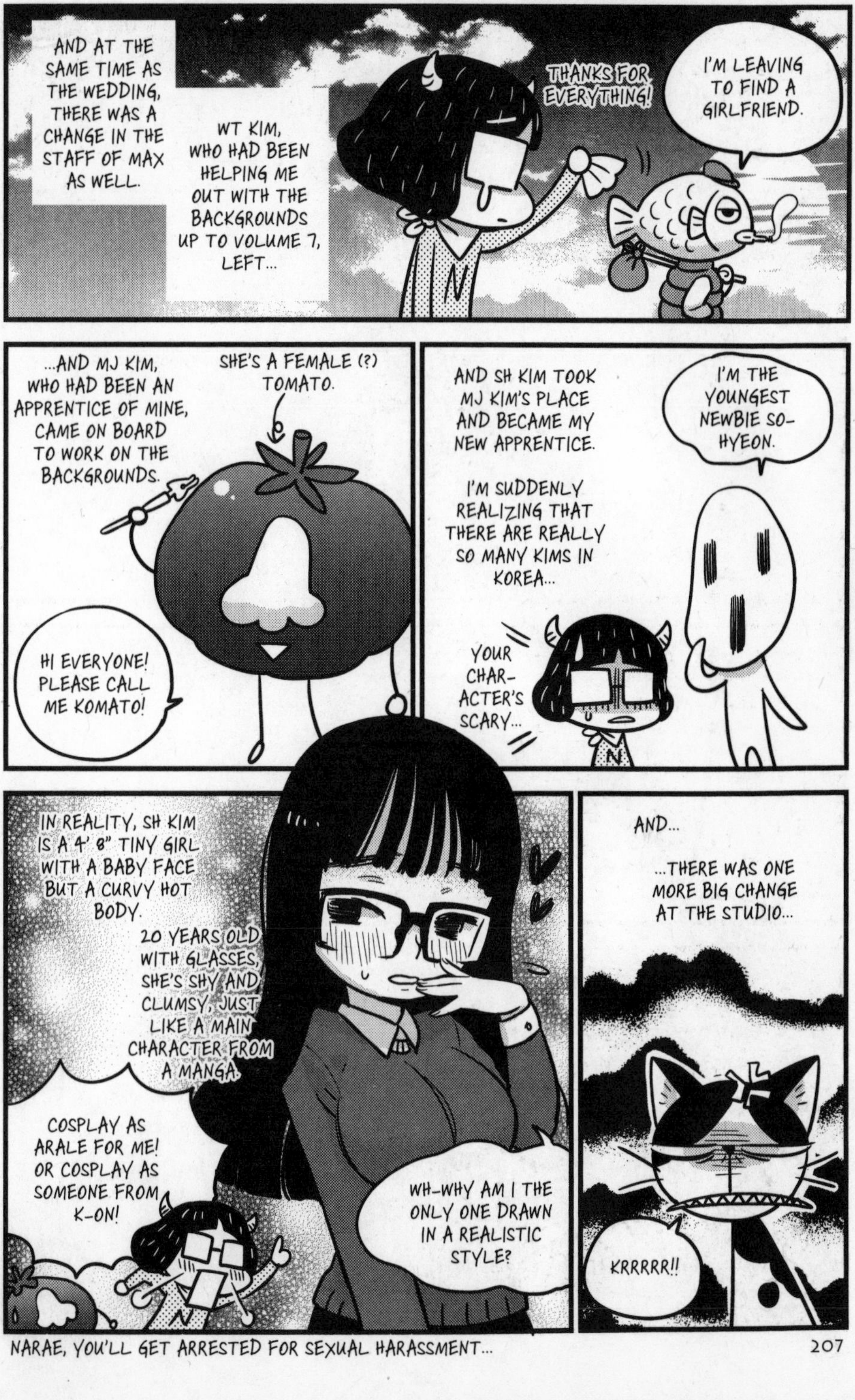
AND AT THE SAME TIME AS THE WEDDING, THERE WAS A CHANGE IN THE STAFF OF MAX AS WELL.
WT KIM, WHO HAD BEEN HELPING ME OUT WITH THE BACKGROUNDS UP TO VOLUME 7, LEFT...
THANKS FOR EVERYTHING!
I'M LEAVING TO FIND A GIRLFRIEND.
...AND MJ KIM, WHO HAD BEEN AN APPRENTICE OF MINE, CAME ON BOARD TO WORK ON THE BACKGROUNDS.
SHE'S A FEMALE (?) TOMATO.
HI EVERYONE! PLEASE CALL ME KOMATO!
AND SH KIM TOOK MJ KIM'S PLACE AND BECAME MY NEW APPRENTICE.
I'M THE YOUNGEST NEWBIE SO-HYEON.
I'M SUDDENLY REALIZING THAT THERE ARE REALLY SO MANY KIMS IN KOREA...
YOUR CHAR-ACTER'S SCARY...
IN REALITY, SH KIM IS A 4' 8" TINY GIRL WITH A BABY FACE BUT A CURVY HOT BODY.
20 YEARS OLD WITH GLASSES, SHE'S SHY AND CLUMSY, JUST LIKE A MAIN CHARACTER FROM A MANGA.
COSPLAY AS ARALE FOR ME! OR COSPLAY AS SOMEONE FROM K-ON!
WH-WHY AM I THE ONLY ONE DRAWN IN A REALISTIC STYLE?
AND...
...THERE WAS ONE MORE BIG CHANGE AT THE STUDIO...
KRRRRR!!

NARAE, YOU'LL GET ARRESTED FOR SEXUAL HARASSMENT...

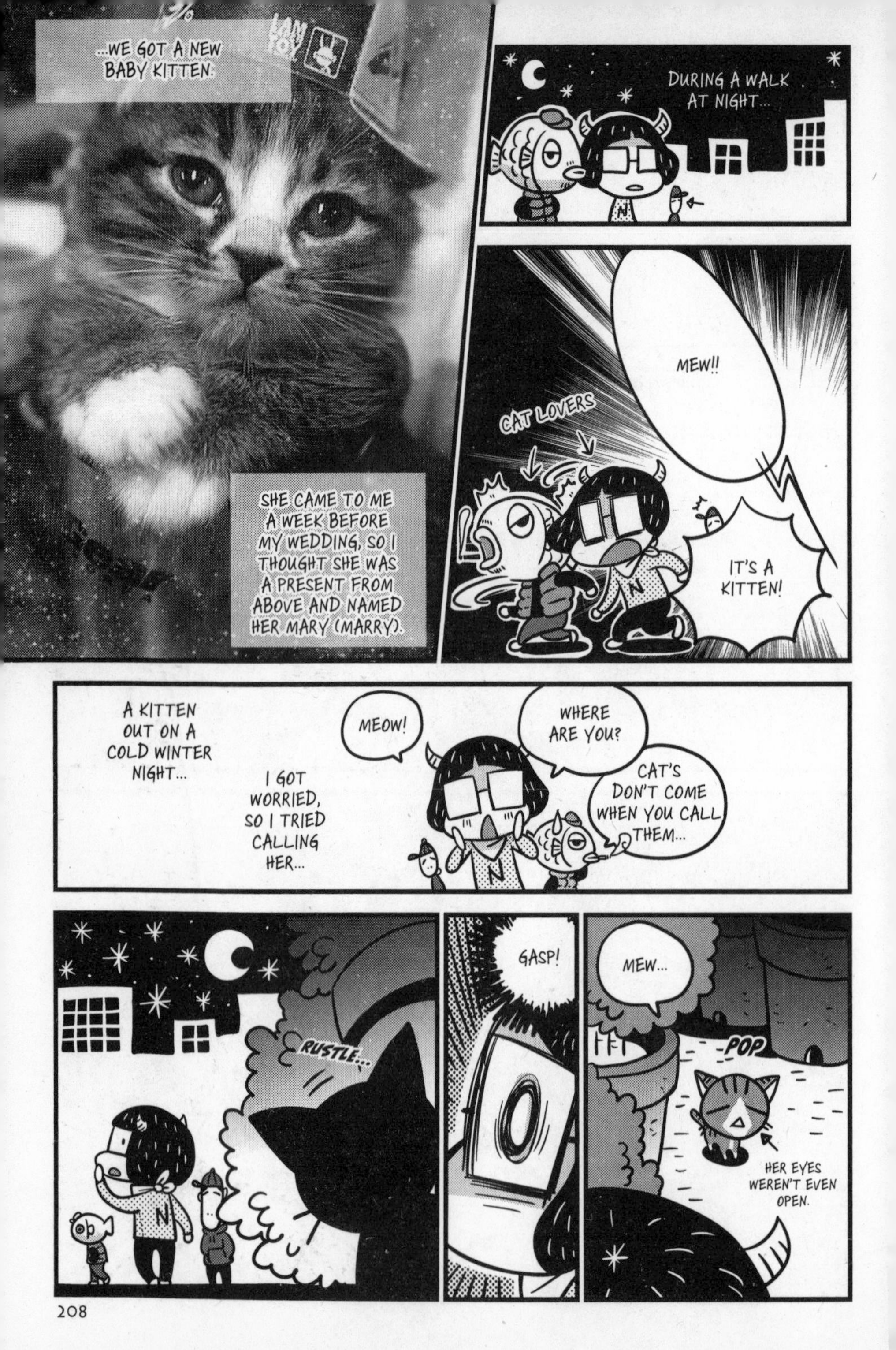
...WE GOT A NEW BABY KITTEN.
SHE CAME TO ME A WEEK BEFORE MY WEDDING, SO I THOUGHT SHE WAS A PRESENT FROM ABOVE AND NAMED HER MARY (MARRY).
DURING A WALK AT NIGHT...
MEW!!
CAT LOVERS
IT'S A KITTEN!
A KITTEN OUT ON A COLD WINTER NIGHT...
I GOT WORRIED, SO I TRIED CALLING HER...
MEOW!
WHERE ARE YOU?
CAT'S DON'T COME WHEN YOU CALL THEM...
RUSTLE...
GASP!
MEW...
POP
HER EYES WEREN'T EVEN OPEN.

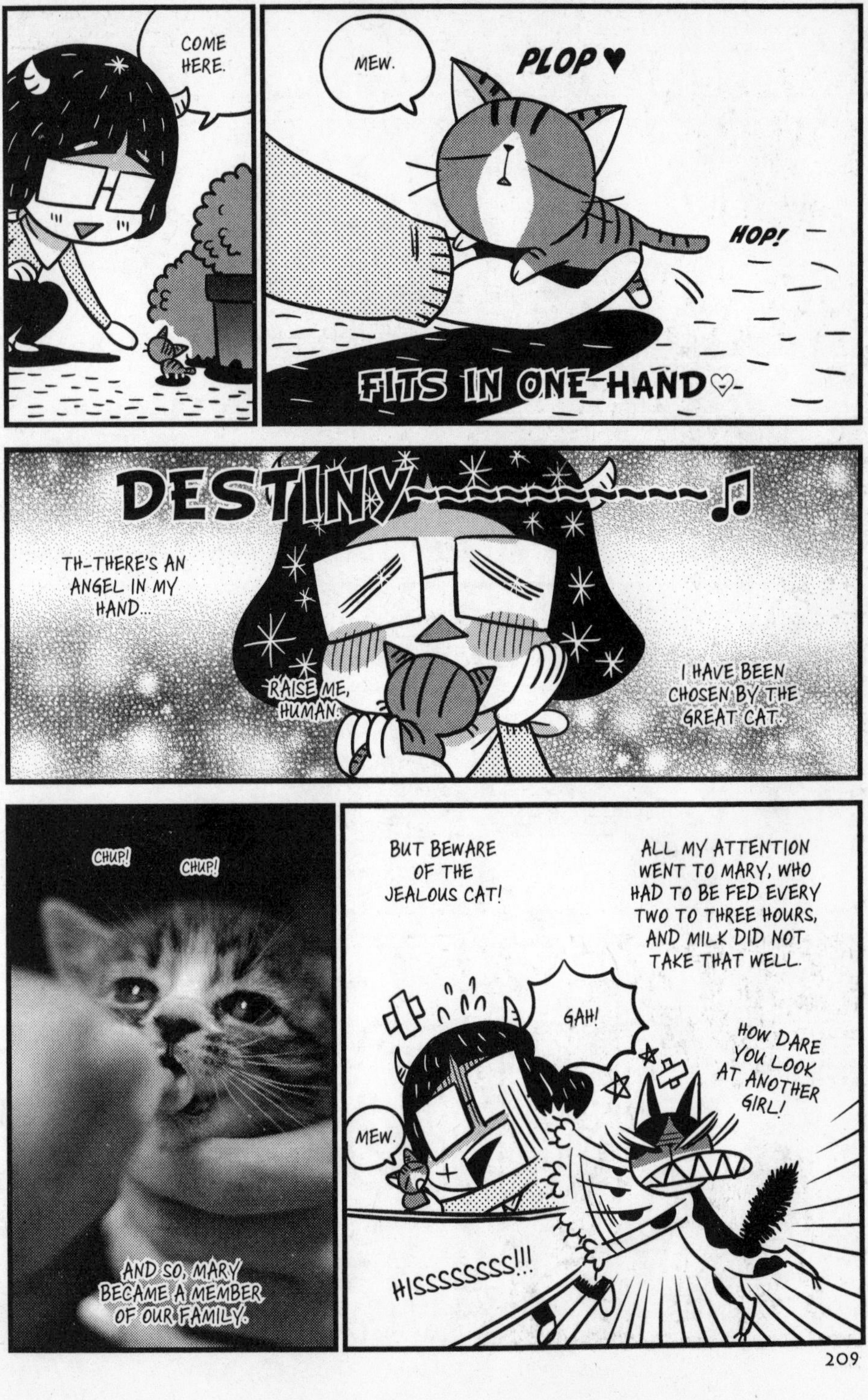
COME HERE.
MEW.
PLOP♥
HOP!
FITS IN ONE HAND♡
DESTINY~~~~~~~~~♫
TH-THERE'S AN ANGEL IN MY HAND...
RAISE ME, HUMAN.
I HAVE BEEN CHOSEN BY THE GREAT CAT.
CHUP!
CHUP!
AND SO, MARY BECAME A MEMBER OF OUR FAMILY.
BUT BEWARE OF THE JEALOUS CAT!
ALL MY ATTENTION WENT TO MARY, WHO HAD TO BE FED EVERY TWO TO THREE HOURS, AND MILK DID NOT TAKE THAT WELL.
GAH!
HOW DARE YOU LOOK AT ANOTHER GIRL!
MEW.
HISSSSSSSS!!!

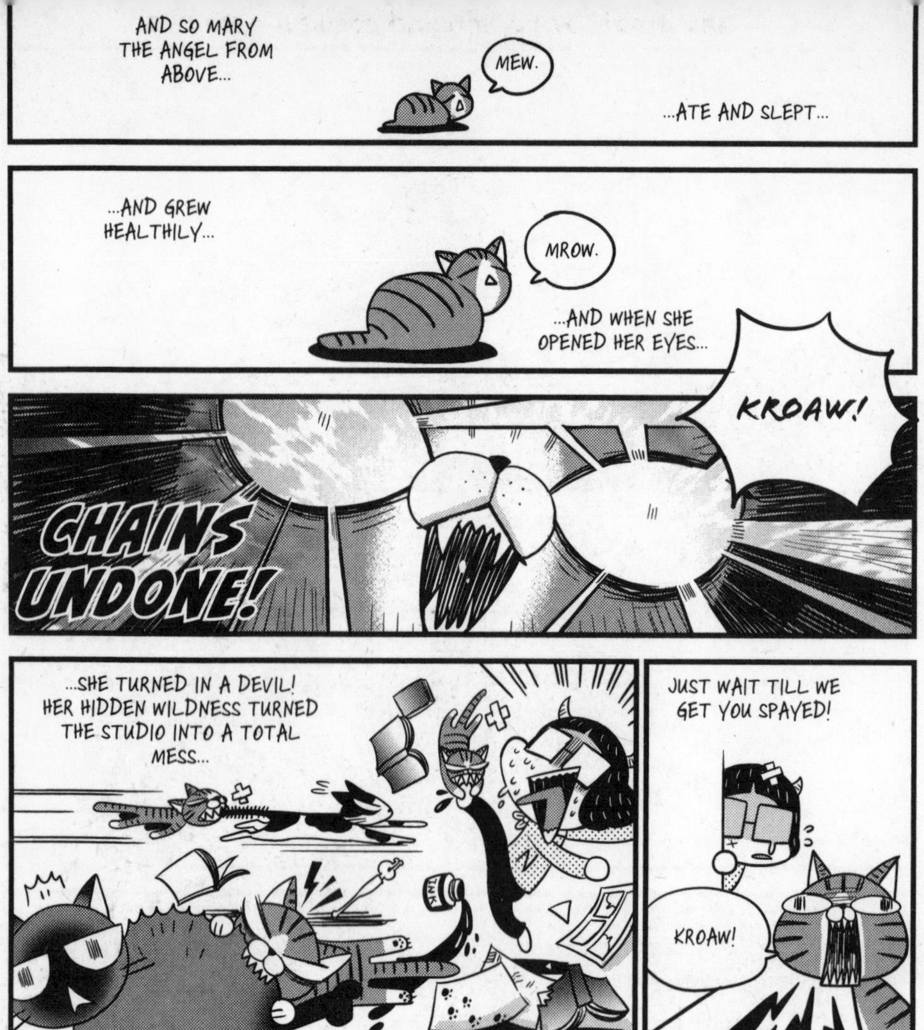
AND SO MARY THE ANGEL FROM ABOVE...
MEW.
...ATE AND SLEPT...
...AND GREW HEALTHILY...
MROW.
...AND WHEN SHE OPENED HER EYES...
KROAW!
CHAINS UNDONE!
...SHE TURNED IN A DEVIL! HER HIDDEN WILDNESS TURNED THE STUDIO INTO A TOTAL MESS...
INK
JUST WAIT TILL WE GET YOU SPAYED!
KROAW!

BONUS WITHIN A BONUS

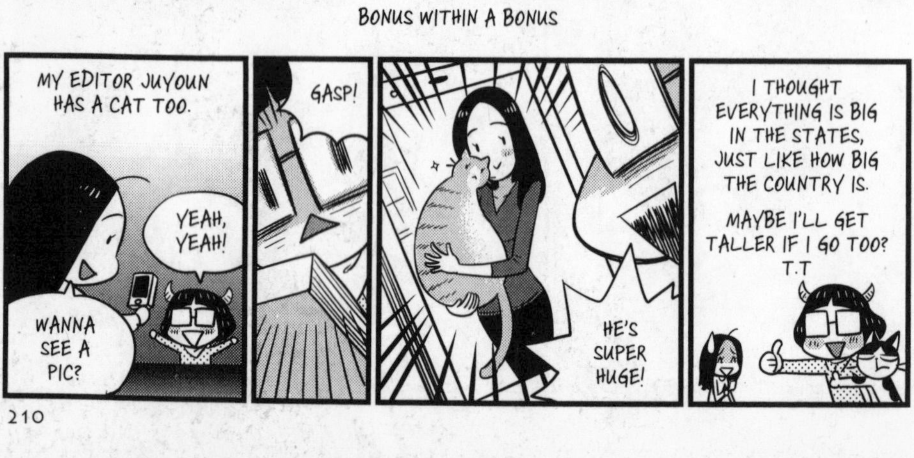
MY EDITOR JUYOUN HAS A CAT TOO.
YEAH, YEAH!
WANNA SEE A PIC?
GASP!
HE'S SUPER HUGE!
I THOUGHT EVERYTHING IS BIG IN THE STATES, JUST LIKE HOW BIG THE COUNTRY IS.
MAYBE I'LL GET TALLER IF I GO TOO? T.T

Max drawn by background assistant MJ KIM

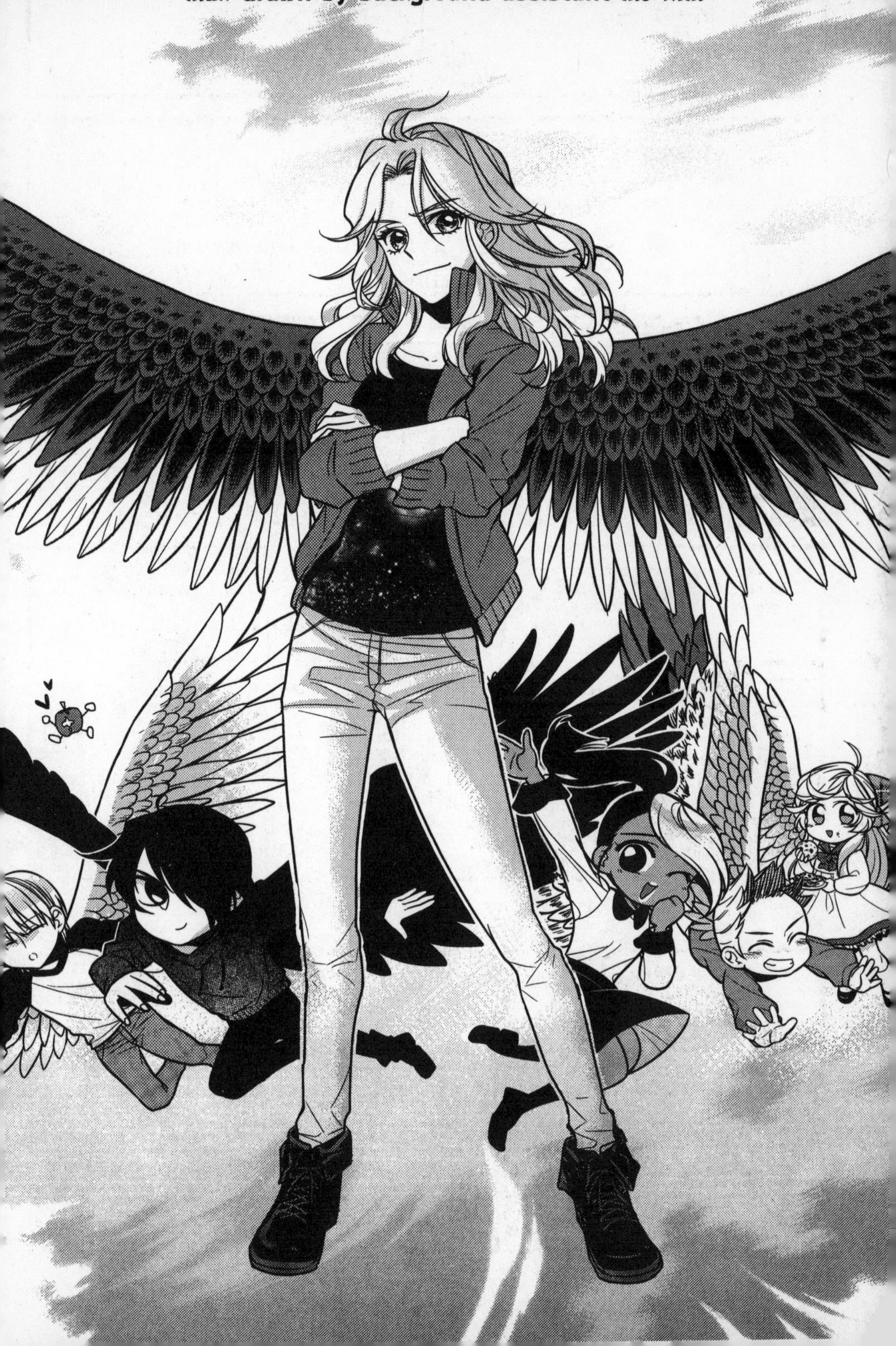

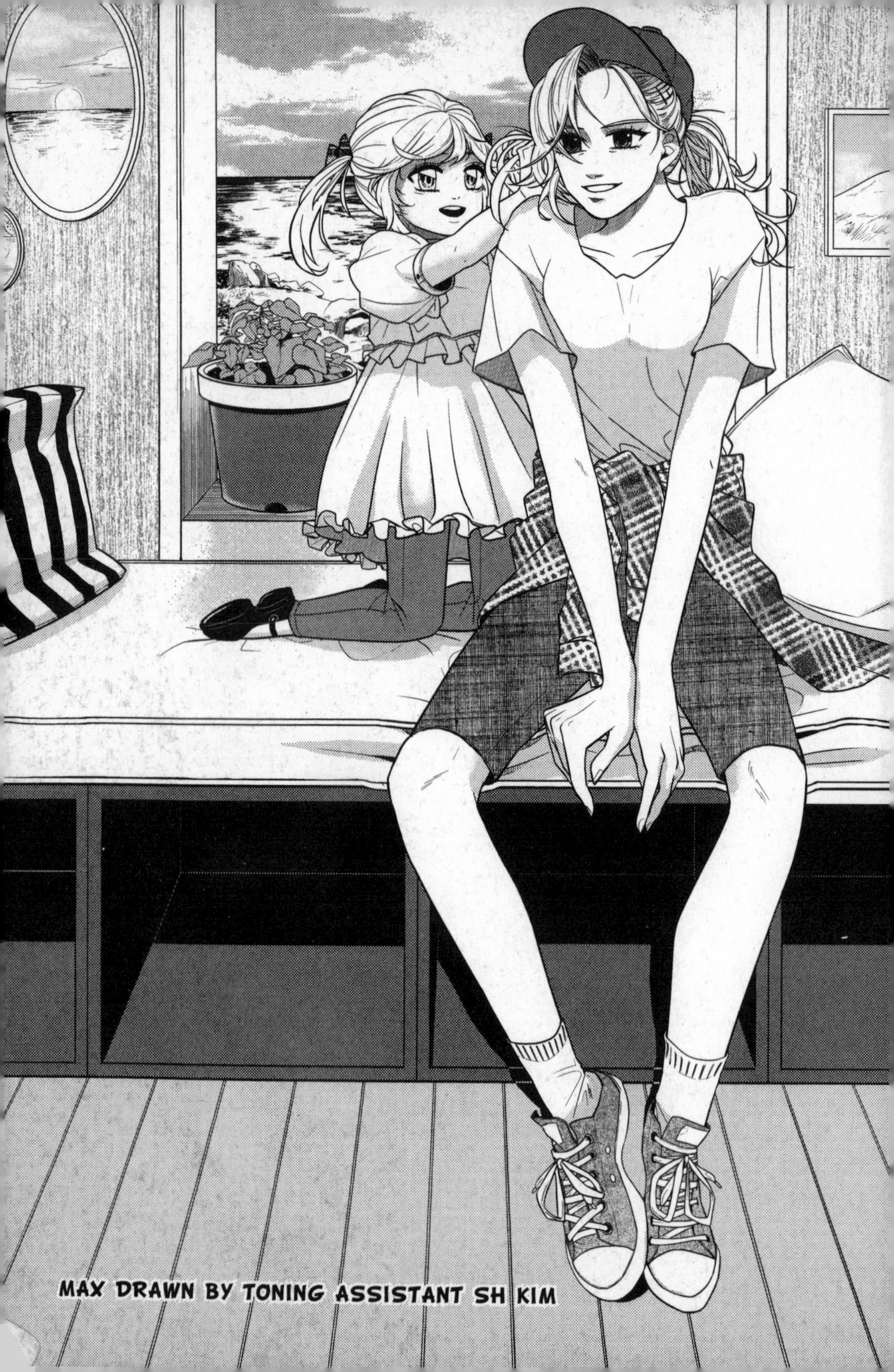

MAX DRAWN BY TONING ASSISTANT SH KIM

MAXIMUM RIDE: THE MANGA

BASED ON THE NOVELS BY
JAMES PATTERSON

ART AND ADAPTATION

NARAE LEE

BACKGROUND ASSISTANCE

WT KIM, MINJOUNG KIM

SPECIAL THANKS

SOHYEON KIM

CAN'T WAIT FOR THE NEXT VOLUME? YOU DON'T HAVE TO!

Follow the latest adventures of Max and the flock each month DIGITALLY!

New chapters go live every month at your favorite ebook retailer, and the Yen Press App!

www.YenPress.com